the organization of society

paul e. mott **THE**

ORGANIZATION

OF

SOCIETY

PRENTICE-HALL, INC., ENGLEWOOD CLIFFS, N. J.

PRENTICE-HALL INTERNATIONAL, INC., London
PRENTICE-HALL OF AUSTRALIA PTY., LTD., Sydney
PRENTICE-HALL OF CANADA, LTD., Toronto
PRENTICE-HALL OF INDIA (PRIVATE) LTD., New Delhi
PRENTICE-HALL OF JAPAN, INC., Tokyo

prentice-hall sociology series · herbert blumer, editor

Printed in the United States of America.   64150-C

Library of Congress Catalog Card No.: 65-17799

Current printing (last digit):
14   13   12   11   10   9   8   7   6   5

for my son paul

preface Two developments
have prompted the writing of this textbook. First, the characteristics of
students in our introductory courses are changing in some important
ways. Today's students have a greater desire to utilize the methods of
science than did their predecessors a decade or two ago. Sociology
becomes more exciting to them when it is presented in propositional
form, which is as rigorous as the present state of the field will permit.
Today's students are also more likely to have a better background in
sociology, having read some of the writing in the field while they were
still in high school. The problem of challenging these students is very
great, and it is compounded in many universities where limited en-
rollments have resulted in a more talented student body. For these
reasons, this book is organized in propositional form—the propositions
being derived primarily from sociological and anthropological research. This form should have the minimal effect of showing students
in introductory courses that the study of human behavior can be
approached more rigorously than they are probably aware.

Second, we are literally inundated with paperback and article
reprint materials of great variety and richness. The student in introductory sociology has much to gain from reading these materials in
their original, unedited form. This textbook was designed to be short
enough to permit the teacher to select a wide range of companion
readings. At the same time it is hoped that the book will provide a

strong enough framework so that students can place their readings in an organized scheme. Correspondingly, many particular subject areas of sociology are introduced in reference to the conceptual scheme of this book, but are not discussed in detail, on the assumption that they can be explored from the paperback and reprint literature. Certain topics, particularly in the area of secondary American institutions, e.g., education, medicine, and the arts, are excluded almost entirely in order to keep the book as short as possible.

The organizing themes of the book are the concepts of social organization and organizational change. I have attempted to extract many of the commonalities among the various types of social organizations and to present them as a set of concepts to organize the study of the specific forms of social organization.

This approach also utilizes a multilineal evolutionary orientation to the study of social organization. Evolutionary theories are currently out of favor among sociologists, the efforts of an earlier generation of evolutionists having proved inadequate. The newer tradition of evolutionism is very strong in anthropology today, but sociologists are taking little cognizance of this trend in our companion field. Modern multilineal evolutionism, particularly as practiced by Julian Steward and Elman Service, makes no ambitious claims that all aspects of social organization and social change can be subsumed under a single general theory. Human organizations are stochastic in that relationships between events are almost always probabilistic rather than deterministic. Human beings have genuine choices; events are often greatly affected by historical accidents. This property of human organizations does not prevent the development of generalizations; it merely suggests that the level of generalization is limited. In this book the *broad outlines* of social organization are derived by use of a series of propositions in which variations in the natural and social environment, economy, and technology are traced to their consequences for the rest of the social organization.

The society is the form of social organization that receives the greatest attention. The variables described above are used to develop outlines of the major types of societies that have existed throughout human history and prehistory. This effort culminates with the development of the outlines of the modern welfare-bureaucratic society. Thereafter, the focus shifts to a consideration of a major force that affects the rate of organizational change in American society: the degree of integration or segmentation of its parts. The final part of this book is also concerned with organizational change, but there the focus is on the organizational responses to the adaptive problems that modern societies face. It is shown that the nature of these internal and external problems is such that some degree of centralization of influence has been required in most modern societies. In the underdeveloped nations, where the desire exists to industrialize rapidly and efficiently, new forms of social organization are being created to assist in the achievement of this objective. In our society, as in many others, the exigencies of modern warfare and the scope of some of the problems have led to increased centralization of influence in order to guide the course of organizational change effectively. Some of these organizational forms are discussed also.

The content of this book is, of course, a synthesis of the author's experience. I am indebted to Professor Gerhard Lenski for demonstrating the value of the comparative societal approach. The environmental and technological emphasis comes from Professor Amos Hawley, who also gave freely of his time to discuss many of the conceptual points of the presentation. The rules about the effects of population size were first presented to me by Professor G. E. Swanson in a form fairly similar to that found here. I have synthesized and expanded these materials in my own way without submitting my final draft to these people; therefore, they share none of the blame for any defects in the presentation and much of the credit for anything that is useful. I am especially indebted to Professor Herbert Blumer, who read the entire manuscript and made many extremely important suggestions for its improvement. Professors Eric Wolf and Neil Smelser also read parts of the manuscript and made suggestions of great value. Professors Robert Carroll, Michael Aiken, and John Leggett helped in the preparation of the manuscript with their extensive comments on earlier versions; the final version was much improved by their efforts. I am indebted to Professor Albert J. Reiss for many useful discussions of social stratification and for making available to me the facilities of the Center for Research on Social Organizations at the University of Michigan. Thanks also go to those at Prentice-Hall who have enhanced the book's clarity and readability: to Mrs. Maurine Lewis, Director of Special Projects; to Mr. Cecil Yarbrough, Special Projects Editor, for his valued contribution—the reader will profit from his efforts; and to Mrs. Eloise Marsilio Lanzana, who designed the book. Finally, I am indebted to my wife, who, besides providing the usual sources of strength, criticized the earlier versions of the manuscript and typed the final version.

PAUL E. MOTT

University of Pennsylvania

contents

PART 4 THE CENTRALIZATION OF INFLUENCE AND THE EMERGENCE OF THE TOTAL SOCIETY

part one THE
CONCEPTUAL
TOOLS
OF SOCIOLOGY

what is sociology?

Sociology is concerned with the study of human behavior. It is therefore a companion field to psychology, political science, economics, and social anthropology. One may well wonder whether five separate fields are necessary for the study of human behavior. Don't they overlap? What is unique to sociology that it merits the status of a separate discipline?

Consider, for example, the relation between sociology and psychology. These disciplines study many of the same types of human behavior, e.g., juvenile delinquency and suicide, and they share an interest in discovering causes. But psychologists develop very different explanations from those of the sociologists. To understand the causes of juvenile delinquency, psychologists use such concepts as *frustration* and *delinquent superego*. Explaining the causes of suicide may involve such concepts as *depression, loss of self-esteem,* and the *death wish.*

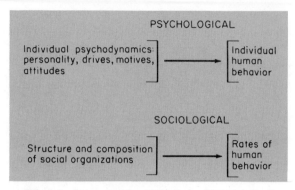

FIG. 1-1   Two approaches to the study of human behavior.

All of these explanations of suicide and juvenile delinquency attempt to explain individual behavior in terms of some characteristic that is internal to the individual—a state of mind or an instinct. The concepts *frustration, superego,* and *depression* are all of this type. The psychological approach to the study of human behavior is schematically represented at the top of Fig. 1-1.

Sociology in its most rigorous form does not consider individual psychodynamics in its study of human behavior. The sociological approach is based on the assumption that much of human behavior can be understood by an examination of the *social situation* in which it occurs. In other words, human groups influence the behavior of their members. Because the word *group* has many popular connotations, let us use the words *social organization* instead. The concept *social organization* will be defined in Chapter 2. Meanwhile, we can represent the sociological approach to the study of human behavior schematically. It is shown at the bottom of Fig. 1-1.

If social organizations do influence the behavior of their members, then they deserve serious study. But that they do should not be accepted without evidence. Let us look at some sociological studies of suicide and juvenile delinquency that make a case for the influence of social organizations on these aspects of human behavior. Then we can begin an analysis of social organizations.

The data in Table 1-1 are taken from a study that relates rate of growth of different communities and some aspects of the behavior of the residents. Wechsler (1) * collected data on fifty communities in the

* Numbers in parentheses refer to entries in the references at the end of each chapter.

TABLE 1-1

INCIDENCE OF REPORTED SUICIDES PER 100,000 POPULATION
BY COMMUNITY GROWTH QUARTERS

| Year | Most rapidly growing communities | | | Least rapidly growing communities |
	I	II	III	IV
1957	20.2	11.4	11.8	6.8
1958	25.7	13.0	9.8	8.9

Source: H. Wechsler, "Community Growth, Depressive Disorders, and Suicide," *The American Journal of Sociology, 67* (1961), 9-16. Reprinted by permission of The University of Chicago Press.

northeastern United States. He calculated the annual rate of increase of the population in each of these communities and divided the communities into four categories according to their rate of increase. The table shows quite clearly that suicide is most prevalent in the most rapidly growing communities.

This finding in itself is not particularly important to us here. What is important is the nature of the relation. An aspect of human behavior—suicide—was studied in terms of a characteristic of the social organization in which the people lived rather than in terms of some characteristic internal to the individual members of the community. In this case, the characteristic studied was the rate of growth of the community (a social organization). Other studies (2) have shown that suicide rates differ according to religious affiliation (there is a higher suicide rate among Protestants than among Catholics) and according to nationality (Denmark has a higher suicide rate than the United States). An examination of these findings reveals an underlying theme —suicide rates differ from one social organization to another. In other words, characteristics of the social organization itself influenced these suicide rates.

A second characteristic of sociology is also evident in Table 1-1. Sociologists seldom try to explain individual human behavior. In Table 1-1 it is the suicide *rate* that varies. Not every individual in a rapidly growing community will commit suicide: only the frequency of suicides per 100,000 population changes.

Should a community seem far removed from what is usually called a social organization, let us look at a set of findings that involves a type of social organization quite familiar to all of us—the family. Nye (3) has related the composition of the family to the prevalence of delinquent behavior among the girl children. Table 1-2 shows one set of his findings. Delinquency among girls was least prevalent in families

TABLE 1-2

BROKEN HOMES AND DELINQUENT BEHAVIOR

Adolescent girls living with	Percentage of girls		Number of girls
	Delinquent	Not delinquent	
Original parents	26	74	921
Mother and stepfather	29	71	102
Father and stepmother	27	73	30
Parents by adoption	33	67	9
Mother only	36	64	53
Father only	59	41	17
Other (relatives, etc.)	53	47	30

Source: F. I. Nye, *Family Relationships and Delinquent Behavior* (New York: John Wiley & Sons, Inc., 1958), p. 44.

where both original parents were present or where one original parent was present, supplemented by a step-parent. When the family contained only one original parent and no substitute for the other, delinquency among the girl children was more prevalent.

We can think of several possible explanations for these findings, but the important idea for us here is that in some way the structure and composition of the family affects the prevalence of delinquent behavior among the girl children. If you are unaccustomed to thinking of social organizations as having structure, consider such characteristics as the patterns of interaction among the members, how the members rank in comparison with each other in terms of income, influence, and other characteristics, and how the different activities the members perform are divided up among them. These and other elements will be discussed in the next chapter.

Let us next examine an aspect of human behavior for which it would seem that only a psychological explanation could be developed: namely, mental illness. Are there aspects of the social structure related to the prevalence of different mental ailments, each of which has its associated kinds of behavior? Working in New Haven, Connecticut, Hollingshead and Redlich (4) divided the population in the community (a social organization) into five categories. The people in each category were essentially alike in three respects: they had similar occupations and levels of educational attainment and lived in similar neighborhoods. The upper class had the highest levels of education, the most prestigious occupations, and lived in the neighborhoods with the "finest" homes. Then Hollingshead and Redlich investigated the prevalence of various types of mental illness in each of these categories. One set of results is shown in Table 1-3.

TABLE 1-3

CLASS, STATUS, AND RATE OF DIFFERENT TYPES OF PSYCHOSES
PER 100,000 POPULATION

Type of disorder	Class			
	Upper and upper middle	*Lower middle*	*Upper working*	*Lower working*
Affective psychoses	40	41	68	105
Psychoses due to alcoholism and drug addiction	15	29	32	116
Organic psychoses	0	24	46	254
Schizophrenic psychoses	111	168	300	895
Senile psychoses	21	32	60	175
Number of people in this class	53	142	585	672

Source: A. B. Hollingshead and F. C. Redlich, *Social Class and Mental Illness: A Community Study* (New York: John Wiley & Sons, Inc., 1958), p. 232.

These findings are rather dramatic. The prevalence of all types of psychoses clearly increased as the level of occupation and education and the quality of the neighborhood decreased. The explanation might be offered that this difference is natural, because sick people are not capable of maintaining a high position in the social structure and, therefore, "drift down." The researchers were able to test this explanation. In their interviews they asked some questions about the family background of the subjects. Using these data, they were able to compare the status of most subjects with that of their parents. They found that 91 per cent of their subjects for whom they could make this calculation were still at the status level of their parents. Of the remainder, more subjects were actually at a higher status level than their parents than at a lower level. Hollingshead and Redlich concluded that something about the nature of social relationships among people at these different levels predisposed them to different rates of psychosis.

These three diverse examples were selected to make the point that the structure of human groups affects a wide range of human behavior.

To study the determinants of human behavior, one must also study the relevant social organizations. *Sociology is the study of social organizations.* This definition has many implications, some of which we can now discuss.

SOCIOLOGY AND THE INDIVIDUAL

Students are often troubled by the basic sociological proposition that the characteristics of social organizations influence rates of human behavior. One source of difficulty centers on the relation between the social organization and the individual. Today's conformity-conscious students are disturbed by the suggestion that their behavior is greatly influenced by their group memberships. Yet, paradoxically, it is the influence of social organizations that really makes us different from one another. Imagine, for example, a room with fifty cubicles in each of which there is a newborn child. Imagine, in addition, that each child's biological needs are being met without his ever coming into contact with another human being. There would be no human voices to mimic, no human behavior to imitate, no exchange of love or affection. The consequences of this situation would be both instructive and saddening. Most of the children would die. But if a few should survive, they would be more alike than different (5, 6). They would all utter the same random sounds associated with small babies, because no one would have taught them which sounds were useful and which were not. Most of them would crawl on their hands and knees, except for the occasional child who accidentally discovered the utility of standing erect and walking (7). This list could be continued, but the point is already apparent: contact with other human beings reduces the similarities and increases the differences in our behavior. It is in group life that the biological entity we call a baby is converted into a skilled person. Because we encounter different patterns of experience in the various groups of which we are a part, we are alike in many ways but different in many more. It is the differences that make us individuals.

But if the individual is defined as a person whose behavior is free of the influences of any social organizational memberships, past or present, then it must be said that such a person does not exist. The development of our basic attitudes, beliefs, linguistic skills, habits of thought, and other kinds of behavior begins during the first months of our lives in the family; it continues throughout our lives in the other social organizations in which we are members.

The effects of the social environment on human development can be seen in a study (8) of monozygotic (genetically identical) twins. The researcher compared monozygotic twins who had been separated since birth with those who had been reared in the same social environment. He found that the separated twins differed more from each other in certain personal characteristics than did the twins who were reared together. This study demonstrates again the profound effects of the social environment on behavior. In summary, social relationships account for many of the similarities as well as differences among people.

Other students are disturbed by the basic proposition of sociology for the opposite reason: they would prefer a science that predicted individual behavior rather than rates of behavior, and sociologists do not appear to make this kind of prediction. But what if a social scientist could show that *all* persons with a certain combination of group memberships and social characteristics always voted for the candidates of only one of our political parties? In effect, he would be able to predict the behavior of *every person* who had the same combination of social organizational memberships and social characteristics. At present, such a situation represents only the goal of sociologists. Whenever this condition is achieved, it will be possible to make *inferences* about individual behavior. But sociologists will not predict from the characteristics of organizations directly to individual behavior; that is the task of social psychologists.

APPROACHES TO THE STUDY OF SOCIAL ORGANIZATIONS

Sociologists approach the study of social organizations in many ways. Not all of them relate aspects of the social structure to rates of human behavior. Many study and analyze the characteristics of social organizations without any reference to rates of behavior. They seek a better understanding of how social organizations function and more useful concepts for analyzing them. The types of social organizations they study are also varied. Some sociologists devote their efforts solely to the study of such small social organizations as the family, the friendship clique, and the work group. Others focus on the community, voluntary associations, or the total society. Still others are interested in the relationships between different social organizations; e.g., between the family and the society, or between the army and the rulers of a country, or among various religious organizations. Others want to know how social organizations function, how they form, or what holds them together. And even these interests account for only a small fraction of the types of research done by sociologists. We will become acquainted with a broader spectrum of their efforts later.

SOCIOLOGY AND THE SOCIAL SCIENCES

We began by observing that sociology is just one of several social sciences interested in the study of human behavior. With the exception of psychology, we have not seen how these other social sciences are related to sociology, and even in the case of psychology the complete picture has not been presented.

Psychologists attempt to predict individual human behavior from the psychodynamics of the individual. Although this emphasis on the individual may seem incompatible with the group emphasis of sociology, a synthesis of the two fields has in fact been made. Many sociologists use psychological concepts to explain sociological propositions. For example, the relationship between community growth and suicide rates might be explained as follows: In rapidly growing communities there are many migrants without family ties and other group memberships. When they get *depressed,* they have no close friends or family members to whom they can turn for help, and they are therefore more likely to commit suicide. This oversimplified argument is strictly hypothetical, but it does illustrate how intervening psychological concepts can be used to understand a social relationship. This explanation is properly labeled social-psychological.

Even in the most rigidly sociological theories and research, some psychological assumptions occur, because the existence of a population or membership of the social organization must be assumed. The population is assumed to have such human abilities as cognizing and responding to stimuli. Although these are minimal assumptions, we need to be aware of them and any other psychological assumptions that are made.

How is sociology related to the other social sciences? At the risk of being accused of academic imperialism, it must be noted that there is considerable overlap between sociology and each of the other social sciences. Social anthropology, for example, is very closely akin to sociology. Social anthropologists study societies and communities; they describe the relationships among the parts of these social organizations. Primarily, they study the so-called simpler societies; e.g., peasant villages, and hunting and gathering tribes. Social anthropologists constitute the greatest single source of information for the sociologist on these simpler societies. Social anthropology and sociology were once separate academic disciplines; but the boundary between them is now artificial.

As formal disciplines, political science and economics have existed much longer than has sociology. But both are concerned with specific forms of behavior and organization. In economics the focus is on the production, distribution, and exchange of goods and services. The institutions of economic behavior—e.g., banking and industrial firms and stock exchanges—have been the preserve of classical economics, and they are still the primary organizational focus. But the field has been broadening rapidly to include concerns that traditionally have been in the provinces of political scientists, sociologists, and psychologists. Economic studies of depressed areas, for example, have taken the economist into the realm of sociology. The role of governmental regulatory agencies, the legislatures, and international political organizations in economic affairs has led economists to use the knowledge assembled by political scientists and to contribute to it. Finally, studies of consumer behavior and attempts to predict purchasing patterns have led to the development of a psychological economics.

Political scientists have also focused on a specific type of human behavior: the exercise of influence by individuals and organizations. Traditionally, they have restricted their research and commentary to political institutions and only to the formal exchanges of influence in these institutions. For example, a study of how Congress passes a law would examine the formal structure of the Congress—the committee system, rules of representation, and the voting system. Similarly, study of international relations would be limited almost exclusively to international law, world courts, and so forth. The same formal approach could be found in the other areas of interest to political scientists: administrative theory and law, political theory, and state and local government. Although the formal school is still very much in evidence, it is gradually being superseded by the so-called behavioralist approach: an orientation similar to that of sociologists. These political scientists are interested in the informal as well as the formal exercises of influence. In their studies of how Congress passes a law, they examine the pressure groups that attempt to influence the decisions of congressmen, the informal social structure of the Congress, and the career patterns and personality characteristics of congressmen. At the community level, studies of city administration are broadened to include an examination of the informal elite structure of the community and the role of various groups in community decision making.

Sociologists are interested in the findings of economists and political scientists because they are interested in studying rates of all types of behavior that occurs in social organizations—political and economic activity is found in every one of them. The boundaries between these fields too are somewhat artificial; in fact, many scholars in each discipline increasingly are ignoring them in their writings. Perhaps the best testimony to the overlap is that many sociology departments offer courses in political sociology and economy and society.

SUMMARY

The basic premise of sociology is that the behavior of human beings is influenced by the structure and composition of the social organizations in which they live. *Sociology is the study of social organizations and their relation to human behavior.*

This chapter has presented evidence to support the basic premise. Having established the importance of social organizations for the study of human behavior, we must learn to recognize the elements that are relevant to such a study. Chapter 2 outlines the major elements common to all social organizations.

REFERENCES

1   H. Wechsler, "Community Growth, Depressive Disorders, and Suicide," *The American Journal of Sociology, 67* (1961), 9-16.

2   M. B. Clinard, *Sociology of Deviant Behavior* (New York: Holt, Rinehart & Winston, Inc., 1957).

3   F. I. Nye, *Family Relationships and Delinquent Behavior* (New York: John Wiley & Sons, Inc., 1958).

4   A. B. Hollingshead and F. C. Redlich, *Social Class and Mental Illness: A Community Study* (New York: John Wiley & Sons, Inc., 1958).

5   J. Bowlby, *Child Care and the Growth of Love* (Harmondsworth, Middlesex; Pelican Books, Ltd., 1953).

6   R. A. Spitz, "Hospitalism," in *The Psychoanalytic Study of the Child* (New York: International Universities Press, 1945), I, 53-72.

7   K. Davis, "Final Note on a Case of Extreme Isolation," *The American Journal of Sociology, 52* (1947), 432-37.

8   H. H. Newman, *Multiple Human Births* (New York: Doubleday & Company, Inc., 1940).

a definition of social organization

The concept *social organization* embraces a wide range of human collectivities. All of these things are social organizations: a surgical team, a family, a hunting and gathering band, a friendship clique, the League of Women Voters, General Motors Corporation, a lynch mob, and the members of a university lecture course.

In this chapter we will identify and define certain characteristics common to all of these organizations. The task is not an easy one because there is considerable lack of agreement among sociologists concerning the definitions and the theoretical usefulness of various organizational concepts. Diverse schools of thought have arisen because of these different ways of looking at organizations. Some sociologists conceive of organizations as systems through which the members can achieve their common objectives. Others argue that organizations are shaped by external forces, the physical and the social environment, and that these same forces even shape the objectives that the members pursue. Still others see organizations as fairly enduring patterns of interaction among the members. Another school studies them as systems of influence in which action occurs as a result of the use of influence by the various parts. A variation of this last approach views organizations as systems of tension and conflict. Another school sees organizations as a division of labor in which each member performs certain specialized activities that are coordinated with the activities of other specialists. Some sociologists view organizations as an interlocking set of institutions—economic, political, educational, legal, religious, and recreational. Others, particularly social anthropologists, conceptualize organizations as patterned sets of behavior: ceremonial activities, political activities, folklore, and so on.

The problem for us arises when we ask the question: What concepts shall we use to analyze and compare organizations? Each of the followers of each specific approach to the study of organizations is very likely to give a different answer. Or even if two people use the same words, they are very likely to have slightly different meanings in mind. For the sociologist who sees organizations in terms of their division of labor, the most important concepts are role, specialization, coordination, and functional integration. The adherent to the influence approach may think that the role concept is important but that such concepts as status, social class, social stratification, elite, and counterelite are more important for understanding human systems.

This lack of consensus should not alarm students beginning the study of sociology. The selection of concepts to use in the study of any form of complex organization is often quite arbitrary. Consider, for example, the organization we call an apple. A biologist might identify its parts as stem, skin, and seeds. A chemist, on the other hand, might talk in terms of its various chemical compounds. The identification of the parts of social organizations is similarly arbitrary, for it depends on the analytical objectives of the sociologist. Furthermore, it must always be remembered that the parts he identifies are *abstractions;* they are labels he applies to collections of phenomena he has observed. Our task is to select from among these concepts and variations in usage a central set of concepts that can be used for the study of *all* forms of social organization, whether they are small groups or total societies.

This chapter begins by identifying and defining the characteristics common to all social organizations. Since the resulting model of a social organization is a static one, the dynamic quality of organizations is also discussed. At the conclusion of the chapter the idea that social organization is a variable concept is introduced and explained.

THE CHARACTERISTICS OF SOCIAL ORGANIZATION

The Parts: Subgroups and Roles

Organizations are composed of people interacting. The interaction takes place among them through the *parts* of organizations (1): the subgroups and roles.

SUBGROUPS.   We label as *subgroup* any part of a social organization that has all the properties of a social organization. Virtually all social organizations contain subgroups. Seen as a social organization, a university contains such subgroups as a faculty senate, student newspaper, sororities, and alumni groups. But on another level of analysis, a university is itself a subgroup within a community social organization. Business organizations contain a variety of sub-groups: bureaus, departments, work teams, and informal friendship cliques.

Subgroups can vary in the degree to which their members perform different activities or functions. Sororities and fraternities are much more similar in terms of the functions they perform than are the various professional departments of a university. There are societies in which the major subgroups are relatively undifferentiated: the various tribes (subgroups) that make up the Nuer society in Africa are an example (2). In our society, on the other hand, considerable differentiation has occurred among the subgroups. If we think of communities as subgroups in societies, for instance, it can be observed that some subgroups specialize in commerce and others in manufacturing, food processing, or education. If a part of a social organization has become specialized in terms of the functions or activities its members perform, then it is dependent upon the other parts for the performance of other functions that are essential to its survival. Industrial communities are dependent upon rural communities for the production and distribution of food. *The greater the differentiation among the subgroups of a social organization, the greater is their mutual dependence.*

ROLES.   If you were to look for regularities in the behavior of the members of a functioning social organization, one observation you might make is that each member performs a certain set of activities repeatedly. When a customer comes into a restaurant, one person brings him a menu, goes away for awhile, returns later and takes his order, gives it to the cook, and still later brings in the prepared food—all in a certain sequence. Other members of the organization perform other combinations of tasks repeatedly. The significance of each set of activities is apparent when it is studied in relation to the other sets. When the waitress takes an order and later brings the food, her actions are significant because they are coordinated with the activities of the cook. Each of these sets of coordinated tasks is performed by a person occupying a position in the organization. In our illustration, the *position* is that of waiter or waitress. *The collection of activities that the occupant of the position regularly performs and that depend for their continuity on the regular performance of other activities by occupants of other positions in the organization* is called a *role*. Some sociologists distinguish roles and positions; others include both ideas within the term *role*. Let us follow the latter practice. When we wish to consider the position aspect of roles separately, we can use the term *position*. The collection of roles (positions plus roles) found in any given social organization are parts of that organization. Examples of roles are student, mother, fiancé, janitor, and policeman.

The utility of the role concept. Perhaps the greatest advantage of the role concept is that it permits us to distinguish a combination of activities and the person who performs them. If *persons* are thought of as parts of a social organization, then we must take into account their nonsocial characteristics in explaining their behavior. A person is a biological entity, and his behavior is affected by genetic and physiological characterisitcs. He is also a psychological entity, and, if we use the person concept, we must study his psychological predisposition in accounting for his behavior. *Roles are parts of social organizations; they are not persons; they are positions in organizations with which certain routinely performed combinations of activities are associated. Persons occupy these positions and perform the activities associated with them; persons occupy roles.*

The role concept is rewarding because of the insights and the predictability it gives to our study of social organizations. Roles greatly influence the social behavior of the people who occupy them. Therefore, we can make more reliable predictions about a person's social behavior by knowing his roles than we can by knowing any other set of information about him. For example, think of how you and your lecturer interact when you go to see him during his office hours. As student talking to teacher, you are probably deferential, cautious, and generally compliant. But suppose this *same person* is a student who sits next to you in class. Your interactions are likely to be different even though he is the same person. Finally, imagine the nature of your interactions if you were the lecturer and he were the student. In each case the persons are the same, but the roles have changed and with them the ways of behaving.

Occupying a given role can even influence the attitudes of the occupant. This relationship was illustrated in a study by T. M. Newcomb while he was a member of the teaching staff of Bennington College in Vermont (3). At the time of his study, the predominant political values among the students at Bennington were liberal. But the student body at Bennington was drawn largely from the relatively wealthy families in the nearby metropolitan areas: families in which the predominant political values were conservative. Newcomb administered a questionnaire about political values to the members of an incoming class of freshmen students before they had had an opportunity to become involved in student life at Bennington. As he had expected, the students' views were generally conservative. The test was administered annually to the same students during their four years at Bennington, and it showed a decided shift in the direction of the liberal values of the Bennington student body. Although it would be interesting to examine the dynamics of this change, it suffices to note that a very important set of political values was affected when a new role was assumed.

People have the greatest effect on their roles when the role is new and consequently undefined by custom, when there are very few other people in the role, or when no one else particularly wants the role. Because most roles are not of these types, knowledge of a person's roles permits us to make predictions about how he will behave and what some of his attitudes and beliefs will be.

The role concept is useful for a second reason: roles remain *relatively* unchanged, even though many different people may occupy them. The roles in a social organization such as the Roman Catholic Church have persisted in essentially their present form over centuries, even though the occupants of these roles have changed many times. Experimentally, when sociologists have removed the occupants of certain roles from groups, they have observed that some other member of the group stepped in to fill the role (4). If the activities of a role are essential to the functioning of a social organization, another person will step in to fill it should it be vacated. It is this stability of the roles in an organization that makes them much more useful objects of study than the individuals who fill these roles.

Role differentiation. The occupants of roles, like the members of subgroups, may perform similar or different sets of activities. In some organizations the roles are more differentiated than they are in others. There are organizations in which the members perform nearly identical sets of behaviors. In the classroom, for example, the major differentiation occurs between the roles of student and professor. On a surgical team, on the other hand, the activities associated with the various roles overlap very little. The particular pattern of role differentiation found in any social organization is generally referred to as its *division of labor*. If the role is highly specialized, it contains only a few of the functions involved in the total task of the organization. To complete the entire task, each specialist must depend on other specialists to perform their functions. Therefore, *the greater the division of labor in an organization, the greater is the mutual dependence of the members.* If we ask what holds an organization together, one answer must be its division of labor.

Privileges and obligations of roles. The activities associated with a role can be thought of as the obligations of its occupant. But there are also privileges associated with roles. The occupants of the more influential roles in a social organization receive deference from its other members. In business organizations, the executive roles may have such privileges attached to them as a private office and secretary, use of a private dining room, and permission to arrive at work later than the other personnel. Usually, the more responsibility attached to a role or the scarcer the skills required to perform it, the greater are the privileges attached to it.

Interaction Among the Parts

Knowing that subgroups and roles are the parts from which organizations are made does not tell us what a social organization is. Organizations are not the mere sum of their parts. To know that an atom of carbon contains electrons, protons, and neutrons does not distinguish it as an organization from any other type of atom. The parts have to be arranged according to some principle before they constitute an organization (1). In social organizations, as in all other types of organizations, we can speak of the spatial and functional relationships among the parts. *The characteristic of structure in a social organization is created by the patterns of interaction among the parts.* In the most general sense, *interaction* indicates only that the parts affect one another. But in most of the discussion that follows, the term is used in a more specific sense: to mean exchanges of communications, goods, or services among the parts. *Communication* refers to the exchange of meaningful symbols among the members of an organization (5). It is not a communication if a person talks to you in French and you do not understand the language. It is a communication only if what is spoken or written evokes the same meaning for the receiver that it does for the sender. Thus, if I use the word *dog,* meaningful communication occurs between you and me if we both are thinking of that category of animals that are furry, four-legged, and prone to barking.

Later in this chapter we shall see how interaction gives structure to the parts of a social organization; but first we must examine the relation between interaction and influence.

INTERACTION AND INFLUENCE.   Whenever subgroups or the occupants of roles direct or control the activities of others, they are exercising influence. Examples of the exercise of influence are commonplace. The administrators of a university decide when students shall return to school in the fall and when their vacations will occur. A doctor prescribes for his patient. A man makes a proposal of marriage. A friend laughs at your joke. A revolutionary group overthrows a government. Every interaction is an attempt to influence the object of the interaction (6). Verbal communication can be used to illustrate this point. No one is more aware of the potential of communication for influencing people than the small child who is just beginning to talk. Before he developed his vocabulary, he emitted random sounds that ranged all over the international phonetic alphabet. When he was happy, he was very likely to make a variety of sounds with his mouth upturned in a smile: "da da" is one of these sounds. When he was sad or uncomfortable, he was likely to make a variety of sounds with his mouth turned downward: "ma ma" is one of these sounds. Over a period of time he found that whenever he made either of these sounds, one of his parents attended to his needs. His father was likely to pick him up and play with him while repeating to him the sound that he had made. His mother usually comforted him. The child had made the biggest discovery of his life: words have force. When he used them, people did things for him. This discovery greatly encouraged him to learn more of the words that his parents were using.

It should not be inferred from this illustration that interaction and influence are identical. Influence is but one component of interaction; interaction also contains information, provides goods and services, and so on.

Influence is a characteristic of interaction that derives from the parts themselves; it is an intrinsic property of subgroups and roles in an organization—and such an important one, in fact, that sociologists often refer to the parts as *centers of influence*. To think of persons as having influence is largely misleading. Although some people do exercise influence by virtue of such personal traits as their physical size or their persuasive abilities, these sources of influence account for little of the total influence wielded in larger organizations. Organizations lock in influence (6). Persons exercise influence primarily by virtue of their occupancy of roles or their membership in subgroups.

Influence, which is intrinsic in organizations, is held in a variety of forms. It is the resources accumulated by an organization or its ability to produce a commodity that is greatly needed by the population. It is the size of the labor force employed or the number of votes controlled.

Influence is distributed among the parts in varying degrees. In some organizations, the subgroups and role occupants have about equal capabilities of influencing one another. But, particularly as the population of the organization increases, differences occur in the amount of influence inherent in the parts. Generally, the greatest influence resides in those subgroups and roles that are primarily concerned with how the organization adapts to its environment (7). In a society, it is the activities of the economy that most influence the patterns of behavior of the other parts.

The exercise of influence is not a one-way street, however. Even the least influential parts of an organization can affect the actions of the most dominant units. College students often feel powerless to affect their own fate; but the decision makers of universities do in fact take student interests into account. If they did not, they might well find themselves making decisions about what to do with empty classrooms.

Because routine and similar exchanges of influence become customary, the exercise of influence is not always apparent to us. Influence is often clothed in the form of rules of behavior for the parts of an organization. As a student (the occupant of a student role), you may seldom think that your teachers are influencing you when you take notes in a lecture. Rather, you are aware of rules of conduct for students—among which are attendance in class, deference to the teacher, taking notes, learning materials, and writing examinations—that you abide by. The distinction is one of words, not of meanings. Any schedule that specifies who will do what and when is a device for regulating the exchanges of influence or the interactions of the parts of an organization: airline schedules and class schedules are examples. The rules of etiquette are formalized means of exchanging influence.

INTERACTION AND ORGANIZATION.   In our discussion of roles and subgroups, we concluded that the greater the differentiation among the parts, the more dependent they are on each other: in other words, the greater is the necessity of having exchanges among them. In a situation as undifferentiated as an audience watching a movie, interaction among the members is seldom necessary: only minimal interactions with ushers and doormen are required. But in a business organization where the specialization of the parts is very great, where each part performs only a small fraction of the total task, much interaction is necessary.

If we were to examine any social organization over a short period of time, we would find that *most* of the relations among the parts (the subgroups and the occupants of roles) are characterized by fairly routine patterns of interaction. There would appear to be a fairly stable principle of organization. *The routinized interaction of the parts constitutes their organization.*

This idea can be illustrated by examining some simple patterns of interaction. The pattern illustrated in Fig. 2-1 is usually referred to as

FIG. 2-1

the chain (8). Here the parts, whether subgroups or roles, can interact only with those to their right or left (except the parts at each end, which can interact with only one other part). This pattern can be found in a somewhat more complex form on certain types of assembly lines. Another example occurs in factories where the workers must wear badges whose color depends on the department in which they work. They are forbidden by the rules to go to departments more than one step removed from their own. The colored badges enable each foreman to determine whether the workers are in their permitted areas.

Suppose we rearrange the chain so that some parts have greater influence than others; that is, they can control the activities of others. Then the chain becomes the hierarchical pattern found in military and many other kinds of organizations (Fig. 2-2).

Yet another structure can be created from these six parts if each part has equal influence and regularly interacts with all the other parts (Fig. 2-3). This pattern is often found in groups with only a few parts. We will see later that an "open" network of this type is extremely difficult to maintain in large organizations.

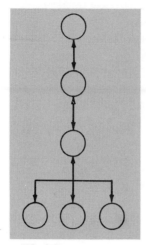

FIG. 2-2

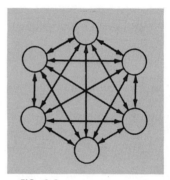

FIG. 2-3

In many organizations, the networks for interacting are designed to minimize the number of open channels. Sometimes barriers to inter-action are imposed between the parts by other, more dominant parts; other times they are self-imposed by the affected parts. One means of minimizing interaction, the central-part pattern, is shown in Fig. 2-4. In this pattern each part can interact with those to its right or left. But in order to interact with a more remote part, it must use another part as an intermediary. As can be seen, this network is simpler than that shown in Fig. 2-3.

INTERACTION, ORGANIZATION, AND CHANGE. Most of the relations among the parts of a social organization are characterized

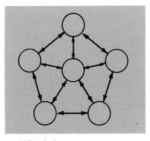

FIG. 2-4

by fairly routine patterns of interaction—over a short period of time. Were we to observe most organizations over a *long* period of time, however, we would find that the routine patterns of interaction change. Even over short time periods, we would be likely to see some change occurring. Why this happens will be discussed in Chapter 5. At this point suffice it to say that the conditions under which the parts operate change. The external environment changes, requiring accompanying changes in the organization of some of the parts and consequent changes in the interactions among the parts. The major content of roles is a fairly routinized set of behaviors, yet *that is not all of the content.* The occupant of a role encounters new or unanticipated problems and often solves them unilaterally. The new pattern of behavior that he develops changes the organization of the roles that are coordinated with his role. The new arrangement, which he may have effected by overt influence, may become routine, creating a new form of organization, but temporarily it represents a change in the routine patterns of interaction.

We must maintain a two-part conception of the organization. On the one hand, there is the stability induced by the routine patterns of interaction among the parts. Usually, the most fundamental aspects of an organization are the most resistant to change. (A society's principle of organization, for example, whether democratic, monarchical, or patriarchal, is usually highly resistant to change.) On the other hand, there is the flux induced by innovation or adaptation by the parts of the organization. (American society has retained its political and economic organizing principles of democracy and free enterprise, but each of them in its various institutional forms has been subjected to a vast number of modifications, which give contemporary society quite a different structural appearance from that of the society of a few decades ago.)

Norms

Interactions that involve similar and frequently repeated patterns of behavior generally become institutionalized; and the institutionalization involves the development of formal or informal rules. Sociologists refer to *the rules or standards that govern interactions* as *norms*. Norms are the "thou shalt's" and the "thou shalt not's" that often govern the behavior of the parts of an organization. College students are subject to a large number of such norms, governing such behavior as when to come to class, manner of dress, and quality of performance of school work. Laws are examples of formal norms that control our behavior.

The actions of parts of an organization may be the results of simple exercises of influence—interactions not governed by norms or only partially governed by them or that occur in spite of the existence of a set of norms. But in other interactions, the element of influence has become heavily overlaid with customary norms. Sometimes these standards of behavior are informal, unwritten customs, often so ingrained in the activity patterns of the members that their response to them is spontaneous and uncritical: we don't eat worms, for example. Other times these standards are formalized norms, such as laws, schedules, or constitutions.

Norms, besides varying between the informal and the formal, can also be classified in terms of the extent to which they are binding on the members of the organization (9). *Prescribed norms* are the "thou shalt's"; they are the standards of behavior to which all of the members of the organization *must* adhere. In our society such norms as wearing clothes in public and being able to speak English are required of all of the members. *Proscribed norms* are the "thou shalt not's"; they specify which activities are forbidden, such as killing, stealing, and adultery. Some norms specify that a certain type of behavior is permitted but not required, such as smoking or joining a sorority. Those norms are referred to as *permissive norms*. Finally, there are *preference norms,* which specify that certain kinds of behavior are preferred, but not required. Your family may prefer that you not smoke, but they will not prevent you from doing it if you want to.

Each norm is enforced by a variety of *sanctions* of differing severity. A sanction is the reward or punishment meted out for adhering to or violating a norm. It is the A given the student for excellent work in a course or the E given for failure to measure up to a *standard of* scholarly *behavior*. The more crucial the behavior is to the activities and objectives of the organization, the more rewarding or costly is the sanction, and the more likely the parts are to adhere to the norm.

NORMS AND COORDINATION. How do the parts of a social organization become *coordinated?* That is, how do they become arranged temporarily and spatially so as to maximize the pursuit of their own tasks as well as those of the total social organization? Many times this development of relatively harmoniously coordinated inter-actions is a result of influence either directly or indirectly exercised. The other parts of the system will arrange their activities to harmonize with those of its dominant unit. Suppose, for example, that a large air-craft manufacturing plant located in a medium-sized community de-cides to double its physical plant and its labor force. This decision will cause compensating alterations in the activities of other parts of the community. Building contractors will construct additional housing for the new workers coming into the community. City planners may propose that additional schools be built in the areas where they an-ticipate residential expansion. They may also propose the widening of the roads that lead to the plant. A myriad of adjustments will occur as a result of the passively exercised influence of one part of the organization.

At the other extreme is the development of formal (written) norms designed to coordinate the activities of the parts of an organization. An executive in a business organization, for example, may develop written rules (formal norms) that specify how the members of certain parts of his organization will interact in the future. Formal coordina-tion of this type involves the creation of norms that generally specify who will do what, when, and how, and with what quality of perform-ance. Between these two extreme types of coordination—the passive ex-ercise of influence and the creation of formal norms—lie types of coordination involving the active exercise of influence or informal, normative solutions to problems of interaction.

NORMS AND ROLES. Social roles are positions in organi-zations with which are associated certain routinely performed activities; they are the means by which the role occupant can participate in his society at the same time that he is achieving his own needs and solving his own problems (10). But the occupancy of a role also places demands on the person: he acquires *obligations*. These obligations range from the performance of highly technical skills (by a doctor, for example) to providing companionship and understanding (by a wife or close friend). These obligations are standards of behavior or norms associated with a role. Much of the content of a role is a collection of norms in the form of role obligations. But many kinds of behavior associated with many roles are not the subject of norms. When role occupants use influence, solve problems associated with performing their roles, or personally select among the options open to them to perform their tasks, their behavior is still associated with their roles, but it may not be normatively regulated.

NORMS AND ROLE CONFLICT. From the time that we are fairly young we occupy roles in different subgroups in our society. Each subgroup is likely to have some associated activities that are different from those of the other subgroups to which we belong. And it is not uncommon for the obligations of one subgroup to conflict with those of another. This situation is referred to as *role conflict*. A student has the role obligation to study and perform well in the classroom and on his examinations. But as a boyfriend he has an obligation to entertain and provide for the emotional needs of his girlfriend. Virtually every evening a situation of role conflict exists for him as he alternates between studying and relating to his girlfriend. The young father who must work from 3 to 11 P.M. in his factory is encountering role conflict. His obligations to his school-age children cannot be met because he must be at work while they are at home and awake.

These situations of role conflict are very unpleasant for the individual, but *sometimes* they are useful for the organizations. In his effort to reduce the conflict, the person often forces a change in the patterns of behavior expected in one or both of the organizations. Sometimes these changes are useful to the organizations as well as to the individual in the roles.

There are many ways of handling these conflict situations, and some of them enjoy considerable social approval (10). The person may leave one or both of the organizations that are responsible for his conflict. He may conform to the demands of each role whenever he is actively in it: the teenager who smokes with his friends but not at home with his family is an example. Occasionally, the person can redefine his role to satisfy the members of both organizations. If, for example, his parents forbid swearing, but his friends believe that swearing is useful, the person with the conflict may use a carefully selected set of words. He persuades his parents that they are really not swearwords and convinces his friends that they are adequate for demonstrating his masculinity. Other means of coping with role conflict include stalling for time, playing off one organization against another, or segregating the two roles completely. Any or all of these devices may be accompanied by the use of tact, lies, or excuses.

NORMS AND CULTURE.   Beginning in the last part of Chapter 4 we will concentrate primarily on one type of social organization: the society. But there is an aspect of the concept of society—its culture—that should be discussed here because of its relation to the concept of norms. Culture is often defined by sociologists as the sum of the norms, values, and beliefs found in a society. Beliefs include the *standards* used to understand the world, other people, and oneself. Belief systems are incorporated into religions and theologies, folklore and science, legends and philosophy. Values are complex sets of norms used as *principles rather than as guides to specific behavior.* They are statements about what is desirable and good and what is undesirable and bad; e.g., it is good to be religious; free enterprise is good. The term *value* is also commonly used to refer to our attitudes about books, money, convertibles, and clothing. Both of these uses of the value concept are heavily social-psychological.

One class of values is of special interest to the functionalist school in sociology. It is those that state the objectives of the organization: free enterprise, democracy, liberty. Some sociologists call these values organizational objectives, goals, or end-values. They are so abstract that they do not imply any definite set of norms (11). Different societies may uphold democracy as a value, but develop different standards of behavior to implement it. There are important differences in the *practice* of democracy in the United States, France, and Great Britain. Although the end-values themselves do not imply any given set of norms, there are standards or statements of standards available that are designed to implement them.

Culture is not synonymous with society. A society is a social organization; therefore it is the ordered, though changing, behavior found in a population. Culture includes much more than ordered behavior; it includes ideas and values, which are not behavior, but part of the psychological structure of the individual members of the society. The relation between society (or social organization) and culture is best understood if they are thought of as interacting. The social organization and the environment in which it is located shape the content of the culture: the values, norms, and beliefs. Conversely, the culture influences the structure of the social organization. For example, we can explain much of the ethical content of American religious institutions in the late nineteenth century as being a consequence of our free enterprise form of economic organization. Ministers declared that unions, collective bargaining, and strikes were contrary to Christian principles. On the other hand, religious organizations probably wield more influence on the affairs of our society than we can account for *solely* on the basis of the resources that they control. The value attached to being religious and to adhering to the ethic of our religious organizations probably increases the influence of these organizations. Thus culture influences the structure of the social organization and is itself affected by it.

One danger in this view of the relation between culture and social organization is that we can become overly enthusiastic in applying it. Every time we study an aspect of human behavior, we can "explain" it quickly and easily by attributing it to some value that the person or organization is trying to achieve. Such explanations are sometimes necessary and proper, but not always. The value explanation avoids the fact that most of our actions are shaped by the behavior of others; by forces external to ourselves. To attribute the behavior to values avoids the long, dirty, analytical task of seeking out other factors in the social organization that *may have* produced the behavior under study. Some sociologists are quick to offer the value explanation whenever a study has failed to explain or predict *all* instances of the behavior. This occurs despite the fact that sociology is still a very young science whose concepts and methods of measurement have not reached their ultimate sophistication. These deficiencies alone might explain the limitations of any set of findings.

A second reason for using the value explanation with great caution is based on logic. We can invent vast repertoires of values to explain all human behavior, but such an approach is hardly parsimonious, and it often creates the illusion, but only the illusion, of having explained something. At the beginning of the twentieth century, social psychologists were explaining every facet of human behavior by invoking an instinct or a combination of instincts. The number and content of the instincts advocated by the social psychologists varied greatly. Obviously, they were not explaining anything; they were just inventing a parallel term at another level—the psychological—and they were not being parsimonious. A similar danger lies in a hasty resort to a value explanation. Values and behavior affect each other, but they are both greatly affected by important environmental and organizational forces, as well as affecting the latter; these larger forces deserve at least as much of our attention as does the general culture.

A third reason for using a value explanation with considerable care is the very elusiveness of the value concept itself. Suppose we attempt to explain the structure of a social organization as the expression of the collective values of the members: for example, educational institutions are developed to achieve the values placed on education by the members of the society or community. But not all people attach value to education, and those who do may still disagree over the desired form of the organization. Whose values are responsible for the shape of the organization? Perhaps those values of the elite of the society? But are not their values in turn shaped in no small measure by the organizations in which they live? Furthermore, can we assume that the values are unambiguous? If they are ambiguous for some or all segments of the population, how then shall we use them?

The culture-organization argument just presented has been the focus for dividing sociologists into at least two camps. On the one side are the functionalists, who understand social organizations as the institutionalization of values. On the other side are the ecologists, who generally disallow that values have any force in human affairs. The ecologists emphasize such factors as the environment, level of technology, and the population in their studies of the determinants of social structure. Let us draw from both camps. Forces such as the environment, technology, and population are undoubtedly the most important for understanding the *broad outlines* of social organization. But just as surely as these factors shape values, the values themselves can become forces that react, to shape the organization and its environment, population, and technology. While the position of the functionalists is extreme in seeing human organizations as the consequence of institutionalizing the values of the population, it must be recognized that there are certain problems that the population must solve organizationally in order to develop and maintain an organization. The population must develop a supply of resources, whether it is food in the case of a society or coal and steel in the case of an automobile manufacturing plant. Subgroups are likely to develop within the organization to solve the problem of obtaining resources. They must develop means of distributing the resources to the members; subgroups will be developed to perform these activities. Similarly, they must develop means of protecting themselves from external and internal enemies and for recruiting new members. The particular shape that these subgroups take is limited *initially* by the environmental, technological, and population givens that confront the society. But solving problems creates values as well as new forms of organization, and then values become a force in human interaction.

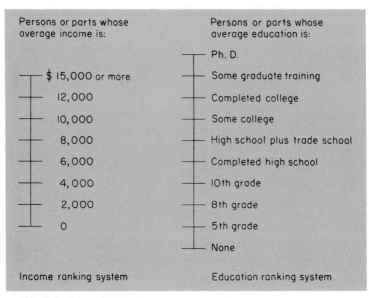

FIG. 2-5 Two ranking systems.

Rank Systems and Social Status

We have already seen that when individuals assume roles, they usually become differentiated from each other in terms of the activities they perform. Subgroups are also differentiated on this basis. But there is another way in which both persons and subgroups are differentiated. A part of the role concept is the position associated with the activities performed: programmer, teacher, daughter. *Positions* vary in the possession of a variety of characteristics; income, influence, educational attainment, and others. These characteristics are usually unequally distributed among the members or subgroups of the organization. We can, therefore, rank the persons, roles, or subgroups above or below one another in terms of *the amount of each characteristic they possess*. These hierarchical systems are called *rank systems. The position of a person or a part in a rank system is called its status.*

Because different persons make different amounts of money, people can be ranked by income. Roles and subgroups can also be ranked in terms of the average income of their occupants. The amounts shown in the income ranking system at the left of Fig. 2-5 are arbitrary but illustrative. Obviously, the status of any given subgroup, role, or person could be between the amounts of money shown, and the distribution of the population or the parts actually would be continuous along the line.

The parts of an organization or its population can also be arranged in a hierarchy in terms of the amount of education obtained by each person, subgroup, or role. The levels shown in the education ranking system at the right of Fig. 2-5 are also arbitrary, but we could expect the occupants of certain roles to have a certain status in the system: the roles of physician, lawyer, and professor, for example, require considerable education, and their occupants therefore are among those with the highest status; most unskilled workers have a low level of educational attainment, and the educational status of their roles is correspondingly low.

As we have just shown above, sociologists often rank populations rather than roles or subgroups on ranking systems. Although this practice is perfectly permissible and often necessary, it can be misleading. Many of the attributes for which people are ranked are obtained *only by their occupancy of roles or their membership in subgroups* (6). A person's income is largely a function of his occupational role. The amount of interpersonal influence that he wields is primarily determined by his occupational role or his subgroup memberships.

For our purposes, the most important of the many possible ranking systems is that of influence (13). Influence, you will recall, is the control that one part has over the activities of other parts. The exercise of influence includes the allocation of resources (14). Therefore, the higher the influence status of a part, the more control it can exercise over the disposition of resources; the lower its status, the less is its control. In business organizations the most influential roles receive the largest amounts of such diverse resources as income and stock options, and high-quality furniture (15). There have been no studies of communities or societies that have treated influence as a variable and shown that the amounts of other resources accumulated by the parts vary with it. But there are community studies (16, 17, 18) that show that the roles with the highest influence status in communities and societies, the *elite,* have larger amounts of such resources as education and income than the other parts possibly could have. In fact, this relation between influence and the accumulation of resources is *assumed* by social scientists to be true. Consequently, sociologists often use the average income and/or education of a part to indicate the amount of influence it contains (19, 20). The influence ranking system is important because it is a factor in any other ranking system that involves the important resources of an organization.

Influence involves the ability of one part to coordinate the activities of other parts. When we order the parts in terms of the amount of influence they possess, we have abstracted the coordinative hierarchy of the organization. When this hierarchy is created or institutionalized by norms, it is referred to as the *authority hierarchy*. Each part in the authority hierarchy is vested by norms with influence over a varying range of parts. The greater the range of institutionalized influence exercised by a part, the higher is its position in the authority hierarchy. The most influential parts or those with the most authority are called the *elite* (14).

Summary

A social organization has the following characteristics:

It has a population.

It is composed of parts, roles and subgroups, which are usually differentiated to some extent by their activities and varying amounts of other characteristics, especially influence.

Its characteristic organization or structure results from the routinization or institutionalization of exchanges of influence and interaction among the parts. This structure of relationships is changing constantly in ways that vary in their significance.

Its parts can be placed in hierarchical rank systems on the basis of differences in influence or other attributes.

SOCIAL ORGANIZATION AS A VARIABLE CONCEPT

Human collectivities vary in the extent to which these organizational characteristics are present (21). In the remainder of the chapter, let us see how this is so.

Social organizations differ in the degree of coordination among the parts. Organizations vary in the degree of specialization of the parts and in the degree of interdependence that arises from specialization. The Nuer society of Africa, as described by Evans-Pritchard (2), is divided into tribes that are located within specific geographical boundaries and are quite independent of one another for the exchange of goods and services. Some of the tribes have more frequent exchange relationships with parts of other societies than they do with their own. There is little functional interdependence and, as a result, little *need* for coordination of economic activities. Nonetheless, the tribes are a part of the same social organization, and they do coordinate other types of exchange relationships. A sharp contrast to the situation in Nuer society occurs when the interdependent parts of a social organization are bound together in a very tight pattern of relationships by the careful coordination of activities. In our society, the communities are highly specialized in terms of the activities their members perform (22). This situation requires a higher level of coordination among the parts to maintain the integrity of the organization. If the adequacy of the coordination for a specific level of specialization varies, the integration of the organization also varies.

Social organizations differ in the extent to which there are barriers to interaction among their parts. In some organizations all of the avenues of interaction are open. In the family, for example, all of the members usually can and do communicate with each other whenever they want to. In other organizations, all of the channels of interaction necessary for effective functioning are open, and others can be opened when they are needed. In the factory where the number of departments to which workers could travel was limited, the amount of unnecessary interaction was reduced. But if a wider range of interaction became necessary, a worker was given a black badge that permitted him to enter any department in the factory. In yet other organizations, some channels that need to be open if the group is to function effectively are closed or have barriers that make interaction difficult. In hospitals, for example, it is essential that the nursing, X-ray, and laboratory departments work together so that the patients' ailments can be diagnosed and treated. If the channels of interaction that connect these departments are obstructed for human, spatial, or mechanical reasons, then the ability of the hospital as a social organization to give adequate care is impaired (23). Barriers in channels of interaction are an especially severe problem for an organization where the parts are highly interdependent.

Social organizations differ in the extent to which the interactions among the parts are institutionalized. Interactions may be pure exercises of influence, or highly routinized and clothed in custom or formal norms, or they may contain some combination of both elements. In the family with a small child, parental interactions with the child are primarily overt acts of influence. But as the child learns what is expected of him—the obligations of his role—his relations with his parents become more institutionalized. The relations between teachers and their students are usually institutionalized. The teacher does not need to order the students to return to school the next day; there are norms that govern these behaviors. Large and very complex subgroups often develop in organizations to regulate and control the interactions among the various parts. Stock exchanges, banks, and law firms are examples of subgroups in our society that specialize in interpreting and controlling economic interactions. Religious subgroups formalize many of our interactions in conformity to a moral code.

Social organizations differ in the degree to which the norms are consistent and the parts conform to them. Imagine a school where the teachers are told to educate their students, but are also told not to suspend too many of them from school nor to permit them to drop out before they are sixteen years of age. The second and third norms make the first one more difficult to implement. The teachers lose some valuable sanctions, and their classes contain some reluctant attendants. In such a case we say that there are conflicting standards of behavior, or inconsistent norms.

The conduct of the parts may or may not conform to the norms of the social organization. The norms of our society oppose killing, the unprescribed use of certain drugs, and having more than one wife. Yet there have been subgroups in our society that have favored one or another of these activities. In social organizations of a given type, the rate of conforming behavior can vary greatly.

Populations without any of the characteristics of a social organization are called *aggregates*. Aggregates in which all the population shares one or more common characteristics are called *social categories*. Teenagers, males, or people who earn $10,000 per year are examples of social categories. In subsequent chapters, we will see that new social organizations often develop within social categories.

Unfortunately, the term *social organization* does not lend itself readily to variable language. We cannot easily or comfortably speak of high social organization versus low social organization (as we can of high versus low pressure, temperature, or volume). But by speaking of integrated versus segmented (unintegrated) social organizations, we can convert the term into a variable. Social organization is represented as a variable in Fig. 2-6.

The variable approach to the study of social organizations allows us to make comparative studies of them. Using the techniques of science, we can compare similar organizations—for example, hospitals or communities—with one another, measuring the degree to which each of the characteristics of organizations is present. Some organizations will be found to have a more normative consistency, greater differentiation, or more adequate coordination than others of a similar type. The consequences of these differences can also be examined systematically.

We can also compare different types of organizations, although this comparison is less easy. The application of a consistent set of concepts to such different organizations as prisons, schools, and families may

CHARACTERISTIC	AGGREGATE	SOCIAL ORGANIZATION	
		Low Integration (Segmented)	High Integration
Has a population?	Yes	Yes	Yes
Adequacy of coordination among the parts	No parts	Inadequate	Adequate
Interaction among the parts	No routinized interaction	Barriers exist between many parts that need to interact	All necessary channels are open; others can open when needed
Institutionalization of interaction	None	Little normative regulation of interaction; overt influence characterizes many interactions	High
Consistency of the norms	No norms	Many inconsistencies	Few, if any inconsistencies
Conformity of population to the norms	No norms	Low	High

FIG. 2-6 Social organization as a variable concept.

permit us to develop some very general propositions applying to large classes of organizations or perhaps to all organizations. Certainly one of the major emphases of future sociological research will be a combination of this approach with the sophisticated tools of mathematics that are becoming increasingly available to social scientists.

REFERENCES

1 J. Feibleman and J. W. Friend, "The Structure and Function of Organization," *Philosophical Review, 54* (1945), 19-44.

2 E. E. Evans-Pritchard, *The Nuer* (Oxford: Oxford University Press, 1940).

3 T. M. Newcomb, *Personality and Social Change* (New York: The Dryden Press, Inc., 1943).

4   The Naval Conference Research Program. An unpublished series of experiments on administrative conferences. Mimeographed copies are in the University of Michigan Library, Ann Arbor, Michigan.

5   A. Strauss, ed., *The Social Psychology of George Herbert Mead* (Chicago: The University of Chicago Press, 1956; a Phoenix book).

6.   A. H. Hawley, "Community Power and Urban Renewal Success," *The American Journal of Sociology, 68* (1963), 422-31.

7   A. H. Hawley, *Human Ecology: A Theory of Community Structure* (New York: The Ronald Press Company, 1950).

8   H. J. Leavitt, "Some Effects of Certain Communication Patterns on Group Performance," *The Journal of Abnormal and Social Psychology, 46* (1951), 38-50.

9   R. K. Merton, *Social Theory and Social Structure* (New York: Free Press of Glencoe, Inc., 1957), p. 133.

10   J. Toby, "Some Variables in Role Conflict Analysis," *Social Forces, 30* (1952), 323-27.

11   N. J. Smelser, *Theory of Collective Behavior* (New York: Free Press of Glencoe, Inc., 1963),

12   A. Cohen, *Delinquent Boys: The Culture of the Gang* (New York: Free Press of Glencoe, Inc., 1955).

13   D. H. Wrong, "The Functional Theory of Stratification: Some Neglected Considerations," *American Sociological Review, 24* (1959), 772-82.

14   H. Lasswell and A. Kaplan, *Power and Society* (New Haven: Yale University Press, 1950).

15   T. Caplow, *The Sociology of Work* (Minneapolis: The University of Minnesota Press, 1954), p. 156.

16   F. Hunter, *Community Power Structure* (Chapel Hill: University of North Carolina Press, 1953).

17   R. S. Lynd, *Middletown* (New York: Harcourt, Brace, and World, Inc., 1929).

18   W. L. Warner, *Democracy in Jonesville* (New York: Harper & Row, Publishers, 1949).

19   G. H. Saenger, "Social Status and Political Behavior," *The American Journal of Sociology, 51* (1945), 103-13.

20   H. H. Hyman, "The Value Systems of Different Classes: A Social Psychological Contribution to the Analysis of Stratification," in *Class, Status and Power*, R. Bendix and S. Lipset, eds. (New York: Free Press of Glencoe, Inc., 1953), pp. 426-42.

21   W. S. Landecker, "Integration and Group Structure: An Area for Research," *Social Forces, 30* (1952), 394-400.

22   O. R. Galle, "Occupational Composition and the Metropolitan Hierarchy: The Inter- And Intro-Metropolitan Division of Labor," *The American Journal of Sociology, 69* (1963), 260-69.

23   B. Georgopoulos and F. C. Mann, *The Community General Hospital* (New York: The Macmillan Company, 1962).

3

some sources of variation
among social organizations

An informal friendship group appears to be quite different from a business organization, and the structure of a family seems quite different from that of a society. What are the reasons for this great variation in social organizations? Three factors account for much of it. One is external to the organization itself—its natural and social environment. The other two are aspects of the organization that greatly influence the structure and functioning of its other aspects—its economy and the size of its population. This chapter develops a series of statements or propositions to explain how each of these factors affects relevant characteristics of the social organization—for example, its division of labor, its normative structure, and its patterns of interaction. By examining the possible variations in the basic factors, we can develop different models of social organizations.

THE ROLE OF THE NATURAL ENVIRONMENT

The *natural* environment in which any social organization is located includes such characteristics as the quality of the soil, the types of mineral and other resources available, the amount and variation in the annual rainfall, the variation in the temperature of the air and the length of the day, and the types and distribution of supporting flora and fauna. But a social organization also exists in the presence of other social organizations, and these constitute its *social* environment.

Each of these environments presents problems for the population living in it. The population must obtain a livelihood in its environment, whether it is by hunting the animals, fishing, gathering the edible vegetation, or farming the land. Floods, tornadoes, violent thunderstorms, or unusually hot or cold weather can pose threats to man's existence. The presence of other social organizations in the environment also poses problems: the existence of a warfaring neighbor can force the members of a social organization to develop measures for self-protection or security. The existence of a neighbor who has desirable goods or services may lead to the development of trade relations that will affect the structure of relations both within the social organization and with the neighbor.

If the population is to survive, it must solve these problems adequately. Let us examine the consequences of the process of problem solving carefully. Suppose the members of a village find themselves under repeated attack by the members of a nearby village. There are a number of ways that they can attempt to cope with this problem: they can surrender themselves to the other village, learn to defend themselves, learn the art of warfare sufficiently to attack the other village, assume a defensive posture and fortify their village, leave the area, or enter a defensive alliance with another village. All these solutions have a common characteristic—they require the development of new patterns of interaction that will probably become institutionalized if they are successful. The solution of the problem requires the restructuring of the patterns of interaction among some or all of the parts of the social organization. The new organization may involve a fundamental adjustment of the whole system or it may require the addition of a new part and some alteration of relationships to account for the presence of this new part. The communal hunting party is an organization created by a population to solve the problem of hunting certain types of game that defy individual hunting. Police forces and armies represent organizational solutions to the problem of defense from enemies.

If the structure of the social organization (the customary pattern of interactions among the parts) represents in part an adjustment to problems posed by the environment, then we should be able to infer some of the characteristics of the social organization from the characteristics of its natural and social environment. Although this is true of any social organization, we shall restrict our discussion to the society. The reason for this restriction is contained in a basic principle of sociology: all other things being approximately equal, *the larger the population of an organization, the greater its influence in relation to other organizations* (1). From this principle it can be deduced that the accommodations a society makes to its environment will greatly influence the structure of its smaller parts (the subgroups). The economy of a society—the means selected to extract sustenance from the environment and to process and distribute it—will exercise great influence on the structure of such subgroups as the family. In an agrarian economy with a primitive technology, the family is likely to contain many members; but in an industrial economy, the value of the large family no longer exists. Thus the economy of the total society affects the size of the family, as well as many other characteristics. This fundamental and pervasive effect of the society on its subgroups leads us to focus here on the relations between the *natural* environment and the society. A discussion of the social environment will be postponed until the end of this chapter, after we have had an opportunity to introduce some necessary concepts.

Environmental Determinism

Populations cope with the natural environment by altering their structure or creating new parts. Because environments differ so greatly in different parts of the world, different types of social organizations may be appropriate for different populations. So we can account for much of the diversity in human organizations in terms of the different environments with which these organizations are trying to cope. But does the natural environment *determine* the structure of social organizations found in it? What aspects of the social organization does it influence most immediately or directly? Let us take each of these questions in turn.

For some time a controversy raged over the extent of the influence of the natural environment on social systems. Some social scientists took the position that the environment determines the structure and functioning of the social system. This proposition seems plausible at first glance, but it does not stand up under closer inspection. The Navajo and the Zuni Indians live in the same arid environment, yet their social organizations are different in some important ways. The Iroquois Indians lived in an environment that is quite similar to that of western Europe, but there the similarity ends. Virtually every social scientist today would agree that the physical environment plays a significant part in shaping social systems, but not that it *determines* their structure.

How great is the influence? We can see it particularly clearly in some of the more extreme environments encountered by populations. The methods of transportation, the tools, and the types of housing built by Eskimos reflect the fundamental effects that the environment has on that society. The paucity of food in the environment precludes the development of a dense population; even the language of the Eskimo is influenced by the environment: several words differentiate among types of snow. The environment of the nomadic Arab can be shown to have had similar effects on his social organization, technology, and language. It would seem that the effects of the natural environment are neither determining nor negligible, but somewhere in between.

The Agricultural Potential Approach

A middle ground between environmental determinism and environmental irrelevancy was developed by Betty Meggers (2). She proposed that "the level to which a culture can develop is dependent upon the agricultural potentiality of the environment it occupies." Note that this proposition concerns the level to which a culture *can* develop, not the level to which it must develop. In other words, the agricultural potential of an area *sets limits* on the degree of elaboration that is possible for its society. This proposition contains a very useful insight. Suppose we divide the occupational roles in a society into two types: food-producing and non-food-producing roles. If the environment has such a limited food-producing potential that every member of a society in it must invest all his time and energy in getting enough to eat, then the society will not be able to support any non-food-producing roles. If a society is to have such non-food-producing roles as miner, carpenter, or digital-computer operator, then some of its members must produce enough food to supply these people or else some outside sources of food must be found.

Aside from this insight, however, Meggers' proposition suffers from some serious problems. First, it is stated in terms of the agricultural potential of the natural environment. It evaluates an environment in terms of its capacity for one type of food gathering—farming. But there are many societies that do not farm their land; instead they hunt or gather the natural flora and fauna. For such societies, the concept of agricultural potential has little relevance (3). Some of these hunting and gathering societies exist in environments that have fairly low agricultural potential, but abundant game. These societies can develop more elaborate social structures than can some other hunting and gathering societies located on land with the highest agricultural potential. The Wishram Indians lived along the Columbia River in Oregon—an area of only fair agricultural potential—and because of the abundance of salmon and other game, they developed a more elaborate society than did many of the Plains Indians, who lived on land of the highest agricultural potential. Betty Meggers' proposition does not permit us to make predictions in this and similar situations because it is based on a specific type of economy—agriculture.

A second problem with the Meggers formulation is that it does not make allowance for the possibility of trade between societies. A society may have a relatively low agricultural potential and still be highly elaborated because it trades its manufactured products for the agricultural products of other societies. Great Britain is an example. Meggers' proposition is adequate only if we assume that the society is isolated from others—a condition that we will see later in this chapter seldom exists.

A Reformulation of Meggers' Proposition

Suppose we consider the food-producing potential of an environment disregarding whether it involves agriculture. If the food-producing potential of the environment is extremely low, then the types of societies that can develop *indigenously* are extremely limited (4). An advanced society with an extensive division of labor cannot develop in a swamp or in a desert. The supply of food is so limited that persons in food-producing roles cannot gather a sufficient surplus to support many non-food-producing roles. In these areas, which Ferdon (3) refers to as submarginal environments, indigenous societies are invariably limited to hunting and gathering economies and rather unelaborate social structures. Environmental determinism is a useful approach for this specific case of the poorest type of environments. We should note immediately, however, that a population in a more salubrious environment can extend itself into areas of submarginal environment and convert them into productive land that will support a greater division of labor. The neolithic Egyptian farmers drained the swamps along the Nile and converted them into land of great agricultural productivity (5, 6, 7).

We may expect, then, that in areas of submarginal environment no native, advanced civilization can develop. But we cannot make the opposite statement, that advanced civilizations *must* arise in regions with superior natural environments. The better the natural environment, the greater is the range of possible solutions to the problem of obtaining food. Regions with marginal environments may contain native societies with hunting and gathering, grazing, or farming economies. Although the problems of farming in a marginal environment are many, they can be solved, and the yields can be fairly reliable (3). Regions of greater environmental potential may produce any of these types of economies, or any of the more advanced agricultural and industrial economies to which we are accustomed. Which type of economy will be found in the better natural evironments cannot be predicted exactly from characteristics of the environment alone; a variety of historical and other factors are also involved. We might expect that a population located at the edge of a body of water with an abundance of edible fish might develop a marine economy, but it is not absolutely certain. Similarly, populations located close to herds of animals or living on easily tillable land may have a high probability of developing respectively a hunting or agricultural economy, but it is not safe to rely too heavily on these environmental guidelines. They make too many assumptions about the rationality of the population and the technology available to it.

What kinds of relations can we expect between the natural environment in which a population is located and the structure of its society? In order to make accurate predictions, we must know the type of economy used by the population, and this can vary widely. There are, however, some general limits: first, agrarian or industrial economies will never originate in submarginal environments. Second, strange as it may seem, agrarian societies will seldom develop in the very best types of environment (3, 8). The best types of environment for agricultural production usually contain prairie, or chernozem, soil such as that found in the American Midwest (3). But this type of soil is so tightly sodded that it cannot be tilled with a crude wooden plow. Generally, a plow with a sharp metal tip is required, and the existence of such plows presupposes the existence of a metals industry. Therefore, the exploitation of excellent environments usually occurs *after* the population has developed a metals industry. The exceptions to this rule are those societies that developed in the Nile, the Ganges, the Tigris, and the Euphrates River valleys. In these instances, however, the population farms soil that is left after the annual river floods, but before anything has grown in it that would make it difficult to till. Most agrarian societies develop in less perfect environments. In forested areas, for example, there is no deeply rooted vegetation other than the trees. Farmers simply burn down the trees using the ashes as a natural fertilizer, and plant their crops after shallow plowing the ground. Societies that use these techniques are said to have *slash-and-burn* economies. In areas where the trees are less dense, farmers may plow the land in irregular patterns around the trees.

THE ROLE OF THE ECONOMY

Economy refers to those parts of the society that are involved in the extraction, processing, and distribution of materials from the natural environment. The term *industries* is often used to refer to the various subunits in the economy that are involved in one *or* another of its functions.

Economy, Environment, and Population

We can develop a close approximation of the size of the population that can be supported in an area if we know the economy selected by that population and the food-gathering potential of the environment given that specific type of economy. Table 3-1 shows some figures of this sort, according to two anthropologists.

TABLE 3-1

TYPE OF ECONOMY AND POPULATION DENSITY

Type of economy	Average population density per hundred square miles
Hunting and gathering	100
Village agriculture	2,500
Urban agriculture	5,000

Source: R. J. Braidwood and C. A. Reed, "The Achievement and Early Consequences of Food Production: A Consideration of the Archeological and Natural-Historical Evidence," *Cold Spring Harbor Symposia on Quantitative Biology*, 22 (1957), 19-31.

There is nothing final about the figures in the table; they are approximations obtained from archeological evidence and from comparisons with similar societies in similar settings in the contemporary world. The table shows that the average hunting and gathering society will support about one hundred people per hundred square miles. But hunting and gathering organizations vary greatly in their population densities, depending on the character of the environment and the level of technology. The highest known population density for this type of economy is the Yokuts of California, who had two hundred people per hundred square miles, but it is far more common for these organizations to have fewer than one hundred people per hundred square miles. In the poorest environments population densities of one to three people per hundred square miles are common: the Caribou Eskimo are an example. If we also know that the natural environment has a very low food-producing potential, then we can expect the population density to be nearer the lower limits of the proposed range; that is, nearer to zero than to two people per square mile. These population-density figures are important, because, as we shall see later, the size of the population is a crucial variable for predicting the society's other structural characteristics. If we can calculate the size of a society's population, we can make some judgments about the configuration of that society.

The Economy and Influence Status

The *key industry* in an economy is the major source of sustenance for the population of the society; e.g., farming in an agrarian society. In some social organizations there may be more than one key industry; for example, in a community with a university and a manufacturing company that employ about the same number of people and spend about the same amount of money. Because it is the key source of sustenance, the key industry (or industries) exerts the greatest amount of influence on interactions among the parts of the social organization. Any change in the ways in which the key industry interacts with the other parts will prompt an adjustment by the latter. If in a community where a university is the key industry it is decided to change the date on which the employees are paid, then corresponding adjustments must be made by the other parts of the community. On the new pay days, extra employees will be added in banks and grocery stores; the police will have to perform special duties because of the increase in the volume of traffic, and restaurants will experience increased business. The literature in the social sciences contains many studies that show the influence of a part of a community to be a function of its relation to the key industry in the community: *the closer and more direct the relation, the greater the influence of the part* (9, 10, 11, 12). The key industries in our largest communities are industrial and commercial, and studies of communities of this type have shown that the greatest influence over community affairs resides in these parts. This influence is concentrated further in the top roles— the elite—in the key industry. The least influence is lodged in roles at the bottom of the role hierarchies of peripheral industries. If the economy is hunting and gathering, the greatest influence is lodged in the role of the best hunter, particularly during a hunting expedition. In a society where the economy is essentially agrarian, the greatest influence resides among the owners of the largest land holdings, and peasants and merchants have little influence. In our society the roles of banker, financier, and industrialist possess the greatest influence (9, 10, 11, 12). Note once again that it is not people who have influence but rather the roles that they occupy. The occupants of roles may or may not exercise the full influence potential of their roles.

The Economy and the Technology

Technology refers to the tools that man uses to manipulate his environment. How does the technology of the social organization articulate with the aspects of the social organization that we have been discussing above? *Implicit in every type of economy is a particular technology.* If the social system has a hunting economy, it will develop such appropriate tools as bows, arrows, spears, or clubs. It may even develop spiked arrows for shooting fish and blunt arrows for shooting birds. If it has a marine gathering economy, it may develop some kinds of nets, boats, hooks, and lures.

Without his tools, man is a rather sorry exploiter of his environment. He is slow afoot, unable to fly, and low in horsepower. Even the technology of the American colonies was sufficiently crude that some frontier farmers occasionally had to use members of their families to pull the plow. These conditions placed severe limitations on the amount of land that could be plowed and, consequently, on the amount of food that could be grown. But with domesticated animals or tractors, or with rifles or bows and arrows, man becomes more a master of the world in which he lives. Tools, then, increase the efficiency with which man can extract food and other resources from his

TABLE 3-2

PERCENTAGE OF THE POPUATION ENGAGED IN
AGRICULTURAL OCCUPATIONS IN SELECTED COUNTRIES

Country	Percentage of population
Congo	85
Honduras	83
India	71
Czechoslovakia	38
France	27
United States	12

Source: *1957 Yearbook of Food and Agricultural Statistics*
(Rome: Food and Agricultural Organization of the United
Nations, 1958), XI, Part 1, 16-17.

environment. *The higher the levels of the technology, the more food and other goods man can produce up to the limits of the environmental potential* (13). Table 3-2 shows that 85 per cent of the Congolese and only 12 per cent of the American populations were engaged in agriculture in 1951. The reason for this difference is, in part, that with his advanced technology the American farmer can produce two hundred times as much food acre for acre as the Congolese farmer. This low productivity per farmer requires that practically the entire population engage in agriculture in order to survive. The number of non-food-producing roles, therefore, is held in check. If these nations are to industrialize, they must develop a farm technology that will increase the food productivity of each farmer and thus release the needed manpower for non-food-producing roles, or they must require the population to assume both food-producing and non-food-producing roles.

The level of technology also influences other parts of the social organization. *The higher the level of technology, the greater the division of labor.* It is not too difficult for most of the members of simpler societies to grasp all aspects of the technology of that society. All of the people can make bows or grass huts. But as the level of technology increases, the amount of knowledge it entails becomes too great for any one person to acquire. Therefore, specialization of roles is required. The division of labor becomes increasingly refined as the level of the technology advances. These relationships are summarized in Fig. 3-1.

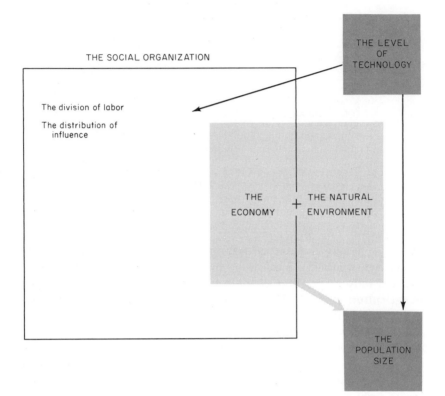

THE SOCIAL ORGANIZATION

THE LEVEL OF TECHNOLOGY

The division of labor

The distribution of influence

THE ECONOMY + THE NATURAL ENVIRONMENT

THE POPULATION SIZE

FIG. 3-1

THE SIZE OF THE POPULATION

The characteristics of the environment and the economy affect the size of the population. But how do variations in population size affect the social structure? Our discussion will parallel the outline of the various characteristics of a social organization presented in Chapter 2; we will see by means of a series of propositions that changes in population size affect most of these characteristics systematically.

Population Size and Interaction Among the Parts

Perhaps the most fundamental effect of increasing population size on an organization is on the patterns of interaction among

TABLE 3-3

SIZE OF AN ORGANIZATION AND THE POTENTIAL
NUMBER OF RELATIONSHIPS AMONG ITS MEMBERS

Size	Relationships *
2	1
3	4
4	11
5	26
6	57
7	120

* These figures are derived by calculating the sum of all
possible subgroups (pairs, triples, etc.) for each organizational size. This total is increased by 1 to account for
the possibility of a simultaneous interaction among all of
the parts.

the parts. Table 3-3 shows the number of paths of interaction possible
in social organizations of different sizes: the size is increasing by addition while the number of paths is multiplying. This finding can be
stated in the form of a proposition.

Proposition 1   *As the population of a social organization increases arithmetically, the number of possible channels of interaction
increases geometrically.*

If the organization is to function effectively, it is obvious that even
in fairly small organizations some means must be found to limit the
use of the available channels. In a classroom situation, for example,
some limitations must be placed on the use of channels of interaction
for effective teaching and learning. The students cannot be talking
with each other when the teacher is lecturing or other students are
reciting, and all of the students cannot be reciting at the same time.
Order is introduced by the use of norms that forbid the use of certain
channels and that require that the student be recognized by the teacher
before he begins to talk. In other words, *the structure of the organization is adjusted to accommodate to the problem of the increased number of channels of interaction.*

Following this same line of reasoning, John James (14) predicted that
organizations that were trying to complete tasks—committees and work
teams—would have fewer members than friendship cliques and other

nontask organizations. He observed 21 organizations in their natural settings, coded them either as action-taking or non-action-taking, and found that the action-taking organizations had an average of 6.5 members, while the non-action-taking organizations had an average of 14 members.

The necessity of limiting the use of available channels was also observed in R. F. Bales' studies of organizations of varying population size in a laboratory setting. He found that as organizations increased in population size, the members began to eliminate some of the channels of interaction. Increasingly, interactions were directed to one person, who decided which of them should receive the attention of the entire membership. Recall Figs. 2-3 and 2-4, which illustrate respectively the situation in which all of the channels are open and that in which some are closed but can be reached through an intermediate part. The latter case illustrates how the specialization of a part as a coordinator of interaction can reduce the number of channels of interaction used and thus maintain the effectiveness of the organization. We can summarize this basic relationship between population size and interaction as follows:

Proposition 1a   *As the population of a social organization increases, some of the potential channels of interaction must be eliminated and the organization restructured.*

The notion of specialization as a means of handling the problem of increasing population size leads us directly to the next proposition.

Population Size and the Parts

Proposition 2   *As the population of a social organization increases, the number of its parts and the degree of their specialization also increase.*

In terms of our earlier definitions, this proposition can be divided into two more specific ones:

> *As the population of a social organization increases,*
> a) *the number of its subgroups and the degree of their specialization also increases;*
> b) *the number of its roles and the degree of their specialization also increase.*

Let us first consider the effects of increasing size on subgroups. If you have ever arrived early at a party, you may recall this proposition in action. When just a few people are present, they usually talk with one another as a single group. But as people continue to arrive at the party, an interesting change takes place. Some of the members come to dominate the discussion, and others do not speak at all. This process usually sets in when half a dozen to a dozen people are present. Some members, dissatisfied with the group life because they cannot involve themselves in it as much as they would like, strike up conversations with the person on either side of them. As the evening progresses, the original group fragments into a series of smaller groups in which the individual has ample opportunity to relate to others. So it is in all our group memberships. In the large groups to which we belong, there are always subgroups present. In student dormitories there are small friendship groups or cliques. Not all of the members of a large community or society can get to know each other and to interact, and in each of these groups are formed vast numbers of subgroups both formal and informal.

This increase in the number of subgroups as the population increases has been noted in several studies. William Ogburn and Otis Duncan (16) reported that the larger the community in the United States, the greater the number of religious denominations it contains. C. Wagely (17) studied the effects of depopulation on the structure of an Indian society (the Tapirape). Originally, the Tapirape were settled in five villages, but owing to epidemics of diseases brought by the white man, the population was greatly reduced. The remaining population was only large enough to support one village. Among his observations, Wagely notes that as the population decreased, the number of feast or ceremonial clubs declined from ten to three. In his study of thirty tribes, R. Naroll (18) found that as the size of the largest settlement increased, the number of subgroups increased.

The relation between the size of the population and the degree of specialization of the subgroups is not so direct. An organization can accommodate itself to an increase in size by creating additional but wholly similar units so long as these units remain fairly independent of each other. In other words, *differentiation among the parts need not occur if there is a minimum of interaction among them.* But as we saw earlier, if interaction is necessary, certain parts must specialize in its coordination. In keeping with this reasoning, Naroll was able to show for his thirty tribes that as the size of the population increased, the number of *types* of subgroups increased, some of them specializing in the performance of police and administrative functions.

Now let us consider the effects of increasing population size on the division of labor. R. F. Bales (15), you will remember, found that the specialized role of coordinator of interaction developed as groups increased in size. In effect, a modified leadership role had emerged, the occupant of which was expected to see that only those interactions took place that helped the group to achieve its objectives. In another study (19), P. E. Slater observed that even in small organizations the leadership role was divided into two specialties: socioemotional and task-leading. The socioemotional leader was concerned primarily with the internal affairs of the group; the task leader, with the relations of the group to the external world.

William Whyte's insightful study of restaurants (20) showed a similar trend to specialization of roles as the restaurants increased in number of personnel. In Fig. 3-2 some of the patterns that he found are diagrammed.

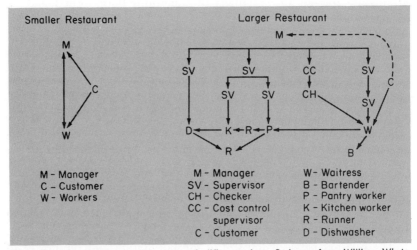

FIG. 3-2   Role structure in restaurants of different sizes. Redrawn from William Whyte, "The Social Structure of the Restaurant," *The American Journal of Sociology*, 54 (1949), 302-8. Used by permission of The University of Chicago Press.

Further support for the increase in specialization with the increase in size of the population can be found in other comparative studies. Using data from the 1940 census, G. K. Zipf (21) found that as the size of American communities increased, the number of occupational specialties also increased. Naroll (18) found that the number of craft specialties increased with the size of the largest settlement in the tribe. Wagely (17) reported that the division of labor declined in the Indian society he studied as the population declined.

The relation between the size of the population and the division of labor is not perfect, however. China, for example, has a larger population than the United States, but it has nowhere near so refined a division of labor. We can give precision to the relation by adding the variable "level of technology." An increase in the level of technology of a social system causes an increase in the division of labor. Therefore, *when an increase in the level of technology is accompanied by an increase in population, then an increase in the division of labor will certainly occur.*

In a large social system with a high level of technology—the United States, for example—the division of labor can become exceedingly refined. H. L. Wilensky and C. N. Lebeaux (22) have illustrated the degree of specialization achieved in our society by referring to the *Dictionary of Occupational Titles* and selecting some occupations listed for the meatpacking industry: eyelid remover, gut snatcher, oxtail washer, hindlegs toenail remover, frontlegs toenail remover, and belly shaver. These are all full-time occupations in that industry.

Because we become highly dependent on one another for the performance of our specialized roles, the content of each role is likely to be made quite clear. We simply cannot afford to have some specialist fail to perform his functions. Furthermore, problems of interaction can occur among highly specialized, interdependent roles if it is not clear which functions are assigned to which roles. Formal statements of the content of each role help to solve this problem. Hence our third proposition:

Proposition 3   *As the population of a social organization increases, the roles become more formalized.*

Population Size and Norms

There is a considerable difference between a sociological definition of the concept *norm* and a social-psychological one. Social psychologists often define *norms* as standards of behavior about which all the members of an organization agree. In other words, there has to be consensus (a psychological state) about a standard of behavior before it can be called a norm. A strictly sociological definition imposes no such standard. Norms are entities in and of themselves. A norm against automobile speeding does not become something less than a norm simply because some fraction of the population does not adhere to it. Therefore, a norm can be an organizational norm even though a part of the population of that organization may not adhere to it. It is possible to talk about the degree to which the behavior of the population conforms to the norm without indicating that something less than perfect conformity revokes the norm. With this clarification in mind, we can make the following proposition:

Proposition 4   *As the population of a social organization increases, variation in norms about a given behavior increases among the subgroups.*

The proof of this proposition is developed from Proposition 2: as groups increase in size, the number and types of subgroups also increase. The combination of problems faced by each subgroup is usually unique—first, because the subgroups are spread out over a varying environment that presents varying problems; second, because each subgroup is bound in a set of interactions with other parts of the organization in ways that are often unique. As we saw earlier, the solution of problems often takes the form of creating norms. Therefore, if a part encounters unique problems, it may develop norms that are in some respects unique (1, 23). In different parts of the world there are some noteworthy differences in the ways that Roman Catholics practice their religion. These differences have arisen as a result of an intermingling of Catholicism and local customs. In our society, the delinquent gang has a subculture that differs in many respects from the parent culture. You have only to look about you to see a subculture with some unique norms—the college student subculture.

It is inevitable, then, that considerable variation from subgroup to subgroup will develop in the evaluation of a given activity. Some groups will be against drinking and smoking, and others will incorporate these activities into their programs. Some groups will advocate making a profit, and others will be against it. Some will favor aggression and violence; others will be utterly opposed to these solutions to their problems.

Often these idiosyncratic norms are difficult to change, even though most of the other subgroups may be opposed to them. First, it must be remembered that the norm is probably useful to the subgroup that adheres to it. Second, the large population of the social organization often protects the anonymity of the subgroup and even permits it to maintain a measure of secrecy (16). Government officials in modern underdeveloped countries complain that they cannot get accurate data on certain behaviors in the peasant villages. When an official arrives in the village, the peasants hide their usual behaviors and conform to the accepted societal standards. But once the official has left the village, they return to their normal patterns of behavior. Third, because of the communication difficulties posed by large size, the members of a subgroup may not know the effects of their action on other subgroups. For these reasons it is easier to maintain normative homogeneity in a smaller social organization.

Despite this difficulty, it is nonetheless essential that the interactions of the parts of an organization conform to certain norms that are essential to the effective functioning of the total organization. In our society, religious subgroups must be tolerant of each other's normative behavior; communication among subgroups should be in English; and homicide is proscribed. School systems could not operate in the manner that we know them if they did not demand the conformity of all of the students to such norms as punctuality, discipline, respect for teachers, and completion of assigned tasks. Yet in spite of the need for universal adherence to these norms, deviance from them is possible for the reasons already stated. As groups increase in size, it is easier for the parts to develop their own patterns of behaviors, to avoid the monitoring of other parts, and to protect themselves from sanctions by the other parts. Furthermore, because of the communication problems attendant on increased population, the norms of the social organization may not be clear to the subgroups. Obviously, if they are not clearly communicated, they are less likely to be obeyed (24, 25). This reasoning suggests the following proposition:

Proposition 5 *As the population of a social organization increases, the proportion of the population deviating from its norms also increases.*

Numerous studies confirm this relationship. They have been summarized by R. G. Barker (26) and are outlined below.

1. As the number of workers in factories increases, several forms of deviant behavior have been observed to appear:
   a) The frequency of lateness to work increases;
   b) The number of threats to strike increases (in spite of the fact that the larger factories pay higher wages);
   c) The number of man-hours lost per employee due to strikes increases.
2. As the number of members in union locals increases, the proportion of the members who attend union meetings declines.
3. As the membership of churches increases, the ratio of the number of children in Sunday School to the total membership declines.
4. As the number of members in Rotary Clubs increases, the proportion of the members who attend meetings of the organization declines.

The effects of increase in population on the norms of the total organization can be summarized as follows: (1) the proportion of members adhering to the norms of the total organization declines, and (2) considerable variation arises in the subgroups' standards for any given behavior, regardless of whether that behavior is the subject of a norm for the total organization.

We saw earlier that the institutionalized pattern of interactions among the parts gives the collection of parts its characteristic of structure or organization. If the different parts do not adhere to common norms governing interaction, the structure of the social organization is less definite. The integration of the parts declines. We can say then that:

Proposition 6   *As the population of a social organization increases, and variation about interactive norms increases among the subgroups, the integration that the organization achieves from sharing common norms declines.*

One final relation between population size and norms is based on Proposition 1 (the number of possible channels of interaction increases geometrically as the population increases arithmetically). If a fairly large organization is to function effectively, appropriate channels of communication among the members must be specified. Use of channels may be limited by a special part charged with the task of coordinating interaction. Or norms may specify which part will interact with which other part, when, and under what circumstances. Or the two methods may be used in combination. If norms are developed, it becomes increasingly necessary to formalize and codify them as the organization becomes more complex. This procedure ensures uniform communication of the norms among the parts. *Robert's Rules of Order* is a formal set of norms that specify the channels and methods of interacting among the members of a fairly large organization. We can summarize the relation between the size of the population and the formality of the norms as follows:

Proposition 7   *As the population of a social organization increases, the ratio of formal norms to informal norms also increases.*

Population Size and Influence

In Chapter 2 we saw that the parts of a social organization can be ranked in relation to one another on any of a number of ranking systems—by the amount of education, income, or prestige possessed by the occupants of roles or by the members of subgroups, for example. The ranking system that is of central importance to sociologists is the amount of *influence* associated with a role or subgroup in an organization. The position of any given part in such a system is the *influence status* of that part.

Influence rank system is a variable concept, ranging from the highly informal and flexible rank system to the formal and rigid *hierarchy*, which is an *institutionalized* influence ranking system. If an influence rank system has not been formalized by traditional or formal norms, then a description of it by a sociologist injects an element of formality that really is not present. In organizations with these uninstitutionalized influence systems, the members are often unaware of how influence is distributed.

In other organizations the members have created *hierarchies* of roles or subgroups, which are *institutionalized influence ranking systems*. In such hierarchies, each role or part is vested with legitimated influence (authority). The creation of hierarchies is a useful device for solving communication and coordination problems in the organization. The Bales experiments with small organizations in laboratory settings (15) show that hierarchies are a useful social invention for handling the problem of the rapidly increasing communication potential that develops as organizations increase in size. The coordinator of the discussion had more influence over the process of interaction than did the other members: he could permit them to interact or prevent them from it. These experiments illustrate the initial stages of the differentiation of influence: if the organization had continued in existence long enough, these differences might have formalized into a hierarchy. The formality and rigidity of these hierarchies varies from one organization to another.

An often-discussed question in the literature on business organizations is: What is the span of roles that a supervisor can supervise? A grade-school teacher, for example, can give a certain amount of individual attention to only so many students. If the number of students increases, the amount of individual attention declines. So as the number of supervised roles increases, the problem of insufficient supervision for effective performance of the roles can arise. Various social scientists have proposed different numbers of roles that a supervisor can effectively oversee (27). The numbers most often proposed vary from three to twelve. But there is a certain artificiality in proposing that a supervisor can oversee a specific number of roles in *any* situation. If the roles are identical—if they involve the performance of the same activities at the same time—then a supervisor can oversee many more than twelve of them.

He can also oversee many more than twelve roles if the occupants are highly proficient in performing their activities—if they require little on-the-job training. A leader of a symphony orchestra can oversee the activities of well over a hundred musicians (with the aid of a coordinative device known as a musical score). In view of these considerations it has been proposed that estimates of the span of control must be modified. S. H. Udy (27) has devised a formula, supported by data from nonindustrial societies, that does just that. He proposes that if the tasks are differentiated and require role specialization and combined effort, then the span of supervisory control is *approximately* five roles. If the number of roles meeting these conditions exceeds five, there must be a minimum of three levels in the hierarchy of organization. Recalling Proposition 2, that the size of an organization is related to the number of its parts and the degree of their specialization, we can generalize Udy's proposition as follows:

Proposition 8   *As the population of a social organization increases, the number of levels in the influence and authority hierarchies also increases.*

This tendency in social organizations can be illustrated diagrammatically. At the left in Fig. 3-3, the number of parts supervised is

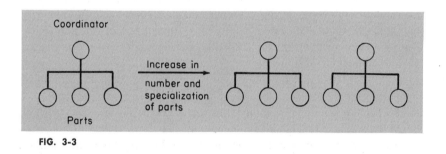

FIG. 3-3

within the span of control of the supervising part. When the number of parts increases beyond that span of control and an attempt is made to maintain the quality of performance of the parts (at the right in the figure), the original organization must be divided into several parts, each with its own leader. But activities of subgroup leaders must also be coordinated. Consequently, a new position must be added to the hierarchy, as shown in Fig. 3-4.

In the average medium-sized hospital (150-350 beds), there are about five formalized influence (authority) levels in the organizational chart. In Bell Telephone there are nine authority levels. In our society, the number of levels defies counting.

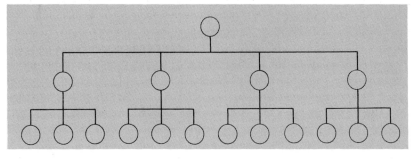

FIG. 3-4

POPULATION SIZE AND THE NUMBER OF INFLUENCE OR AUTHORITY RANK SYSTEMS. In his study of the social organization of the restaurant, William Whyte observed a change in hierarchical organization that was associated with size. In very small restaurants there was little differentiation of functions or activities. The manager was a generalist; he cooked, waited on the customers, and served as the cashier. In terms of authority status, his was the only superordinate position; he could easily oversee the activities of the other employees. But in very large restaurants, the complexity of the tasks and the increase in their number made the manager more of a specialist, and increased the number of levels in the hierarchy. But the complexity of the tasks had another consequence: the manager no longer contained within his person all of the skills essential to the successful operation of the restaurant or chain of restaurants. He had, therefore, to hire specialists to handle these tasks. If an organization becomes large enough, it is possible for hierarchies to develop centered around some of these complex activities (28). Fairly autonomous hierarchies of roles may develop around such functions as employee relations and auditing. This tendency can be stated in the following form:

Proposition 9   *As the population of a social organization increases, the number of influence or authority rank systems also increases.*

This proposition can be illustrated further in such large organizations as communities. In a small community the functions that need to be performed can be handled by a small group. But as the community increases in size, this is no longer possible. Consider city management. Nominally, at least, the mayor is the chief executive officer, but while he may be skilled in the ways of politics, he is probably less skilled in the complexities of city management. Municipal legal problems, budgets, taxes, and the myriad other functions associated with running a municipality require the services of trained specialists. Often the mayor and the council solve the problem by hiring a city manager to supervise a group of specialists in the affairs of the community. Although the mayor and the members of the council may have the authority to give orders to these specialists, the latter still have considerable influence over the affairs of the city by virtue of their expertness in running a municipality. Consequently, separate centers of influence and hierarchies within them develop.

If we consider the community as a whole, rather than just the administrative apparatus of the municipality, the number of hierarchies and informal influence rank systems we find can be even greater. The literature on community elites is a large one. Most of the early studies (9, 10, 11, 12) assumed the existence of more than one ranking of influence, but their results indicated that one elite, that which controlled the economic sector of community life, dominated the others. More recently (29, 30), social scientists have found that the noneconomic elites are becoming independent of the economic elite. It has been suggested that the conduct of political affairs and the technical problems of managing a community are so complex that in many communities the economic elite has withdrawn from active participation. An additional factor surely is that, in our largest communities, the political sector becomes a key industry, controlling billions of dollars and tens of thousands of jobs.

The increasing autonomy of the political elite has been accompanied by the division of the economic elite into a number of autonomous elites. In a study of a suburban community of 24,000 residents (29), R. O. Schulze found two economic elites, the owners of the various downtown commercial enterprises and the managers of local plants of large national corporations. He found that the political elite exercised considerable authority independent of the interests of the economic elites. In their study of decision making in Chicago (31), Martin Meyerson and E. C. Banfield found numerous economic elites limited by their very number in their ability to affect the political leaders of the community, who were bound together in a tight organization. In

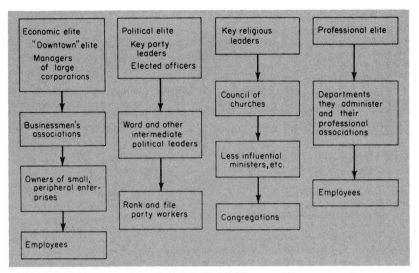

FIG. 3-5 Influence rank systems in a medium-sized community.

Fig. 3-5 are represented some of the influence rank systems and hierarchies that might be found in a medium-sized community.

POPULATION SIZE, HIERARCHIES, AND INTERACTION. The multiplication of hierarchies and of levels in each hierarchy creates problems for interaction among the parts of an organization. In a laboratory study in which hierarchies were created (32), it was found that status differences between communicators were responsible for inaccuracies and distortions in the messages. This problem of communicating up and down hierarchies was also encountered in a study of a large American business organization (33). The investigators requested certain factual information from a vice-president of the company. The vice-president sent messages to the relevant departments, but received no answers. In spite of further inquiries no answers were ever obtained. Countless illustrations of this problem are reported in newspapers and magazines. The plot of these stories centers on the difficulties experienced by presidents, kings, and prime ministers in finding out what is going on in their own bureaucracies.

Proposition 10 *As the population of a social organization increases, the problems of interacting vertically in the same hierarchy or between hierarchies also increase.*

That "the problems of interacting" increase need not mean a large organization must have a less effective interaction network than a smaller one. The members of the large organization may *solve* the problems that increasing size poses for their interaction network. If the problems are solved effectively, then interaction may be no more difficult in a large organization than in a smaller one.

These problems of interaction spring from three sources. First, increased size is likely to bring about *increased physical distance* between the hierarchically arranged parts. X-ray and laboratory departments, for example, are often located in the most remote parts of hospitals. The heads of these departments often complain that they have considerable difficulty communicating with the administrative section of the hospital. It is not that they cannot talk with the administrators, but rather that the administrative personnel are not so familiar with these departments as they are with other departments located nearer to them.

Second, the population at any given level in the hierarchy is very likely to be homogeneous in many respects. The members may earn about the same amount of money, have the same amount of education, or have essentially the same sort of job. In other words, they are in some *common social categories*. Problems often find their locus in social categories (23). People who earn $1,000 a year face problems not encountered by those who earn $100,000 a year. People who are over 65 years of age encounter different problems from teenagers. The fact of encountering similar and in some respects unique problems can result in the formation of many common norms among the members of a social category. It can also result in important differences in the norms of subgroups in different social categories (hence, at different levels in a hierarchy). Since norms are institutionalized means of interacting, it is much easier to interact with others who share the same norms as well as the same problems. It is easier, for example, to interact with others who share similar manners of speech and dress and with whom we "have something in common." Doctors prefer to discuss their professional problems with other doctors, manual workers with other manual workers, and teenagers with other teenagers. In his study of a high-school population (11), Hollingshead found that children at the same status levels (in terms of the father's occupation) tended to choose each other as friends. Occasionally, a person would choose as a desired friend someone of higher status, but this choice was seldom reciprocated. Barriers to communication then arise out of this tendency to prefer to interact with others in the same or similar parts of the organization. The lack of sufficient common norms tends to reduce communication between dissimilar parts.

Third, different parts of the population may be pursuing *different objectives* in the organization. Some parts may be organized primarily for the efficient production of a commodity; others may be organized to maintain the job security or promotional opportunities of the members. Therefore, when an order that conflicts with one or another of these objectives comes down a hierarchy, parts of the population may try to neglect or sabotage it. Barriers to the transmission of communication may develop.

When serious barriers to effective interaction exist among the parts of a social organization, the system is *segmented*. These barriers may result from the process outlined above—the development of unique norms and objectives within status levels—or they may develop as a result of force exercised by the more dominant parts on the less influential parts (1). One society may conquer another, force its population into slavery, and prevent any but the most necessary contacts with the conquering group. Parts of the population may be segregated because of some characteristic that they possess. Ghettoes of Jews, Negroes, or guild merchants are examples of some segments created by force rather than by some evolutionary process.

Some interesting conditions develop in segmented organizations— particularly if the segments·exist over long periods of time (25, 34). The combination of unique norms and insulation from the other parts of the social organization fosters the development of significant subcultural differences. Because of the different norms, it is often difficult for the population in one part to understand the behavior of the population in another part. And misinterpretation of the behavior can lead to conflict among the parts. If this condition develops, then interaction between parts will decline further and segmentation will be increased (25, 34). A cycle of increasing conflict is generated.

Segmentation between the elites of the organization and the other members with less influence is especially serious. When it occurs, the relatively uninfluential members of the organization may receive little information that would make the acts of their remote leaders accurately comprehensible. As a result, they may come to distrust the elites and to question the sincerity of their actions. Citizens often doubt the honesty of their political leaders, and workers often are suspicious of the intentions of management. Since the organization is segmented, the elites are less likely to know or understand the needs and problems of the less influential people under them. Lacking qualitative understanding of these people, the elites may develop rather callous attitudes toward them. In this situation, the potential for conflict between the elites and the other elements of the population is very great. A vicious cycle is created in which increased conflict leads to increased segmentation, and so on.

This process of declining interaction and increased segmentation and conflict can also be illustrated by lower-working-class cliques of boys who spend their evenings standing around on a corner sharing their boredom and waiting for something to happen (23). Their behavior may be interpreted by others in a different way—they are troublemakers. So the other elements of the population simply avoid contact with them—or someone calls the police. Generally, both of these events occur during the life of a corner gang. As a result, the members of the gang develop increased resentment toward the other parts of the society and find themselves isolated—voluntarily or otherwise—from it. When this segmentation occurs, the boys become more dependent on each other for entertainment and other activities. In other words, the influence of the group on the life of its members increases.

Much of the conflict and tension that can be observed in our society between labor and management, whites and Negroes, various religious groups, and so on can be explained in terms of the process just outlined. It is on the basis of this process that we can formulate our next proposition:

Proposition 11   *As the population of a social organization increases, the potential for conflict and friction among the parts also increases.*

Populaton Size and Coordination

We have seen that increased organizational size is usually accompanied by an increase in the number of parts, communication channels, levels of status in a hierarchy, hierarchies, and in the degree of specialization of the parts. If the organization is to be effective in pursuing its objectives, then the number of channels of communication must be limited to those deemed necessary. But when the parts are highly specialized, each part is performing fewer of the functions necessary for the completion of the total task, and if the organization is to achieve its objectives, the parts must be coordinated. (A sundial is a timepiece with only one part and so needs no coordination. But a spring watch has many specialized parts that must be related to each other according to some principle of organization if they are to function together as a timepiece.)

The increased possibility of segmentation in larger social organizations makes the need for adequate coordination especially great. If the problems that exist between subgroups can be discovered early, before they cause the outbreak of conflict and friction among the affected parts, then the process of segmentation can be arrested.

The role of adequate coordination in the functioning of an organization can be summarized in the following proposition:

Proposition 12 *As the population of a social organization increases, the number of coordinative problems and the need for coordination also increase.*

Up to this point we have used the terms *leader, coordinator,* and *supervisor* interchangeably, to refer to the people in the higher positions of influence or authority who run the organization. But with the increased complexity of an organization and of the social environment, it becomes extremely difficult for the leaders to perform both control (decision or policy-making) and coordinative activities. The president of a large automobile-manufacturing company has to be concerned about such decisions as the type of car the company should produce five years hence, the expansion of the company, the relations of the company with the rest of the society, and so forth. These problems are extremely complex, and they demand the combined effort of many specialists who advise the president. He cannot be concerned with problems of coordination between departments or plants in the company; these tasks become the assignments of specialists. In large organizations, therefore, the controller-coordinator role is separated into two roles: controller and coordinator.

The problems of coordination tend to increase at a more rapid rate than the rate of increase in the population of the organization. Two of our earlier propositions explain this phenomenon. First, the number of potential channels of interaction among the parts increases more rapidly than the number of parts (Proposition 1). Second, the increasing potential for conflict among the parts (Proposition 11) contributes to the problem. For these reasons, it is possible that the *proportion* of coordinators in the total organization can increase. F. W. Terrien and D. L. Mills found in their study of the California secondary-school system (35) that the proportion of persons in the administrative departments increased with the increasing size of the school system. Other studies have not supported this finding, but they have led to the development of an important insight. The leaders of large organizations often try to overcome the coordinative problems caused by increased size by turning some of their functions over to independent organizations (36). General Motors has turned over to independent companies the task of manufacturing many of the parts for its automobiles. In this way the company seeks to minimize the number of parts that it must coordinate. In effect, the organization is smaller than it would be otherwise. As a consequence, although General Motors produces about twice as many cars as Ford Motor Company, it actually has fewer workers in its administrative section than does Ford. A second means of minimizing the effects of large size on coordination is the decentralization of the authority of the controllers of the organization. *Authority is legitimated influence*—a pattern of influence that is prescribed by norms. As the population of an organization increases, authority is usually decentralized. With the increased specialization that accompanies increased size (Proposition 2) comes an ability of some parts to handle specialized problems (28)—an ability the controllers of the organization may not share. Their ability gives these parts special influence that, when institutionalized, becomes authority. In some organizations the dominant part delegates its authority according to some plan. But regardless of the means of decentralizing authority, its occurrence changes the structure of the organization considerably. As the amount and span of the decentralized authority increases, the organization becomes much like a collection of small, fairly autonomous organizations held together by a part that controls and coordinates certain of their activities. By creating these "small" organizations, the total organization is able to minimize some of the effects of increasing organizational size.

If decentralization of authority frequently accompanies increase in size, the amount of influence possessed by the parts that delegate the authority does not necessarily decrease. The dominant parts do not lose any influence, because they can rescind the delegation at any time (37). Factory owners can always replace a factory manager. Also, the dominant parts usually retain control over policy questions, delegating authority over the relatively minor problems of coordination. This is, in actuality, a device for the *maintenance or increase* of influence of the dominant part in the organization. Our final proposition summarizes the situation.

Proposition 13   *As the population of a social organization increases, decentralization of authority also increases, but at the same time the most influential parts may maintain or increase their influence.*

THE ROLE OF THE SOCIAL ENVIRONMENT

Up to this point our discussion has focused on the individual social organization without any reference to the social environment in which it exists. We have developed a series of propositions that will permit us to make predictions about the structure of a social organization given a few fundamental facts about its situation, its economy, and its population size. If we were to rely on these propositions for outlining the structure of a social system without making any allowances for the effects of the social environment, our predictions would have a fairly high probability of being accurate. But greater accuracy can be obtained if we take the social environment into account. With social organizations, the whole is more than the sum of the parts; if the principle of organization of the parts is changed, the social organization is changed. How one part is specialized is a function of how the other parts are specialized.

Yet studies of single communities without any reference to the social environment abound in both anthropology and sociology. Indeed, taking the relevant social environment into account is a recent development in the social sciences. The failure to examine the field of social relations in which social organizations are bound can be traced in part to the assumption that primitive communities and societies lived in isolation. Betty Meggers' law of agricultural potential (2) assumes relative isolation of the society, as do most of the single-community ethnographic studies. This assumption has not been supported in contemporary research on primitive societies. In fact, the opposite assumption is made today—interaction occurred among social organizations during all of man's history (39, 40) and may even have occurred among organizations of pre-Homo sapiens or homonids (41). Primitive man made war on his neighbors, provided them asylum, and visited, traded, feuded, and intermarried with them (40). Let us illustrate the extent of this interaction with some examples of economic exchanges between primitive societies.

Perhaps the most complex trading system among the paleolithics existed in Great Britain (39). In three different locations in Britain and Ireland hunting and fishing groups mined stone that was shaped into axe heads by specialists who devoted part of the year solely to this activity. These axes were then traded with other primitives in some rather distant places. Axes made in Ireland have been found in southern Britain. Axes made in northern Wales have been found as far away as the islands off the coast of France and in Scotland. Examples of these trading systems could be multiplied many times. Our stereotypes of primitive man as a parochial and unimaginative creature are difficult to maintain in the face of the evidence of his sophisticated trading systems. Primitive man was no less of an adventurer than his modern brother. The prospect of crossing an unknown sea to trade with unknown people seems quite analogous to our current attempts to explore our solar system. As a general principle it must be said that *in any region where social organizations differ in what their members produce, exchange between the social organizations is probable* (40).

What is the significance of this social field approach for the study of social organizations? It increases our ability to predict accurately the structure of the organization. We can illustrate this with the fundamental exchange system between societies—trade. Only surpluses are traded. Thus, if the members of a society wish to trade with another society, they must produce a surplus of a commodity that the other society wants. In effect, each of the organizations in the trade relationship must specialize with reference to the other. Surpluses can be created by nontechnological as well as technological means (40). The simplest way to create a surplus of food is to clear more fields and plant more crops. This method requires an increase in the population. Thus, entrance into a trade relationship may be occasioned by an increase in the size of the population. A second means of creating a surplus is to divert some members of the society into specialized pursuits such as making axe heads to trade for food. If this occurs, we will find more specialization than we would have expected on the basis of the size of the population and the available food supply and the level of technology. Finally, a surplus can be created by hybridization of the crops or animals or by improving the technology so that more produce can be obtained for the same amount of effort. Some primitives did learn to hybridize certain types of crops (40). That they did so can be understood adequately only in the light of the social field in which their society was located.

We can think of the division of labor as containing two classes of roles: *intercommunal* roles, those that the population develops to create a surplus of products and carry out exchange activities with other organizations; and *intracommunal* roles, which are all the others. Differences in the products exchanged result in differences in specialization in the organizations involved. More specifically, product differences result in differences in the intercommunal specialization of the involved organizations. Our thirteen propositions do not account for the intercommunal roles. But if we take into account the specialization of the organization for the larger field of relationships, it is much easier to predict accurately the characteristics of the division of labor of the organizations.

This point is no less true in our own society, where, because each community plays a specialized role in the total pattern of exchanges, the occupational role structures of various communities are quite different (42). We cannot understand these differences if we study each community in isolation.

SUMMARY

Most of what this chapter has said is summarized in Fig. 3-6. We have by no means exhausted all of the possible rules relating environment, economy, technology, and population size to the

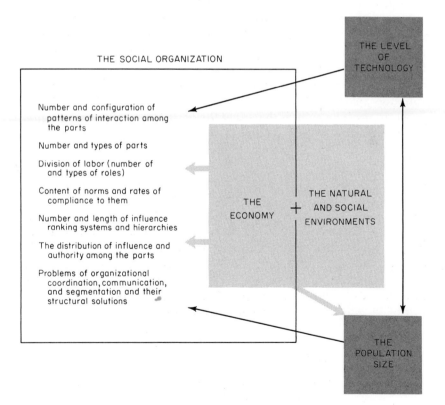

FIG. 3-6

other characteristics of social organization. But we have outlined a sufficient number of them to permit us to understand the basic outlines of social organizations. There are, however, two important qualifications that we need to make regarding the rules that have been developed so far.

First, we must remember that all of the parts of a social organization are connected by some means, and, therefore, any change that takes place in one part will spread in a chain reaction to affect the other parts. The more integrated the social system, the more immediate and strong this effect will be. This idea will be discussed in considerable detail in Chapter 5.

Second, you may have noticed in the preceding discussion and in the summary diagram that the relationships all moved in one direction: from the environment and the economy to the technology and population size, and from there to the rest of the social organization. But if it is true that the parts of social organizations are interrelated, then we must expect that changes in the norms, division of labor, or status systems will affect the population size, technology, economy, and the environment. Therefore, there are characteristics of social organizations that we will not be able to predict with our thirteen propositions, because these characteristics were shaped by forces other than the environment, economy, technology, and population size. *Most* of the variation among social organizations *can* be accounted for with our propositions. The point is that *all of the parts of any social organization are dynamically related. The most powerful influences run from the environment to the economy, technology, and population size, and from there to the other parts of the social organization. But there are important influences that run in the opposite direction.* Man creates social organizations in order to cope with the problems posed by his environment. He creates concentrations of influence. He also creates culture: the values, norms, and beliefs found in an organization. These latter creations have force; they can react on the environment, economy, technology, and population size. In Chapter 5 this process of mutual modification will be discussed in some detail. In Chapter 9 the dynamic relationship between population size and social organization will be investigated on a broader basis than it was here.

REFERENCES

1   P. Sorokin, *Society, Culture, and Personality: Their Structure and Dynamics* (New York: Harper & Row, Publishers, 1947).

2   B. J. Meggers, "Environmental Limitation on the Development of Culture," *American Anthropologist, 56* (1959), 801-24.

3   E. N. Ferdon, Jr., "Agricultural Potential and the Development of Cultures," *Southwestern Journal of Anthropology, 15* (1959), 1-19.

4   R. B. Dixon, *The Building of Culture* (New York: Charles Scribner's Sons, 1928).

5   J. A. Wilson, *The Culture of Ancient Egypt* (Chicago: The University of Chicago Press, 1951).

6   V. G. Childe, *Man Makes Himself* (London: Watts and Co., 1939).

7   L. Mumford, *The City in History* (New York: Harcourt, Brace, and World, Inc., 1961).

8   E. A. Hoebel, *Man in the Primitive World* (New York: McGraw-Hill Book Company, 1949).

9   R. S. Lynd, *Middletown* (New York: Harcourt, Brace, and World, Inc., 1929).

10 F. Hunter, *Community Power Structure* (Chapel Hill: University of North Carolina Press, 1953).

11 A. B. Hollingshead, *Elmtown's Youth: The Impact of Social Classes on Adolescents* (New York: John Wiley & Sons, Inc., 1949).

12 R. J. Pellingrin and C. H. Coates, "Absentee Owned Corporations and Community Power Structure," *The American Journal of Sociology, 61* (1956), 413-19.

13 L. A. White, *The Science of Culture* (New York: Grove Press, Inc., 1949).

14 J. James, "A Preliminary Study of the Size Determinant in Small Group Interaction," *American Sociological Review, 16* (1951), 474-77.

15 R. F. Bales, "Some Uniformities of Behavior in Small Social Systems," in *Readings in Social Psychology,* G. E. Swanson, T. M. Newcomb, and E. L. Hartley, eds. (New York: Holt, Rinehart & Winston, Inc., 1952), pp. 146-59.

16 W. F. Ogburn and O. D. Duncan, "City Size as a Sociological Variable," in *Contribution to Urban Sociology,* E. W. Burgess and D. J. Bogue, eds. (Chicago: The University of Chicago Press, 1964).

17 C. Wagely, "The Effects of Depopulation upon Social Or-
    ganizations as Illustrated by the Tapirape Indians," *Trans-
    actions of the New York Academy of Sciences, 3* (1940),
    12-16.

18 R. Naroll, "A Preliminary Index of Social Development,"
    American Anthropologist, 58 (1956), 687-715.

19 P. E. Salter, "Role Differentiation in Small Groups," in
    Small Groups: Studies in Social Interaction, A. P. Hare,
    E. F. Borgatta, and R. F. Bales, eds. (New York: Alfred A.
    Knopf, Inc., 1955), pp. 498-515.

20 W. F. Whyte, "The Social Structure of the Restaurant,"
    The American Journal of Sociology, 54 (1949), 302-10.

21 G. K. Zipf, *Human Behavior and the Principle of Least
    Effort* (Reading: Addison-Wesley Publishing Co., Inc., 1949).

22 H. L. Wilensky and C. N. Lebeaux, *Industrial Society and
    Social Welfare* (New York: Russell Sage Foundation, 1958).

23 A. K. Cohen, *Delinquent Boys: The Culture of the Gang*
    (New York: Free Press of Glencoe, Inc., 1955).

24 E. Jaques, *The Changing Culture of the Factory* (New
    York: The Dryden Press, Inc., 1952).

25 P. E. Mott, "Sources of Adaptation and Flexibility in Large
    Organizations" (Unpublished doctoral dissertation, The
    University of Michigan, 1960).

26 R. G. Barker, "Ecology and Motivation," *Nebraska Sym-
    posium on Motivation: 1960,* Vol. III of *Current Theory
    and Research in Motivation,* M. R. Jones, ed. (Lincoln:
    University of Nebraska Press, 1960), pp. 1-49.

27 S. H. Udy, "The Structure of Authority in Non-Industrial
    Production Organizations," *The American Journal of
    Sociology, 64* (1959), 582-84.

28 V. A. Thompson, *Modern Organization: A General Theory*
    (New York: Alfred A. Knopf, Inc., 1961).

29 R. O. Schulze, "The Bifurcation of Power in a Satellite
    City," in *Community Political Systems,* M. Janowitz, ed.
    (New York: Free Press of Glencoe, Inc., 1961).

30 R. A. Dahl, *Who Governs?* (New Haven: Yale University
    Press, 1961).

31 M. Meyerson and E. C. Banfield, *Politics, Planning and the Public Interest: The Case of Public Housing in Chicago* (New York: Free Press of Glencoe, Inc., 1955).

32 H. H. Kelley, "Communication in Experimentally Created Hierarchies," *Human Relations, 4* (1951), 39-56.

33 A. H. Hawley, Professor of Sociology, The University of Michigan, in a personal communication.

34 J. Cummings and E. Cummings, "Social Equilibrium and Social Change in the Large Mental Hospital," in *The Patient and the Mental Hospital,* M. Greenblatt, D. Levinson, and R. Williams, eds. (New York: Free Press of Glencoe, Inc., 1957), pp. 51-76.

35 F. W. Terrien and D. L. Mills, "The Effect of Changing Size upon the Internal Structure of Organizations," *American Sociological Review, 20* (1955), 11-13.

36 P. F. Drucker, *The Practice of Management* (New York: Harper & Row, Publishers, 1954).

37 H. H. Gerth and C. W. Mills, "A Marx for the Managers," in *Reader in Bureaucracy,* R. K. Merton, *et al.,* eds. (New York: Free Press of Glencoe, Inc., 1952), pp. 165-78.

38 R. K. Merton, "Bureaucratic Structure and Personality," in *Reader in Bureaucracy,* R. K. Merton, *et al.,* eds. (New York: Free Press of Glencoe, Inc., 1952), pp. 361-71.

39 J. G. D. Clark, *Prehistoric Europe: The Economic Basis* (New York: The Philosophical Library, 1952).

40 A. Lesser, "Social Fields and the Evolution of Society," *Southwestern Journal of Anthropology, 17* (1961), 40-48.

41 H. L. Movius, Jr., "Old World Prehistory, Paleolithic," in *Anthropology Today: An Encyclopedic Inventory,* A. L. Krocher, ed. (Chicago: The University of Chicago Press, 1952), pp. 163-92.

42 O. R. Galle, "Occupational Composition and the Metropolitan Hierarchy: The Inter- and Intra-Metropolitan Division of Labor," *The American Journal of Sociology, 69* (1963), 260-69.

4 some important types of organizations

The primary focus of this book is the society. In the chapters that follow this one, the structures of various types of societies will be elucidated from the definitions of Chapter 2 and the propositions of Chapter 3. But since societies are large—ranging in population from 50 to 600 million or more people—from our first rule of organizational size we can expect subgroups to be present. This chapter, therefore, discusses some of the more important subgroups found in societies. Remember that the power to shape human organizations flows *mainly* from the larger organization to the smaller subgroups found in it. The structure and functioning of subgroups, therefore, will be greatly affected by the environment, economy, technology, and population size of the society in which they are found. With this reservation in mind, let us begin our discussion with the smallest groups and move later to increasingly larger ones.

SMALL ORGANIZATIONS: CLIQUES, FAMILIES, TASK ORGANIZATIONS

John James observed organizations of persons in their natural settings, primarily to determine how many organizations existed of what sizes (1). Less than 0.1 per cent of the organizations he observed had a population in excess of seven people. Nine out of ten of them were composed of only two or three people. Since James's sampling techniques were not ideal, his figures can be considered only as approximations of the actual distribution of organizations of different sizes in our society. The only conclusion that we need to draw, however, is that small organizations are likely to contain seven or fewer members.

All societies contain small organizations: cliques of friends, workers who interact daily while performing a series of interrelated tasks, families, or committees. Because they are organizations, they must possess the characteristics of organizations outlined in Chapter 2, and they may vary in the extent to which these characteristics are present or absent according to the propositions presented in Chapter 3. Some small organizations, such as surgical teams or string quartets, exhibit considerable specialization and coordination; in friendship groups the division of labor may be difficult to discern. This variation in the division of labor can be explained when the economy, or, more specifically, the technology of the organization is considered. But despite variation caused by the technology and other factors, small organizations have many common attributes because of their small population. First, interaction among all of the members is possible, and each person has ample opportunity to take part in organizational life (Proposition 1).* Compared to members of other organizations, then, the members of small ones are in a fairly intimate relationship with each other. The extreme case is called a *primary group*. But more about that later.

Second, the norms of small organizations are almost always informal and unwritten (Proposition 7), and, for many reasons, deviation from them is minimal (Proposition 5). The members themselves adopted or created the norms and so believe in them; further, the members are under regular and intimate surveillance by one another, and because they are likely to value their membership in the organization very

---

* This notation means that the statement preceding it is based on Proposition 1, discussed in Chapter 3 and printed for your convenience on the end papers of the book. Interaction among all the members of a small organization is possible because the number of possible channels of interaction is small. You will be seeing proposition numbers in parentheses throughout this book.

highly, they dread the thought of being punished by the other members. In summary, normative integration is very high in small groups (Proposition 6).

This solidarity of small groups, and particularly of primary groups, has been documented in numerous studies. Interviews with American soldiers in World War II showed that the major motivation to fight and risk being killed was not patriotism, but rather a desire "not to let my buddies down" (2). Similarly, the German Wehrmacht remained an effective fighting force in spite of severe deprivations near the end of the same war until the primary groups within it broke down (3).

Third, unless the members of the organization use an intricate technology or perform a complex task (that is, are a task organization), the division of labor is not extensive. Interrelated roles are present, but they are sufficiently vague and ambiguous to make them undiscernible to all but practiced observers of organizational life (Proposition 2). We saw earlier that the role of leadership is one of the first to emerge in a small organization. Even in a two-person organization one member may dominate (4). Other roles are likely to develop: that of joker or date procurer in a male friendship organization, for example. If it is difficult for the unsophisticated observer to perceive these roles, they are nonetheless present and persistent.

The Primary Group

A primary group is a small organization characterized by the nearly total involvement of the members. Interactions are more likely to be informal and affective than they are in nonprimary or larger organizations. *Most*, but not all, friendship cliques, engaged couples, and families are primary groups. In larger organizations our interactions are likely to involve little other than the functions associated with our roles there. This type of participation is called *segmental*.

Some authors use *primary group* to refer to *any* small organization. Let us restrict our definition to those that are characterized by a high degree of member involvement. This will permit us to distinguish our clique of friends from, say, a committee to which we belong that meets frequently but with which we are not affectively involved. There are many differences in structure and function between these two small organizations, and these differences are obscured by a purely *quantitative* definition of primary *group*.

Primary groups play a crucial role as subgroups in the larger organizations in which they are found. To understand their role, we must know the concept of *organizational objectives*. This is, in a way, an unfortunate term, because organizations do not have objectives—people have them, and to study "organizational" objectives is to study a psychological property of the population. A rigorous sociology is concerned with rates of behavior, not with any attitude in the population. The sociological parallel of the notion of objectives is *what the members are actually organized to do*. Rather than invent a new term to denote this concept, let us use *organizational objectives,* but note the definition very carefully.

Implicit in the structure of a social system is the pursuit of a set of objectives. If the objectives of the primary groups, as reflected in the behaviors of the members, support the norms of the parent organization or at least do not interfere with its functioning, then the efforts of the entire population will remain effective (5). If, however, the primary group socializes its members into a set of norms that conflict with those of the parent organization, then the efforts of the latter will be less effective, because more disrupted and conflict ridden. Families may train their children to take socially useful roles in the society or they may socialize them into a pattern that results in their becoming deviants from the society's norms. In the former case the family enhances the effectiveness of the social organization; in the latter case it hinders it. In business organizations the workers often do not share management's norms; they may, for example, develop patterns of activity that reduce productivity. Members of the German Wehrmacht and U.S. GI's developed norms that increased the effectiveness of the German and American armies during World War II; but the strength of these primary groups could also reduce the effectiveness of the parent organizations when there existed norms that supported goldbricking or being absent without leave. The organizational objectives of primary groups can present problems of such magnitude that larger organizations have developed specialists to handle them—human relations specialists, in-service trainers, personnel officers, and counselors.

ASSOCIATIONS, INDUSTRIES, AND INSTITUTIONS

The Association

In very small societies the only subgroups found are the family and friendship cliques (6). Associations and industries, which often recruit people from the same social category, are not found in small societies because there simply are not enough people in any social category to form a large organization. In Wagely's study of the effects of depopulation on the Tapirape Indians (7) it was shown that as the population decreased, the ceremonial clubs for young adults began to recruit children and old men. Only by abandoning their restriction on membership to a certain social category (young adults) could the clubs remain in existence. Several of them were disbanded anyway for lack of members.

But as societies increase in size, there is an increasing number of people in most social categories, especially those of age and sex. In these larger societies we find a new type of organization—the association. Among the American Indian tribes this type of organization was fairly common. Most of them were ceremonial clubs designed primarily to socialize the young members of the tribe and characterized by secret rites and formality of the interactions among members. Among the Blackfoot Indians there was a regular progression of a dozen ceremonial clubs through which a young boy might pass on his way to manhood. He first joined the Pigeons, then the Mosquitoes, moved to the All-Brave Dogs, and ultimately to the Bulls. Our society has a modest replica of this pattern in the Cub Scouts and Boy Scouts. In American society, as in all large societies, there are thousands of associations. Fraternities and sororities are proximal examples, but there are also such organizations as the National Association of Manufacturers, country clubs, political parties, the League of Women Voters, and the Blizzard Men of '88. The association is larger than the small group, ranging in size from about a dozen up to many thousands of members. Knowing their size and that they are subgroups in a society, what basic characteristics can we expect of them from the propositions developed in Chapter 3?

In organizations of this size complete interaction among the members is not possible (Proposition 1). Several consequences follow from this fact. It becomes necessary to formulate norms that specify the channels of interaction and their use. This necessity lends to the association its characteristic formality (Propositions 3 and 7). It is likely to have formal norms governing the organizational behavior of the members ("Members who wish to speak shall rise and ask for recognition from the chairman"). The parts (roles and subgroups) are more differentiated and their activities more formalized than in most small groups ("This club shall have the following officers . . .") (Propositions 2 and 3). In order to coordinate the activities of the organization, these formalized parts are generally arranged hierarchically in an authority structure ("The actions of standing committees shall be approved by the executive committee and then by the president") (Proposition 8).

These formal elements of the association are often embodied in a formal document—a constitution—the preamble to which often contains a statement of the objectives of the members of the association; e.g., to protect the rights of the worker, inform the voter, do God's work, or provide for the common defense. There may or may not be some correspondence between the formal statement of objectives and the actual activities of the members of the organization (the organizational objective, as we have defined it) (Proposition 4). The members of an association may proclaim formally that they are organized to perform charitable activities, yet even a cursory look at what the members actually do might indicate that they are organized primarily for social activities.

Formal subgroups (e.g., committees) and informal ones (usually friendship cliques) exist side by side in the association (Propositions 2 and 10). Similarly, there are informal roles as well as the formal ones. The members of associations seldom create formal roles for injecting humor or relieving tension, yet these roles usually appear. The existence of informal parts and relationships in an association can create problems for its members. If the members of informal subgroups engage in activities that interfere with the formalized interactions among the parts of the association or if they create their own patterns of interaction, they may reduce the effectiveness of the organization. Often, too, there are members who did not join the association voluntarily: few, perhaps, in an organization like the League of Women Voters, probably a higher proportion in most labor unions. Segmental participation or nonparticipation in the affairs of the association is more prevalent among these involuntary members and among those whose interactions are detrimental to the activities of the total population; they are less "involved" in the association than the other members. Union leaders are disturbed by the fact that only 1 or 2 per cent of the members come to union meetings. The president of a college housing unit can't understand why more people don't help to build the homecoming sign and participate in other house activities.

Associations play a vital role in the affairs of the larger social organization. The activities of church members or of the members of charitable organizations such as the American Cancer Society can contribute to the well-being of a larger population. The association often serves as a channel of communication from individuals or small groups to larger units in the society. Indeed, in large and complex societies, the association may be the individual's only effective means to influence the decisions of large social units. Labor unions, associations of manufacturers, and medical associations, for example, can communicate the problems of their members to governmental and private organizations to obtain relief. And communication can move in the other direction as well. At a union meeting, members hear an analysis of some community problem, or a congressman addresses a meeting of the League of Women Voters. We will discuss this communicative function of associations in some detail in later chapters.

The Productive Organization

Industries are subunits in the economy that contain organizations engaged in the extraction, processing, or distribution of materials from the environment. These productive organizations can be classified according to the activity they perform:

Primary industries are involved in the extraction of raw materials from the environment. Mining, farming, hunting, and gathering are examples.

Secondary industries are involved in the processing of raw materials. The manufacture of steel, automobiles, and pottery are examples.

Tertiary industries are involved in the distribution of goods and services. Railroads, public relations agencies, and universities are examples.

A specific productive organization can crosscut the types. Ford Motor Company mines iron ore, converts it into steel, and manufactures and distributes automobiles and other commodities.

Productive organizations range in size from the family that has a farm or weaves rugs to an organization like General Motors with over 600,000 employees. The size of the organization and the complexity of its technology determine its structural characteristics. Let us here discuss the characteristics of large, technologically complex productive organizations.

Large productive organizations with a fairly high level of technology have an elaborate division of labor (Proposition 2) and a corresponding degree of interdependence among the roles. Norms exist to specify the content of each role (Proposition 3), often to the most minute muscular actions to be performed. By this means, an interlocking of the highly specialized roles can be maintained.

Norms also govern the interactions among the roles. These are the coordinative norms that regulate who will interact, when, and with what quality of performance (Proposition 12). Like associations, then, large productive organizations are characterized by formality and impersonality of the interactions among the parts (Propositions 1 and 7).

As the number of interrelated tasks to be performed increases, the number of levels in each influence rank system also increases (Proposition 8). And the factors that formalize the content of the roles are likely to formalize the influence hierarchy into an authority hierarchy (Proposition 8 *et passim*). In fact, productive organizations often have the most clearly delineated authority-hierarchies found in social organizations. As size and complexity of productive techniques increase, a multiplication of the number of hierarchies can be expected (Proposition 9).

The ability of a part of a social organization to affect the activities of other parts is a function of its size and its proximity to the major means of coping with the physical environment. Large productive organizations engaged in vital economic activities have the greatest influence over the affairs of the social organization. Where the key industry is agriculture, the timing of religious activities is geared to the seasons so as not to interfere with planting and harvesting. The key industry or industries even condition the structure of the smaller parts of the social organization. In agrarian societies with limited technology, families are larger than they are in a society such as our own. The need for manpower to perform the varied farm tasks is responsible for this.

The Institution

You probably have most often heard *institution* used in phrases like "the institution of the family," "the institution of banking," or "our religious institutions." When some sociologists use the term in phrases like these, they are thinking of institutions as categories of subgroups in a community or society that share some characteristic (or characteristics). The American family is an institution because American families share a set of characteristics that make it profitable for us to consider all of them together. We could, similarly, study together all of the organizations involved in criminal activities as "the institution of crime."

Other sociologists define *institution* as a product of interaction between the population and its culture. When they use the word, they are thinking of organizations that were created to implement values. According to this usage of the term, organizations that implement values are called institutions and it is said that the values are institutionalized. Such organizations as legislatures and courts are called institutions because they may implement the democratic value placed on the peaceful resolution of conflict.

It is doubtless true that organizations are created to implement values that are in many respects unique to a given society. But it is also true that a great many more organizations are created to solve problems *common to all organizations*: survival, distribution, safety, and recruitment. Despite the commonality of these problems, their solutions vary greatly from one organization to another. The usefulness of the value approach to understanding the origins and structure of organizations is, therefore, questionable. The problem is similar to the old school in psychology that sought to derive motivational explanations of human behavior from the basic human drives for food, sleep, sex, and protection. The ineffectiveness of this approach is apparent when it is realized that all people have these drives, yet the means by which they are expressed are extremely variable.

For these reasons and those already discussed in Chapter 2 (in the section "Norms and Culture"), let us become members of the former school and define *institution* as a category of subgroups with some common characteristic (or characteristics). However, you should expect to see the term being used the other way in many of the articles and books written by sociologists. The collective term *institution* embraces such diverse forms of organizations that it does not lend itself to analysis using our propositions.

COMMUNITIES AND SOCIETIES

The Community

A community is a social organization through which a *localized* population provides for its *daily requirements* (8). The parts and their relations reflect this objective. Industries exist to provide sustenance for the local population. Protection from deviants is provided, if the community is large enough, by a police force, night watch, or court system. The need to recruit new members versed in the skills essential to the community's survival is reflected in the development of educational organizations or such associations as the ceremonial clubs found among the Blackfoot Indians.

These parts are coordinated, passively or actively, by the key industry (or industries) of the community. As the size of the community increases, a part develops that specializes in the coordination of many community affairs; that is, a government (Proposition 2). In small communities, this government may take the form of a council of elders, who are only part-time specialists. In large communities, we find much more complex structures administering large school systems, road construction, traffic control, and police and fire protection (Proposition 2). Large communities, in effect, have several important status hierarchies:

political, economic, religious, and professional, among others (Proposition 9).

Just how small can a community be? Among the Shoshone Indians, the family is *the* localized population that provides for the daily needs of its members (6). During most of the year, the family scours the countryside alone in search of food; it combines its efforts with those of other families for social and hunting activities only rarely. The Shoshone family nonetheless meets our definition of *community*. Logically, then, communities range in size from very few to many millions of people.

What are the boundaries of the community? The community includes all of those people who are reliant upon each other for their daily needs. The suburbs around a city are included in the community as long as the majority of the residents there are reliant on the central city for most of their daily needs. They may work in the central city or purchase goods there. The timing of activities in the suburb will likely be regulated by the central city, which will generally provide such services as transportation systems, water, and sewage facilities.

The Society

The anthropologist studying primitive societies may define *society* as all of the tribes that share a common culture. To the social scientist who is interested in the study of human interaction in all its forms, society may be the sum total of all of the human relationships in which a person is involved. We will try only to make our definition consistent with the other definitions in our system.

As a social organization, a society contains a population and interrelated parts. The population includes all of those people who share a way of life, who have a common cultural tradition. (Americans, for example, share a common language and other norms and values that govern their interaction.) This *distinctness* of the organization of each society is a product of the history of interactions among the factors discussed in Chapter 3. Environmental and economic problems that were in some respects unique were solved, and a unique combination of interrelated parts resulted. Our political institutions are in *some* respects similar to those of England, and our economic and familial institutions are similar in *some* ways to those of Canada. But the combination of characteristics sets us apart as Americans.

Communities can be distinguished from societies on this basis. Communities *share* in the way of life that characterizes a society; they do not have a separate one. A community such as Chicago has many characteristics that differentiate it from our other communities, but it shares in the culture of American society. Most residents of that community speak English, participate in our national electoral processes and in all the other societal culture traits. While the Shoshone family may conform to our definition of a community, it does not constitute a society. Shoshone families share a way of life with the other Shoshone families, including a common language, technology, and economy, among other things.

The population of a society, like that of a community, is involved in economic activities, control and protection, and the recruitment of new members. How the various parts of the society perform these activities will be the subject of analysis in following chapters.

SUMMARY

In this chapter we have outlined the characteristics of the major forms of social organizations by means of the propositions presented in Chapter 3. The society is the most encompassing social organization in which we live. Depending on its size, however, it may contain a variety of other types of organizations, which are subgroups in it. The most common are the family and friendship cliques, found in every society. They are the major source of socialization as well as recruitment of new members. But many other types of small organizations may be found in the society: work teams, committees, and other task units.

Units of intermediate size include associations and productive organizations, whose structure is complicated by the increased population size and, sometimes, the higher level of technology. The subgroups, roles, and their patterns of behavior are likely to have a formal basis of organization. Their objectives are usually more limited than those of small organizations. Associations play a vital role in larger societies by creating a means of communication between elements in the population with low influence and those with great influence. Some of them, particularly educational organizations, are also responsible for part of the socialization of the members of the population. The term *institution* embraces many types of subgroups, ranging from small ones such as the family to large associations and many types of productive organizations. Institutions are categories of subgroups found in a society.

A community is a form of organization within the society through which a localized population can provide for its daily requirements. The structure of these units varies with their size, but it is here that the basic problems of obtaining sustenance, distributing goods, maximizing safety, and obtaining recruits are dealt with.

REFERENCES

1   J. James, "A Preliminary Study of the Size Determinant in Small Group Interaction," *American Sociological Review, 16* (1951), 474-77.

2   S. A. Stouffer, *et al., The American Soldier: Combat and Its Aftermath,* Vol. II of *Studies in Social Psychology in World War II* (Princeton: Princeton University Press, 1949).

3   E. A. Shils and M. Janowitz, "Cohesion and Disintegration of the Wehrmacht in World War II," *Public Opinion Quarterly, 12* (1948), 280-315.

4   F. L. Strodtbeck, "Husband-Wife Interaction over Revealed Differences," *American Sociological Review, 16* (1951), 468-73.

5   The classic discussions of the formal and the informal aspects of associated life are E. Mayo, *The Human Problems of an Industrial Civilization* (New York: The Macmillan Company, 1933) and F. J. Roethlisberger and W. J. Dickson with the assistance and collaboration of H. A. Wright, *Management and the Worker: An Account of a Research Program Conducted by the Western Electric Company, Hawthorne Works, Chicago* (Cambridge: Harvard University Press, 1939).

6   J. H. Steward, *Theory of Culture Change* (Urbana: University of Illinois Press, 1955).

7   C. Wagely, "The Effects of Depopulation upon Social Organizations as Illustrated by the Tapirape Indians," *Transactions of the New York Academy of Sciences, 3* (1940), 12-16.

8   A. H. Hawley, *Human Ecology: A Theory of Community Structure* (New York: The Ronald Press Company, 1950).

5 organizational change

Up to this point our model of organizations has been a static one. We have described the elements common to all social organizations and then discussed the effects of changes in the environment, technology, and population size on these elements. But social organizations change almost constantly. This dynamic character of organizations is seen most readily in our cities. The process of urbanization, which has been occurring since the formation of American society, is continuing. People continue to migrate from the rural areas into the cities in large numbers. Within the cities themselves, urban renewal programs are perhaps the most dramatic testimony to change, but the flow of people into the suburbs is another evidence. Small towns that were once a day's ride from the central cities now find themselves in the forefront of the advancing urban population. Some of these satellite communities have experienced population growth rates that severely strain their ability to adapt.

Economic organizations have exhibited a similar penchant to change. These organizations, like those in government and other spheres of our life, are becoming increasingly bureaucratized. New levels of hierarchy are being added, and increasing use is being made of highly formalized procedures of interaction, promotion, and recruitment. Changes in the technology of these organizations, particularly through the coupling of electronic data-processing equipment and servomechanisms, have altered the patterns of relations among the workers, their skill levels, and even their numbers.

Even the family has been the object of significant change: the patriarchal family is becoming less common than the equalitarian pattern of organizing influence; methods of child training have changed greatly; and the family has seen many of its functions taken over by such bureaucratic organizations as schools, churches, and governments.

The remainder of this book examines some of the major changes that have taken place in this and other societies; urbanization, industrialization, and bureaucratization. The final part examines the attempts of the elites of contemporary societies to control and plan the process of change. Let us begin in this chapter by examining the causes, the processes, and some of the consequences of change in large organizations, defining *organizational change* as an alteration in the pattern of relations within or among the parts of an organization.

THE NECESSITY OF CHANGE

Do organizations *have* to change? Do their members have to alter their patterns of behavior? Let us ask the opposite question: Under what conditions could an organization avoid changing? Certain types of organizational structures are highly resistant to change. A molecule of argon, for example, is an organization that is "saturated." Interaction between an argon molecule and other molecules is extremely difficult, but it can be accomplished. Similarly, we can imagine a "perfect" social organization in which all of the parts are in an ideal relationship with each other: a utopia. If such an organization were created, there would be no internally evoked problems to give rise to a need for change. Unfortunately, the existence of problems that can cause change is an almost endemic condition in organizations, as we will see. But even if such ideal conditions did exist, the organization would have to change, because the natural and social environments pose their own repertoire of problems over which the members can have but limited control. Hurricanes, tornadoes, desiccation, warfare, the loss of markets, and other such events are forces that the members of a social organization can hardly ignore. An unchanging organization, therefore, would have to have a utopian social structure in an unchanging environment; and these conditions simply do not exist in earthly social organizations. The structures of organizations are such that problems and other change-generating conditions always exist. If the members elect to resist the introduction of a change that is crucial to their continued existence as an organization, the organization will nonetheless be changed—because of its altered relationships with other organizations or because it simply disappears.

THE PROCESS OF ORGANIZATIONAL CHANGE

Earlier we saw that one way we can conceive of social organizations is as centers of varying amounts of influence, each with its own rhythms of performing its activities. We also saw that exchange of influence among these parts is a two-way street in which the members of the less influential parts are capable of affecting the behaviors of the members of the more influential parts, as well as vice versa. But the major direction of the exchange of influence is from the more influential to the less influential parts, from those that are *societal in scope* to those that are *more limited in their area of activity*. Therefore, a full understanding of the change processes in any subgroup of any organization requires that they be examined in the context of the changes that are originating in the other parts of the organization. Our examination of the process of organizational change must begin, then, with the forces that cause changes in the parts whose influence is societal in scope and then turn to an examination of the processes by which these changes are reflected in the other subgroups of the society. We must also discuss the reverse process by which changes in the less influential parts of the society react and alter the structure of the more influential parts.

The Sources of Societal Change

Natural environments are extremely dynamic, and they have fundamental effects on the structures of the societies located in them. The Ice Ages of prehistoric Europe and the desiccation of the grasslands that are believed to have occupied the area that is now the Sahara have had pervasive effects on the societies located in these environments (1).

Man's interactions with his natural environment are another source of change. Man often changes his environment and then must learn to cope with the new conditions that he has created. Repeated one-crop farming without the use of soil conservation techniques, practiced by neolithic as well as contemporary farmers, depletes the soil, forcing the farmer to move on to other areas of greater fertility. The depleted soil, without a deep root system to hold it intact, is easily eroded by the action of rain or wind. Large areas of the American South and West stand as tributes to these practices; in China, too, once fertile lands stand barren and rilled with deep gorges, the products of centuries of erosion. Even in North Africa, where desiccation was probably the major malefactor, the neolithic farmer's slash and burn farming techniques contributed to the denuding of the area. Once man has caused these changes in his natural environment, he must either leave it or learn how to live in it.

Other changes are introduced into the society from its social environment: the other societies that exist in its social field. In any region where social organizations differ in what their members produce, exchange between them is probable. Specialization of productive activities is a basis for developing exchanges and for further changing the structure of parts in the trading organizations. This process of disseminating and adopting items of technology or patterns of behavior is called *diffusion*. Many more things than economic goods can be diffused from one society to another: belief systems, for example, can be exported. If these belief systems are accepted by the local population, they become institutionalized. New parts are created or overlaid on older ones, older parts disappear through disuse, and the pattern of relations among the parts is adjusted to accommodate to the changed situation. Warfare, invasion, and immigration are other sources of social change emanating from the environment.

The environment may also affect parts of societies. The natural environment, for example, may have greater direct effects on the patterns of activity of a part than of the whole. Hurricanes change Florida more than they do the whole United States. The parts also exist in a social environment, particularly that made up of the other parts of the same society. Diffusion among them is a major source of change in their internal structure and in their patterns of relations with each other. The communications media—trade journals, closed circuit television, newspapers—and associational meetings are two of the many ways that the parts of societies can formalize the process of diffusing information and ideas. Stealing is another. Just as invasion and immigration can change the society, corporate consolidations or outright acquisitions change the patterns of activity in the affected units. Belief systems can also be exchanged among the parts of a society. The human relations tradition of democratic supervisory-subordinate relations was created by social scientists but diffused into industrial and educational organizations, where it has become institutionalized. Whether it is the arrival of southern migrants in the cities or taking roomers into the family household, the juxtaposition of interacting people in the same arena will produce changes in the patterns of behavior in the resulting unit.

Change occurs, finally, when the parts that are societal in scope alter their own internal patterns of activity. The introduction of new items of technology, new forms of organization, or new types of legislation can have fundamental effects on the organization of the whole society.

The Spread of Change

The greater the degree of interdependence among the parts for the performance of specialized activities, the greater is the need for coordinating the rhythms of their activities (Propositions 2 and 12). If the temporal rhythms of activity of an influential part of the organization are changed, compensating changes are required of the other interdependent parts. The existence of established channels of interaction facilitates this change. The spread of change from part to part is referred to as the *chain-reaction* effect of organizational change. Many changes in the natural environment, intersocietal diffusions, and inventions have their most fundamental impact on the parts of society that are societal in their scope: economic, political, and religious organizations. The changes that are worked in these extremely influential parts of the society then produce compensating changes in the other parts. The invention of the internal combustion engine illustrates the chain-reaction effect. This new source of power quickly transformed many industries; milling, mining, drilling, sawing, pumping, and many other productive activities could hereafter be performed more easily. The application of the internal combustion engine to problems of transportation was quickly realized, and only twenty-five years after its discovery, the automobile was invented. Robert Heilbroner illustrates some of the chain-reaction effects of the invention of the automobile on the American economy (2).

By 1905 there were 121 establishments making automobiles, and 10,000 wage earners were employed in the industry. By 1923 the number of plants had risen to 2,471, making the industry the largest in the country. In 1960 its annual payroll was as large as the national income of the United States in 1890. Not only that, but the automobile industry had become the single greatest customer for sheet steel, zinc, lead, rubber, leather. It was the buyer of one out of every three radios produced in the nation. It absorbed twenty-five billion pounds of chemicals a year. It was the second largest user of engineering talent in the country, bowing only to national defense. It was the source of one-sixth of all consumer spending in the country. In fact, it has been estimated that no less than one job out of every seven and one business out of every six owed their existences directly or indirectly to the car.

Even this impressive array of figures by no means exhausts the impact of the internal combustion engine and its vehicular mounting. Because of the existence of the car, some fifty thousand towns managed to flourish without rail or water connections, an erstwhile impossibility. Seven out of ten workers no longer lived within walking distance of their places of employment but drove to work. Of the nation's freight tonnage, 76 per cent no longer moved by rail but by truck.*

Impressive as these statistics are, they only begin to enumerate the effects of this one application of the internal combustion engine. Think, for instance, of its effects on family life, styles of entertainment, and even the structure of our cities.

The introduction of the horse into Blackfoot Indian society had effects just as dramatic on that society as the invention of the internal combustion engine had on ours (3). The most immediate effects were on the economy, for the hunting techniques of the Indians were greatly changed. Distance became a less important factor in pursuing the buffalo, hunting territories increased in size, and warfare became more commonplace among the tribes competing for the buffalo herds. The Indians could now kill many more buffalo than their personal needs required, and they began to trade them with the white man for rifles and other goods. This change altered the structure of the Blackfoot family; since buffalo skinning was women's work, the more wives a hunter had, the more buffalo he could have skinned to trade with the white man. Polygamy became a common form of family organization.

In sum, changes in the patterns of behavior in the major centers of influence produce a chain-reaction effect; the lesser centers of influence alter their rhythms to adjust to the changes in the more influential parts. Some parts may resist the change, but the costs of continuing the old patterns of behavior in the changed situation may be so high that a change will occur in the structure of the organization anyway. Many parts may not be affected by the change because of their limited interdependence with the changing part.

* Robert L. Heilbroner, *The Making of Economic Society* (Englewood Cliffs, New Jersey: Prentice-Hall, Inc., 1962), p. 104.

The Reverse Process: Changes from the Lesser to the Greater Centers of Influence

Change originating in the lesser centers of influence in the society can be traced to certain characteristics of their structure and situation—characteristics such as the costs of interaction that are inherent in every organization. If one part is moved a greater distance from the others, the cost of member time spent traveling from one part to the remote part is increased. In our large cities the cost of moving employees from their homes to their places of work is far greater than it is in a small town because of the greater distances that the people must travel. Costs can also take the form of loss of functions. The worker who moves from the day shift to the night shift at his job will find that he has greater difficulty maintaining his social life. Thus, we say that the structure of an organization has both temporal and spatial elements, and changes in these elements change the costs of interaction among the parts. If a part exercises its influence, it is by definition directing or controlling the rhythms of the other parts. It is forcing them to change the temporal or spatial character of their activities. This change may reduce the costs of interaction for the part exercising its influence, but it may also change the costs of interaction for the part that it has affected. If it increases the costs of interaction for other parts, it creates a conflict situation, and members of the affected parts may seek to change the relationship in order to reduce their own costs to the previous level. When a factory changes from an eight-hour to an around-the-clock operation, it forces drastic changes in the rhythms of the families of its shift workers. Meal schedules are inverted, the wife is forced to do her housework in the evening when her husband is at work, and social life with friends is altered. The costs to the family of this new pattern of life are enormous. The family can attempt to reduce its costs in several ways. The husband can get a daytime job in another company, or he can bid for a daytime job in his present company, or through his union he can force the company to pay him more money to compensate for his increased costs. Any of these solutions will change his cost situation and that of the company for which he works. The exercise of influence, then, increases costs and can serve as a basis for conflict among the parts of an organization. In conflict-ridden organizations the members of some of the affected parts devote a considerable share of their collective time and energy to the accumulation of influence in order to change their cost position (4). This accumulation of influence may vary from the formation of mobs to the creation of more stable organizations. Labor unions, the National Association of Manufacturers, the Communist Party, the Congress on Racial Equality, and the Black Muslims are examples of organizational responses to conflict situations. Throughout human history, social movements formed out of conflict have shaped the course of events. Some of the Protestant organizations of the Reformation won adherents because of conflicts between the Catholic Church and the nobility of medieval European societies. The origins of the Communist social movement can be traced to the conflicts between the owners and workers in early industrial enterprises. The current civil rights movement is a product of the conflict situation that has prevailed because the existing pattern of relationships in our society has greatly disadvantaged the Negro.

It should not be assumed that conflict is always reduced when the less influential parts are successful in their attempts to influence the more influential parts. The solutions proposed by the less influential parts may not be the best ones for the situation; conflict will continue to exist (5).

Changes can also originate in the less influential parts because the members usually have some behavioral options (5). In large organizations, it is virtually impossible for the dominant parts to specify norms to guide the conduct of the members in every situation they will encounter. The dynamic body of common law that exists in our society illustrates our inability to legislate all human behavior. Parents are free to choose how they will organize influence within the family or socialize their children. Teams of nurses often have wide latitude in organizing their work. When these people encounter problems and create new patterns of behavior to solve them, they may cause changes in the larger organization, depending on the prevalence or importance of the change that was introduced. The coffee break illustrates the accumulation of small changes that affect the total organization. Originally, the coffee break was installed by management groups in their respective companies because studies of fatigue showed that giving the employees a break increased productivity. But in many organizations the original fifteen-minute coffee break approved by management has been stretched gradually into the half-hour break by the cumulative actions of the employees. Since the additional fifteen minutes does not add appreciably to the productivity of the employees, this change has increased the costs of operation for the company and forced other minor changes in its patterns of behavior.

When the elites of the organization, whether a society or other large organization, *do* attempt to specify the detailed behaviors of the members, other problems can arise. The people who are faced with unique problems that the leaders did not anticipate may find their efforts to solve them thwarted by the detailed regulations. In such a situation the less influential members may utilize their informal friendships in the organization to skirt the rules and solve the problem. The informal network of relationships then becomes a very influential part of the organization. In the Soviet Union, the central planning agencies imposed rigid production quotas on factory managers, but the managers often could not fill these quotas because the necessary supplies were not available in the quantities needed (6). As a consequence, an informal network of supply procurers has developed among the factories in the Soviet economy. Despite the illegality of this practice, it has not been stopped by the central planners—probably because it is essential to the effective functioning of the economy.

Organizational change can originate in the less influential parts because of the different *cohorts*, or age categories, to which the members belong. Each cohort is born into a world that is different from that into which its predecessors were born. The cohort born at the turn of this century did not enter a world where one nation could destroy another within a matter of minutes. These differences in the organizations into which cohorts are born affect the values and the behaviors of the members; naturally, then, when people in different cohorts belong to the same organization, conflict can result, with each cohort attempting to change the organization in such a way as to solve its particular problems. As members of one cohort die or retire, those of another come into the positions of influence in the organization and are able to change patterns of behavior. But sometimes the members of a cohort are not willing to wait to infiltrate the role structure of the organization —they form subgroups to promote a set of changes. The Student Non-Violent Coordinating Committee, organized by college students and recruiting its members from the same group, is an example.

The cohort phenomenon is a special case of a more general source of organizational change. A cohort is a social category, and the members of any social category are likely to encounter unique problems (see page 62). In their effort to solve them, they may form organizations to promote change.

Change can originate in the lesser parts of the organization because of the subcultures of the subgroups. A change initiated by the elite may be resisted by the members of some of the parts because it violates one or another of the norms, values, or beliefs to which they adhere. Agricultural experts in India have experienced great difficulty and limited success in introducing new techniques of farming in the peasant villages, because the villagers simply prefer to continue the time-honored techniques of their ancestors. This unwillingness to accept an important change has forced some modification of the objectives of the planners in underdeveloped societies.

Summary of the Process of Organizational Change

All parts of an organization can influence all the others with which they interact, but the major flow of change is from the more influential, societal parts to the less influential ones. The major changes, therefore, are generated in the social or natural environment or within the major units of the organization and spread to other parts in a chain-reaction effect. Change sometimes occurs in the opposite direction when the lesser parts, finding it difficult to adjust the rhythm of their activity to that of the more influential part, accumulate influence in order to force a change in the larger unit. Mobs and stable social movements are examples. The behavioral flexibility that exists in many less influential parts can sometimes result in change in the whole organization; members of social categories may also force changes in the whole, often by forming organizations. And occasionally the dominant part may have to change because the lesser parts refuse to.

THE RATE OF ORGANIZATIONAL CHANGE

The United States Patent Office cannot keep abreast of incoming patent requests. A new electronic computer or a new weapon of destruction makes another one obsolete by the time it is produced. Members of many social movements demand major changes in the social order. Within our subgroups, change is as rapid. Automation is changing the patterns of work behavior. Medical techniques, drugs, and forms of hospital organization change so rapidly that no doctor can call himself knowledgeable. Change is not only constant in our society; it is also amazingly rapid. Why is this so? What accounts for the *rate* of change in social organization?

The factors that are responsible for change—interpart conflict, behavioral flexibilities, the existence of dissident cohorts—also affect its rate. Since population size is related to the amount of conflict (Proposition 11) and the size of cohorts (Proposition 10), *as the population of an organization increases, the potential rate of change also increases* (5). Increasing population size creates problems that can be solved by changing the structure of the organization. One population factor particularly relevant for a society is the absolute number of people with the ability to create a new pattern of behavior or item of technology. As the size of the population increases, the number of these people also increases. Thus, where a hunting and gathering society of 150 people will have an average of seven or eight creative people, American society will have 9 million people with creative potential.

As the number of behavioral patterns and items of technology increases arithmetically, the number of possible *combinations* of these items increases geometrically (7). Therefore, the organization with the greater number of different patterns of behavior and items of technology available to it will have a disproportionately greater opportunity to combine these items into new patterns of behavior and items of technology.

Complexity and population size are intrinsic to the structure of an organization. Whether these "natural" causes of change are permitted to operate depends on other characteristics of the organization. The activities of the elite in the organization can facilitate or thwart the process of change. In very large business organizations the rate of organizational change is often lower than it is in smaller, less complex organizations in the same field. The elite of a large company with its sizable markets prefers a minimum of change. It has a tremendous investment in equipment, personnel, and routinized practices that can be altered to produce newer products only at very great expense. Its strategy therefore centers on slowing the pace of innovation and convincing people that newer products represent no improvement. Smaller, less complex companies try to use innovation as a means of capturing markets by offering superior products. The elite of one company fosters change while the other seeks to limit it. Elites can inadvertently limit the rate of change through the overuse of their rule-making power. They can make such detailed specifications of what is acceptable behavior that some valuable innovations are discarded by the members because they violate one or another of the rules. Lack of understanding of this factor has inhibited the industrialization of some nations. Before the industrial revolution, French political leaders imposed detailed standards on manufacturing. The weight, width, and color of woven materials were subject to detailed regulations. A new machine that produced a wider piece of cloth more cheaply could not be adopted because it would violate regulations about the width of the cloth.

The rate of change can also be increased by the creation of parts of the organization whose members are specialists in innovating and in discovering the ways that other organizations are solving problems. The Egyptian pharoahs used a part of the food surplus in that society to support craftsmen who were expected to innovate. These specialists were able to advance mathematics, engineering, and other fields at a more rapid rate than had been previously possible. The extremely high rate of social change that characterizes our society is largely a product of this type of specialization. Industrial firms, universities, and government agencies employ thousands of people who are specialists in innovation. In some of our large corporations, inventions are mass produced. We also have specialists in social planning who are expected to make innovations in the social structure itself.

The usefulness of an invention also affects the rate of change. The members of parts of an organization are constantly encountering problems some of which can be solved only by changing the patterns of activity in the organization. If this need exists, greater activity is likely to be directed to making the invention and incorporating it into the activity patterns of the parts. In England, for example, inventions in the area of transportation—macadam roads, canals, and railroad trains —were quickly adopted because they served the objectives of influential elements in the population. The nobility had found that the lack of good roads prevented the army from quashing rebellions promptly (8). The owners of the developing industrial enterprises encouraged the development of transportation systems to facilitate commercial activity. These systems were considered so useful that they were developed despite violent resistance from other parts of the population.

The rate of change is also affected by the cultural values the population attaches to change. If there has been a steady rate of change in an organization, then the value attached to acting in the traditional way using the traditional tools is likely to be weakened. If there is a cultural value attached to progress, then the pace of change is facilitated. And a negative value attached to change will surely impede it.

The Bursting Effect of Organizational Change

When we study history as a process of social change, we sometimes get the impression that there are periods of quiescence followed by bursts of rapid innovation and adaptation. Examples of events that have been interpreted as sudden bursts of change are readily available. One anthropologist has referred to the emergence of towns and cities in the prehistoric world as the "urban revolution" (9). The rapid industrialization of parts of Europe in the eighteenth century is often treated as one of those periods of extremely rapid social change. The emergence of Protestantism and communism provide further illustration of seemingly sudden breaks with the traditions of the medieval period. Our own observation that the rate of social change is currently accelerating may even contribute to this impression. But the appearance of quiescence followed by rapid change is more illusion than fact (5). If social change is accelerating, yet it seldom moves from one plateau to another through a period of rapid change. Part of this illusion is due to our penchant for focusing on the most dramatic changes. Certainly the development of the great urban centers of the ancient world captivates the imagination, but behind that development stand centuries of social and technological innovation and experimentation that set the stage for what we read about in our history books. There was no revolution; there was only a slow process of evolution, marked by small changes, that was consummated in the urban center (10). Similarly, many of the doctrinal points promulgated by Luther and Calvin were "in the air" before they were even alive. The writings of Augustine, Thomas Aquinas, and many other Roman Catholic thinkers contained many of the ideas that the early leaders of Protestantism advocated, including the doctrine of predestination (11). The work of Karl Marx was built upon a combination of ideas and methods of reasoning that had been developed beginning with the ancient Greek philosophers. Many of the ideas integral to his work were also "in the air." It is a mistake generally to conceive of the Dark Ages as a period of changelessness. If few of the changes of the period were dramatic, they were numerous, and they were essential to the emergence of industrial society.

THE ACCEPTANCE OF ORGANIZATIONAL CHANGE

That new ideas, techniques, and tools are available does not mean that the members of an organization will accept them or adjust to them; they may resist them. The difficulty of introducing changes in agricultural practices in India has already been noted. Factory workers have a long history of resisting changes that eliminate jobs; the resistance to automated equipment is only the most recent instance of this longstanding struggle. The elites of corporations often resist innovations that threaten to upset their productive routines. New laws, which create new patterns of behavior or forbid old ones, are sometimes resisted by the population. Among competing organizations, if one is able to reduce its costs of interaction by making changes and the others cannot reduce theirs because of resistance to change, the consequences can obviously be important.

Temporally unpredictable events can create even more serious problems of accommodation for the members. Such disasters as fires, chemical plant explosions, tornadoes, and undeclared wars may threaten the very existence of an organization. Its survival often depends on how quickly the members organize to cope with them. Other important temporally unpredictable situations are work overloads. A multiple-car collision or a bus accident may overload the local hospital, and people's lives depend on its success in coping with the overload. Handling a crisis of this type usually requires that the members perform some activities other than those usually assigned to their roles. Registered nurses may be making preliminary evaluations of the victims' condition until the physicians arrive; practical nurses may be giving medications that they are not legally permitted to give.

The instructions for handling disaster situations given to the state policemen in Texas also illustrate this requirement of flexibility. These police are ordered to *assist* the organizations that have formed to handle the disaster rather than assume direction and control of their activities (12). If several people have formed a line to remove debris from people trapped beneath it, the state policemen are expected to take a place in the line and pass debris. If they exercised their usual role requirements, precious time would be lost while they took over the direction and control of the rescue workers. If the people coping with any such crisis situation are unwilling to be flexible about what activities they will perform, their handling of the problem will be less adequate (12).

Accommodating to unusual situations and accepting changes are so essential to many organizations that social scientists have invested considerable research time studying the problems involved. Most of these investigations have focused on the problem of overcoming member resistance to new routines and equipment—a problem appropriate for study from a sociological point of view. If the structure of social organizations influences rates of human behavior, it may be that differences in the proportion of the members of various organizations who accept new routines and equipment are due to certain structural characteristics of the organizations themselves. The weight of the existing evidence suggests that *the more integrated the structure of the organization, the larger will be the proportion of the members who will accept changes in their routines and equipment* (13, 14, 15, 16). Characteristics of the integrated organization, you will remember from Chapter 2, include the adequacy of coordination among the parts, the consistency of the norms governing routine behaviors, and the lack of barriers to communication among the interacting parts. When the opposite condition, segmentation, prevails, several forces are set in motion to increase member resistance to changes. If the parts are segmented, adequate communication channels do not exist to disseminate a change from one part to another; the members simply are unaware of the availability of new routines and equipment (13, 14, 15). The potential for conflict and friction among the parts is greater in segmented organizations (see page 62), so that if a change is introduced in one part, it will not be accepted in the other parts *because* of the hostility between the members of the parts. In a segmented organization, the members of each segment zealously guard their influence and always seek to increase it. It becomes very difficult for one part to exert sufficient influence to alter the behaviors of the members of other parts. Influence is not pooled or concentrated; it is fragmented. The pooling of influence in a segmented organization is achieved by bargaining, which means that the part desiring the change must give up a resource to obtain it. Thus the part may obtain the change, but it loses some influence in the process—something it is most unwilling to do.

The most crucial concentration of influence for gaining acceptance of changes is among the elites of the various hierarchies in an organization. If these elites are segmented, then influence is not sufficiently concentrated for the *pursuit of a unified set of objectives*. Influence is fragmented, and each elite can use its influence to nullify the attempts at change made by the other elites. In this situation, the people at lower positions in one hierarchy will be able to resist changes advanced by the elite in another hierarchy because they will be protected by their own leaders. In a university, for example, administrative officials will have great difficulty changing the practices of faculty members if the latter are protected by the most influential faculty members. But if the elites are integrated and their influence is pooled or concentrated, there is no protection available for members who would resist an order to change their routines or equipment. *If the elite of an organization is integrated, the proportion of members who will accept a change and the promptness with which they will accept it also increase* (16).

Much of the popularity of socialist and communist organizational models among the leaders of many underdeveloped nations can be explained in terms of the propositions just advanced. The leaders of many of these nations want to improve the standards of living of their people *as rapidly as possible*. If they can devise governmental structures that create an integrated elite and centralize influence, they can maximize the prompt acceptance of changes that they propose to make in the structure of their societies. These leaders devise programs designed to increase the integration of the parts of the nation because they understand the necessity of integration for winning acceptance of changes. Roads and railroads are built, radios are made available, illiteracy is reduced, and competing elites are rendered impotent. The stage is set for rapid industrialization.

But the popularity of integrated forms of organization, particularly involving the centralization of influence, is not restricted to the underdeveloped countries. Modern industrial countries also face problems so vast in scope that their parts cannot cope with them unilaterally—controlling the flood waters of the Mississippi, for example. General acceptance of effective solutions to these problems often requires some increased integration of the parts and greater centralization of influence.

The organization that copes most adequately with temporally unpredictable overloads of work has an integrated elite that, in addition to its usual planning, builds plans for emergency situations. Each role contains behaviors that are contingent upon the situation. When emergencies of different types occur, the occupant of the role is expected to utilize the contingent behaviors. Studies of community disasters have shown that in addition to these flexible features built into the roles, successful coping with unusual situations is maximized if the members, are given ample opportunity to practice their contingent activities (12).

Unfortunately, it is not common for an organization to have programs for these emergencies. Often the leaders are so busy with routine activities that they do not have time to plan for them. Even when such plans exist, it is seldom possible for the leaders to take into account every problem or emergency that may arise and plan a program for it. Therefore, to the extent that drilled plans do not exist or the plans are not perfectly appropriate for each emergency, effective handling of emergencies requires that influence be sufficiently decentralized during the emergency so that the people who are coping with it can make the necessary decisions to organize their work. Of organizations that lack adequate plans for emergencies, segmented organizations are most likely to cope effectively with the situation that confronts them—because influence is decentralized and the leaders in each segment are accustomed to making decisions independently of the formal elite of the organization (16).

Temporally unpredictable events are among the problems faced by modern societies that require increased centralization of influence. The threat of nuclear or undeclared war that can completely destroy any society is one of these grave problems, and it has prompted increased interest in organization for disasters. Our increased *ability* to create systems that warn the members of a community or nation of the approach of tornadoes, hurricanes, nuclear bombs, and other disasters has been partially responsible for the heightened interest in planning for them. These problems and the need to adjust rapidly and effectively to them are another reason for the increased centralization of influence in modern societies; they will be discussed in Part 4.

SUMMARY

Social organizations change constantly, and in complex ways. Most frequently, the major changes in any organization originate among the most influential parts: those with the greatest control over the resources essential to the organization. These parts are the major point of entry of problems from the environment both natural and social. Their adjustment to these problems affects their own rhythms of activity and those of other, less influential parts. These parts are also the points of origin of many technological and social innovations that force other parts of the organization to alter their patterns of activity. Since the parts of the organization are integrated to some extent, these changes spread in a chain reaction from their points of origin to the other parts of the organization. The less influential parts can also originate changes. Often the changes these parts must make to adjust to changes in the major parts increase their organizational costs and thus become a source of conflict among them. By pooling their influence the members of the less influential parts often can force the major parts to alter their patterns of activity. In addition to conflict as a source of change are the behavioral flexibilities that are found in most organizations, the effects of accumulated small changes, and the cohort and social category problems.

The process of organizational change is so complex that it is sometimes difficult to distinguish cause and effect. The rate of change is currently accelerating, owing to the growing number of items of technology and organization that are available to combine in new forms, to the increasing population size of the organizations, and to the specialization of innovative activity. It is a mistake to conclude, however, that change is cyclical, with periods of quiescence and others of rapid innovation. As a rule, the particular change we are studying occurred because of a long period of other changes that, accumulating, brought it about.

That change is available to the members of an organization does not mean that they will accept and utilize it. They often resist it. The proportion of members who accept and adjust to change is highest in integrated organizations. The greater the centralization of influence, the more promptly will the innovations be accepted. Organizations whose elites have planned for emergencies and drilled the members in their emergency roles cope most successfully with temporally unpredictable work overloads. But if a plan is lacking or is unrehearsed, organizations in which influence is relatively decentralized are most likely to cope with the situation successfully.

In the remainder of this book, we will study societies, deriving their characteristics from the definitions in Chapter 2 and the propositions in Chapter 3. The outline for that analysis will, with some variation, be the following:

Basic Information

1. In what type of environment is the society located?

2. What is the key industry?

3. What is the level of technology?

4. What is the population size?

Using this basic information and applying to it the rules we developed in Chapter 3 we can derive a great variety of further information about societies.

Derived Information

5. Roles: What is the degree and nature of the division of labor found in the society?

6. Norms: *(a)* What types of norms are present? *(b)* What is the ratio of formal to informal norms? *(c)* How much variation is there among the sub-groups in the norms about a given behavior, or, conversely, how extensive is normative integration?

7. Subgroup formation: *(a)* What types of subgroups are present in the society? *(b)* What is the structure of these subgroups? *(c)* How are the sub-groups related to one another?

8. Status: How many and what types of status systems are found in the society?

In Part 3 we will discuss American society as a case study of a modern industrial society. The effectiveness of this society, like that of any organization, is dependent on the effective solution of the major problems that confront its members and the willingness of the members to adapt to these solutions (17). Since the degree of integration of the society is related to the willingness of the members to accept changes, our discussion of American society will be organized *in terms of the segmenting and integrating forces that are at work in it.* Since many of the nations of the world face problems similar to those faced by the members of American society and many underdeveloped nations are seeking organizational models that will hasten the pace of change in their societies, Part 4 is devoted to a discussion of the centralization of influence as a means of coping with these problems.

REFERENCES

1   J. A. Wilson, *The Culture of Ancient Egypt* (Chicago: The University of Chicago Press, 1951).

2   Robert L. Heilbroner, *The Making of Economic Society* (Englewood Cliffs, N.J.: Prentice-Hall, Inc., 1962).

3   O. Lewis, *The Effects of White Contact upon Blackfoot Culture*, Monograph No. 6 (Washington: The American Ethnological Society, 1942).

4   R. L. Kahn, "Introduction," in *Power and Conflict in Organizations*, R. L. Kahn and E. Boulding, eds. (New York: Basic Books, Inc., 1964).

5   W. E. Moore, *Social Change* (Englewood Cliffs, N.J.: Prentice-Hall, Inc., 1963).

6   J. S. Berliner, "The Informal Organization of the Soviet Firm," *The Quarterly Journal of Economics, 66* (1952), 342-65.

7   W. F. Ogburn, *Social Change* (New York: Huebsch, 1922).

8   P. Mantoux, *The Industrial Revolution in the Eighteenth Century*, rev. ed. (New York: Harper & Row, Publishers, 1961).

9   V. G. Childe, *The Prehistory of European Society* (Harmondsworth, England: Penguin Books Ltd., 1958).

10 R. J. Braidwood and G. R. Willey, *Courses Toward Urban Life: Archeological Considerations of Some Cultural Alternatives* (Chicago: Aldine Publishing Company, 1962).

11 K. Samuelsson, *Religion and Economic Action: A Critique of Max Weber* (New York: Harper & Row, Publishers, 1964; a Torchbook).

12 N. Demerath, "Some General Propositions: An Interpretive Summary," *Human Organizations, 16* (1957), 28-32.

13 J. Cummings and E. Cummings, "Social Equilibrium and Social Change in the Large Mental Hospital," in *The Patient and the Mental Hospital*, M. Greenblatt, D. Levin-

son, and R. Williams, eds. (New York: Free Press of Glencoe, Inc., 1957), pp. 51-76.

14   E. Jaques, *The Changing Culture of a Factory* (New York: The Dryden Press, Inc., 1952).

15   R. Lippitt, J. Watson, and B. Westley, *The Dynamics of Planned Change* (New York: Harcourt, Brace, and World, Inc., 1958).

16   P. E. Mott, "Sources of Adaptation and Flexibility in Large Organizations" (Unpublished doctoral dissertation, The University of Michigan, 1960).

17   B. Georgopoulos and F. Mann, *The Community General Hospital* (New York: The Macmillan Company, 1960).

part two   THE
URBANIZATION AND
INDUSTRIALIZATION
OF SOCIETIES

the social organization
of the pre-urban society

6

In this chapter let us assume that there is an organization X located in a submarginal environment. Let us also assume that X's neighbors (the organizations that form its social environment) are quite similar to X. What characteristics can we expect this organization to have, from our rules and propositions?

Before we begin, let us see what our assumptions entail. A submarginal environment is one where the food supply is so limited that a society that evolves indigenously in it can support no non-food-producing roles—a swamp, for example, or a very arid or wet or hot or cold area. Such an environment severely limits the economy and technology of a society. Our second assumption—that X's neighbors are much like X—minimizes the effects of the social environment on the organization. It simplifies our task of characterizing X, but it keeps X from being typical of real, existing societies. This assumption, therefore, would have to be altered if we wanted to obtain a closer approximation of the characteristics of empirical organizations. All societies have been "discovered," and all have been irrevocably affected by the experience. In characterizing X, we will nonetheless draw on examples from real societies in submarginal environments. But we must remember that their social environments differ.

SOME DERIVATIONS

The Economy

Agriculture will be possible in organization X only if considerable effort is made to interfere with the natural environment; and a fairly advanced level of technology is necessary to accomplish this. For reasons that we will see later, the level of technology required for agriculture is beyond the capabilities of the population of a submarginal environment. Small gardens may be maintained, but they usually demand more human energy to cultivate than they are worth. The Siriono sometimes maintain small gardens for the cultivation of yams, but their enthusiasm for gardening is dampened by the constant encroachment of the jungle on their cleared plots (1). They find it much easier to pursue a hunting and gathering economy in their environment. The women collect wild fruit, nuts, and vegetables. The men hunt the animals that inhabit the area or fish the streams. The diet of the Paiyute Indians, who live in the arid basins east of California, is composed mainly of nuts, roots, grasshoppers, and rabbits. The Yokuts of California live primarily on nuts that they grind into a mash and carry about in small bags (2).

Hunting and gathering economies are the most common types developed indigenously in submarginal environments. Less common economies are pastoral (the population obtains its food by keeping herds of domesticated or semidomesticated animals) and predatory (the population obtains sustenance by raiding or bribing other populations). We will concentrate here on the hunting and gathering economy; but the logical development that we follow could also be used to develop the outlines of predatory or pastoral organizations.

Level of Technology

The use of a hunting and gathering economy in a submarginal environment limits the density of the population to approximately 2 or less people per square mile (3). In fact, unless the game is plentiful and fairly easy to catch, there will usually be nearer zero than 2 people per square mile. The amount of edible materials that a natural environment contains is limited. It is for this reason that so many hunting and gathering organizations are nomadic.

The efficiency with which members of a hunting and gathering organization can obtain food from the environment is a function of the level of their technology. If they have obtained rifles from some outside source, they can approach the upper limits of efficiency and support a relatively dense population. Sometimes the native technologies are quite elaborate, permitting fairly efficient exploitation of the environment. The hunter may have different types of arrows for different tasks: arrows with egg-shaped heads designed to stun birds, and arrows with a cluster of barbed points for fishing. Elaborate snares, traps, and nets are often used. On the other hand, the level of technology may be so low that hunting and gathering are very difficult and the population density is correspondingly low. The Kung Bushmen, who inhabit the Kalahari Desert region of Bechuanaland in Africa, use a bow whose pull is so low that the arrows often do not penetrate the hide of large game (4). So they have developed a poison that, put on their arrows, makes up for the inadequacies of their bows. In some organizations the technology is so poorly developed that members must resort to such tactics as driving the animals over a cliff to be killed on the rocks below. A. R. Holmberg (1) reports that the Siriono have forgotten how to make fire and consequently carry a torch with them whenever they move the location of their village.

We will assume here that organization X has a modest level of technology: one that is only moderately effective for its intended purposes. Most hunting and gathering organizations in fact develop only moderately effective technologies; first, because an advanced hunting technology presupposes a metals industry, and such an industry is unlikely to develop in an organization where all of the members must have food-producing roles. Second, the population is probably nomadic, and the elements of the technology must be light and easily transported. Therefore, tools must be limited in their complexity. Futhermore, the range of implements is so restricted that there are few ways in which they can be combined to form more complex and efficient tools. J. H. Steward (5) reports, for example, that the Shoshone Indians have only 3,000 elements, or items, of culture and technology, while American society contains many millions of such elements.

To summarize our assumptions thus far: organization X is located in a submarginal natural environment, surrounded by similarly structured organizations, employing a hunting and gathering technology, and possessing a moderately effective technology.

Population Size

Using the assumptions just made, we can estimate the size of the population of organization X. The use of a hunting and gathering economy in a submarginal environment will ordinarily result in a population density of two or less people per square mile. With only a moderate level of technology the population density is further reduced, to approximately one person or less per square mile. These figures are only approximations because there is very little accurate data on the relations between level of technology, type of natural environment, and population size. But if this data were available, we would use the same method of reasoning to arrive at an estimate of the population density.

Having estimated that there will be one or less persons per square mile, we must now calculate the size of the area in which the population can gather food. It is reasonable to assume that hunters can walk about fourteen miles a day while searching for game. They can travel, therefore, about seven miles away from their settlement and still get back by nightfall. They can travel even greater distances from their settlement if they extend their trip beyond a single day. But the area that they can cover per day will be about the same by either option. Using seven miles as an estimate of the radius that the hunters can cover, a simple computation tells us that the area available for exploitation is roughly 150 miles. Therefore, hunting and gathering organizations that meet our assumptions will probably contain less than 150 people. Populations of 25 to 75 people are most common in this situation. This information permits us to invoke our rules of population size to develop further characteristics of the hunting and gathering organization. But before we do that, there are a few observations to be made about the problems of population size that exist for the members of hunting and gathering organizations.

A significant population increase will bring about a serious situation for the people. If the population outstrips the available food supply, then the possibility of starvation becomes a reality. Ordinarily, however, the death rates in these societies are about equal to the birth rates (45–50 deaths or births per thousand people), so the population size remains fairly stable. The birth rate is very high because of the minimal contraceptive techniques available. The only reliable method of preventing pregnancy is abstinence. Another method often used by mothers to prevent an immediate recurrence of pregnancy is to continue breast-feeding the child well past the time when he is capable of eating other foods. They believe that this practice will reduce the probability of becoming pregnant during the nursing period. Contraceptive magic is often used, as are a variety of herbs that are thought to have contraceptive properties.

The death rate is high for two reasons. First, the infant mortality rate is usually extremely high. Only a fraction of the children survive the first years of life. The technology and professional skills available for parturition are minimal. In many hunting and gathering organizations the children are seldom washed, and little or no effort is made to keep flies or other disease bearers off their skin. Some children die because they are fed solid foods before they are old enough to tolerate them; others are repeatedly fed salt water. Vitamin deficiency, hookworm, and other maladies take their toll too. Second, even if the baby survives this intimate relationship with so many sources of disease, he faces an adult life that is unbelievably harsh. The inability to store food and the recurring cycles of feast and famine mean that the hunter must work hardest when he is most undernourished. He is exposed to disease in the water he drinks and in the bites of the insects and other animal pests. His shelter is often inadequate for severe weather, and, therefore, he spends much of his life exposed to the harsher elements. During the rainy season, the Siriono spend their nights huddled sleeplessly around the fire because their huts will not keep out the rain (1). To fall from a tree could be disastrous. There are no effective techniques available to help the person recover from his injury. He becomes a social burden because he cannot help in the search for food. But if the death rate should drop in spite of these odds, then the members of the organization usually invoke measures to limit the population density. Extreme measures include infanticide and gerontocide, but the population usually tries to avoid them. The most common solution is for some of the families to move to another area where the environment will be adequate to support them. This is one reason that many hunting and gathering organizations have as neighbors in their social environment other similar organizations to which they are related by kinship and/or by cultural ties. All of these organizations can be said to belong to the same society because they share a common way of life.

This side-by-side existence of culturally similar hunting and gathering organizations can develop another way. The population may not increase in size, but the supply of food may decrease in the natural environment. In some hunting and gathering organizations—the

Semang of Malaya (2), for example—the members divide into smaller units on the basis of kinship, and each subgroup seeks out a different region in which to find food. In effect, the social density is reduced. When the food supply increases again, the subgroups will rejoin each other.

Subgroup Formation

An organization that contains 150 or fewer people is large enough to be divided into subgroups, but not so large that they can be either numerous or greatly differentiated (Proposition 2). Hunting and gathering organizations of this size are primarily familial organizations, but informal cliques will also be found. If there are enough people in some age and sex categories, a few associations may be found in organization X (5, 6). These will be fairly unelaborate associations, however, bordering on being cliques.

It has been demonstrated that the size of the family most commonly found in a social organization is a function of the size of the food supply (7). Hunters cannot feed regularly a large family and exploit the additional manpower efficiently. The nuclear family which is composed of the father, mother, and children is the most economically rational type of family in hunting and gathering organizations and it is the most common type found in them (7).

Males have primacy in hunting and gathering organizations of this size for two reasons (5). First, they occupy the key role of hunter because of their superior strength and other physical skills. Transportation is restricted to human carriers; because of his physical strength, the male's performance of these tasks is essential. Second, in hunting and gathering organizations that emphasize the hunting of nonmigratory, scattered animals, it is advantageous for the males to remain in the area of their birth. Hunting animals of this type is very difficult; by remaining in the area of their birth the males can profit by their knowledge, gained in childhood, of the area and of the animals. For these reasons, the family in organization X is likely to be patrilocal as well as nuclear. A *patrilocal family* is one in which the children are members of the father's blood-related kin organization and reside at the place of residence of his family rather than the mother's family. Spouses are recruited by males residing there, while the female children move somewhere else when they marry.

Some hunting and gathering organizations have families organized in ways other than nuclear and patrilocal. Social anthropologists, greatly interested in explaining the causes of the different forms of family organization, have studied these various forms extensively. In the process, they have recognized a bewildering array of types of family and kinship organization, most of which are not of immediate utility for us.

We can now identify organization X more specifically. It is a band, a collection of families which are probably patrilocal in their organization. Unless there is an extended period of famine or some other disaster situation, the patrilocal band is a fairly stable and integrated form of organization. It usually numbers between 25 and 100 persons. Contrasting with it is the composite band, which is about the same size, but is less stable and integrated. The composite band is a loose collection of families that forms temporarily either to hunt large game or for mutual protection. This type of band also can form as a result of warfare; the surviving families from several bands may form a composite band for safety.

The Division of Labor

From our knowledge of the rules that relate technology and population size to the division of labor, we expect very little differentiation in the role structure of a hunting and gathering band (Proposition 2). Case materials of actual hunting and gathering settlements that meet our assumptions support this expectation. The only significant division of labor is by sex and age categories.

The reason why is very easy to see. The level of technology is so low that any normal person can grasp it in its entirety. Further, because there is no food surplus and so small a population, there can be no non-food-producing specialists. There may be a shaman, a person believed by his fellow bandsmen to have certain supernatural powers, but he will perform all of the other activities of an adult male and serve as a shaman only on special occasions. There may also be a chief. But he also will perform the activities of other adult males. The members of the organization may be required by norms to give part of their food to the chief. Among the Siriono this practice is adhered to begrudgingly (1). But the gain to the chief is shortlived: he is required by the norms to redistribute the food to others or to call a feast for all of the members of the tribe.

In some hunting and gathering organizations the role of chief is inherited or ascribed. But whether the role is simply honorific or actually influential depends very much on the skills of the occupant. In a subsistence organization where starvation is a constant threat, the population cannot afford to trust such crucial activities as hunting to an unskilled occupant of an ascribed role. Leadership is usually bestowed on a man because of his personal characteristics: primarily because he is an unusually skilled hunter.

Since the level of specialization is low, it is not the source of integration for the band. To discover what unifies a band, we will have to look elsewhere. We will also have to look elsewhere to discover how this type of organization is coordinated. The leaders seem to have very little authority beyond the coordination of a hunting expedition. There must be some other means for maintaining order.

Norms

Remembering our rules of population size, we expect a hunting and gathering patrilocal band to have informal norms (Proposition 7). We also expect very little variation from one subgroup to another in the norms that govern a given behavior (Proposition 4). Robert Redfield (8) has characterized the norms of hunting and gathering organizations as traditional and the members' response to them as spontaneous and unquestioning. By traditional he means not easily changed—there is a premium placed on doing things the same way generation after generation. Spontaneous and unquestioning response implies that the norms are so internalized and so ingrained into the members of the population that they largely determine their decisions about their behavior. Redfield's position is somewhat extreme, but it is essentially correct. Some people exhibit deviant behavior in these organizations, but highly ingrained conformity is the common pattern.

Obviously, the sanctions for violating the norms are powerful, and deviance is minimal (Proposition 5). The life of a deviant in a small social system is very unpleasant. When the occupant of a role deviates from the norms that govern his role, he experiences declining or negative interactions with the rest of the population. He has no place that he can go and start afresh. He is trapped forever in the small band in which he lives. In a large society, the deviant can and often does find social support, because he can always find others like himself who will provide it. Further, he can move away from the place of his offense and make a fresh start.

It is the norms of a hunting and gathering organization that unify it and coordinate its activities (Proposition 6). Ideally, the people go through their daily activities with virtually every act determined by some norm. In this way they avoid creating problems for each other.

The chief, rather than coordinating the daily affairs of the members of his society, finds his own behavior determined by the norms. We say then that these societies are highly integrated normatively.

Status

Since there is very little differentiation in the roles in the band, there is little basis for the development of status differences (Proposition 8). Therefore, bands are essentially equalitarian organizations (6). A man with a reputation for being a good hunter may exert considerable influence on the other hunters, especially during a hunting expedition. In other pursuits his influence is not so great. Another role that is often vested with considerable influence in communal activities is that of the shaman. In some tribes the shaman is believed to have a magical power that permits him to work his way into a herd of animals and drive them into traps or toward the other hunters. Other than in these special cases, influence is decentralized and located primarily at the family level (Proposition 13).

The Economy Revisited

We have now seen the basic characteristics of organization X. In the light of what we know, we can elaborate on our discussion of its economy.

An examination of the history of man's economic relationships reveals a fairly common theme: economic activities are intended to serve the needs of the total organization and are not an end in themselves (9). The economic system has often been used to achieve the noneconomic objectives of the total population. In most hunting and gathering societies, wealth is not accumulated as an end in itself, as it can be in our society, where a wealthy person is given deference by others simply because he has accumulated wealth. In most hunting and gathering societies the wealthy person gains deference from his fellow bandsmen by redistributing his accumulated wealth.

A social anthropologist once gave an illustratation of this point (10). Several pygmies were invited to engage in a contest for a package of cigarettes. The package was placed in a notch in a tree, and the pygmies were asked to try to hit it with their arrows. Whoever hit the package first won it. After several tries, there was a winner. By winning, the pygmy won more than the cigarettes; he won increased deference from his fellow tribesmen. None of them would dispute his ownership of the cigarettes nor would they ask for any of them, but he would have lost some of his newly won deference if he had not shared the cigarettes with the others. By sharing them, which he did, he gained even more deference. The redistribution of material goods was used to enhance social standing.

Economic activity has a similar value in many agrarian societies. Eric Wolf (11) reports that the inhabitants of the Indian villages of Mexico save money to provide a celebration for the other members of the village. To use a lifetime's savings for a single celebration does not seem irrational to the Indian: it has immense social value for increasing his importance in the eyes of the other members of the village. Our own medieval ancestors had a similar set of norms. It was sacrilegious to make a profit by one's work. Charging interest for lending money was also contrary to the norms, and the religious tax—the tithe—was calculated to be approximately the amount of surplus food that a farmer could produce in an average year. The accumulation of wealth as an end in itself does occur in hunting and gathering and agrarian societies—the opulence of many Asian elites attests to that—but it really becomes prevalent in Europe only with the rise of commerce and industry at the close of the medieval period.

Like all other behaviors in hunting and gathering organizations, the distribution and exchange of goods and services are completely governed by traditional norms. Consider first the activity of distributing goods. If a party of hunters kills a particularly large animal, who owns the meat from it? The answer is dictated by a set of norms. Usually, the hunter who actually killed the animal receives the largest share, how much and from what parts being determined by norms. But he is required by rigid norms to distribute his share among certain members of the village. He may be required to give the ribs to his first cousins, the right shoulder to his wife's parents, and so on. In some societies he shares his portion of the meat with the members of the village who did not even participate in the hunt.

In a hunting and gathering organization, norms specify that for any service rendered or for any goods given, there must be some goods or services given in return. This is the phenomenon of reciprocity (12). Norms specify the value of a service or of goods so that an appropriate exchange can be made. Suppose, for example, that X owns a fishing canoe. Y and Z give X a service by serving as his front paddler and his back paddler, respectively. A set of norms exists that dictate which parts of the catch Y and Z will receive in exchange for their services. There is no notion of profit. All exchanges are governed by strict norms that specify the worth of any item or service.

THE SPECTRUM OF HUNTING AND GATHERING SOCIETIES

By making some fairly specific assumptions about the natural environment, the economy, and the technology of organization X, we were able to outline its most obvious characteristics. Organization X was found to be a patrilocal or a composite band, probably the former. It was part of a larger society of similar organizations, probably created by splitting off of families whenever food was difficult to find or when the population grew too rapidly for the food supply.

But if we changed any one of the assumptions, the characteristics of the resulting society would differ in many ways. The great number of possible combinations of assumptions suggests the diversity of types of nonagricultural and nonindustrial societies. The variations in the social structure of societies with hunting and gathering economies alone is very great. This fact was not always understood by social scientists. Robert Redfield (8) placed all "primitive" societies in one category, which he called the folk society and for which he developed a single model that had a long vogue in the social sciences. It has fallen into disuse as a concept as the great variation in hunting and gathering societies has been recognized.

To give some indication of the spectrum of nonagricultural and nonindustrial societies, we will now look at two extremes on the continuum. The more primitive of the two societies is the Shoshone-speaking Indians of the American Southwest. An example of the other end of the continuum is provided by the Wishram Indians of Oregon.

The Shoshone Indians

J. H. Steward (5) tells us that some Shoshone Indians inhabited an extremely arid natural environment (one in which there are large areas with no vegetation at all). The supply of such game as antelope and rabbits was limited, and rats, mice, gophers, locusts, ants, ant eggs, snakes, and lizards were the main sources of meat. The Shoshone were primarily gatherers of the edible flora rather than hunters. A population can survive in this type of environment only if it has an extremely low density. Steward reports that there was an average of only one person to every twenty or thirty square miles. Under these conditions, a patrilocal band would be too large a unit of settlement for the available food supply. The nuclear family was the only feasible unit of settlement, although when food was more plentiful, two or three related families might form the unit of settlement (Proposition 2). Shoshone society was composed, then, of essentially independent nuclear families that were isolated during 80 or 90 per cent of the year. These families were nomadic, constantly moving about their habitat in search of food.

Occasionally, several of the families came in contact with one another, and if food was available, they would stay together for awhile. But there was no fixed pattern to interfamilial activity and no fixed suprafamilial leadership (Propositions 2a and 8). Hunting for larger game, such as rabbits and antelope, formed the basis of some communal activity. During rabbit hunts, leaders, called "rabbit bosses," were selected to coordinate the activities of the participants. The higher influence status of the rabbit bosses lasted only for the duration of the hunt, however. The Shoshone had "antelope shamans" who were believed to have a magic power that rendered the antelope helpless to escape the hunters. The antelope shaman had high influence status during an antelope hunt, but only during that period. The only other communal activities of the Shoshone were dancing and gambling.

The Wishram Indians

The characteristics of Wishram society provide a great contrast to those of the Shoshone (13). The Wishram were located by the Columbia River in Oregon. The natural environment was capable of supporting a very large and dense population. There were salmon runs on the river, and the Indians used a variety of fairly efficient methods to catch the fish. They also knew how to process the salmon so they could store them for later use. When the salmon were not running, the men hunted, elk, deer, and bear in the neighboring forests, and the women gathered huckleberries, acorns, and edible roots. The population probably reached about 1,500 people located in several villages along the edge of the river.

In terms of subgroup formation, Wishram society was much more elaborate than the patrilocal bands and Shoshone families (Proposition 2). Families and cliques were present, of course. But ceremonial clubs were also numerous and constituted an integral part of Wishram life, being involved in the socialization of the young and honoring the role of the warrior. Political institutions were not well developed, however.

Very little is known about the division of labor in Wishram society. It is clear that the roles of chief and shaman had become full-time activities (Proposition 2). There was usually more than one full-time shaman in each village. Status differences were quite pronounced in the population (Proposition 8), with the greatest influence being possessed by the village chiefs, and other males in the society being graded according to their skill as hunters and warriors. The lowest status was held by the slaves: the prizes of successful warring expeditions. There was no elite that ruled over all of the villages. Each village was independent in that respect (a condition usually referred to by sociologists as a stateless society).

The Shoshone and Wishram Indians illustrate the great diversity found among so-called primitive societies. Their basic characteristics, however, could have been derived very easily from our basic rules once we had made some assumptions about the natural environment, the economy, and the technology.

SUMMARY AND CONCLUSIONS

In this chapter, the definitions of Chapter 2 and the rules of Chapter 3 have been used to describe the major characteristics of organization X, a hunting and gathering society located in a submarginal environment, amidst similar organizations, and possessing a modest level of technological development. The size and density of the population was calculated, and the rules of population size were used to develop the remaining characteristics of the organization. To show the diversity of hunting and gathering societies, illustrations of societies with more extreme environments were given.

Our propositions give us a *first approximation* to the major features of hunting and gathering organizations, but they do not permit the development of detailed statements of all of the characteristics of these organizations. For example, although the family is very likely to be nuclear and patrilocal, it does not *have* to be. There are hunting and gathering organizations with other forms of familial organization, and there are even some with more than one form of organization. Similarly, the propositions guide us to the probable distribution of influence in the organization, but they do not tell us how it is structured specifically. In the case of a band, for example, we expect influence to be decentralized, but some bands have roles with ascribed status while others do not. Our ability to make more refined statements concerning the structure of these organizations depends on the continuing development of theory in this area. Some anthropologists and sociologists currently are attempting to extend the scheme used in this chapter to account for the more detailed aspects of life in hunting and gathering organizations. The approaches of these social scientists vary from studying the size of the game hunted to examining the value systems. Ideally, these efforts will eventually permit us to explain most of the specifics of organization in these societies. But because of the element of indeterminacy in historical events and human decision making, we are unlikely ever to be able to formulate rules that explain every specific.

REFERENCES

1   A. R. Holmberg, *Nomads of the Long Bow: The Siriono of Eastern Bolivia,* Bulletin No. 10 (Washington: Smithsonian Institution, Institute for Social Anthropology, 1950).

2   C. D. Forde, *Habitat, Economy, and Society: A Geographical Introduction to Ethnology* (New York: E. P. Dutton and Co., Inc., 1956).

3   R. J. Braidwood and C. A. Reed, "The Achievement and Early Consequences of Food Production: A Consideration of the Archeological and Natural-Historical Evidence," *Cold Spring Harbor Symposia on Quantitative Biology, 22* (1957), 19-31.

4   E. M. Thomas, *The Harmless People* (New York: Alfred A. Knopf, Inc., 1959).

5   J. H. Steward, *Theory of Culture Change* (Urbana: University of Illinois, 1955).

6   E. R. Service, *Primitive Social Organization: An Evolutionary Perspective* (New York: Random House, 1962).

7   M. F. Nimkoff and R. Middleton, "Types of Family and Types of Economy," *The American Journal of Sociology, 66* (1960), 215-25.

8   R. Redfield, "The Folk Society," *The American Journal of Sociology, 52* (1947), 293-308.

9   K. Polanyi, *The Great Transformation: The Political and Economic Origins of Our Time* (Boston: Beacon Press, Inc., 1957).

10   Horace M. Miner, Professor of Sociology and Anthropology, The University of Michigan, in a personal communication.

11   E. Wolf, "The Indian in Mexican Society," *Alpha Kappa Deltan, 30* (1960), 3-6.

12   B. Malinowski, *A Scientific Theory of Culture and Other Essays* (Chapel Hill: University of North Carolina Press, 1944).

13   D. French, "Wasco-Wishram," in *Perspectives in American Indian Culture Change,* E. H. Spicer, ed. (Chicago: The University of Chicago Press, 1961), pp. 337-440.

the social organization
of agrarian societies

Although the hunting and gathering band has been the dominant form of organization during most of the human period on earth, other forms of organization did appear in the paleolithic age. Canoe or fishing cultures flourished, and predatory bands exploited their less warlike neighbors. Some populations developed specialties in stonecraft and commerce. Interaction among these different societies was prevalent.

THE DEVELOPMENT OF NOMADIC AGRICULTURE

How and when man discovered and utilized the techniques of agriculture will never be known. That event is condemned to prehistory by the very impermanence of man's technology—a technology that could not withstand centuries of exposure to the natural environment. The paleolithic hunter may have discovered the relationship between seed and cereal long before he was willing to use it extensively. The Wishram Indians grew tobacco, but did not expand from one-crop gardening to agriculture. The Siriono occasionally cultivated yams, but their environment forced them to rely primarily on hunting and gathering.

The cultivation of cereals must have begun in Southwest Asia. Wild barley and emmer originally grew only in the area now contained in southern Turkey, Iran, and Palestine (1). Nomadic bands in this area must have made the shift to agriculture. The agricultural technology of these people was probably no more complex than that of their hunting and gathering neighbors (2). With their crude tools these early farmers could not have farmed grasslands or prairies because the sod would not yield to their plows. They were forced to farm less productive, but more easily worked land. Whenever trees dominate the natural environment, grass is sparse, and therefore the land is easier to plow. The neolithic (i.e., early agriculturalist) farmer either plowed around the trees, or he burned them down. If the trees were dense, he burned a clearing, used the ashes as a fertilizer, and scattered his seeds on the fresh soil. The cleared patch was reused to grow the same crops until the soil was depleted; then the farmer moved on to a new area and repeated the process. This type of economy is called *slash and burn* agriculture. The slash and burn economy forced the neolithic farmers into a nomadic pattern of life. Slowly they migrated in all directions from their starting point in Southwest Asia. They entered Europe via the Dardenelles, the northern coasts of the Mediterranean, and possibly through northern Africa into Spain (1). They converted densely forested Europe into the fairly open land we know it to be today.

THE DEVELOPMENT OF SUPRAVILLAGE ORGANIZATION

The arrival of the Asian farmer in Europe set the stage for a period of heightened cultural diffusion. Trading goods, exchanging techniques, and waging warfare became more common. Given a similar technology, the farmers were no match for the hunting and gathering bands. The latter had the advantage of mobility and very little property that was worth capturing or destroying. The farmers had forsaken warfare in favor of agriculture and, consequently, were not as skilled at fighting as were the hunters. They could protect themselves by living in villages, but their crops were impossible to protect. This problem of vulnerability was often resolved by submitting to extortion or by enlisting the aid of one band to protect the farming population from other bands (3). But the farmers often found themselves captured by their protectors. By increasing the number of villages under its control, the predatory band was able to increase the amount of food it could expropriate for its own use. For the first time in man's life on earth a level of integration above that of the band appeared. The hunters assumed all the elite roles: they coordinated the internal affairs of the villages, provided protection from other bands, and exacted their price in the form of food and other goods.

THE DEVELOPMENT OF SEDENTARY AGRICULTURE

Early farmers were forced into their nomadic way of life because they had not learned how to replenish the soil with the nutrients removed by their crops. Sedentary agriculture requires use of fertilizers, rotation of crops, or a natural environment that replaces depleted soil periodically. The annual floods of such rivers as the Nile and the Tigris provided fresh soil and a basis for settled agriculture. In other areas, the discovery of the use of fertilizers permitted permanent agricultural settlement. The oldest of these settlements found thus far is Jericho I, which is believed to be 9,000 years old (1). Jericho I was built on six acres of land. The threat of violence from other bands was apparently very great, because the village was surrounded by a ditch that was twenty-seven feet wide and eight feet deep. On the inside perimeter of the ditch there was a stone wall with a twenty-five-foot tower on one corner. Archeological evidence suggests that the population of the village was about 600 people and that the roles of chief and priest were at least part-time specializations.

The original technology of these permanent villages was just as crude as that of the hunting and gathering bands, but since the necessity of nomadism was removed it could and did develop to more complex levels. Pottery making was developed, as was metallurgy. A settled life permitted more elaborate housing and gave rise to the intricate science of construction. As the level of technology increased, the efficiency of farming increased too. The population of each village grew (if slowly) because deaths due to starvation declined while the birth rate remained high. When the size of the population came to exceed what the available land would support, some of the families left the parent village and formed new settlements nearby. This pattern of small, culturally similar villages can be seen in many parts of the world today.

A level of integration higher than that of the independent village did not develop until conquest or changes in the natural environment required it. One of the probable natural events that engendered the multivillage society was mentioned earlier: the desiccation of North

Africa. The change may have forced the neolithic farmers and the hunting and gathering bands into the Nile valley; the density of the population increased greatly. The existence of diverse social organizations in close proximity along the banks of the river led to intense interaction among them. Amalgamations and alliances grew out of these interactions. A similar chain of events was started by the use of slash and burn farming techniques, which forced growing populations to compete for the decreasing supply of arable land.

Conquest was a major factor in the development of the multicommunity state. The process was essentially the same as for nomadic farmers. The victorious tribe assumed all of the elite functions in the villages (3). The security of the victors was also enhanced because the conquered villages formed a buffer against potential enemies, and the defeated population supplied soldiers for the army. The losers were often reduced to slavery: a role that is very useful in a society still heavily reliant on human sources of energy.

It would be illogical to expect warfare as a form of interaction among these small states to cease; and, indeed, the technology and way of life of warfare became a permanent part of the culture of the conquering elites (3). Masculinity and bravery were exalted in the norms. The story of the development of the great empires of Egypt and Babylonia is one of successive conflicts among increasingly large political units. In no case is the process well documented. We do know, though, that, in Egypt, a clan from the region of the Upper Nile eventually amalgamated all of the populations along the Nile up to contemporary Sudan (1, 4). The number of generations required to complete this amalgamation is not known (4). In the area that was to become Babylonia, King Sargon emerged as the leader of the triumphant elite. In what is now India, successive waves of Indo-European conquerors came out of the area northwest of India and defeated the peoples in the Ganges and Indus river valleys. Each wave of conquerors took over the elite functions of the society, forced their predecessors into lower statuses; thus was created the caste system of classic Indian society.

Farming was still the predominant occupation in these early empires, but the basis for a more elaborate division of labor had arisen. The peasants were forced to deliver their surplus produce to the storehouses of the elite. In Egypt the pharoah used two very effective devices to claim the food surplus of his people. The threat of police action was probably sufficient to make virtually all of the peasants comply. But the Egyptian elite also took advantage of the religious inclinations of the peasants; the pharoah was declared to be a living god. By this means a tax became a religious tribute, which was much easier to collect. It became a part of the religious duties of the peasant to turn over his surplus to the agents of the pharoah: the priests. The temples of Egypt originally served as storehouses as well as places of worship. As the keepers of the enormous surplus of food that flowed into their temples, the priests were in a very influential position.

The surplus was used to support the elite, the army, the priesthood, and a variety of craft specialists. The science of metallurgy was given great impetus by the allocation of resources to the pursuit of that activity. The crafts of carpentry, masonry, pottery, and the sciences of medicine, mathematics, and astronomy were also advanced because they could now support full-time specialists.

The influence of these various roles and subgroups varied. Influence ranks contained many statuses. At the top of the influence ranking system was an elite composed of the king or pharoah, the landowning nobility, and the religious and military leaders. The members of this elite were interlocked by ties of kinship. Arrayed below this elite were the subelites of the landholding, religious, and military elites: the lesser nobles, priests, and officers. Professionals of many kinds formed another level: government officials, temple scribes, and doctors. The craftsmen were located at the next level of influence, and the laborers, whether urban or rural, had the least influence.

THE STRUCTURE OF AGRARIAN SOCIETIES

We have cursorily looked at the evidence provided by archeologists, historians, and classical scholars for the emergence of agrarian social organizations and their development into the larger and better known societies of Egypt, Babylonia, and India. Even from this brief introduction it is apparent that there is considerable variation among agrarian societies. Nomadic bands engaged in slash and burn agriculture and existed in relative independence of other bands. Settled villages had a larger population and slightly more elaborated social structure. The multicommunity state followed, composed of two or more villages with subgroups that specialized in the conduct of political affairs for all of the villages. Varying only in degree from the multicommunity state was the elaborate social structure that was found in classical Egypt, Babylonia, Rome, and in some modern agrarian societies. We shall refer to the most elaborate of these multicommunity organizations as *urban-agrarian societies*.

Other variations on the agrarian theme have not been mentioned. One is the stateless agrarian society: a collection of quasi-independent villages whose members share a common language and way of life, but who have no well-developed supracommunity political institutions. The special case of the agrarian village in an industrial society, so common in the world today, should also be noted. This chapter characterizes two types of agrarian societies: the settled agrarian village and the urban-agrarian society.

The Settled Agrarian Village

We shall assume that the economy is agrarian and the technology is at a relatively low level of development. Hoes or crude plows are used. The major source of power is human, because the domestication of animals is minimal. Fertilizers are utilized to refurbish the soil, so the population need not change its location periodically. The density of the population can be approximated using the figures shown in Table 3-1 on page 44. An agrarian organization with a crude technology will have a population density below the figure given in the table: less than 25 people per square mile. The size of the population of the organization cannot be determined, however, until we know the settlement pattern. If the people are fairly safe from external threats of violence, a decentralized pattern of settlement, in which each family lives on the land that it farms, is often used. A broken terrain also fosters this pattern, although it will not by itself cause it. When this decentralized pattern exists, the population of the "village" can be extremely large. In Africa there are communities containing thousands of persons in which each family farms and lives on a small plot of land. Japanese villages are often organized this way. Remembering our notion of social organization as a variable concept, we can say that the village with this type of settlement pattern represents a very low level of integration.

A centralized village is necessary when other organizations in the social environment threaten the safety of the population. The peasants live in villages, walk to their fields to work, and return to the safety of the village at night. Since this latter situation is more common, we will develop its structural implications.

The approximate size of the population of a centralized village can be determined by calculating the area around the village that will be farmed. Under certain circumstances, farmers have been known to travel great distances from their homes to work their land. Sometimes during the busy seasons of sowing and harvesting they minimize the time lost commuting by sleeping in the fields at night. The usual situation, however, is for the farmer to cultivate land at most only two or three miles from the village. At the lowest level of population density for an agrarian organization (less than 25 persons per square mile) farming within a radius of two or three miles, the resulting population would number about 100 to 700 people. A slight rise in the level of technology, permitting the support of 200 or 300 more people, would result in a village population of around 1,000.

POPULATION GROWTH. A population practicing subsistence agriculture will have a lower death rate than a hunting and gathering organization because it has a stable and storable source of food. Although starvation remains an annual threat, it is less immediate than it is for the hunting and gathering band eking out an existence in a submarginal environment. The birth rate will continue to be maximal because the means of limiting family size are still crude, and because a large family becomes more essential as the size of the farm increases. The additional family members are used to help with the plowing, sowing, reaping, and other farm tasks. As a consequence of the reduced death rate and the high birth rate, the population of the village will grow—slowly, because violence and famine will still provide checks in addition to the usual ones of disease and accidents. When the population exceeds its food supply significantly, some of the families will form a new village, perhaps only a few miles away. This practice creates the now familiar pattern of several culturally similar villages located near each other. If the area is free of predatory bands, this stateless pattern of social organization persists.

SUBGROUP FORMATION. The smaller settled agrarian villages (pop. 100-200) have about the same population size as the hunting and gathering band studied in Chapter 6. Because of this small size, the number and types of subgroups are not very great (Proposition 2). The family and the clique still account for most of the subgroups found. The family is the unit in which all important individual needs are met. It is primarily an economic unit. Etymologically, in fact, the word *economy* (from Greek *oikonomia*) *means* householding (5). Since it is a productive organization, it employs its own members and provides their food, clothing, and shelter. Marriages are made, not for love and companionship, but to maintain the economic well-being of the family. Few activities are performed by units external to the family: religion is primarily a family affair and the education of the children and the recreation of all the members are ordinarily family activities. Often it will incorporate features that provide security for elderly relatives, who are no longer physically able to perform the harder farming tasks, and would starve if they had to provide for themselves. A common form of organization is the *extended* family in which other relatives share the household with the nuclear family and form a single productive organization. In another pattern, several related households of large nuclear families are tightly bound together in a higher level of integration: the clan or the corporate family. The children are tied closely to the family unit, because as soon as they are able, they share in the duties of their parents. The boys travel to the fields and work with their father, and the girls assist the mother in her household duties. The care of very small children is often shared by the mother and the grandparents. This arrangement minimizes interaction within cohorts of young people and often prevents these cohorts of youngsters from forming associations of their own.

In the larger villages, there are enough people in various social categories, particularly age categories, for the development of associations. Associational life takes many forms. The most significant unit often is a council, composed of the leaders of each clan, that may perform some political functions for the whole village. Religious and educational subgroups are sometimes found in these villages, although the family often performs these activities too.

THE DIVISION OF LABOR.   The small size of the population, the simple technology, and the lack of sufficient food surpluses preclude the development of an extensive division of labor in the subsistence agrarian village (Proposition 2). With rare exceptions, all of the adult male villagers are farmers. The village will generally have a headman or chief who has the power to make certain types of decisions with or without the aid of the council, but he must work in the fields just as the other villagers do. Another common part-time specialist is the priest. The deities of agrarian societies reflect the fundamental concern of the population with the problems of farming. Religious observances are closely tied to the change of the seasons, and the aid of the deities is sought to ensure the abundance of the crops. In all of these activities the family plays the major role, but a part-time priest often performs a few functions in village religious ceremonial activities. In Jericho I, which was very similar to the type of village we are describing here, the population worshiped a maternal fertility deity and supported a part-time priest (1).

THE DISTRIBUTION OF INFLUENCE.   If the village is composed of independent farmers, there is little need for specialized roles to coordinate their activities (Propositions 12 and 8). The chief or headman usually controls the external relations of the village. Strangers are required to get his permission before interacting with other village members. In our contemporary underdeveloped societies the cooperation of village headmen is essential to government plans to increase agricultural productivity and industrialize the society; they are not always cooperative. Any outsider who is seen by the headman as a threat to the status quo is unable to accomplish his objectives in the village. Daniel Lerner (6) records an example of the extremes to which the village headman will go to protect his position. In a village he studied, the headman owned the only radio. Although he invited others to hear the news programs, he followed each newscast with his own interpretation of its meaning.

In the simple agricultural village, the influence of the headman is usually restricted to the areas mentioned above. But as the diversity of the crops produced, the division of labor, and trade with other social organizations increase, the influence of the chief or headman expands over broader areas of village life (Proposition 13). A specialized role emerges: that of chief as redistributor of the food and other products produced by the villagers. This role is also useful for the regulation of trade with the members of other social organizations who may be producing different and desired products. Given a sufficiently steady surplus of food, this role may emerge as a permanent full-time specialization, and its occupant's influence may border on despotism.

Urban-Agrarian Society

The urban-agrarian society is the product of centuries of warfare and amalgamations. It is essentially a collection of peasant villages the members of which are ruled by an elite. The elite is able to mobilize part or all of the food surplus of the peasants for its own use.

THE SPECIALIZATION OF COMMUNITIES. The most influential community is the administrative center—the residence of the elite (Proposition 2 *et passim*). To this city or to regional market centers the peasant takes his tribute of produce. He may also take additional goods for barter with the merchants who inhabit these cities. The food from the storehouses of the elite is used to support soldiers, government officials, religious personnel, craftsmen, and other non-food-producing specialists. It is also used to trade with merchants from other societies, in marketplaces in the regional and national capitals. Other communities, such as seaports, develop at the crossroads of natural trade routes and become specialized in commercial activities. Mining, religious, and educational centers also develop.

The existence of a food surplus that can be redistributed gives rise to specialized subgroups and roles in urban-agrarian society (Proposition 2). In the cities, particularly the capital, guilds of craftsmen form to develop and protect their skills. These crafts may vary from working silver and other metals to carpentry and construction work. And each of these occupational subgroups will contain many differentiated roles. The specialization of activity greatly enhances the rate of technological change as the craftsmen seek new techniques to improve their arts.

RANK SYSTEMS AND SOCIAL STATUS.   With the increased population size of the urban-agrarian society, we expect the number of rank systems and the length of each to increase (Propositions 8 and 9). In the small village, the absence of occupational specialization precludes distinctions among roles on the basis of influence. In larger villages, the specialized role of chief or headman possesses more influence than that of the other peasants (Proposition 13). In the urban-agrarian society, more gradations of influence appear. The most influential rank system is that centered on the key industry of the society—agriculture. In this system the most influential roles are held by the owners of the largest acreages of land—the ruler and the nobility around him. In Iran, where land reform programs have been initiated by the king, some of the nobility had land holdings that included several hundred peasant villages. In Egypt before the revolution, 2 per cent of the population owned 50 per cent of the arable land (7). Arrayed below this landholding elite in terms of influence are the freeholding peasants, the farm laborers, and the slaves, in that order.

Historically, the landowning elite has usually been an absentee one, preferring to live in the more cosmopolitan urban centers rather than in the rural areas. The management of the farms was left to professional overseers. This pattern is still found in modern Spain and Italy, as well as in many of the underdeveloped countries. It was also found in medieval Europe until the commercial revival led the nobility to forsake the cities in order to escape the tradesmen who were settling there (8). Because it lived in the cities, the elite was largely ignorant of the problems and conditions of the peasant. The value systems of most of these societies also prohibited any interest on the part of the nobility in understanding the peasants' problems. Sociologists refer to value systems that are used to justify an existing distribution of influence as *legitimating myths*. In most agrarian societies the legitimating myth was based on the divine right of the ruler. He ruled because he was chosen by the god or gods to rule; indeed, the legitimating myth may have conferred on the ruler the status of a god. The nobility, in their turn, profited by the holiness of the ruler; they were selected by him; therefore they must be superior. This myth of divine right was ingrained in virtually all the members of the society. The peasants would not think of questioning the decisions of their rulers because it would be irreligious to do so. Daniel Lerner (6) records an incident in which a student of his was interviewing a shepherd in rural Turkey. The student asked the shepherd what he would do if he were prime minister. The shepherd became extremely agitated and refused to answer, because no person as lowly as he should question the actions of so superior a person. The low regard in which the elite and sub-elites hold the peasant is reflected in the following passage from Ayrout's study of Egyptian society. The attitude was prevalent among the Egyptian nobility of antiquity as well.

Contempt for the fellah has become so deeply rooted in the mind of the townsman that the very word has become the worst of insults. Call anyone "fellah" and it is as if you had called him "lout," "scum" or even worse. The rich assume a striking indifference to the fellahin. To them, they are only "things" in which there is no point in interesting oneself and which it is considered good form to ignore. Faced with the simplest queries about them, the rich often display an ignorance which shows quite clearly that such questions have never occurred to them and arouse no curiosity at all. Others among the better type deplore the dullness and hidebound habits of the fellah, but will attempt nothing to help him which will lessen their own incomes.*

The legitimating myth and the geographic separation of the elite and the peasantry are the major segmenting influences in agrarian societies (Proposition 10). The segmentation is so nearly complete that it is common to refer to *the national life* and *the peasant life* in these societies. *The national life* refers to the activities of the elite, but it also includes those of government, religious, and commercial subgroups in the cities. The national or urban life exists in an almost frictionless relationship with the peasant life. The peasant seldom travels to the city, except to trade a few items. If he has problems that require official action, he will appeal to the *local* official, but if that fails, he will seldom carry his case higher (9).

Other rank systems are based on military, religious, and governmental activities (Proposition 9). An immediately impressive characteristic of these rank systems is the way in which the landowning nobility manages to dominate them. Agrarian societies, it must be remembered,

---

* H. H. Ayrout, *The Egyptian Peasant*, trans. J. A. Williams (Boston: Beacon Press, 1963), p. 19. Reprinted here by permission.

are kinship societies, and the importance of kinship is as binding on the behavior of the members of the elite as it is on the peasants. Relatives of the landowning elite assume the most influential positions in all of the key areas of economic, political, and social activity (10). In western societies, it was customary for the first son to inherit the family lands and titles, and the second and third sons bought or assumed elite positions in the church and military organizations. The implications for controlling the population are very great. The families of the nobility can enforce the religious legitimating myth, and, failing that, can use the police and military units to put down any insurrections.

A number of factors combine to limit the occupational opportunities of the population and thereby the opportunities of people to increase their influence. First, because agrarian societies are kinship societies, considerable emphasis is placed on assuming one's father's occupation. Indeed, occupations are thought of as belonging to a family and are passed from one generation to the next. Second, there is no premium placed on migrating from one part of the country to another. The outlook of the peasant is so parochial that he has great difficulty even thinking about the world outside his village; his village *is* the world. The difficulties and dangers of traveling dictate against it for all but the most venturesome peasants. Even on the American frontier, a woman who married and moved thirty miles away was unlikely to see her family again. The parochial character of life depresses any desire to move in yet another way: the role of stranger in another village or town greatly disadvantages its occupant. Third, the legitimating myth often contained the value that everyone should be satisfied with his station in life, perform well the duties associated with that station, and not aspire to a higher one. For these reasons, in the classic agrarian society we find rigid boundaries between the various occupational status levels. When there is *no* mobility between status levels, we say that there is a *caste system*. In this system, which is found in India, the occupations of the fathers are passed on to the sons in perpetuity. In most agrarian societies, such as classic Roman, Egyptian, and Chinese society, some mobility was possible. Although the elite roles were generally closed, a peasant's son could achieve a fairly high rank in the military, religious, or governmental organizations.

When barriers to ocupational mobility are sufficiently high, as they are and were in agrarian societies, each status level becomes something more than a social category—it acquires properties of organization. The population occupying a given status level shares similar problems and similar allocations of resources and rewards. Social interaction is often restricted by the norms to persons at the same level in the occupational rank system (Proposition 10). Inevitably, normative similarity increases, and subgroups based in each level of status appear. Manners of speech and dress often serve to identify the status position of the person. In other words, status levels become the basis for the formation of sub-cultures (see page 62). When status levels have these organizational and cultural properties, *social classes* are said to exist.

NORMS AND DEVIANCE.   In spite of the relatively strong integration of agrarian societies at the national level, the primary level of integration for the peasant is still the family and the small village in which he lives. The character of the norms in the village is still quite similar to that of the hunting and gathering society and the subsistence village that it emulates (Proposition 4). The norms are traditional, and responses to them are still uncritical and spontaneous. Formal norms now appear, because the central government creates them to coordinate and control the affairs of the society (Proposition 7). The development of professions such as engineering and medicine also increases the number of formal norms, because the members seek to develop standardized procedures for their activities.

In spite of the strong forces for obedience to the norms, deviance does appear in agrarian societies (Proposition 5). The development of occupational specialization provides a basis for this deviance. The investigations of a scientist may run counter to the sacred traditions of a society, as they did for Galileo and Socrates. Some professionals can afford a certain amount of deviance, however, because their services are too valuable for the elite to impose drastic sanctions.

The itinerant merchant who visits foreign lands and sees the different cultures is also a source of tension in the traditional society. Even the lowly peasant, tradition bound and passive as he usually is, is a source of deviance from the formal prescriptions of the rulers. As was noted earlier, the peasants often fail to conform to the demands of government officials who come to their village. Occasionally, they are given to violence. In Czarist Russia the peasants sometimes burned the barns and homes of their absentee masters. The red glow on the horizon often served as a signal for similar acts by peasants on other manors. In modern agrarian or underdeveloped societies, two additional sources of deviance appear. The most dangerous category from the point of view of the ruling agrarian elite is the disaffected middle class. This group is composed of the trained professionals who do not have an opportunity to practice their chosen profession because of the backwardness of the society. It includes the teachers who have no schools or students, the engineers with no buildings or roads to build, the lawyers with no clients, and the students who see no hope of achieving these rewards. In the Near East these people usually went into the army where they could experience some mobility and approximate the style of life that they wished to lead (11). In other areas of the world they have entered the trade union movements or political parties (9). In any of these organizations, they become a potential source of rebellion. In the army they find that they seldom can rise above the rank of colonel because all of the general staff ranks are the property of relatives of the elite families. The similarity of their positions, problems, and backgrounds facilitates interaction and the planning of revolution. It is no accident that many of the rebellions in the Near East and elsewhere are the work of colonels with backgrounds in other professions.

The second source of deviance in the contemporary urban agrarian society is the urban peasant (9). Many peasants leave their native villages and emigrate to the cities in the hope of escaping the grinding poverty of peasant life. Usually they are greeted by grinding poverty in the urban slums. In or around most of the cities in most of the underdeveloped countries there are slums composed of these displaced peasants. Disenchanted with their lot, they are susceptible to the entreaties of revolutionaries. They form the backbone of urban mob violence.

PEASANT LIFE.   In virtually all agrarian societies peasants comprise 80 per cent or more of the population. What is life like for this vast majority of the population? We have already seen that the peasant is tradition bound and oriented in his loyalties to the family and his village. The most revealing characteristic of his life is that he lives on the borderline of poverty. An array of social forces seemingly are designed to keep him poor by preventing him from building up a surplus of wealth. Occasional crop failure can force him to borrow money at exhorbitant rates from a moneylender in order to buy the seed for next year's crops. Unless he is very lucky, he is unlikely to free himself of this type of debt. In some societies he is required by the norms to provide a dowry for his daughter. The dowry is usually larger than he can afford, and he is once again driven to the usurer. In other societies the norms require that whatever money he saves be used to pay for a celebration for the villagers (12).

The struggle to stay alive is so omnipresent that life in the peasant village has a distinct competitive side. Although the peasant may participate in certain communal activities that enhance his chances of survival, he is in reality a short-range economic opportunist (13). He thinks in short-range terms because he cannot afford the luxury of thinking any other way. E. C. Banfield (13) observed that the peasants in southern Italy frequently switch their voting allegiances from the Christian Democrats to the Communists to the Monarchists and back again. He explains this behavior in terms of the peasant's short-range economic thinking; the peasant votes for the party that promises or has given him the most rewards. The strategy of the Chinese Communists for winning control of the countries in Southeast Asia is based on this proclivity of the peasant (14). By giving the villagers presents of medicine and food and by working with them in the fields, the Communists secure the passive cooperation of the villagers. Should these measures fail, there is always the threat of violence to ensure their cooperation.

Even within the family, poverty has serious effects. The family is not completely characterized by the warmth and friendliness of a primary group. The parents are often remote and domineering with their children, and marriages are made for economic reasons, not for love. Certainly the family is the major source of affection, but this aspect of it has been overemphasized.

Although the life of the peasant is physically hard because of the lack of tools, this aspect also has been overemphasized. We tend to think of our own society as one in which the amount of leisure time available is increasing, but we have far less leisure than the agrarian peasant. H. L. Wilensky (16) has observed that peasant life is studded with religious holidays, and the peasant demonstrates a penchant for converting them into feast days. Wilensky also states that one out of every three days was a holiday in Roman society.

REFERENCES

1   V. G. Childe, *The Prehistory of European Society* (Harmondsworth, England: Penguin Books, Ltd., 1958).

2   J. H. Steward, *Theory of Culture Change* (Urbana: University of Illinois Press, 1955).

3   L. Mumford, *The City in History: Its Origins, Its Transformations, and Its Prospects* (New York: Harcourt, Brace, and World, Inc., 1961).

4   J. A. Wilson, *The Culture of Ancient Egypt* (Chicago: The University of Chicago Press, 1951).

5   K. Polanyi, *The Great Transformation* (Boston: Beacon Press, Inc., 1957).

6   D. Lerner, *The Passing of Traditional Society: Moderniz-ing the Middle East* (New York: Free Press of Glencoe, Inc., 1958).

7   H. H. Ayrout, *The Egyptian Peasant,* J. A. Williams, trans. (Boston: Beacon Press, Inc., 1963).

8   H. Pirenne, *Medieval Cities* (Garden City: Doubleday & Company, Inc., 1958).

9   G. A. Almond and J. S. Coleman, *The Politics of the De-veloping Areas* (Princeton: Princeton University Press, 1960).

10   G. Sjoberg, "The Preindustrial City," *The American Jour-nal of Sociology, 60* (1955), 438-45.

11   Majīd Khaddūri, "The Role of the Military in Middle East Politics," *American Political Science Review, 47* (1953), 511-25.

12   E. Wolf, "The Indian in Mexican Society," *Alpha Kappa Deltan, 30* (1960), 3-6.

13   E. C. Banfield, *The Moral Basis of a Backward Society* (New York: Free Press of Glencoe, Inc., 1958).

14   *Essays on Communism in Asia: Papers from the CENIS China Project* (Cambridge: Massachusetts Institute of Tech-nology, 1955).

15   W. F. Willcox, *Studies in American Demography* (Ithaca: Cornell University Press, 1940), p. 54, Table 23.

16   H. L. Wilensky, "The Uneven Distribution of Leisure: The Impact of Economic Growth on 'Free Time,'" *Social Prob-lems, 9* (1961), 32-56.

organizational change: industrialization

In order to understand industrial societies, let us first examine the process of change that led to their development. In so doing we may also gain insight into the process of organizational change itself.

There are two ways that an industrial society can develop. It can evolve naturally with little planning on the part of members of the population, as it did in England and other nations of Europe and the United States. Or it can evolve as a result of the concerted efforts of planners in a society. This latter approach is currently being used in the Soviet Union and in some of the underdeveloped countries. In keeping with the historical and evolutionary emphasis of this book, we will describe the natural evolution of industrial and commercial societies that developed in Europe. In Part 4 of this book the creation of an industrial society by planning will be discussed.

There are certain prerequisites to an industrial society. A large population is required to serve as markets for the large volume of goods that can be produced with a machine technology. A good transportation system is essential in order to move the large volume of goods great distances cheaply. The transportation of manufactured products must be protected from piracy and robbery. Machines and efficient sources of power to drive them are required. Finally, the farmers must produce a food surplus sufficient to feed the workers in the factories. These prerequisites were not developed in any neat order as if in accordance to some plan; they evolved—sometimes by design, other times quite independently of each other. By the mere act of organizing them for discussion here, we are injecting more order into the actual historical process than it possessed.

Industrialization began in Europe and particularly in England in the latter part of the eighteenth century. We shall trace here the development of industrial forms of organization, using England as an example because the advent of industrialism is well documented there.

THE PROCESS OF INDUSTRIALIZATION IN ENGLAND

Prior to the Industrial Revolution, England was an agrarian society modeled on the feudal pattern. Although there was a central government in the person of a king, his influence was dependent upon the coalition of feudal lords that surrounded him. The nobility and the landed gentry controlled the major locus of governmental influence—the Parliament. The most potent political unit was still the feudal barony.

In A.D. 1700 the population of England was estimated to be about 6 million people, an increase of only one million since A.D. 1600 (1). Gregory King estimated that at that rate of growth the population would reach 11 million by the year A.D. 2300 and 22 million by A.D. 3600 (1). Virtually all of the population was involved in agriculture, and urban development was correspondingly low. London was about the size of present day Buffalo, New York. A cottage wool industry had developed, as it had in Europe. The pattern was the familiar one in which the merchant sold the raw materials to the farmer and bought them back after they had been processed in one or more ways. This system gave the farmer an additional source of income: one that he could increase by making all of the members of his family work on the looms or spinners. He simply carried over the time-honored agrarian practice of having the children work the farm to the manufacture of cloth. It was the farmer who invented the long work day for children; the industrialist merely continued and perhaps found new ways to abuse the practice.

The woolen industry was suffocating under the weight of governmental protectionism that specified the length, width, and weight of the pieces of cloth (1). The processes of dyeing and stretching were also regulated minutely, as were the methods of folding and packaging. As a consequence, technical improvements in methods of manufacture were not possible because such improvement invariably violated one regulation or another. Government regulation of commerce and industry in this period was much greater than we experience today; in fact, it accounts for the emphasis that the value system of capitalism places on minimizing governmental interference in the affairs of the economy.

The low volume of innovative activity is also apparent in the fact that an average of fewer than 12 patents were recorded for each year during this period (1). In 1720 there were only 17,000 tons of crude pig iron produced in all of England, compared to the quarter of a million tons that were to be produced less than one century later.

Transportation systems in England were extremely backward. The roads were poor because it was easier to travel by any of the abundant water routes. The only important technological advance that had occurred in transportation during the entire medieval period in Europe was the invention of the horse bit. Prior to the invention of the bit, several animals were required to pull a load that only one animal with a bit could pull, because the pressure of the raw thong had to be distributed over the mouths of several horses. With the invention of the bit it was possible to substitute carrier wagons for pack horses on the crude roadways. The roads were so narrow that only one wagon could fit on them at one time. Whenever two wagons passed each other, it was necessary for one to get off the road. The abundance of chuck holes forced the wagoner to use much of his valuable space to carry spare axles to replace the ones that were inevitably broken. Rain and snow reduced the roads to ribbons of mud and prevented their use in any season except the summer. In the less accessible parts of England in A.D. 1700 transportation was so poor that the peasants did not know of, never mind eat, such commodities as sugar (1).

Population Growth and The Food Surplus

In the interval from 1700 to 1750 the population of England increased at its normal rate, from 6 to 6.5 million. But between 1750 and 1801 it increased to 9 million. In the same period the population of London had increased by a similar percentage, to 900,000 persons. This dramatic population growth signaled the fact that England had entered what is known technically as the *demographic transition:* the period when the death rate drops more rapidly than the birth rate, resulting in an increase in the size of the population. The transition is illustrated in Figure 8-1.

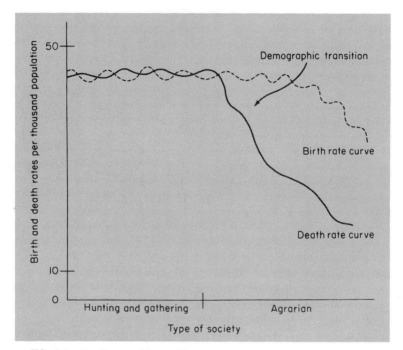

FIG. 8-1   The demographic transition.

The birth rate declines somewhat during this period because means are found to limit the size of families. The decline in the death rate is not due, however, to medical advances. The medical advances that are affecting the death rates in most industrialized countries today did not occur until the turn of the present century. Smallpox was conquered in the latter part of the eighteenth century, and legislation was passed to train midwives, care for poor children, and require the burial of the dead in coffins, but these improvements had but minor effects on the death rate. The major cures recommended by doctors for the treatment of tuberculosis were horseback riding and drinking crocodile blood. The commonly used medicines that are still considered to be of some medical value were sulphur, digitalis, and mercury. The modern profession of medicine had not emerged. Quacks moved from village to village offering to cure the village idiot of his mental problem by removing an offending stone from his head. A collection was taken among the villagers to pay for the surgery. In the village square the hapless idiot was subjected to head surgery without benefit of anesthetic. At the conclusion of the operation, the surgeon triumphantly held up a stone that he had palmed in his hand, patched up the head of the idiot, and moved on to another town before his chicanery was discovered.

Hospitals during this period were places to go to die. The nurses of that era were often arrested prostitutes who had a choice of serving their sentences in the jail or the hospital. The neophytes unknowingly chose the hospital. Bandages were made from rags collected in the neighborhood and were put on the patient's wounds without benefit of sterilization, there being no germ theory in those days. Fifty percent of the patients in the larger urban hospitals died from an infection after their legs were amputated (2).

Agricultural Advances

The decline in the death rate was due to the increased supply of food that was available to the population. Prior to the agricultural revolution of the eighteenth century, English agricultural techniques were little advanced beyond those of neolithic farmers. Each farmer worked a series of tiny patches of land that were geographically decentralized. This spatial arrangement had many drawbacks. A multitude of paths were required to get from one patch to another, wasting arable land. The small patches greatly limited the farmer's ability to innovate, and he wasted time walking from one patch to another to work or inspect them. The farmers also used three-crop rotation—a system that divided land into four quarters, one of which was left fallow and, therefore, unproductive each year. Means of feeding large numbers of animals through the winter were unknown, so each fall the farmers slaughtered almost all of them, preventing any growth in the size of their herds.

On virtually every manor there was a parcel of land called the commons that, although owned by the lord of the manor, was actually used by the peasants or yeomen. The yeomen were allowed to farm this land and to graze animals on it. Some of the poorer yeomen lived in cottages at the edge of the commons.

It was the commercial revival that set off a chain of events culminating in a drastic alteration in the practice of agriculture and the life of the yeomen. We noted earlier that the growth of the commercial town occurred at the expense of the nobility. Alarmed at the behavior as well as the increasing economic power of the merchants, some of the English nobility decided to build up countervailing power by leading from their strength—the land (1). Ways were sought to increase their wealth by increasing the agricultural productivity of their lands. In 1731, a man named Jethro Tull published a book on agricultural practices based on thirty years of research on his estate. In his book he advocated several new practices (1). Instead of leaving a fourth of the land fallow each year, Tull recommended planting a useful crop that would put back into the soil the nutrients that previous crops had removed. By this means alone the productivity of the land could be increased by a third. Deep plowing rather than shallow plowing was also advocated, along with a system for foddering animals during the winter. Some of the nobility, notably Lord Townshend, tried these techniques with dramatic results, and others followed their lead.

Another advance suggested was the selective breeding of animals. Previously the animals were simply turned out to pasture, and nature was allowed to take its course. Now it was discovered that animals could be bred selectively for certain traits. The effects of selective breeding are apparent to us when we look at the average weights of the animals sold at the Smithfield fair (1). In 1710 the average oxen sold weighed 370 pounds; by 1795 the average weight was 800 pounds. In the same period, the weight of calves increased from 50 to 150 pounds; that of sheep, from 38 to 80 pounds. It is difficult for us to imagine the scrawny, long-legged animals that bore the names of cows and sheep in the period before 1710.

The nobility also used their power in the Parliament to force the yeomen off the commons. Eviction orders called Enclosure Acts were passed. Whereas in the decade from 1720 to 1730 only 33 such acts were passed, 642 enclosures were made between 1770 and 1780 (1). Since the more efficient farming techniques of the nobility required fewer workers, large numbers of yeomen found themselves unemployed as well as evicted. Many of them sought to make a living for themselves and their families by contracting their services in one of the cottage industries. Others migrated to the urban areas in great numbers and looked for jobs in the newly developing industries. Unwittingly, the nobility had created the labor force of the industrial revolution. But the supply of labor exceeded the demand, and the life of the displaced yeomen was generally a miserable one. The cities were ill equipped to handle their burgeoning populations, and many people died from one or another of the plagues that were endemic to the times. Although the plagues decimated the urban population, the yeomen came on to the cities in such great numbers that the cities grew rapidly in size.

The Development of a Machine Technology

The cotton industry was among the first of the English industries to experience the technological advances that are the mark of an industrial revolution. Before 1720 this industry was organized at the familiar cottage level. The simple knitting frame was the usual tool, and the farmer could rent it from a merchant. When it became illegal to buy cotton products from India, the cotton industry in England received considerable impetus (1). In 1733, John Kay invented the fly shuttle that permitted the weaving of broader pieces of cloth more rapidly. Weaving was done so rapidly with this machine that the spinners could not keep up with the demand for cloth, and many weavers had to be laid off. In 1765 James Hargreaves invented the spinning jenny, which solved the problem of the lag in the spinning operation. Replacing the one-spindle manual model that is now a much sought after antique, Hargreaves' model had eight spindles. In his own lifetime the number of spindles in a single jenny was increased to eighty. Today it is possible to have hundreds of spindles on a single jenny. A decade after the invention of the jenny, the spinning "mule" was introduced. This machine combined all of the technological advances in the spinning operation into one complex piece of machinery that permitted the spinning of yarn that was stronger and finer than earlier techniques had permitted. The steam engine, invented in 1767 by James Watt, was eventually incorporated with the other machinery to provide an efficient source of adequate power for the cotton industry.

In the early stages of this development, the farmer could afford to buy or lease the equipment necessary to process cotton. Old barns and carthouses were converted into spinning factories where the early spinning jennys could be used. But as the machinery increased in size and complexity, the investment required to purchase it became prohibitive for the farmer. The necessary capital was possessed by the merchants, a few willing members of the nobility, and other enterprising individuals. Mills employing 150 to 600 people sprang up all over England, particularly in the extremely humid area of Lanchashire. These mills were located near sources of power, such as waterfalls. The working force was composed largely of yeomen and other less successful farmers who left their birthplaces and migrated to the growing industrial centers. Rather than working on his own land or for a wealthy farmer, the city laborer worked in a factory, for an unknown employer who had no obligation to him beyond paying his wages.

The experience in the cotton industry was duplicated in other industries. As was noted earlier, only 17,000 tons of crude pig iron were produced in England in 1720. This is less pig iron than can be produced by a single modern blast furnace. Furthermore, the quality of the pig iron was so poor that machinery made from it broke down easily. Through the inventive efforts of Abraham Darby and Henry Cort the predecessor of the modern blast furnace and the associated technique of puddling were discovered (1). English iron manufacture quickly leapt ahead. By 1881 England *exported* 3,820,315 tons of steel. The development of the steel industry gave added vigor to industrialization in England because it permitted the construction of durable machinery and iron bridges.

The Development of Transportation Systems

The means of transportation that existed in England at the opening of the eighteenth century were clearly inadequate for the transport of the products of the factory system. During that century great emphasis was placed on the construction of various systems of transportation. The national government in the person of the king and the Parliament had an interest in the development of adequate road systems. It had been found that it was difficult to put down insurrections in remote parts of the country because of the poor roads. The lesson was not lost on the elite, and support for the construction of roads was given quickly. The practice was to create trusts of private builders who were given a franchise to build a road connecting certain cities and towns and to charge a toll for its use. Between 1748 and 1760 the number of Turnpike Trusts rose from 160 to 530 (1). By 1790 the country had a good network of roads. The creation of adequate roads was implemented by the innovations of McAdam and Telford. These and other road engineers discovered methods of road construction that led to the building of all-weather, permanent roads.

Other means of transportation were also utilized during this period. In 1750 there was not a single canal in England, although the geography of the country was ideal for the use of this form of transportation (1). By the close of the century canal building had taken on the proportions of a craze. England was crisscrossed with a canal system that joined its abundant rivers. The introduction of the canal greatly reduced the cost of transporting such bulky materials as coal. But the importance of the canal system was quickly reduced by the invention of the rail-road train. The locomotive is a relatively simple and logical applica-tion of the steam boiler or engine. The engine was placed on a wheeled platform and attached to the wheels by means of pistons and levers. Regular carriage coaches then commonly in use were simply attached serially to each other and to the locomotive. Since this system was much cheaper to construct and maintain than a canal system, it quickly superseded the latter.

The Development of the Nation-State

In feudal societies, the lord is able to maintain order within his small principality. But the leaders of an industrial economy have wider interests and markets than the small principality. They are interested in the maintenance of order in all areas where their trade routes extend. In the fragmentary system of feudalism, the merchant industrialist found himself greatly disadvantaged. He had to pay a toll in each principality he crossed with his goods, and this made them unduly expensive to transport. Furthermore, paying the toll was no guarantee of safe transport. The merchant was still subject to robbery by the lord as well as by independent operators. The merchants had, therefore, a vested interest in the development of the strong nation-state. This form of political organization had three major advantages for them. First, it could remove internal barriers to trade and intro-duce order and law into economic activity. Second, a strong nation-state could maintain armies and navies that could protect the overseas trade routes. Third, this social arrangment could be used to eclipse the influence of the natural enemy of the merchant: the landed aristocracy. Very early in the commercial revival the emerging middle class, com-posed of merchants, threw its growing influence behind the claims of the king to sovereignty over the affairs of England: an alliance that was eventually triumphant. The movement of the major center of influence away from the landed aristocracy continued as the merchant class gradually undermined the influence of the king. Because of their con-trol of vast wealth, the merchants and the emerging industrialists were able to extract concessions from kings in exchange for loans. Once the members of the merchant class had wrested the major share of political influence away from the aristocracy, they used the institutions of gov-ernment to further their interests and activities.

It must be remembered that the original members of the merchant class were outsiders in an essentially hostile world. The nobility dis-dained them socially and indeed often threw the full weight of their military as well as their economic power against them. The norms of feudal society also prohibited the making of profits or lending money for interest; the merchants were clearly deviants.

Another source of problems for the merchants was ingrained in the very nature of feudalism: the principle that all phases of life should be integrated. The economy was not a separate entity free from the regulation of the nobility. Thus when commercial and manufacturing activity increased, it was logical from the point of view of the feudal culture that these new activities would be regulated by the elite. The intricate system of state protectionism arose and had the effect of slowing the pace of the industrial revolution. All of these lessons were not lost on the merchant-industrial class when they captured the political institutions. The new philosophy of the independence of the economy from the regulation of government represented an attempt to nurture the developing industrialism. It was easy for the new class to argue that the economy should be free of the influence of the other institutions of the society because the merchants and industrialists had never really been parts of the older system. Furthermore, the capitalists and the feudal elite saw the world organized in entirely different ways. For the capitalists all of the aspects of a society—its population, land, and property—were organized into markets (3). Markets were the most meaningful groups, and as such they should be free of the influence of other, older, feudal organizations. The only laws that were to govern the markets were the laws of economics: the laws of supply and demand. Human considerations were foreign to the marketplace; labor was subject to the same economic laws that regulated land and goods. If the government passed laws that interfered with the workings of the markets, they were wrong to do so. The role of the government was to facilitate the natural workings of the marketplace. It was in this spirit that they took over the operation of the government and used it to further their interests. This philosophy of the role of the government in relationship to the economy was given the name *laissez-faireism.*

The Development of Corporate Forms of Social Organization

A final invention of an organizational nature facilitated the development of an industrial society: the joint-stock corporation. During the early phases of the industrial revolution, businesses were owned by individuals or partners. Neither form of organization was particularly suitable for large-scale industrialism. Both forms of organization limit greatly the amount of money that can be invested in a business. The partnership suffered the added disadvantage of lasting only for the lifetime of the partners. In the event of the death of one of them, the partnership was legally dissolved, and the surviving partner was left to reorganize his company. The widow of the deceased partner often found her position somewhat tenuous and dependent upon the honesty of the remaining partner. Each partner was also liable for the business behaviors of the other. If one partner embezzled the funds of the firm, the other partner was a party to any resulting lawsuits that might be brought against the company.

The corporation overcomes these disadvantages. First, it permits the pooling of the large amounts of money essential to the purchase of expensive equipment and buildings. It does this by issuing stock or certificates of ownership in the corporation, which large numbers of people may purchase. Second, the corporation is viewed under the law as a fictitious person, and so can continue to exist beyond the lifetimes of any of the individual owners. Third, each stockholder is liable for the actions of the corporation only up to the limit of his investment. Without this form of organization, the development of the giant productive organizations that are a part of life in modern industrial societies would not have been possible.

SUMMARY

This chapter has traced the development of some of the factors that led to modern industrial society, using England as a case study. The industrial revolution was triggered by increased agricultural productivity that permitted an increased proportion of non-food-producing specialists. In pursuing their objective of increasing their wealth, the landed nobility forced the peasants off the commons. In so doing they created a large unemployed category of persons who migrated to the urban areas and the factories in search of work and a means of staying alive. During this same period—the latter half of the eighteenth century—technological advances in the cotton and iron industries proceeded at a rapid pace. Transportation systems were invented, and existing ones were improved immeasurably. The development of the nation-state form of political organization and the corporate form of business organization also augmented the development of modern industrial society.

We need now to look at the consequences of the development of industrialism for the structure of society. This task is taken up in the next chapter.

REFERENCES

1   P. Mantoux, *The Industrial Revolution in the Eighteenth Century* (New York: Harper & Row, Publishers, 1961).

2   R. W. Revans, "Human Relations, Management, and Size," in *Human Relations and Modern Management,* E. M. Hugh-Jones, ed. (Amsterdam: North Holland Publishing Co., 1958), 177-220.

3   K. Polanyi, *The Great Transformation* (Boston: Beacon Press, Inc., 1957).

the social organization
of the mass-industrial society

9

Chapter 8 discussed the events that brought about the industrial revolution, but did not present an analysis of the *organization* of the new type of society; that is the objective of this chapter. Using our earlier rules and some additional ones, we will deduce the characteristics of the mass-industrial society.

THE MASS ORGANIZATION

As a part of our tools for developing models of social organizations, we have been using a set of rules about what happens to organizations as they increase in size. The number of these propositions would be multiplied many times by answering the question: *What happens if the rate of increase in the size of the population is varied in relation to the total number of roles available in the organization?*

151

We can simplify the question by dividing it into three smaller ones. What would be the effect on the social organization if the population increased so slowly that it actually lagged behind the number of roles that were available to be filled? This question has been studied empirically and has produced some very interesting findings both in terms of effect on the social structure and psychological characteristics of the members (1). But these findings are not relevant to our interests in this chapter.

We might also ask what the effect on the social structure would be if the population and the number of roles both increased so that the additional members of the population could be absorbed into the role structure easily? Actually, our earlier propositions were predicated on this assumption; we assumed that the organization was not too disrupted by the population increase, and that it was able to cope with the increase in size.

Finally, what would be the effect on the social organization if the population should increase very rapidly in size: more rapidly than the role structure could be expanded to accommodate the growth? This question reflects the situation that existed in English cities during the early phases of the industrial revolution. Unemployed farmers were migrating to the urban centers in search of work. The rapidly expanding factory system provided new occupational roles for many of these displaced yeomen, but it could not take in all of them. Because of the historical appropriateness of the third question, we will discuss it here.

This problem of a rate of population increase greater than the role structure of the organization can handle is faced by many organizations. A husband and wife who are blessed with triplets or quadruplets when they had expected but one child have had a first-hand experience with the problem. The growth of a suburban development is often so rapid that the churches and schools cannot absorb all of the persons seeking admission. Our society may not have enough occupational roles for our rapidly growing population.

Whenever this problem occurs, it has certain predictable effects on the structure of the organization, regardless of its type. To illustrate these effects, we will use as our unit of analysis a community that has experienced an influx of migrants that outstrips the capacity of the community role system. In this hypothetical example, we will assume that the rate of *solo* migration is high, which is usually true. When migrants bring their families as well as their culture along with them, their normative and kinship ties often enable them to overcome the problems that will be detailed below. In the total subculture, however, the rates of all the characteristics we will discuss will vary considerably from those of a stable population.

Subgroup Formation

The very nature of the question posed implies that the community cannot assimilate the migrants into the role structure immediately. The spatial problem of finding adequate room for them to settle is very great. Space is usually available either on the edge of the community or in a section with large dwellings that can be converted into multiple dwelling units. In South America the first solution is generally used. The shacks of former peasants can be seen today perched on the hillsides on the edge of Rio de Janeiro or around Lima, São Paulo, and the other large cities. In the United States, England, France, and most western societies, newcomers have moved into the centers of the cities, where large homes have been divided into smaller units.

Grouped in this manner and not having developed interdependencies with the older residents, the migrants are a separate unit. They cannot be called a subgroup because initially they have none of the properties of an organization. They are an aggregate.

One of the most outstanding characteristics of this aggregate is its *lack of subgroup formation*. Often the newcomer has made the trip alone; he has left his familiar way of life, his family, and his friends. His immediate problem is finding a means of livelihood, not social relationships. At the earliest stages of settlement, only those ubiquitous subgroups the family and the friendship clique are found among the migrants. These subgroups assume added importance for these people because of the loneliness and competitiveness they encounter. Associations do not develop at this *early* stage for temporal as well as economic reasons: the immigrant must devote most of his time to finding a job. The exception would be the case of migrants from another culture, whose members might institute their old associations rather rapidly. The elite of the community controls access to all major sources of influence. Since the newcomers have no basis of influence other than their physical strength, political associations among them are generally ineffective. Recognizing this fact, the elite of the community has good reasons to retard the development of associations among the immigrants. Economically, the migrants represent a source of cheap labor. If they are unorganized, they can be exploited, but if they become organized, they can threaten the superior influence and security of the members of the host community.

Interaction Patterns

The development of subgroups and of institutionalized patterns of interaction among them takes time. Initially, the number of institutionalized channels of interaction among the newly forming subgroups is minimal. In the language that we used in Chapter 2, the subgroups are unintegrated or poorly integrated.

Institutionalized patterns of interaction between the members of the host community and the migrants also develop slowly. At first, only fragmentary economic interactions take place. The newcomers contract their services with individual businessmen in the community. More elaborate economic relations develop later. Social relations generally evolve more slowly than economic ones. The absorption of the Italian immigrant population into city jobs in New Haven, Connecticut, illustrates this process (2). In the first two decades after their arrival, the Italians made almost no penetration into city administrative roles. A few of the more highly skilled migrants did obtain jobs as teachers, professional workers, clerical, and protective workers. By the end of the third decade of their residence, they were moving into jobs at virtually all levels of the city government. But in terms of their proportion in the total population, they were still greatly underrepresented in these jobs. Even fifty years after their arrival in New Haven (1940) they were in an improved, but still underrepresented, position.

Norms

With the exception of the norms they derive from a common cultural heritage, we expect by definition that there will be very few common norms in the migrant population. Norms develop through the institutionalization of interaction, and we have already seen that interaction is minimal within the aggregate. The process of developing common norms is greatly complicated if the immigrants are a culturally heterogeneous population.

Similarly, norms develop between the older residents and the newcomers only when patterns of interaction between them become routinized and institutionalized. Since this does not happen on any significant scale in the early stages, there are few common norms in the population. The term *anomie* has been applied by some sociologists to these situations in which there are relatively few common norms.

Role Differentiation

We have stipulated that the role structure cannot absorb all of the newcomers. If they are farmers who have emigrated to a city, they have few if any skills to offer in an urban economy. They can be employed only as unskilled laborers. In view of the relative lack of subgroup formation, they have few, if any, roles in social groupings within the community. In other words, the population is relatively *undifferentiated*.

The Influence Ranking System

If we rank all of the parts—either roles or subgroups—in the community in terms of the amount of influence they possess, the highest status positions would be held by the old residents of the community, and the newcomers would occupy the lowest positions. The elite is composed of the owners of the major key industries in the community. The migrants, having only a physical basis for influence, are essentially uninfluential. The distribution of influence among the roles in a mass organization approximates that shown in Fig. 9-1. The major share is lodged in the few roles at the top of the key industries.

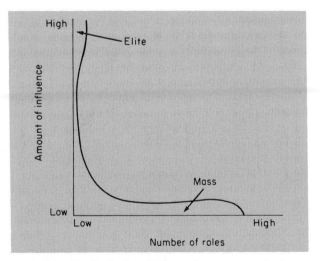

FIG. 9-1   The distribution of influence in a mass organization.

In the example we discussed above, some of the other established roles in the community are vested with intermediate amounts of influence, but the actual amount of influence they can exercise is not great. It is conceivable that virtually all influence is in the hands of the elite. As we will see later, this concentration of influence is precisely the objective of a totalitarian elite. At the bottom of the influence hierarchy is the bulk of the population. In our example, the migrants and the less skilled and more peripheral roles in the host community occupy this position.

A Summary of the Characteristics of the Mass Organization

This form of organization, given the name mass (3), can be characterized as follows. It is *unintegrated*—there are few subgroups, and a large portion of the population does not have any subgroups at all. The two major subgroups in the organization are the elite and the mass. Among the elite we expect normal subgroup formation, but not among the mass. As a consequence, the organization is *anomic*—the development of norms among the members of the mass and with the older residents of the organization is minimal. It is *undifferentiated*—while the role structure of the older residents may be highly differentiated, that of the mass is not. The major set of interdependencies exists between the elite and the mass. Influence is highly concentrated because the mass has no basis for influence other than their collective physical strength. The lack of influence in the mass is further aggravated by the fact that they have no legitimate means by which they can communicate their problems to the elite. Since the mass is unintegrated, there are few or no voluntary associations such as labor unions, the leaders of which could communicate with the elite. The elite is, in effect, *inaccessible by legitimate means*. Mob demonstrations, violence, sit-ins, and other forms of collective action have to be used. Because of their control of the means of communication, the elite can reach the mass more easily. The mass is *available*. The term *mass* sums up these characteristics rather nicely.

Other Methods of Forming a Mass Organization

To derive the characteristics of the mass organization, we used as an example a community that was experiencing an increase in population size that exceeded the number of roles available in the community. This illustration is appropriate historically. The rapid industrialization and urbanization that occurred in some European societies produced conditions in the cities similar to those that we described.

A mass organization can be developed by other means. The production techniques used in a factory can produce a mass organization. On some assembly-line operations, the total operation has been divided into a series of simple and repetitive behaviors. The workers can be trained to do their jobs efficiently in a few days. They are sometimes isolated from each other because of the layout of the machinery. Given these conditions, the factory will have some mass characteristics (4). The work force contains a very high proportion of undifferentiated workers. They possess little influence over the decisions of management because they do not have a scarce talent. Since it only takes a few days to train a person to optimum efficiency, the individual worker can be replaced with ease. The situation can be improved or worsened by the management group. If their actions minimize legitimacy, then the mass condition of the workers is increased. The less legitimate the actions of the elite, the greater is the likelihood of segmentation, conflict, and distrust between the elite and the mass. If the managerial elite prevents the formation of associations of workers, they deny them independent sources of influence and security, and they aggravate the mass condition. They also reap the consequences of a mass organization—the propensity to strike is increased in a mass factory (4).

A mass organization can also be created by using the techniques of terror and caprice (5). In a later chapter, we will see how these techniques are used by the elite in a totalitarian society either to create a mass or to maintain the existence of one.

Students often experience considerable difficulty with this concept because it seems foreign to their own organizational experiences. Yet many students have lived in mass organizations, particularly in some of the larger universities. In these schools the mass organization is sometimes found in the student dormitories. The student body is composed primarily of migrants from other communities. They have left their home towns, friends, families, and other attachments behind. At the university they all occupy essentially the same role—student—so they are undifferentiated. During this initial stage they are also unintegrated. Most of the students will eventually form friendship cliques, but some will not, and only a few will join associations. The students are easily replaced, and while university officials must take their needs into account in their decision making, the students have few institutionalized means of influencing these decisions. The associations that exist are designed to give the student a feeling of belonging to the university without giving him a basis of influence to use on the university elite. This type of mass is a product of the size and characteristic role structure of a large university. It is also a consequence of the fact that students are thought of as incompletely socialized individuals who are not yet prepared to make organizational decisions.

Finally, it should be noted that an urban-agrarian society has many of the characteristics of a mass organization. There is an elite and an undifferentiated and powerless peasant mass. There are also few effective voluntary associations to serve as channels of communication and negotiation between the elite and the peasants. But there are other characteristics of the urban-agrarian society that ameliorate these mass characteristics. The peasant's situation is integrated; he lives in the village of his ancestors and has a family and friends. There are very few peasants who are devoid of any subgroup affiliations. For this reason the situation in which he lives is not anomic.

The Importance of the Concept of Mass

The concept of the mass organization is particularly important because of certain types of behavior that it generates in the population. We established in Chapter 1 that social organization influences rates of human behavior; the mass organization is no exception. The mass, for one thing, is given to restive or milling behavior (6). Like all social categories of any significant size, its members have problems that are in some ways unique to the category. Whether it is the economic insecurity or deprivation of their position, the loneliness of their lives, the competitive struggle in which they must engage, or the powerlessness of their position, the problems are often severe, and the members of the mass can do little to alleviate their condition without the aid of the elite. Any one of these problems would be sufficient to make most aggregates in which they were lodged restive.

Events in the world around the members of the mass are very difficult for them to interpret accurately or consistently. The members also have difficulty developing consistent guidelines for their own behavior in new situations. These problems result from the unintegrated character of their situation. Most of our understanding of social reality comes to us through our organizational memberships. It began in the family, where our parents demonstrated an uncanny skill at predicting the consequences of our actions. During the rest of our lives we use the family, our friendship groups, and associational memberships to help us to interpret the world around us and to provide guidelines for our behavior. You might speculate on the organizational sources of any decision you might make about a political candidate in an election. The members of the mass have no such organizations. For these reasons they are particularly susceptible to two sources of influence: the elite, and the leaders of mass-based organizations. The elite can use its wealth and its control of the technology of the society to expose the mass to its point of view. If radio or any of the other media of communication are available to it, the elite can use them exclusively to indoctrinate the mass. Another source of interpretation of events and recommendations for action is the mass-based organization. The leaders of such organizations understand the condition of the mass; they provide an explanation for this condition and a course of action for changing it. The source of the problem is usually attributed to the elite, and the course of action often proposed is the removal of the elite, generally, though not necessarily, by violent means. The repetition of these themes and the lack of other sources of interpretation often result in the successful recruitment of large segments of the mass into these organizations. For quite practical purposes, the program of action proposed by the leaders often emphasizes violence. First, this is the only source of influence available to the mass. Second, the use of violence has a certain appeal because it would provide an outlet for the restiveness that the mass experiences.

The Transitoriness of the Mass Organization

One of the most interesting characteristics of the mass organization is its volatility; social forces which pressure for change in the structure are very powerful. First, the pressure to develop organizational memberships is very great; with the passage of time, if there is no restraint imposed by the elite, these memberships *will* develop. This fact has not always been apparent to sociologists, who once thought that slums contained perpetual masses. Studies of an Italian slum neighborhood in Boston (7) and of a Jewish community in Chicago (8) refuted this point of view. In both of these studies it was shown that extremely complex subgroup and intergroup relationships had developed in these neighborhoods. Second, roles will become more differentiated with the passage of time. In both of the neighborhoods mentioned above specialization was extensive. Third, the activities of the mass-based organization may cause changes in the structure and functioning of the social organization in which they are found.

An elite can attempt to prevent the mass from evolving into a more complex organization. To accomplish this objective the elite must use the techniques of terror and economic manipulation.

Now we should recognize the mass organization in terms of our earlier definitions. The mass organization is really a variation on our notion of a poorly integrated organization. If you review those characteristics from Fig. 2-6, you will see the general correspondence. But more important here is that this relationship reminds us of the variable nature of social organizations. We can conceive of different social organizations as containing mass and nonmass characteristics in varying degrees. Thus while no social organization may have all of the characteristics of the ideal mass organization, most are likely to have them to some degree. Although contemporary American society is not a mass society, it does contain some mass elements. Some of our cities, labor unions, industries, and other types of associations are more mass than others.

The concept of *integrated organization* will be used to refer to the polar opposite of the mass organization. The term *pluralist organization* is often used in this respect, but actually this term has been defined to refer only to the characteristic of subgroup formation. Pluralist organizations are those in which there is an abundance of subgroups in which most of the members of the organization are qualitatively involved. The membership of these subgroups is diverse in terms of social categories: labor unions contain Republicans as well as Democrats, Roman Catholics as well as Protestants, Negroes as well as whites. We will see in later chapters that these pluralist characteristics also produce some interesting effects on the rates of behavior of the members. But before we can develop that theme, we must summarize the characteristics of the mass-industrial society, by combining the characteristics of the mass organization with those of an industrial and commercial economy. Because of our extensive discussion of the mass organization above, we can do this rather quickly.

THE MASS-INDUSTRIAL SOCIETY

The mass-industrial form of organization can occur when a society that has developed an industrial economy experiences rapid urbanization. If urbanization is not rapid, the mass characteristics are less likely to appear.

For reasons already explained, industrial societies seldom develop in excellent natural environments. The cultivation of prairie soils requires a metal and machine technology, which is most likely to evolve *after* industrialization. The urban-agrarian societies that developed in the river valleys in the Middle East and Egypt lacked many of the resources needed to industrialize (9). But regardless of the environmental origins of industrial societies, the most fundamental fact of the relationship between the natural environment and industrialization is that industrial societies quickly free themselves of the influence of their environments. The population devises a complex technology to manipulate the environment. Dams, irrigation, artificial fertilizers, specialized machinery, and new techniques permit the conversion of submarginal and other types of environments to arable lands. The effect of the application of new techniques and technology to farming is an enormous increase in the productivity of the land. We have seen how productivity increased in England during the time of its industrial revolution. This increase in food productivity creates the conditions for an expansion in the number of non-food-producing roles. It also creates a farm labor surplus, as the less efficient farmers are driven out of commercial farming and must either regress to subsistence farming or move into the cities in search of work. The shift from farming to industrial occupations is reflected in the following statistics. In 1800, 70 per cent of the population of the United States was involved in the primary industries of farming and mining; by 1900 that figure had been reduced to 35 per cent. Correspondingly, in 1800 only 10 per cent of the population earned its living in the secondary or manufacturing industries; by the turn of the century that figure had risen to 30 per cent. The remaining workers in both periods were in the tertiary, or service and distribution, industries.

The concentration of the population in cities is also a concomitant of an industrial commercial economy. Industries must be located near markets, materials, avenues of transportation, and sources of energy; therefore, they tend to concentrate in the optimal geographic locations. In 1790 only 5 per cent of our population lived in urban areas; by 1920 the urban population exceeded the rural population.

Since industrial populations have largely freed themselves from the threat of starvation, the death rate drops. A decline in the birth rate also occurs, but it usually lags behind the death rate, and population growth is maintained. The birth rate declines because the means and the need to reduce family size now exist and because of the improving medical technology. The agrarian family was large because the presence of several male children increased the survival chances of the family by providing needed human energy. But the urban family does not need children for economic functions; in fact, they become a liability. They are additional persons for whom the family must provide on one or two incomes.

This rapidly increasing urban population has important effects on the structure of the society. The number of types of subgroups increases (Proposition 2), but not so rapidly as the population. The reasons for this lag were explained in our discussion of the mass organization. The small family and the friendship clique are still the most prevalent units found. As the effects of the rapid increase in size in the cities are coped with, the development of associational relationships increases.

Interaction in the mass-industrial society is also inhibited by the mass element of the society. Relationships in the city tend to be impersonal and secondary rather than primary. This impersonality of city life continues to disturb many urban dwellers and social commentators alike.

The sacred norms of agrarian societies give way to more secular norms (Proposition 7). The old solutions to the problems of life in the agricultural village are inappropriate in many respects to the new urban life. Furthermore, the external controls of community, family, and friends disappear and facilitate a secular attitude. In this period of limited controls, new solutions are being tried and new norms are being formed. Problem solving becomes a less collective, more individual activity. In England and the United States individualism was advocated in pulpits and pamphlets. The elite supported the new emphasis on individualism because it served their long-range economic interests. The members of the mass adopted it because it was essential to their short-term economic well-being.

On the basis of the increase in population size and the development of the new technology, we would anticipate an increase in the division of labor (Proposition 2). New roles in the manufacturing industries do emerge, but the actual increase in the degree of specialization lags behind our theoretical expectations because of the *nature* of the technology and the very rapid increase in the size of the population. In this period of innovation, the new technology is not very complex; it does not require any great degree of specialization. Furthermore, the tasks are fractionated so that they can be mastered by unskilled or semiskilled laborers, who can be replaced easily. The rapid increase in community size ensures that there is a large, unemployed, and equally unskilled labor supply available to replace the workers.

This unusual situation in the division of labor has its effects on the rank systems of the society (Proposition 9). Two major bases of influence exist: one based on the land and the other on the new industrial and commercial activities. The industrial influence ranking system resembles that given in Fig. 9-1. There is an elite composed of the owners of the new enterprises. This category of persons possesses virtually all of the influence and wealth lodged in this rank system. At the bottom is the mass of unskilled and semiskilled laborers. Between them are remarkably few status levels containing relatively few people with very little influence. For this reason and those developed earlier (see pp. 62-64), relationships between the elite and the mass are highly segmented.

Competition between the landowning elite and the industrial-commercial elite for control of the institutions of government and other sources of influence is very great. Eventually, it is won by the industrial-commercial elite because the bases of its influence grow much more rapidly than those of the agrarian elite. Segmentation can certainly be expected to exist between the occupants of these two rank systems (Proposition 11).

SOME CONSEQUENCES OF INDUSTRIALIZATION

Industrialization alters the lives of the members of an agrarian society in some fundamental ways (10). In agrarian societies, a person's various roles are integrated. Religious activities are a part of all facets of life, and work roles are bound intimately with those of husband and father. In industrial societies these roles become more segmented. The husband leaves home to travel to some other place of work. He cannot set his own pace of work, but must adjust it to some external norms. The timeclock becomes the symbol of this adjustment. Children know less about their father's job, and one basis of relating to each other is removed. The absence of the father from the home also diminishes his control over his children, particularly the boys.

The loss of community ties of various kinds also poses problems (11). The small and familiar village is replaced by the large and strange city. The guild gives way to the factory, and the extended family with all of its ceremonial overtones is supplanted by the nuclear family, with many fewer functions.

The larger size of industrial societies creates other problems. Influence is increasingly centralized in the hands of a small elite and is often exercised through giant bureaucratic organizations. Individualism may be espoused, but the individual can do little to affect his fate in the face of the large productive and political organizations that he now encounters.

This chain of events is occurring now in various parts of the world. It has already occurred in western Europe and the United States; it gave rise to the problems that are the heritage of the present century. In the next two chapters, we will examine more closely some of the major effects of the industrial revolution on societies.

SUMMARY

A mass organization exists when social and normative integration and role differentiation are minimal. There is an elite that has a virtual monopoly over all of the influence lodged in the organization, and a mass that is relatively powerless.

REFERENCES

1 R. G. Barker, "Ecology and Motivation," *Nebraska Symposium on Motivation: 1960,* Vol. III of *Current Theory and Research in Motivation,* M. R. Jones, ed. (Lincoln: University of Nebraska Press, 1960), pp. 1-49.

2 J. K. Myers, "Assimilation in the Political Community," *Sociology and Social Research, 35* (1951), 175-82.

3 W. Kornhauser, *The Politics of Mass Society* (New York: Free Press of Glencoe, Inc., 1959).

4 C. Kerr and A. Siegel, "The Interindustry Propensity to Strike—An International Comparison," in *Industrial Conflict,* A. Kornhauser, R. Dubin, and A. Ross, eds. (New York: McGraw-Hill Book Company, 1954), 189-212.

5 H. Arendt, *The Origins of Totalitarianism* (New York: Harcourt, Brace, and World, Inc., 1951).

6 H. Blumer, "Collective Behavior," in *New Outlines of the Principles of Sociology,* A. M. Lee, ed. (New York: Barnes & Noble, Inc., 1946).

7 W. F. Whyte, *Street Corner Society: The Social Structure of an Italian Slum* (Chicago: The University of Chicago Press, 1955).

8 L. Wirth, *The Ghetto* (Chicago: The University of Chicago Press, 1956).

9 V. G. Childe, *Man Makes Himself* (London: Watts and Co., 1939).

10 H. L. Wilensky and C. N. Lebeaux, *Industrial Society and Social Welfare* (New York: Russell Sage Foundation, 1958).

11 R. A. Nisbet, *The Quest for Community* (New York: Oxford University Press, 1953).

the social organization
of the welfare-bureaucratic society

The industrial revolution in Europe left a lasting impression on the behavior of man and the thought and writings of intellectuals. It gave rise to the problems that are the basis for much social thought and action to the present day. The poverty and powerlessness of the factory worker, the abuses of child labor, and the seeming callousness of the owners of industry were recorded accurately or with distortion, brilliantly or methodically in countless works. The revolution was the basis for the social protest novels of Dickens and Zola. It was charged with violating the tenets of modern humanism: of destroying human initiative, stifling creativity, and preventing self-fulfillment. It led to movements for social reform; it gave rise to the trade unions and vitalized the various socialist movements in England and on the Continent. But it found its most powerful commentary in the writings and political activities of Karl Marx and Friedrich Engels. Engels provided money and a description of the excesses of the industrial revolution, while Marx gave an interpretation of it (1, 2). Both founded a social movement that was to have profound effects on contemporary society (3).

MARX'S THEORY OF SOCIAL CHANGE

Karl Marx formulated the communist ideology: an ideology that is a vital factor in the present struggle for power between the Soviet Union and the United States. Because of his integral role in this movement, which threatens our contemporary way of life, his image has become distorted. Occasionally, his portrait appears on the cover of a national magazine replete with red eyes, wildly disorganized hair, and superimposed on a red background as if he had just sprung straight from hell—the very incarnation of the Devil himself. An honest portrait of Marx is less stereotyped.

Marx was born a German, a Jew, and a member of a fairly wealthy family. His brilliant mind was oriented to scholarly activities; he spent several years in the British Museum working on his central work, *Das Kapital*. He married, raised a family, and had a reputation for being a devoted family man. In later years, when he was devoting himself to political and journalistic activities, he developed some interesting attitudes toward the United States and Russia. He admired the United States and advocated moving his political headquarters to that country because it was moving the most rapidly of all western societies toward the freeing of the proletariat. His admiration for Abraham Lincoln was very great. He wrote enthusiastic letters to Lincoln, and when the President was assassinated, Marx published his newspaper with a black border around the front page. Marx harbored that suspicion and condescension toward Russians that characterized the German culture of his day. He was engaged in a fierce struggle with the Russian revolutionist, Bakhunin, who sought to capture control of the Communist or Workingman's Party. This struggle only deepened his distrust of Russians, and he disdained their participation in his party. Marx was more than a political activist; if we are to understand the full importance of his work for sociology, we must discuss Marx the moralist, economist, and sociologist.

Marx's work was motivated by the same moral standards possessed by most English churchmen and other reformers. He was opposed to drunkenness, adultery, the dissolution of the family, and other forms of deviance. He believed passionately that every man should have the opportunity to realize his full potential as a human being. But around him he saw little of these virtues and an abundance of the vices. He

asked himself the same fundamental question that was being posed in
books and from pulpits all over western Europe: why has man fallen to
such a low state? His answer was different from that of most intellectuals because Marx operated on the premise that man's morality and
his condition are a function of the society in which he lives. If the
society is corrupt, then man will be corrupt; if it is moral, then man
too will be moral. This premise is a clear departure from the Christian
premise that man is born evil and must strive for goodness; that society
is not an important factor.

Marx's major contribution to sociology and economics was his theory
of social change. At the core of this theory were several assumptions
besides that of the societal sources of human morality. First, he assumed
that history moved in a dialectic pattern from *thesis* to *antithesis* to
synthesis. Any given society is labeled a *thesis*. But every society (thesis)
contains defects—the seeds of its own destruction (the antithesis). The
interaction of these social forces would yield a new or modified society,
called the synthesis. Second, the major forces of change in a society
originate in its economy. Marx's theory has been given the label dialectic materialism because of this fundamental emphasis on the economy and the dialectic processes of history. Third, the *sine qua non* or
essential characteristic of a society is its system of social classes. Fourth,
the basis on which people can be assigned to social class positions is
their relationship to the means of production: in other words, their
occupations. Marx also defines the concept of *state* in a way that is uncommon to us. The state according to Marx is the instruments of violence and coercion found in a society.

Using these assumptions, we can trace Marx's theory of social change.
Marx's thesis is the classic feudal period in Europe. Since the essential
characteristic of society is its system of social classes and one's position
in that system is determined by one's relationship to the means of production, then the class system in feudal society had the following status
levels:

Thesis: Feudal Society
Feudal lords
Vassals
Guild-masters
Journeymen
Apprentices
Serfs

But every system contains the seeds of its own destruction, and these
seeds are located in the economy. The economic force that was to alter
feudal society drastically was the revival of commerce with the East and

the consequent growth of the new merchant class. Even the old guild system would be undermined by the newer factory system, because the guild system was too inadequate a productive mechanism to keep up with the demand for goods. The rapidly growing economic influence of the new merchant-industrial class—the bourgeoisie—was accompanied by increasing political influence. The eventual ascendance of the bourgeoisie resulted in a new synthesis: the capitalist nation-state. Since the essential characteristic of any society is its social classes, and positions in that system are a function of the person's occupation, the capitalist nation-state can be represented as follows:

Synthesis: The Capitalist Nation-State
Bourgeoisie
Professionals
Small businessmen (petit bourgeoisie)
Proletariat

The proletariat includes all of the industrial laborers; the other connotations Marx attached to that concept make it quite similar to our notion of the *mass*. But every system contains the seeds of its own destruction, says Marx, and the capitalist nation-state is no exception. The economic forces that lead to the destruction of the capitalist nation-state are overproduction and the profit motive. The techniques of modern industry permit the production of goods on a scale more vast than ever before in human history. But the workers cannot consume as much as they produce because of the profit system that pays the worker less for making the commodity than he can buy it for himself. Marx's thinking on this point was based on the best economic theory available during his time, but from the point of view of modern economics it was not sufficiently sophisticated or accurate.

The problem of overproduction causes the bourgeoisie to search for new markets: a search that is facilitated by achievements in the fields of transportation and commerce. The efforts of the bourgeoisie result in exploitation of colonial areas for raw materials and as a place for selling manufactured goods. In this worldwide distribution and consumption system only the very large industrial organizations can continue to exist. Therefore, worldwide monopolies or cartels develop, whose leaders control the societies in which they do business. Small businessmen are driven into bankruptcy, and craftsmen and professionals are forced to work for the great monopolies rather than for themselves. As a result, the middle class is forced into the proletariat. The result is the social structure known as finance-imperialism. The social class system of this new synthesis can be represented as follows:

Synthesis: Finance-Imperialist Society
Bourgeoisie
Proletariat

The bourgeoisie decrease in number as the less successful competitors are driven out of business and their organizations are absorbed into the larger ones. But the influence and wealth of this class increases at the expense of the proletariat. For its part, the proletariat gets poorer and less influential. The social distance between the two classes increases steadily. The members of the proletariat cannot improve their situation by peaceful means because the bourgeoisie controls the state.

Every system contains the seeds of its own destruction, however. The defect in the finance-imperialist system is the economic oppression of the proletariat and forcing the middle classes into the proletariat. The more intellectual members of the old middle class provide the sense of direction, the inspiration, and the leadership to galvanize the less imaginative factory workers into a revolutionary force. Violent overthrow of the bourgeoisie is the only course open to the proletariat, says Marx, because the bourgeoisie control the state. Such a revolution could never occur in an agrarian society, according to Marx, because the means of communication are too primitive for the organization of a revolution. The violent overthrow of the bourgeoisie by sheer weight of numbers can occur only in an urban-industrial society that is a world rather than a national organization. After the revolution, a new synthesis—the dictatorship of the proletariat—is set up. In this system there are only two classes: the dictators and the proletariat. The dictators are the leaders of the revolution who must create the moral social organization—which you will note will be a worldwide society—and prepare the proletariat to live in it. The cornerstone of the new system is the negation of private property and profits. They are replaced by public ownership of the means of production. The proletariat is educated for the new society, and deviants are removed from the population. As society and man become increasingly moral, the state or the instruments of violence become less necessary. Gradually and irrevocably the state withers away and the dictatorship of the proletariat gives way to a new synthesis: the world communist society. In this society man is moral because he has a social consciousness—an internal gyroscope that keeps him on a moral path—and because the society is moral. The instruments of violence are unnecessary.

THE VALUE OF MARXIAN THEORY

Marx actually had very little to say about the ultimate communist society: that task remained for Lenin and the neo-Marxists. But the outcome of the dialectic is not so important to us here as some of the earlier and more fundamental aspects of his reasoning. Marx's interpretation of the shift from feudal to industrial society agrees with modern interpretation on many major points. It agrees with newer versions because there are many useful elements in his assumptions about the process of social change. His assumption that conflict among social classes is inevitable still wins modified adherence in sociology (4). Support for this assumption is modified because sociologists disagree about a definition of the concept of social class itself. This point will be discussed in Chapter 12.

The importance of the economy in shaping the other parts of the society is also recognized. This assumption is the cornerstone of a type of sociological theory called human ecology (5), and it is obviously the assumption made early in this book. Studies of community and national elites generally support this assumption. However, Marx's doctrinaire assumption that the economy affects the rest of the social structure but that nothing of importance arises independently of the economy and that the noneconomic aspects of society have no effect on the economic structures is no longer considered tenable by most sociologists. Noneconomic institutions can have effects on the society, although not so fundamental as those of the economy. Churches can obtain the passage of legislation to prohibit some kinds of economic activity completely or to limit it to certain days of the week. One social scientist has shown that Japan industrialized before China for reasons lodged in the value systems of the two countries and not primarily in the economy (6). Modern sociology accepts the notion that the economy has a fundamental role in shaping the rest of the society. But it also holds that the other parts of the society have effects on the structure and functioning of the economy.

Marx's notion that the occupational system (one's relationship to the means of production) is the core of the system of social classes in a society receives modified concurrence today. Occupation is still considered by most social scientists to be the best single *indicator* of social class position. The problem arises in defining social class. Most social scientists do agree, however, that regardless of what it is, social class is a more complex concept than Marx made it.

This point of view is overdone sometimes. Some social scientists contend that certain occupational roles, such as physician, for example, have greater influence than one would expect from Marxian theory because the population *values* that occupation. In this dissent, a partially noneconomic factor—the prestige of the occupation—affects amount of influence. The choice of the physician as an example by the advocates of a less Marxian orientation is unfortunate. In medieval societies, the role of physician was neither influential nor prestigious. The physician's prestige and influence have grown as his success at treating human ailments has increased. It is undeniable that the successful treatment of illness is an important activity in a society. Also, the ability of the physicians to organize into associations and use their collective influence has been overlooked. By using their influence to obtain the passage of legislation restricting certain activities to themselves, they have been able to increase their influence. Finally, the central value system of physicians is similar in many respects to those of the persons in the major centers of influence in our society—the economic elite. The natural alliance of these two groups on some issues has sustained the influence of the physicians.

The real usefulness of occupational prestige rank systems is that they are a relatively easy way to approximate the amount of influence possessed by a role. But they are at best only an approximation. An ex-President or ex-President's wife has far more prestige in the society than influence. The concept is also a social-psychological one that is concerned with people's attitudes about other people, not about how they behave.

THE LIMITATIONS OF MARXIAN THEORY

In spite of its usefulness, the fact is that Marx's predictions were not correct. Instead of a mass society with a decreasing middle class, industrial societies have developed large and growing middle classes. The conditions of the workers improved rather than worsened, and no violent overthrow of a world-sprawling capitalism has occurred.

Marx had expected the workers to develop a class consciousness, but they did not. In England the Conservative Party gets a large proportion of its vote from the working class. In the United States the worker has disregarded the pleas of union leaders to be militant, exhibit solidarity, and attend union meetings.

Marx erred because, like so many social class theorists, he failed to appreciate the ability of aggregates of low influence status to increase their influence by peaceful means. Violent encounters between workers and owners have occurred, but they have been sporadic battles and skirmishes rather than outright wars. Labor conflict was prevalent during the nineteenth century in all western societies, but these encounters resulted in significant concessions from the owners of industries and from the government. The most fundamental of these concessions was the right to vote. The possession of this right is a very powerful source of influence: *one that can invert the influence ranking system at election time* (7). The workers have many more votes than the economic elite; if they mobilize them, they can use the agencies of government as a means of winning further concessions from the economic elite. Many members of the economic elite recognized this fact and sought to use their resources to win the labor vote. During the latter half of the nineteenth century they were successful with this tactic. But in the twentieth century the government has emerged as a *third force* in relationships between labor and management. Among the concessions that were won by the workers (who were allied with the farm organizations at the turn of the century) was antitrust legislation that eventually blunted the growth of the industrial organizations in American society.

THE EMERGENCE OF WELFARE-BUREAUCRATIC SOCIETY

To account for the development of modern industrial society, we must move beyond Marxian theory and examine three major trends in some detail. The first is the shift from small to large subgroups, particularly in the economy. Marx predicted this trend, but he did not anticipate that growth would stop short of or retreat from the formation of monopolies or cartels. The second trend is the shift from a mass to an integrated form of social organization, which Marx did not predict at all. Finally, there has been a trend away from an individualist value system to a welfare-collectivist one: an equally un-Marxian occurrence. These trends are highly interrelated, but we shall examine each of them in turn, detailing their consequences for the structure of modern society. This chapter will conclude with an outline of the characteristics of the welfare-bureaucratic society.

The Increasing Size of Subgroups

In industrial societies, growth in the size of business organizations is virtually an economic necessity. The technology becomes complex and costly: only very large organizations with extensive markets can afford the necessary equipment.

A second reason for organizational growth is supplied by the relationship between business volume and *variable* costs. In most industries there are certain costs that decrease as the number of units manufactured increases. In the newspaper business, the cost of making the original plates from which the newspapers are printed can be spread over the number of papers printed because only one set of plates need be made. Therefore, the more newspapers that are printed, the lower will be the cost per paper that must be charged for the plate. This type of cost is referred to as a *variable cost. Fixed costs* are constant per unit regardless of the number of units produced. The ink and the paper that are used to make newspapers are fixed costs, although even they may become variable if the printer can buy larger amounts of them at a reduced price per pound. An economic principle is involved here: the greater the volume of goods produced in most industries, the lower is the cost of producing them. And the lower the cost of producing them, the lower will be the price of the product or the greater will be the profit (if the price is not lowered). Finally, the lower the price charged for a product of the same quality as that of a competitor, the greater the business volume is likely to be and the more likely the company is to survive. If the fixed versus variable cost problem is not sufficient to encourage the managers of a company to increase its productive capacity, the fact that their competitors might expand does encourage them.

In many fields the outcome of competition has been the emergence of a few successful giant organizations controlling most of the business and many very small organizations controlling an even smaller fraction of the market. Over half of the steel produced in the United States is made by the four largest companies (8). Similarly, 78 per cent of the canned milk, 94 per cent of the baby food, 80 per cent of the cigarettes, 90 per cent of the finished thread for home use, 96 per cent of the linoleum, 99 per cent of the passenger cars, 90 per cent of the electric lights, 95 per cent of the window glass, and 64 per cent of the zippers manufactured in this country are produced by the four largest companies in each industry. There are, of course, a great many industries where the degree of concentration is not that great.

The increase in organizational size occurred primarily after the turn of the present century. One of the key methods of increasing size and business volume was the merger, or consolidation. There were five times as many mergers between 1919 and 1930 as there were between 1877 and 1904 (9). The size of some organizations was also increased at the expense of less successful organizations. Between 1919 and 1930, 12,000 public utilities, banking, manufacturing, and mining concerns that had existed before 1919 went out of business (9). The remaining organizations increased in size to accommodate the business of their defunct competitors. A third means of increasing size is simple growth or expansion. The A&P chain grew from 5,000 stores in 1922 to 17,500 stores in 1928 (9).

By one means or another, we became a nation of large organizations. In the life insurance business 50 firms do 80 per cent of the business, while the remaining 20 per cent is handled by 1,000 companies. The two largest insurance companies—Metropolitan and Prudential—have total assets of over $32 billion. American Telephone and Telegraph Company has assets of over $14 billion and has 745,000 employees. The largest automobile manufacturer—General Motors—produces better than half of the automobiles manufactured in the United States and employs 625,000 people.

This phenomenal growth in size is not restricted to business organizations. We have witnessed the growth of giant union organizations also. The structure of unions *has* to parallel that of the businesses whose workers they represent. If a union represented the workers in only one plant in a large corporation, it would be in an extremely poor bargaining position. The threat to strike would not bother management personnel particularly, because they could simply shift their production emphasis to another plant where a different union represented the workers. Logic dictates that unions must represent not only all of the plants in a company, but also all of the companies that manufacture the same products. Today over 18,000,000 people are affiliated with labor unions, and all but one-sixth of these are affiliated with the AFL-CIO (9).

Organizations in other areas have experienced concomitant increases in size. The federal government has grown very rapidly, particularly since World War II. Today the budget of the United States Meteorological Service is larger than that for the entire federal government during a single year of the Jackson administration. Twenty universities have 400,000 students, which is 20 per cent of the total college enrollment in the United States. Even farms have increased in size. Since 1900 the number of farms containing an excess of 1,000 acres has increased threefold (9). In 1949, 10 per cent of the farms produced over 50 per cent of the food. Or, to put it another way, 9 per cent of the farms earned more than the remaining 91 per cent.

More Americans are living in large cities than in small communities. The population increase has occurred primarily in the suburbs which ring the urban center. In these suburbs large organizations have sprung up to attend the needs of this automobile-driving population. Suburban churches are larger than the urban ones that they replace, and supermarkets containing thousands of items have supplanted the neighborhood grocery store. It would seem that large organizations have become a part of our way of life—and in a deep and subtle way that we often do not recognize.

Another economic reason for the growth in industrial organizations can be understood now that we have some appreciation of the size to which they have grown. Consider the costs and the problems involved in starting a new business that is capable of competing successfully with the giants found in most industries (10). It would cost $265 to $665 million to start a competitive steel mill, $250 to $500 million to start an automobile-manufacturing plant that had a chance of being successful, and $125 to $150 million to start a cigarette company with some prospects of a business future. These costs border on being prohibitive. Small wonder that these particular businesses are among the most oligopolistic in our society. Only about $500,000 is required to enter the shoe business; it is interesting that this business is among the least oligopolistic in our society.

SOME EFFECTS OF THE INCREASING SIZE OF SUBGROUPS. The large size of modern business organizations and the increasingly complex technology that they have used has altered the labor force of industrialized societies in ways that Marx did not anticipate. The repetitive and simple tasks were still present. But because of the enormous productivity made possible by technological advances and because of automation, the demand for semiskilled workers has not increased so rapidly as Marx expected. In 1910, 14 per cent of the labor force was composed of semiskilled workers; the proportion rose to 21 per cent by 1940, but as the effects of automation began to be felt, it dropped to 18 per cent. There has also been a mild decline in the proportion of skilled workers in the labor force since the beginning of the present century, because techniques of production have been invented that made their skills obsolete.

Correspondingly, there has been an enormous growth in the so-called white collar occupations. These occupations include primarily the professional and semiprofessional roles and the clerical and sales jobs. This development can be attributed directly to the growth in the size of organizations. We saw in Chapter 3 that very large organizations have more potential problems of communication, coordination, and legitimacy than do smaller organizations. These problems generally result in an increase in the proportion of people in the organization who are concerned with paper work, coordination, and the distribution of goods. Clerical workers are needed to process in fairly routine ways the external and internal communications. Specialized departments with specialized personnel are added to the organization to handle interpersonal problems that emerge because of the increased size: labor and dealer relations and community problems, for example.

The complexity of the technology as well as that of organizational life increases the need for specialists. The advent of the computer technology and of automation has created such new and highly specialized roles as computer programmers, operators, and maintenance men. Even innovation, which is often crucial to the success or failure of a company, has been put on a mass production basis. Thousands of chemists and engineers are hired by our largest corporations to make highly coordinated and mass attacks on problems. The enormous rate of innovation in our society has led to the creation of new industries that require work forces of their own. The electronics industry is essentially a post–World War II phenomenon, although many of the inventions occurred prior to that period. The need for electronic tools gave rise to many new corporations and to many new owners, managers, and professionals. As a result of these and other factors, the white collar segment of our population has increased dramatically. The number of professionals—engineers, doctors, lawyers, advertising specialists—in our labor force has increased more than four times over since 1910, during a period when the labor force has not quite doubled (11). Furthermore, the supply of persons for these roles has not kept pace with the demand; many more professionals would be hired if they were available. Between 1910 and 1960 the number of clerical and sales workers increased a little less than three times. About 10 per cent of our population works in primary industries, 35 per cent in secondary industries, and 55 per cent in tertiary industries. Instead of the mass of unskilled or semiskilled blue collar (manual) factory workers that Marx had expected, we have developed a labor force in which specialization is essential. Were it not for the retarding forces of government and other groups, there would be even fewer farmers and unskilled and semiskilled workers than there are currently. The undifferentiated role structure found in a mass society is far less prevalent in a welfare-bureaucratic society.

The growth in the size of organizations has been accompanied by the bureaucratization of their structure. In the smaller firms of the industrial revolution, there were so few workers in the office that all of them could be supervised by the owner or manager (12). But the enormous increase in the number of people involved in the coordinative activities of the enterprise is greater than the span of management of any single person (Proposition 8). To handle this and associated problems, an organizational structure called a bureaucracy is employed. These structures have existed since antiquity, but never on the scale that they exist today. A bureaucracy has several characteristics. It is composed of specialists who are arranged hierarchically in terms of authority: the higher the position of the role, the greater the authority attached to it (Proposition 9). Rules governing role behavior and coordinating activity are formal and, hopefully, clear (Propositions 3, 7, 12). Standards exist by which judgments are made about the promotion of persons up the hierarchy. In the ideal bureaucracy all of the formal norms that govern behavior are clear and conducive to effective functioning, and the employees' responses to them are disciplined.

Many activities earlier performed by smaller groups have been taken over by bureaucratic organizations. Church organizations now perform functions formerly in the province of the peasant family. Education, care for aged relatives, and recreation were also family activities; now schools, government agencies, Little Leagues, the communications media, and other large organizations have assumed a large share of them. Modern industrial society has certainly become bureaucratic society.

Rather than living by means of individual enterprise, we now look to the large organization for a livelihood. Rather than starting our own university, we pursue career patterns up the bureaucratic hierarchy of an ongoing school. Rather than start our own business, we join the large corporation and hope to work into a position of great authority. The professions of medicine, dentistry, and the law and small businesses have become the last of the truly attractive refuges for the modern entrepreneur. But even in these cases, the pressures to join large organizations are often very great.

For the professional, the bureaucratic organization poses many questions. Will he be able to use his professional skills on problems that interest him or will he be "a cog in a machine"? Will his professional standards be sacrificed to those of nonprofessional persons in positions of greater authority? Will he lose his sense of mission? Will he have an opportunity to interact with colleagues in the same profession?

The problems of working and developing a career in a large bureaucratic organization are also new and perplexing. The struggle for promotion is often fiercely competitive; what are the rules of survival? The rules governing decision making are often unclear. What is to be done in these instances: make a decision that may incur the wrath of your supervisor or make no decision at all?

The problems created by the development of large bureaucratized organizations and the behavioral responses that they have engendered can never be described adequately here. The important point is that this form of organization has emerged, created new problems, and led to new cultural responses.

The Shift From Mass to Integrated Organization

Following the industrial revolution, individuated man found his way back into group life. In part, it was essential that he join organizations. For most of the population, the only way to affect the decisions of the large bureaucratic organizations was to approach them in league with other people. Unions and other associations of workers served this purpose. Local and national governments had not escaped the trend to larger size, and often the only way the decisions of the elites in these organizations could be affected was by association. In our society, associations for farmers, physicians, laborers, and industrialists, to mention but a few, press the political decision makers for favorable legislation.

Associations were also formed by occupational groups to protect their functions, to create standards, and to exchange information and ideas relevant to their calling. Associations to promote social, religious, and other activities number in the thousands.

Among its other effects, the proliferation of associational memberships has stabilized the behavior of the members of the society. First, it has provided a setting in which a person can learn the meaning and significance of various events: an opportunity that was not sufficiently open to the population of the mass-industrial society. Second, members can be mobilized for only a limited range of activities because of the heterogeneity of their composition. The leaders of most of our associations could not use them to achieve the violent overthrow of the government because very few of their members would support them. The membership includes people of various religious groups, political parties, and other associations with norms of their own that do not support the idea of overthrowing the government. The potential revolutionist must maintain a homogeneous membership in the early stages of his revolution, and, in so doing, he usually limits his organization to an ineffectively small size. Finally, the leaders of associations have greater opportunities than their members to interact with the leaders of other associations. Union leaders have a better opportunity to interact with the members of management than do the workers. Through this regular interaction, the leaders develop a better understanding of each other's problems, needs, and objectives than do their members. For this reason the leaders of the associations often are more tolerant of their opposites in other organizations and more willing to bargain with them than are their members.

This diversity of group life does result in considerable variation in approved behaviors in the society. One group may advocate a certain activity while another abhors it. But there are norms, and that is an improvement over the anomic situation found in mass-industrial societies. Furthermore, the leaders of associations often encourage their members to abide by the norms of the communities and the society in which the members live.

In summary, life becomes more integrated. Subgroups form, voluntary associations provide a link between the people at the bottom of the influence rank system and those at the top, and the groups become generally *more* articulated with each other (Proposition 2). Although normative variation is often great, there is a minimal set of norms that govern the fundamental aspects of life (Proposition 4). Because of the variation in norms governing many behaviors, however, they are not the vital force that integrates the society, as they are in hunting and gathering and in agrarian societies (Proposition 6). It is the extremely refined division of labor, which makes us so dependent on the performances of others, that maintains the integration of the welfare-bureaucratic society.

The Shift From Individualism to Welfare-Collectivism

The rationale for the return to collective rather than individual solutions to problems has already been discussed. In the face of the great size of modern bureaucratic organizations, collective action is often the only effective means by which problems can be heard and solved.

But the shift to welfarism has other origins, and other reasons propelled its development. By the term *welfarism* is meant the use of collective wealth to provide for people with certain economic needs. In value terms, welfarism refers to the belief that the members of a society have an obligation to protect each other's welfare. Historically, in industrial societies the individual and his family were responsible for their own welfare. If you were injured at work, the responsibility for medical expenses was yours, not the company's. You were also responsible for your own retirement expenses: your company was not, nor was your society.

Three major factors are causing the shift from individualism to welfare-collectivism. The first is the increasing specialization of the labor force. The supply of specialists is often scarce, but even if their services are obtained, long training periods are often required before they become profitable members of the organization. For these reasons, management personnel develop ways to attract specialists and to keep them. Attractive retirement, medical, and insurance programs have been devised. A specialist with fifteen years of service in his company will think twice before leaving his job if he knows that he can retire on half pay in five or ten years. The managers had no equally compelling reasons to extend these programs to their less skilled employees. But the latter had every reason to insist on participation in these programs. The issue was a source of conflict for many decades, but it was eventually won by the workers. It was a simple and logical next step to insist that the government use public monies for the same purposes.

A second factor made the new welfarism easier to accept. Industrial societies have the necessary surplus wealth. Compared to agrarian societies, with all their occasional but highly concentrated opulence, industrial societies are extremely wealthy, producing goods in unprecedented quantities. The development of welfare programs neither prevents companies from making a profit nor members of governments from performing their other duties.

A third factor also implements welfarism: it is the development of the concept of commercial risk pools called insurance companies. These companies provide risk pools not only for individuals, but for companies as well. A company faced with a worker demand for a medical compensation program is more willing to participate because it can share the risks with other companies. Such a program is likely to be less costly than a private insurance program in which a company must create its own insurance pool. As a result of this shift to welfarism, life in welfare-bureaucratic societies is far less likely to be marked by the personal insecurity and attendant problems than it was or is in mass-industrial societies.

THE WELFARE-BUREAUCRATIC SOCIETY

One of the fundamental advances that leads to the creation of a welfare-bureaucratic society is the enormous productivity of its complex and ever changing technology. The technology and techniques of farming become so advanced that less than one in ten members of the population needs to be engaged in the production of food. The American farmer produces twelve times as much food as his Soviet counterpart; this statistic helps us to account for the fact that approximately half of the Soviet labor force is engaged in farming occupations. The productive capacity of welfare-bureaucratic societies is not restricted to agriculture. The output of other industries is very great, creating so much wealth that part of it can be diverted for public use without impairing the operation of the economy.

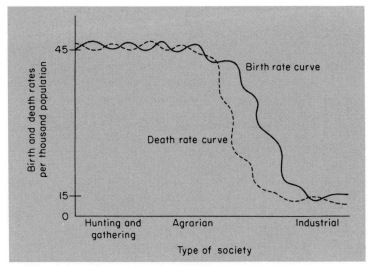

FIG. 10-1   Birth and death rates in different types of societies.

As Fig. 10-1 shows, the death rate drops close to the biologically permissible low point. Medical advances and the abundance of food are the major factors in this decline. The population would increase at a very rapid rate if it were not for a concomitant decline in the birth rate. The latter declines because there is no particular virtue to a large family in a society where human sources of power have largely been replaced by machine sources. The development of reliable techniques of contraception implement the economically rational desire to have a small family. Since the birth rate normally stays above the death rate, the population grows steadily. In the United States there were 192 million people by October, 1964; it is expected that there will be between 250 million and 350 million people by the year 2000.

Societies of this size would be expected to have elaborate subgroup formation (Proposition 2). The greatest development is in the area of associations: literally thousands of associations emerge, serving a wide variety of objectives. In one out of two American families, at least one member belongs to at least one association (13). These subgroups provide a channel by which the members can exert their collective influence on other large subgroups in the society: labor unions can affect the decisions of government, dealers can influence the companies they serve, and voters can influence the positions of candidates for political office.

The division of labor in these societies is very great (Proposition 2). No one person can master anything but the smallest fraction of the knowledge essential to maintain the complex technology. Since many operations can be performed more efficiently if the total task is divided into a series of extremely simple activities, task specialization increases. A person can make a career of mounting the wheels on the right-hand side of automobiles as they come down the assembly line. Because of the increasing complexity and productivity of the technology, fewer unskilled and semiskilled roles are required. Instead, there is an increasing proportion of white collar roles. The proportion of clerical workers increases to handle the more routine aspects of coordination and distribution in large organizations. The proportion of managers and professionals also increases greatly, because the technology and highly bureaucratized organizations that are being created demand highly trained persons for their operation.

A society with such diversity and differentiation in its role structure can be expected to have rather lengthy status hierarchies (Proposition 8). There are a great many levels of status between the president of a large university or business corporation and the occupants of the least influential roles there. The distance between the elite of a large organization and its least influential members becomes so great that distrust between workers and managers, students and university administrators, and between the electorate and government officials becomes more likely (Propositions 10 and 11).

The number of status hierarchies also increases, because there are more bases of influence in this type of society (Proposition 9). Cities and national governments develop such complex and ambitious programs that they become a key industry in their own right. The politician can claim a measure of independence from the economic elite because of his specialized knowledge and the vast resources that he controls (14, 15). The economic elite is often divided into separate hierarchies of influence. In a community, for example, the managers of the absentee-owned corporations may act quite independently of the elite of Main Street businesses (14). Military, religious, and professional centers of influence also develop. The elites of each hierarchy bargain, compete, and form shifting coalitions in a never ending struggle for access to the key resources of the society. The existence of different centers of influence and long hierarchies of status provides a basis for the segmentation of the society. This topic will be discussed in considerable detail in the chapters that follow.

SUMMARY

Marx's predictions about the directions in which in-dustrial societies would develop proved to be wrong. Instead of a dwindling middle class, that category of people has increased impressively in size. The proletariat was able to improve its position without resorting to open rebellion. Negotiation marked by occasional violence was the route used by the unions to improve the conditions of the workers.

Modern welfare-bureaucratic society arose as a result of three developments: the growth of large organizations, the shift from mass to integrated social organizations, and the shift from individualism to welfare-collectivism. Welfare-bureaucratic society is characterized by large bureaucratic organizations that take over many of the functions formerly in the province of smaller organizations. The norms become secularized, and the division of labor becomes exceedingly refined. Because of the high degree of specialization in this type of society, there are several bases of influence. Hierarchies of status develop on these different centers of influence. Segmentation among the hierarchies and between levels in each hierarchy becomes a problem for the society.

REFERENCES

1   K. Marx, *Capital*.

2   F. Engels, *The Conditions of the Working Class in England in 1844* (London: George Allen & Unwin, 1952).

3   K. Marx and F. Engels, *Communist Manifesto*.

4   D. H. Wrong, "The Functional Theory of Stratification: Some Neglected Considerations," *American Sociological Review*, 24 (1959), 772-82.

5   A. H. Hawley, *Human Ecology* (New York: The Ronald Press Company, 1950).

6   Marion J. Levy, Jr., "Contrasting Factors in the Modernization of China and Japan," *Economic Development and Cultural Change*, 2 (1953), 161-97.

7   B. Walter, "Political Decision Making in Arcadia," in *Urban Growth Dynamics in a Regional Cluster of Cities*, F. S. Chapin and S. F. Weiss, eds. (New York: John Wiley & Sons, Inc., 1962).

8   Committee of the Judiciary, United States Senate, *Concentration Ratios in Manufacturing Industry, 1958: Part I* (Washington: U. S. Government Printing Office, 1962).

9   R. Presthus, *The Organizational Society* (New York: Alfred A. Knopf, Inc., 1962).

10   J. Bain, "Economics of Scale, Concentration, and Entry," *American Economic Review,* cited in Presthus, *The Organizational Society,* p. 75.

11   Figures for 1910 calculated from *Historical Statistics of the United States;* data for 1960 from *Census of Population: 1960,* Final Report PC(1)-1C, Tables 89 and 90.

12   C. W. Mills, *White Collar* (New York: Oxford University Press, 1951).

13   C. R. Wright and H. H. Hyman, "Voluntary Association Memberships of American Adults: Evidence from National Sample Surveys," *American Sociological Review, 23* (1958), 284-94.

14   R. O. Shulze, "The Bifurcation of Power in a Satellite City," in *Community Political Systems,* M. Janowitz, ed. (New York: Free Press of Glencoe, Inc., 1961).

15   M. Meyerson and E. C. Banfield, *Politics, Planning and the Public Interest* (New York: Free Press of Glencoe, Inc., 1955).

part three ORGANI-
ZATIONAL
INTEGRATION AND CHANGE
IN AMERICAN SOCIETY

an introduction to american society

American society is a welfare-bureaucratic society; it is also partially integrated. But it does not represent the extreme of these dimensions. British society is probably more integrated than our own; French society is undoubtedly more bureaucratic; Swedish, Israeli, and Soviet societies are more imbued with welfare-collectivism.

In American society the older value system of individualism has not been completely superseded by welfare-collectivism. Individualism became a popular value system at a time when it really had very little utility for the less influential members of our society. Large organizations had supplanted smaller ones: guilds gave way to factories and duchies to the nation-state. Personal relationships, clothed in traditional norms, became impersonal and secular. There were few moral imperatives in the relationships between the individual and the large organizations that controlled much of his fate. In this new cultural atmosphere the individual was an inadequate lever to move the bureaucratic organizations. Stripped of his earlier subgroup relationships, alone, told to be an individual, to make his own decisions, he shrank from an essentially hopeless task. Sometimes the problem of powerlessness was handled by withdrawing from active participation in the affairs of the society and the community. We will see later that this type of behavior is most prevalent among the members of the lower working class. Another option was, as R. A. Nesbit termed it, the quest for community: joining organizations of various kinds to avoid the terrible aloneness and powerlessness he experienced (1). The object was not qualitative involvement in the activities of an association, but rather relief from the omnipresent sense of aloneness. Bridge clubs, P.T.A., leagues for the preservation of almost anything became an integral part of the lives of many people. Americans join religious organizations where the emphasis is less theological than social. The flight into marriage occurs at an increasingly early age despite the fact that longer training periods are required before a person can earn a living in modern society. The high divorce and desertion rates testify to the mirage-like qualities of the vision of community in marriage.

While some people withdrew from active participation in the affairs of the society, and others formed numerous superficial group relationships, still other people organized associations designed to influence the decisions of large organizations. Labor unions are a most noteworthy example of the collective response to the problem of interacting with large organizations.

The complexity of our society also impedes our search for qualitative group life. The problems of communication are so great that it becomes very difficult for people to understand and relate to one another. Qualitative interactions are inhibited and replaced with "lowest common denominator" conversations; we begin by talking about the weather, then move to sports and other current events, but we seldom develop truly primary relationships. The problem is not restricted to strangers; it occurs among people who have known each other for years. When you write home to your parents, you probably fail to tell them about the truly significant events of your week because you know that your life is so different from theirs that they will not appreciate the significance of your week's events. The lack of qualitative communication is so pronounced that Americans use the word *friend* to include acquaintances. When people are asked in interviews "How many friends have you got?" many of them will say "Hundreds" or "Thousands."

If our group relationships are superficial rather than qualitative, how can we say that the society is more integrated than a mass society? Is it adequate to count the number of associations in the society and because that number is increasing assume that we are becoming more integrated? These questions remain to be answered by social scientists. It is clear that several forces at work in American society operate to prevent it from becoming highly integrated.

THE SEGMENTING INFLUENCES IN AMERICAN SOCIETY

The most fundamental segmenting influence in American society is its size. According to our rules of increasing population size, we expect that vast numbers of subgroups will form (Proposition 2). These subgroups are encountering different problems and are often arriving at different solutions to those problems. Although the solutions may seem perfectly appropriate for the problems faced by the subgroup, they may have deleterious effects on others (Proposition 5). Yet often the members of a subgroup do not realize the effects of their behavior on others because of the problem of inadequate communication in large populations (Proposition 10). This same problem of inadequate communication may also lead to hostilities among subgroups; the members of each do not really care whether their behaviors hurt others (Proposition 11). In this segmented situation deviance from the common norms of the society takes many forms. Juvenile crime is one manifestation; white collar crime is another, more costly, form. But perhaps more perplexing is the passive acceptance of deviance by large segments of our population (2).

Our interest in segmentation in this part of the book is based on the relationships between organizational segmentation and change, costs, and conflicts. We saw in Chapter 5 that segmentation impedes the rate of change. In a segmented organization, changes that are initiated in one segment do not spread easily to other segments because of the barriers to interaction that exist. If hostility and conflict are present between the members of different segments, then mutual rejection of each other's innovations is likely. Finally, the protection that the members of a segment can receive from the elite of the hierarchy in which they are located can minimize their acceptance of change. As we saw in Chapter 5, organizations must often change their patterns of behavior or experience rising costs of interaction. These costs can become so high that the organization's survival can hinge on its ability to adapt to certain classes of problems when they occur. American society, as an organization, must maintain a certain level of adaptiveness if it is not to suffer from the effects of increased costs of interaction and conflict and friction among the parts. It is for this reason that we will study the forces of segmentation and integration that are at work in this society.

Our rules concerning the environment, economy, technology, and population size have taken us as far as they can. The technology will continue to become more complex, and the population may continue to grow, and these factors will continue to affect the organization of society, but they add only small increments to the gross characteristics that we have examined until now. They have helped us to outline the major characteristics of the industrial and bureaucratic form of organization in which we live. Henceforth, our discussion will examine the details of American social structure within this organizational format.

The major forces in our society that segment us horizontally are influence status differences (social classes) and racial and nationality differences. The most important vertical segmenting influence is religious differences. Each of these factors will be discussed in turn in the following chapters.

REFERENCES

1   R. A. Nesbit, *The Quest for Community* (New York: Oxford University Press, 1953).

2   E. O. Smigel, "Public Attitudes toward Stealing as Related to the Size of the Victim Organization," *American Sociological Review, 21* (1956), 320-27.

social classes in american society

Few aspects of society have received more attention from social scientists than social classes. Yet there is considerable disagreement about how to define the concept. Some social scientists think of social classes as social organizations. Warner, for example, distinguishes among social classes in terms of the patterns of interaction among people; those people who are engaged in routinized social interaction are in the same social class (1). In this approach to social classes social relationships are characterized by what has been called *corporateness* (2): the members of a social class limit routinized social interaction to those people who are in social categories similar to their own. The white Protestant professional develops social relationships with other people in the same social categories. Social contact with Negroes, Roman Catholics, and manual workers is minimized. Once social categories are used to set boundaries on social relationships, corporateness exists;

relationships are closed to outsiders. You can sense the quality of corporateness when you move to a new town or are a newcomer in a social group. The other persons interact with each other easily and freely; they are much less willing to relate to you. Sometimes the group is so corporate that outsiders who seek to join it are called "social climbers" or some other term with an equally derogatory connotation. Marx's conception of social classes differs from Warner's only in degree. He defines social classes in terms of occupational roles. But he also assumes that, normally, the higher the social class, the more likely it is to be a social organization with the characteristic of corporateness. The following passage from the *Communist Manifesto* (3) illustrates this point:

> The bourgeoisie, wherever it has got the upper hand, has put an end to all feudal, patriarchal, idyllic relations. It has pitilessly torn asunder the motley feudal ties that bound man to his "natural superiors," and has left no other nexus between man and man than naked self-interest, than callous "cash payment." It has drowned the most heavenly ecstasies of religious fervor, of chivalrous enthusiasm, of Philistine sentimentalism, in the icy water of egotistical calculation.

According to Marx, the bourgeoisie is a social organization: it has objectives, a division of labor, a collective consciousness, and common norms. But eventually even the proletariat becomes more than a social category; it too becomes a social organization. When the members of the middle class are forced into the proletariat, they supply the leadership and ideology and create the division of labor essential for the revolution.

The political scientist Harold Lasswell defines *social classes* in a manner similar to that of Marx: a social class is "a major social group of similar function, status, and outlook" (4). Lasswell, however, is less interested in whether classes are social organizations than he is in the process by which they become social organizations.

More recently, a criticism of the social organizational definition of social classes has been offered. Research in a New England community has shown that when people are asked to assign other members of the community to social classes, no consistent boundaries appeared that would indicate the existence of social classes (5). In other words, instead of finding stratified layers of influence or resource differences, a continuous distribution was obtained that indicated the so-called class boundaries were difficult to locate. Regardless of where horizontal lines were drawn, there were people on either side who were essentially similar and might engage in social interaction with one another. The search for class consciousness within each of the so-called classes in our population has really demonstrated that classes have not developed very well in the United States (6).

The argument between the adherents of these two extreme schools of thought continues, with one side arguing that our society is run by a small group of likeminded men and another group maintaining that because of the complexity and size of the society, it is virtually impossible for a single elite to dominate it.

A DEFINITION OF SOCIAL CLASS

It is not too difficult to understand why Marx and Lasswell conceived of social classes as social organizations. Marx lived at an interesting juncture in history when Europe was undergoing the transition from feudal to industrial society. The feudal social organization was still very much in evidence, and that organization was characterized by an elite with many of the characteristics of a social organization. Ties of kinship bound together the military, religious, and landholding elites. The great families had a division of labor: one that was designed to give them control over all of the important parts of the society. It was very easy to transfer this idea to the bourgeoisie. Furthermore, both Marx and Lasswell were either studying or participating in revolutionary activities, and it is during such events that social classes are most likely to have organizational characteristics. The "counter-elite," to use a Lasswellian term, is an organization that supposedly represents the interests of some class of people. When there is a threat of revolution, the elite is also more likely to be organized than it is at any other time.

These observations point to the fact that social classes have been social organizations at certain times in history. But we cannot overlook the evidence presented by the representatives of the other school of thought. Some resolution of these differences is obtained if we assume that *social class* is a variable concept. We will assume that social classes can vary from being unbounded social categories to poorly integrated classes to such highly integrated classes as the caste system of India. We will also continue our assumption of Chapter 2 that variation in the amount of influence is the essential characteristic of a class system. We expect that variation in the accumulation of resources and rewards is highly, though not perfectly, correlated with amount of influence. Therefore, differences in income or occupation can be used as *indicators* of differences in amount of influence. But the best *indicator* of influence status is one's role in the economy.

On the basis of Proposition 8, we expect that influence will be distributed unevenly among the parts in very large organizations. From anthropological evidence we also expect that the greater the per capita wealth found in a society, the more likely there are to be differences in influence among the roles (7). American society is both large and wealthy: facts that help to explain the variation in influence of our roles. Other reasons for this variation will be developed later. Because the variation exists, we can array the roles or their occupants on an influence rank system. Since large numbers of roles or occupants are involved when entire populations or role systems are ranked, many of them will have about the same amount of influence. Therefore a characteristic curve representing the distribution of influence among

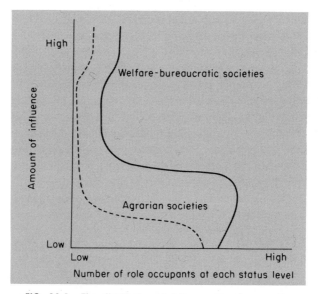

FIG. 12-1   The distribution of influence in urban-agrarian and welfare-bureaucratic societies.

the roles or role occupants of the society can be obtained. Figure 12-1 illustrates these curves for hypothetical welfare-bureaucratic and agrarian societies.

In agrarian societies most of the influence is held by the land-owning elite and their families.* There are very few roles or occupants with intermediate amounts of influence. At the bottom of the influence

* It is desirable to think of the family as a unit, giving the wife and children the same influence position that the husband attains.

system in these societies is the peasantry, which is both numerous and uninfluential. In welfare-bureaucratic societies, such as ours, there is a slight leavening effect; there are many roles invested with a modest amount of influence (8). Nonetheless, the greatest influence is still possessed by a very small proportion of the total population (Proposition 13). Figure 12-1 also illustrates one reason why social scientists seldom use measures of influence as a means of studying social classes: the bulk of the population has about the same amount of influence and so cannot be differentiated on that basis.

If there are social classes in a large society, we would expect some breaks in the distribution shown in Fig. 12-1. If classes exist, they must have boundaries, and they cannot have boundaries if there are subtle shadings of influence. Another indication of the existence of social classes is the degree of relationship between the influence status of a role occupant and that of his father. We expect the position of the son to approximate somewhat that of his father for genetic reasons. Intelligent people are more likely than unintelligent people to produce intelligent offspring. Therefore, even in a system with no social classes, there is a minimal but significant probability that a child will achieve the same position as his father. But as the relationship between the father's position and that of the son increases, the likelihood increases that there is a class system of the social organizational variety. A high relationship indicates that barriers have been created around status positions that permit monopolization of these positions by the families involved. Roles are ascribed by birth rather than achieved.

CLASSES AS ORGANIZATIONS: INFLUENCING FACTORS

Up to this point we have considered influence status levels simply as social categories. How do they become social organizations? The major factors are conquest, immigration, skill, and similarity of social category positions among interacting people.

The more rigid social classes are often the products of conquest; the conquerors assume a monopoly of the positions of greatest influence in the combined society. In medieval Europe, when a warlord conquered an area, he and his vassals assumed the positions of greatest influence and control over the key resources. Eventually, they became the nobility and transmitted their positions to other members of their families. A similar process led to the development of the class systems in virtually all of the classical agrarian societies.

Immigration can also produce class distinctions. The older members of the society may organize to maintain control over the important centers of influence or to deny the immigrants access to them. The immigrants who came to the United States during the last half of the nineteenth century formed the majority of the working class in our society for generations.

But even if conquest or immigration does not occur, class systems are likely to develop in agrarian and industrial societies. Some powerful factors usually lead to the development of social classes even though the members of the society prefer an equalitarian form of organization. One factor is that the members of the population vary greatly in their ability to perform the functions of any given role. Not all of us can be concert pianists, engineers, mathematicians, or textile spinners. How this difference in ability can lead to the development of perpetuating status differences is illustrated by the collective farms of Israel: the kibbutzim (9, 10). The kibbutzim were organized in a society whose members were dedicated to equalitarianism. To maintain the equal distribution of influence, the members of the collective farms devised a system in which the leadership roles were to be rotated among the members. A person might serve a term of office as manager of the collective farm and then return to ordinary farm labor. This ideal could not be retained in practice because of the scarcity of people capable of performing the more skilled roles. Because of the marginality of their existence, the population on a typical kibbutz could not afford the luxury of an ineffective leader. Therefore, the same persons tended to be elected repeatedly to the most influential roles.

Robert Michels called this phenomenon of permanent concentration of influence in a small group of persons the iron law of oligarchy (11). There are reasons why oligarchy will develop other than differences in personal ability. Experience in an influential office develops one's ability to perform its functions (12). With experience, a person develops routinized patterns of interaction both with his constituents and with the members of other organizations. To replace this person or group of people with other equally talented but less experienced persons could make the organization less effective for a long period of time. In labor unions, for example, when the elected leaders have developed skills at bargaining and other difficult and crucial union activities, the members are not too willing to replace them (12). They are even less willing to replace them if the leadership has been successful in achieving the objectives sought by the workers.

These factors help to account for the existence of oligarchies, but they do not account for the transmittal of influence status across generations. One factor that brings us closer to understanding the development of a social organizational class system is the social category differences between more influential and less influential parts of the population. People in influential roles are encountering different problems and probably receiving greater rewards for their services than are the people they lead. As a result, they have little in common with these members of the organization. A union leader who rises from the ranks of the workers or a political leader who traces his origins to a lower-working-class family has less in common with his constituents than with other union or political leaders. His income, intellect, and problems are more like those of people in roles similar to his own (see p. 62). With the passage of time, the leader is increasingly likely to interact with other persons at his influence status level than he is with those at lower levels (13). Persons at essentially the same position in influence or reward rank systems will face some problems in common about which they might interact and develop common solutions or norms. The development of common norms gives the status level one of the properties of a social organization. Associations come into existence that are designed to solve the problems faced by the people at any given status level. Labor unions develop among factory workers; stock clubs, country clubs, and other organizations appear and recruit members from the higher income status levels. Media develop that cater to the populations at different income and educational levels; e.g., *Vogue, Harper's, The Wall Street Journal.* These media provide needed information, reinforce the subculture that is developing at a given status level, and provide new solutions to problems. As an influence status level takes on the characteristics of an organization, a cycle develops (14). The development of norms peculiar to a particular status level increases the differences among role occupants at different status levels; a further decline in communication across status levels occurs, and differential association becomes more apparent. Persons at the same status level find themselves living in the same neighborhoods, reading the same newspapers, sharing some similar problems, and electing some similar or common solutions to those problems.

The use of the influence lodged in a role and the resources accumulated by its occupant to assure the future position of his children is the next logical step in the development of a class system. When influence is used to prevent occupants of lower status roles from achieving higher ones, a class system has emerged. In the Soviet Union an elaborate system of rewards has developed to perpetuate an equally elaborate class system (15).

A Poorly Integrated Class System

Returning now to our conception of social class as a variable, we can describe briefly some of the characteristics of class systems of different degrees of integration. In the poorly integrated class system there will be some differential association by status level. The persons at a given level are somewhat more likely to associate with one another than they are with persons at different influence status levels. Neighborhoods and associations will show some homogeneity of characteristics among the members. A few specialized subgroups and roles will emerge to serve the needs of the population at a given status level. Some normative homogeneity will also appear. There will also be a higher relationship between the positions of the fathers and the sons than one would expect on the basis of genetic factors alone, but the barriers to mobility are still fairly low, and it will be relatively easy for a person to move from one influence status level to another. Clique and associational memberships still cross over any arbitrarily drawn status boundaries.

A Highly Integrated Class System

Differential association and corporateness is now marked. A. B. Hollingshead (16) illustrated this situation in his study of high school students in a small midwestern town. He asked the students to indicate whom among the other students they would like to have for friends. Almost no one picked a person at a lower status level; most choices were people at the same status level; some picked persons at a higher level, but these choices were seldom reciprocated. Homogeneity of membership in associations is also high. There are social clubs, restaurants, political groups, and even occupations that are restricted to the persons at certain status positions. A division of labor appears at some levels. Kinship may provide the basis of this division of labor, as it does in urban-agrarian societies, or the division of labor can take the form of highly specialized associations serving the needs of the population in each class. Finally, there is a very high relationship between the status position of the father and his sons. If this relationship becomes nearly perfect—so that you can predict almost exactly the position of the son from the position of his father—the class system is called a *caste* system. In India, where the caste system was highly developed, the basis of the system was occupations. Certain occupations were reserved for the people in a given caste, and children were expected to assume the positions held by their fathers. The caste system represents, therefore, the most extreme form of social organization that man has created on the basis of status differences.

SOCIAL CLASSES AS A SOURCE OF SEGMENTATION

The factors we have been discussing that lead to the formation of some degree of social classes are fundamental and almost universally operative. Therefore, we expect all societies of great size and ample wealth to develop social classes of varying degrees of integration. We shall now see that a class system of middling integration has developed in the United States.

The very behaviors that lead to the development of social classes are by definition segmenting influences. By engaging in differential association and preventing the mobility of persons from lower influence status levels to higher ones, communication barriers are being erected among the roles of the system.

Class differences are also likely sources of conflict in the society. If a part of the population is prevented from improving its position by the members of a higher social class, a natural basis for conflict and hostility exists. The function of legitimating myths is to justify the superior position of the members of one class to the members of lower ones so that the latter are less likely to seek to change their position or to increase their share of the influence in the society. Conflict among social classes will often lead to increased segmentation in the society.

SOCIAL CLASSES IN THE UNITED STATES

What evidence is there of the presence of social classes in the United States? First, we will establish that there are influence and reward status differences in this society and then we will examine the extent to which these differences are permanent.

Influence Differences

No studies have attempted to array all of the roles or role occupants of a large American community, much less the society, on an influence ranking system. W. L. Warner and his students did it for smaller communities (17, 18, 19). Warner's studies showed that there were status differences in these small communities, so, on the basis of Proposition 8, we expect that larger communities also exhibit status differences. Community influence studies are unanimous in their conclusion that influence differences do exist (20). At the societal level there are studies that attempt to show the existence of a quasi-organized national elite that controls the major activities of the society (21, 22). Objections to these conclusions are not on the grounds that an extremely influential collection of roles does not exist, but rather on the assertion that the occupants of these roles work in concert with one another (23). On the basis of our rules of increasing organizational size, the existence of a unitary elite is unlikely. In large social organizations we expect a number of elites based on different sources of influence: economic, political, religious, and military, for example. In view of the different interests and problems of these elites, it is unlikely that they act in league with one another on anything approaching a permanent basis. Support for this last assertion is supplied in the literature on the structure of influence in communities. There it has been shown that the various elites have vied with each other in the exercise of influence, pursuing their different interests, forming ephemeral coalitions, and bargaining with each other for the allocation of resources and rewards (24, 25). If the level of integration is this low at the community level, it is difficult to maintain that it is higher at the national level. Shifting coalitions and bargaining are the more likely pattern of interactions among the elites at the national level (26, 27). Most of the segments of the population, except perhaps the lower working class, are represented in these maneuvers.

Resource and Reward Differences

Occupation, education, and income are the key resources and rewards available to the American population. The data showing how they are distributed in the population are more abundant than are data on the distribution of influence. An occupation is a resource because it provides access to influence and to such material rewards as income. Table 12-1 shows the distribution of occupations in the American population.

As we saw earlier, the major shifts in the occupational structure during this century have been the rapid increase in the proportion of people involved in the white collar occupations and the decline in the proportion of people in farm occupations. In spite of this upward shift in the labor force we shall see in the next section of this chapter that the opportunities to improve occupational status are less than perfect.

Table 12-1 does not really give us an adequate picture of the extremes in resource accumulation that exist in our society. Among the

TABLE 12-1

DISTRIBUTION OF THE POPULATION OF THE UNITED STATES
ACCORDING TO OCCUPATION

Occupational category		Percentage of population
Professional, technical, and kindred workers	11	
Managers, proprietors, and officials, excluding farmers	9	
Skilled, white collar		20
Clerical and kindred workers	15	
Sales workers	7	
Semiskilled, white collar		22
Craftsmen, foremen, and kindred workers	14	
Skilled, blue collar		14
Operatives and kindred workers	20	
Service workers	12	
Laborers	6	
Semiskilled and unskilled, blue collar		38
Farmers and farm managers	4	
Farm laborers and foremen	2	
Total farm		6
Total		100

Source: Department of Commerce, Bureau of the Census, *Census of the Population: 1960*, Final Report PC(1)-1C, Tables 89 and 90.

very wealthy, there are persons who do not have an occupation because it is not necessary for them to have one. Each person or family in this small fraction of the population (less than 0.5 per cent) has an average of $1,000,000 invested in property (28) that produces an average annual income of $50,000. Some of the very wealthy do work, but they derive only about $15,000 from this source.

Except for the case of the very wealthy, occupational status is highly related to income. Average income earned from employment varies from $30,000 for executive positions in large organizations to less than $3,000 for the unskilled worker. Because of their greater income and their role in large organizations, the executives can invest part of their income in stocks and other income-producing property. This source augments their income by an average of $20,000 each year. The unskilled worker has no such opportunity. A part of the reason that his income is so low is that he is usually unemployed during part of the year. His wages are inadequate to support him above the poverty level. Ninety per cent of the income-producing property in this country is owned by 15 per cent of the population (28).

The distribution of income in our society can be illustrated another way. In Table 12-2 the families and individuals in the United States have been arrayed on an income ranking system. Then they are divided into five segments, each including an identical number of people. In the lowest fifth are the families with the lowest income in each of the three time periods shown. The most remarkable features of this table is the stability of the distribution of income over the twenty-three-year period. One fifth of our population receives about 5 per cent of it. If we assume that a minimum income of $2,500 is required for a family of four persons to obtain the essentials for living, then approximately 32 million persons are living below that minimum. If we make the more realistic assumption that $3,000 to $3,500 is required, then 50 million persons are living in poverty (29).

TABLE 12-2

DISTRIBUTION OF TOTAL FAMILY INCOME
BEFORE TAXES 1935-36, 1944, AND 1958

Families by fifths	Percentage in each fifth			Average income per family, 1958
	1935-36	1944	1958	
Lowest	4.1	4.9	4.7	$ 1,460
Second	9.2	10.9	11.1	3,480
Third	14.1	16.2	16.3	5,110
Fourth	20.9	22.2	22.4	7,020
Highest	51.7	45.8	45.5	14,250

Source: Department of Commerce, Bureau of the Census, *Statistical Abstract of the United States: 1963*, 84th ed., p. 337.

The key means of gaining access to the highest status occupations in our society is getting an adequate education. The complexity of the social and technological problems of running large organizations is such that long training periods are required before a person can perform the tasks involved in a great many jobs. The importance of education in determining a person's occupation is demonstrated by the fact that 75 per cent of all technical and professional workers have gone to college, but only 5 per cent of the semiskilled and unskilled blue collar workers had similar training. Almost three-quarters of the latter category of workers did not even finish high school (30).

An increasing proportion of our population is completing high school today, but they are probably just maintaining pace with the upswing in the demand for skills in the labor force. In spite of this upswing in the demand for skills, 24 per cent of the nonwhites and 7 per cent of the whites who had completed their educations by 1960 *did not get as far as the fifth grade in school* (31). The reasons for this situation will be discussed in the next chapter.

Status Mobility

"Success," "ambition," and "equality of opportunity" have been important themes in the American value system. In the period between the Civil War and the economic depression of the 1930's these themes were a part of the value system of almost all Americans. At home, in school, in church, and in ordinary conversation the slogans of the success ethic were repeated. They can still be heard today, but primarily from the older persons in our society. The force of this ethic is reflected in the popularity of the Horatio Alger novels published after the turn of the present century. Millions of copies of these novels were bought and read despite the unbelievably uniform plots and the poor dialogue. What was the attraction? Each novel followed the career of a man as he moved "from rags to riches." In each case a poor boy possessing all of the virtues—he worked hard, and was obedient and courteous—became a successful businessman. The Horatio Alger stories sustained every young man's desire to "make something of himself." Other information was supplied in newspapers and magazines to support the success theme. The careers of successful executives were recounted to show how they had "risen from the ranks." It seemed possible to start at the bottom in a large corporation and advance to the rank of executive officer. But is it really possible? What are the probabilities that a person can improve his occupational status?

The answers to these questions are not clear. It is certain that the opportunities for mobility are greater in our society than they are in Japan or England. It is equally certain that they do not approach the American ideal of unrestricted opportunities to move upward through the class system.

One reason that mobility trends are not clear is a by-product of the crude occupational categories used in mobility studies. Usually the *entire* occupational structure is divided into a few categories such as those shown in Table 12-1: "professional, technical, and kindred workers," "managers, proprietors, officials," "clerical and kindred workers," and so forth. Using these categories, the data might show that 12 per cent of the sons of "semiskilled" workers had become "skilled" workers and 2 per cent had become "professional, technical, and kindred workers." It would seem by these data that there is considerable upward mobility: that we are not in danger of developing a highly integrated class system: that democracy is safe for another generation. But when we look at the *actual* occupations achieved by the sons, a different picture emerges. The son who had moved into the "professional, technical, and kindred worker" category was actually an X-ray technician and not a lawyer or doctor. The son who had moved into the "skilled" worker category was a "semiskilled" worker who had become a foreman in his shop.

A. J. Reiss, Jr. has shown that virtually all of the sons of manual workers who move into the so-called "professional" category are in semiprofessional jobs: X-ray and laboratory technicians, engineer's assistants, surveyors (32). Rarely does a manual worker's son become a doctor, lawyer, or college professor.

The other son's mobility is not as impressive as it seems, either. Foremen are traditionally chosen from the ranks of semiskilled workers in factories. But for many reasons they usually have a short career in their new jobs before "falling back" into their old jobs.

While these moves are truly significant, their real importance is masked by the unrealistic categories used to study mobility. No accurate conclusions about mobility in American society can be reached until detailed occupational categories are used.

Another reason that mobility trends are not clear is that there are many kinds of mobility, and the trends in some of them cancel the effects in others. Persons can move upward, downward, or laterally through the occupational ranks. They also can change their positions in the course of their own work careers—*intra*generational mobility— or they can improve their position over that of their father—*inter*generational mobility.

The most obvious fact about mobility in our society is that the son is very likely to have the same occupational position as his father or to be one rank above or below him (6). Movement from one extreme of occupational status to the other is very unlikely. In 1900, 39 per cent of the people who possessed $30 million or more came originally from blue collar families; in 1950, only 9 per cent of these very wealthy people could claim similar origins (21). Most of the mobility that does occur involves short steps upward or downward.

A second characteristic of mobility in our society is that it occurs primarily within the blue collar or white collar categories. There is very little movement across the manual-nonmanual gap (33). Blue collar workers and their children may improve their position, but they usually move from one manual job to a better manual job. The gap between the blue and white collar categories is usually crossed by the most adjacent groups: the children of skilled and semiskilled manual workers who obtain clerical and sales jobs and the children of clerical and sales workers who obtain skilled manual jobs. There is a mild upward movement, but it is accounted for by the shift from secondary to tertiary industries. The children of blue collar workers are getting better educations and moving into the more abundant clerical and sales jobs. While this shift is considered as evidence of mobility, this conclusion is questionable. The clerical worker actually earns less money than the skilled manual worker. The improvement is in working conditions: offices and stores are cleaner and less dangerous and noisy. Also, the American value system accords greater deference to white collar workers than it does to blue collar workers.

Another trend is for considerable lateral movement in the social system. It is estimated that the average worker holds about nine to twelve jobs during his work career and virtually all of them have the same occupational status (33).

The evidence about the amounts of intra- and intergenerational upward mobility is less clear. The present trend indicates that intra-generational mobility is declining (33). It has become increasingly difficult for a person to improve his occupational position in his own lifetime. The demands of his present job and of supporting and participating in a family limit the time he has available for self-improvement. The increasing complexity of modern industry requires that managers and professionals have specialized training (34). The manual worker cannot expect to climb the hierarchy into a managerial role unless he gets the required training. The costs of starting a private business are also prohibitive for someone who earns about $5,000 a year. Yet annually, thousands of factory workers try to start a small business of their own, usually a gasoline station or similar low-investment small business, and, annually, most of these workers return to the factory (34). The major avenue of mobility for the manual worker and his clerical and sales counterpart is smaller movements within his company. A machine operator may strive for a job as a supervisor or foreman or simply for work in a cleaner, quieter place in the plant (34). If this route is blocked, some workers direct their energies into other channels. A few workers seek to move up the status hierarchies of associations—unions or political parties, for example (35). Others get a second job and use the added income to live the style of life they desire (36).

It is questionable whether intragenerational mobility was ever so easy as the media indicated at the turn of the century. William Miller (37) has shown that the "rags to riches" theme of the Horatio Alger novels did not apply to the executives of that period. This theme is still very much with us today and is even less likely to be true. In 1954 Bell Telephone placed an advertisement in which the careers of the nineteen top executives in that organization were traced. The point of the advertisement was that all of these executives had moved from very low positions in the company to their positions of great influence. A study of the educational backgrounds of these people showed that all but two of them had been to college at a time when only 2 per cent of their age cohort had received similar training (38). In other words, their backgrounds were anything but ordinary.

Intergenerational upward mobility does occur more frequently. It tends to be in short moves, primarily among white collar workers, and among young people (33). These moves are facilitated by the general upward shift in the occupational role structure and the increasing availability of money to provide scholarships and loans to needy students.

One final trend deserves attention. There is still some downward mobility in our society despite the upward shift in the occupational role structure. In a study of the Detroit labor force it was found that "19 per cent of the 495 men were intergenerational skidders, and 20 per cent were worklife skidders" (39).

SUMMARY

The concept of social class can be treated as a variable. At one extreme, social classes are simply categories of people who have similar amounts of influence or rewards. This situation is not found empirically in large organizations because of the operation of several very powerful forces. The size and complexity of the social system operate to develop an elite. The scarce supply of adequately skilled people for the more difficult roles leads to development of oligarchies. The skill they develop from experience in their roles makes it more imperative that they stay in their positions. Differential association and the transmission of roles across generations lead to the development of a more rigid class system. Warfare, subjugation, conflict, and immigration have a similar effect. At the other extreme of the class continuum is the caste system found in some agrarian societies.

The American class system represents an intermediate development. It is clear that there are great differences in influence and rewards in the population, but the class system has not become highly integrated. The position of the son is most likely to be the same as the father's or within one level of it. The upward mobility that does occur tends to be within the major occupational categories: blue and white collar. Extreme movement has become relatively uncommon, as has movement within one's own lifetime. The greater availability of white collar jobs has induced a mild upward mobility in the population. But in spite of this fact, a significant proportion of the population is still experiencing downward mobility.

REFERENCES

1   W. L. Warner, *Social Class in America* (Chicago: Science Research Associates, 1949).

2   M. Weber, *The Theory of Social and Economic Organization,* A. N. Henderson and T. Parsons, trans. (New York: Oxford University Press, 1947).

3   K. Marx and F. Engels, *Communist Manifesto.*

4   H. D. Lasswell, *Politics: Who Gets What, When, How* (New York: McGraw-Hill Book Company, 1936), p. 98.

5   G. E. Lenski, "American Social Classes: Statistical Strata or Social Groups?" *The American Journal of Sociology, 58* (1952), 139-44.

6   R. Centers, *The Psychology of Social Classes* (Princeton: Princeton University Press, 1949).

7   E. A. Hoebel, *Man in the Primitive World* (New York: McGraw-Hill Book Company, 1949).

8   J. A. Kahl, *The American Class Structure* (New York: Holt, Rinehart & Winston, Inc., 1961).

9   E. Rosenfeld, "Stratification in a 'Classless' Society," *The American Sociological Review, 16* (1951), 766-74.

10   M. E. Spiro, *Kibbutz: Venture in Utopia* (New York: Schocken Books, 1963).

11   R. Michels, *Political Parties,* E. Paul and C. Paul, trans. (New York: Collier Books, 1962).

12   S. M. Lipset, "The Political Process in Trade Unions," in *Freedom and Control in Modern Societies,* M. Berger, T. Abel, and C. H. Page, eds. (New York: Van Nostrand, 1954).

13   M. Weber, "Class, Status, and Party," in *From Max Weber: Essays in Sociology,* H. H. Gerth and C. W. Mills, trans. and eds. (New York: Oxford University Press, 1946), pp. 186-93.

14   A. K. Cohen, *Delinquent Boys: The Culture of the Gang* (New York: Free Press of Glencoe, Inc., 1955).

15   A. Inkeles, "Social Stratification and Mobility in the Soviet Union, 1940-1950," *American Sociological Review, 15* (1950), 465-79.

16   A. B. Hollingshead, *Elmtown's Youth: The Impact of Social Classes on Adolescents* (New York: John Wiley & Sons, Inc., 1949).

17   W. L. Warner and P. S. Lunt, *The Social Life of a Modern Community* (New Haven: Yale University Press, 1941).

18   A. Davis, B. B. Gardner, and M. R. Gardner, *Deep South: A Social-Anthropological Study of Caste and Class* (Chicago: The University of Chicago Press, 1941).

19   S. C. Drake and H. R. Cayton, *Black Metropolis* (New York: Harcourt, Brace, and World, Inc., 1945).

20   C. Press, *Main Street Politics: Policy Making at the Local Level* (East Lansing: Institute for Community Development, Michigan State University, 1962).

21   C. W. Mills, *The Power Elite* (New York: Oxford University Press, 1956).

22   F. Hunter, *Top Leadership U.S.A.* (Chapel Hill: University of North Carolina Press, 1959).

23   K. B. Mayer, *Class and Society,* rev. ed. (New York: Random House, 1962).

24   M. Meyerson and E. C. Banfield, *Politics, Planning and the Public Interest* (New York: Free Press of Glencoe, Inc., 1955).

25   R. O. Schulze, "The Bifurcation of Power in a Satellite City," in *Community Political Systems,* M. Janowitz, ed. (New York: Free Press of Glencoe, Inc., 1961), pp. 19-80.

26   S. Lubell, *The Future of American Politics* (New York: Harper & Row, Publishers, 1952).

27   R. A. Dahl and C. E. Lindbloom, *Politics, Economics and Welfare: Planning and Politico-Economic Systems Resolved into Basic Social Processes* (New York: Harper & Row, Publishers, 1963).

28 J. C. Bowen, "Some Aspects of Transfer Taxation in the United States" (Unpublished doctoral dissertation, The University of Michigan, 1958).

29 M. Harrington, *The Other America: Poverty in the United States* (New York: The Macmillan Company, 1963).

30 *Manpower: Challenge of the 1960's* (U.S. Department of Labor, 1960), p. 17.

31 U.S. Department of Commerce, Bureau of the Census, *Statistical Abstract of the United States: 1963,* 84th ed., p. 120.

32 A. J. Reiss, Jr., "Occupational Mobility of Professional Workers," *American Sociological Review, 20* (1955), 693-700.

33 S. M. Lipset and R. Bendix, *Social Mobility in Industrial Society* (Berkeley: University of California Press, 1959).

34 E. Chinoy, *Automobile Workers and the American Dream* (Garden City: Doubleday and Company, Inc., 1955).

35 H. L. Wilensky, "Work, Careers, and Social Integration," *International Social Science Journal, 12* (1960), 543-60.

36 P. E. Mott, "A Profile of the Moonlighter" (Ann Arbor: Institute for Social Research, mimeo).

37 W. Miller, "American Historians and the Business Elite," *Journal of Economic History, 9* (1949), 184-200.

38 S. J. Kaplan, a note in the *American Sociological Review, 24* (1959), 79-80.

39 H. L. Wilensky and H. Edwards, "The Skidder: Ideological Adjustments of Downward Mobile Workers," *American Sociological Review, 24* (1959), 215-31.

13 class differences in american society

Assigning people to social classes is at best a perilous enterprise. First, American social classes have not become highly integrated, and any method of dividing the population into classes is bound to be somewhat arbitrary. Each class will be composed of many heterogeneous elements that share only influence or occupational status. Often a valid case can be made for putting some categories of people into more than one social class. Second, since the population in each social class is heterogeneous, it is virtually impossible to make generalizations that apply to all members. If it were not for the problem of monotonous repetition, every description in this chapter of a class behavior would be modified by such words as *tends* or *in general*. But in view of our proclivities for making stereotypes about the different classes, it may be a useful learning experience if the heterogeneity of the populations in our social classes is demonstrated.

A third problem emerges from the type of data that we will discuss. There are two types of data collected by social scientists: theoretical and descriptive. Collecting descriptive data is similar to taking a photograph; it provides us with a description of reality, but that description may not obtain at a later period of time. In a dynamic society, the relationships between social classes and behavior that are found in today's descriptive data may not be found tomorrow. The quality of education, the availability of the media, or the condition of the economy can change the findings drastically from one time period to another. Theoretical knowledge is designed to test propositions, and it permits the social scientist to account for some of the important changes that occur over time. Virtually all of the information about social class behavior is descriptive and, therefore, subject to drastic revision with the passage of time. When we examine the data available today, it is absolutely essential to remember that the same findings may not hold tomorrow. If we fail to realize this fact, we can create stereotypes about social classes that bear as little resemblance to reality as some of the popular stereotypes. As the social sciences move toward maturity, they will develop more studies of a theoretical nature that will account for the changes over time.

One final point before we begin the description of the class system: when a social psychologist studies social classes, he is often interested in the effects of the different class positions on the *attitudes* of the people in those positions. His findings are often very interesting, and for that reason some of them will be discussed in this chapter. You should keep this distinction in mind, however.

THE LOWER WORKING CLASS

One of the unique features of American society as compared with other welfare-bureaucratic societies is the existence of a lower working class that has many of the features of a *mass*. The bulk of the Negro population is located in this class, and many Puerto Ricans and Mexicans are at least temporarily located in it. There is also a significant number of white Anglo-Saxon Protestants in this class, whose presence is due primarily to their failure to complete their educations.

If we use personal income as well as lack of influence as a yardstick for measuring a person's class position, then there are other categories of people who must be included in the lower working class. Business failures, technological changes, and the moving of factories nearer to markets and sources of cheaper labor have caused chronic unemployment among the middle-aged, less well-educated workers. Ironically, one of the reasons that many of these people "fall" into the lower working class is their middle class values. During their work careers, they married, raised and supported families, met their responsibilities, and perhaps bought homes. When the factories where they worked closed down, they could not easily leave town and go to other cities where work was available. They could not sell their houses in a depressed market nor could they leave their families behind while they looked elsewhere for work. Modern welfarism can work to the disadvantage of these workers, too. When an employer hires a person, usually he must make a contribution to his retirement fund. If he hires a middle-aged worker, he is required to make a larger contribution than if he hires a younger man. Therefore, the middle-aged worker is more costly than equally skilled younger workers. For these reasons, the middle-aged unemployed worker is likely to stay in the same town or city, looking for any kind of work regardless of the amount of the pay, and he often accepts jobs that will not provide him with a retirement income.

One of the common stereotypes of the lower working class is that they don't work because they prefer to live on relief. This stereotype applies only to a very small minority of the people in this class, and it certainly does not apply to the unemployed middle-aged worker just described. Virtually all of the unemployed actively seek work, preferring any kind of job to unemployment relief. Evidence of the means used by unemployed persons to avoid taking relief money is given in a nationwide study of financial management by unemployed families during the 1958 recession. These persons used up their savings, borrowed money from relatives, delayed making some purchases, moved into cheaper housing, or simply let the bills pile up (1). At the time of the survey only 10 per cent of the unemployed workers had accepted any form of relief; prior to that survey the figure had been only 3 per cent. Either figure is extremely low, reflecting in part the onus that members of this class attach to relief. The segment of the lower working class that prefers relief to work is an extremely small and over-publicized fraction of the lower working class population.

Another category of persons who would have to be included in the lower working class if we use low income as a criterion is the large and growing number of old people in our population who must retire on marginal incomes. Welfarism is a *developing* phenomenon in American society; it is not as pervasive as it is in some other countries. Many industries do not have retirement programs for their workers, and the social security program does not cover all of the occupational categories in our society. For these and other reasons, many oldsters retire on inadequate incomes.

Social security is the most common source of income for this category of people; others work, but advancing age soon terminates that source of income. Contributions from other members of their families are also a source of income, but the amount of the contribution is related to the social class of the children; the lower the social class of the children, the less they can and do contribute to the care of their parents (2). This group naturally has the most severe health problems found in the population. They require longer periods in the hospital to recover from their ailments than do younger people, and their health insurance rates are correspondingly higher. These and other factors conspire to make the lives of many of our oldsters one of poverty.

Tenant farmers are traditional residents of the lower working class. Many but not all of the people in this occupational category are non-whites. The tenant farmer is engaged in subsistence farming, living from crop to crop, farming marginal land, and always in debt. Living a comparable existence is the migrant farm laborer who sells his services to the owners of large commercial farms. The migrant farm worker has seldom had the support of a union, he is not protected by minimum wage laws, his work is seasonal, and his wages are low. Because he follows the crops, his children have little opportunity to get an education. For this reason the way of life of the migrant farmer is passed from fathers to sons over several generations.

Objections could be raised to the inclusion of oldsters and unemployed, middle-aged persons in the lower working class. The values of these people are usually more like those found in the upper working class. But they do have influence, resource, and reward statuses similar to those of the other members of the lower working class. There is evidence that skidding affects them in ways that increase their resemblance to the other members of the lower working class (3, 4, 5).

Life Chances in the Lower Working Class

Living in the lower working class affects a person's life chances: his life span, health, education opportunities, and ability to obtain justice. The people in the lower working class live an average of eight years less than members of the highest classes (6). The major difference in life span is between Negroes and whites, and much of this difference is accounted for by the higher infant mortality rate of Negroes.

MENTAL AND PHYSICAL HEALTH.   The mental and phys-
ical health of the people in this class is also significantly poorer:
lengthy disabling illnesses are 57 per cent more prevalent in the lower
working class than in the other classes (6). In spite of this great difference, the middle classes obtain proportionately twice as many services
from physicians and seven times as many from hospitals (6). In Chapter 1 we saw that psychoses are eight times as prevalent in this class
as in the middle class. Neuroses have been shown to be about three
times as prevalent in this class as in the upper middle class (7). The
class that can least afford to pay for illnesses is the one most likely to
suffer from lengthy and costly ones. The serious health problems found
in this social category have caused some associations to advocate the
extension of governmental welfare programs to include members of
the lower working class.

EDUCATION.   The lower the social class, the less likely
the members are to finish high school (6). Among nonwhites, who are
found predominantly in the lower class, 47 per cent of those old
enough to have completed their educations had never gone beyond
the seventh grade. This figure is an improvement over the comparable
one for 1950 when over two-thirds of the nonwhite population failed
to go beyond the seventh grade (8). The failure to get an adequate
education severely limits the occupational opportunities of the dropout. Less than 5 per cent of the dropouts become skilled workers; two
out of every five of them become laborers.

In view of the occupational fate in store for the dropout, we might
suppose that the children of lower working class families would strive
for better educations in order to improve their position over that of
their parents. This is not the case. Interviews with children in different
social classes show that the lower the social class, the less likely the
children in that class are to complete their education (9). There are
several reasons for this. Lower working class children may be less
bright than the children in the higher social classes. IQ scores are
correlated with social class: the lower the social class, the lower the IQ
scores (10). It is difficult to know whether differences in IQ reflect
differences in native intelligence, because IQ tests measure the child's
ability to take a test, and that ability is cultivated in children in the
higher classes and not in lower working class children. But the number
of working class children who drop out of school exceeds the number
that would be predicted on the basis of IQ differences. There are
other factors that are at least as important to account for the dropout
tendency.

There is a value system prevalent in the lower working class that does not include a prescription for education. Parents who follow this value system do not prepare their children for the requirements of a school system, nor do they support or reward their children for their accomplishments in school.

Economic problems are the major reason for the failure of so many children in the lower working class to complete their educations. The earning power of the family is so marginal that the children must quit school, get a job, and contribute to the support of the family. Lower class school children also want to have the clothing, cars, and pocket money that their middle class classmates have, so they quit school to get them. Here again they are victims of their value system, which emphasizes short-term thinking and de-emphasizes self-denial.

Lower class children often find themselves discriminated against in the schools by teachers and other students alike (10). The children from higher class families exclude them from the extracurricular activities of the school. The teachers give them less attention, fewer honors, poorer grades, and more punishment for a given infraction of the rules than they give to students from higher class families. The school is not a pleasant place when seen from the point of view of the lower working class child.

JUSTICE.   There are also class differences in the attainment of justice. Lower class persons are more likely to be arrested, tried, convicted, and serve the maximum sentence for violating a given law than are members of the upper middle and upper classes (6). The greater influence of middle class families partially accounts for this differential treatment. Another reason centers on the expected role of a police force in a community—it is often conceived as a means of protecting the upper class families from the lower class ones. The fact that the police arrest more people from the lower class than from any other attests to their effectiveness. Many so-called *white collar crimes*— price fixing, issuing inadequately supported stock, using fraudulent advertising claims, selling inadequately tested drugs—involve more money than burglary and robbery, but the offenders seldom receive proportionate jail sentences or fines (6).

Another reason for the differences in jail terms and fines is the quality of legal services that the members of each social class can command. Upper class people can afford the services of the best lawyers; the members of the lower working class cannot. Legal aid societies are an interesting attempt to solve this problem, but the lower working class person who uses this service is likely to be represented by one of the newer, less experienced lawyers in the community who has not yet built up his own private practice.

The Formation of the Lower Working Class Value System

In earlier periods in our history, the lower working class was populated by the migrants from Europe and elsewhere and by people with little or no education. Most of them overcame their initial position and moved into higher class positions. Negroes are the exception; they have been virtually permanent residents of this lowest class.

Lacking adequate skills for the better jobs or the right color of skin, the members of the lower working class were forced to accept the unskilled jobs. They were day laborers, sweepers in factories, and household service workers. These jobs provided low income and were sensitive to economic conditions. When the volume of business declines, they are the first to be laid off; when it rises, they are the last to be rehired. This problem may not be insurmountable to someone who was socialized in a different culture or against whom there are no discriminating norms. For the ambitious migrant his lowly position was "only temporary." But for the person who was a product of generations of discrimination or residence in the lower working class, the problems were quite different. Upward mobility did not seem a realistic possibility. As a result, an appropriate value system was developed and transmitted from one generation to another.

This value system is based on the assumption that mobility is not really possible. Therefore, why strive to get ahead? The lower working class person often decides that getting an education will not expand his job opportunities appreciably. An educated Negro, particularly, often finds himself working at the same type of job as a Negro who dropped out of school. During the 1940's, Pullman porters were often men with medical and law school degrees (11). This position may be less true today than it was formerly, but the ingrained value system it produced is not going to change in a generation.

The core of the prevalent value system is based on a choice of one of two types of behavior: withdrawal from the participation in the affairs of the society or fighting back. The more common choice is withdrawal. Members of the lower working class are less likely to have friends and to belong to associations than are the members of the higher social classes (12). The code of behavior places value on living for today and not worrying about tomorrow. There is no virtue in self-denial; the "good things" in life are scarce and should be enjoyed whenever they are available.

It would be a mistake to think that the members of the lower working class do not value the middle class norms. They know that they should respect the property of others, not be physically aggressive, sacrifice in the short run in order to maximize long-term goals, and discipline their behavior, but there is inadequate support for these values in the lower class culture. The father mouths the value of an education but does nothing to support his children's educational achievements. The child knows the value of completing his education, but he can't seem to get started on his homework. The children in higher class positions have the same conflicts (shall I study or go to the movies?), but in their case the financial and normative support of their parents makes the choice easier and even a little less crucial. It is ironic that the lower working class child is the only one who needs an uncompromising middle class value system if he is to get ahead. Continuing in school will involve real deprivations for him and few for the middle and upper class child.

Given his lower class value system, the child develops a style of life appropriate to it. Social scientists have perhaps been slow to recognize that this style of life has its pleasant as well as its unpleasant side. The boundaries of the important part of life are roughly the same as those of his neighborhood. There he can express freely his physical and mental skills. He can experiment in sexual relations easily and often. He can win the deference of his friends using skills he has developed: strength, wit, and sexual prowess. He can have fun. Reading Boswell or Coleridge is of little value for his style of life, and school is a waste of time. The lower class child bides his time in the school system until he can get out and get a job.

Because of this value system, a vicious cycle exists in the lower working class. A pattern of values that was appropriate for that class was developed and passed on through socialization to the children. In spite of changing conditions, these children cannot easily change their basic patterns of behavior; they are not equipped to assume more skilled occupations. They transmit their own ambiguous value system to their children, and the process is repeated.

Problems of legitimacy occur in this situation. The members of the lower working class believe that there are two sets of rules: one for them and a different one for the members of the higher classes. The police and courts are understood as agencies designed to repress them, "while the big operators get away with murder." The phrase "You can't fight City Hall" has special meaning for them.

Some members of the lower working class do not advocate withdrawal as a solution to their problems. A few try to move up through the occupational ranks. Others advocate violence or "fighting back." Destruction of property, physical crimes, robbery, and other acts of violence are committed. Social class differences can be sources of segmentation, conflict, and hostility.

THE UPPER WORKING CLASS

The upper working class also contains some diverse elements. In it are the semiskilled operatives who work in the mass production industries: the automobile assemblers, the operators of grinding, edging, and facing machines, instrument readers, and furnace tenders. The aristocrats of the working class are the foremen, tool and die makers, and building trades specialists. Despite some important differences among the people in this class, they share some fundamental characteristics. Virtually all of them are manual workers who usually work for someone else rather than for themselves; they are less likely than the members of the lower working class to be unemployed during an economic recession. The average income for the upper working class family is a little over $5,000 per year: about the same as that of the lower middle class. The highest wage earners are the more skilled workers—plumbers, electricians, and foremen— who earn more than most members of the lower middle class. Like so many other people in our society, the members of the upper working class are consumption oriented. Between this penchant for spending their surplus income for a variety of commodities and the limited size of that income, they have very few savings. Most families have a few hundred dollars in savings accounts and government bonds.

Life is divided into two highly segmented areas: work and living. Work and the income it provides is a *means* used to achieve free time objectives. Work can have few other meanings because it is repetitious, uncreative, and dull. On an automobile assembly line the worker mounts right wheels on cars using a semi-automatic bolt tightener that tightens all five bolts simultaneously, or he mounts the battery on the battery stand and bolts it into place (in 54 seconds), or he lowers the motor from an overhead carrier into the front part of the chassis where it is bolted into position by a man who works in a well under the assembly line. Because of the simplicity and repetitiveness of the task, many workers achieve a trance-like state in which they perform all of their tasks but pay little mental attention to the job.

The workers attempt to relieve the monotony of their jobs by interacting with each other, but this is not always possible. The nature of the technology may be such that interaction is minimized (13). Workers may be strung out serially along an assembly line or at opposite ends of an automatic broaching machine. The problems posed by the technology merely tax the ingenuity of the worker because ways are usually found to relieve the monotony. Pranks are quite commonplace, and the worker is expected to be able to "take it." Notes are passed along the line, usually of a humorous or cynical nature. Relief and lunch breaks are the high points of the work day when the workers can relax and talk with each other.

These problems are less bothersome for the skilled worker. If he works in a factory, he is free to move about, to talk with other workers, and most important, to set his own work pace. The superiority of his position does not make him a zealous worker, however. Workers have their own norms about the amount of work that they will produce. They will lay a specified quota of bricks each day, test a certain quota of wheels, or box a certain number of products. The norms may be lower than what the managers would prefer, but tacit agreement usually develops around the workers' norms (14). The low production norms are partially the result of the depression consciousness of blue collar workers. They do not want to overproduce and lose their jobs. They believe that if they produced as much as management would like, many of them would be laid off. The worker who violates the informal production norms is negatively sanctioned by the other workers.

Noneconomic Roles

The upper working class has often suffered from a kind of guilt by association. Social scientists often ascribe the same value system to the upper working class as to the lower. Perhaps at one time this position was correct, but it is no longer. Many factors strengthen the blue collar family's adherence to the middle class value system, particularly education and the media. Today's blue collar worker obtained a better education than did his father a generation ago, and his children are improving on his performance. Since our educational institutions function to instill the middle-class ethic in children, increased exposure to formal education has helped to achieve that objective. The media, particularly television, have penetrated deeply into our lives. Every hour or half-hour a middle-class morality play is presented in which good triumphs over evil and honesty and fairness are rewarded.

As a result of these and other factors, the members of this class generally place great emphasis on stability and responsibility. Primarily home-oriented in their outlook, they strive to become home-owners, to provide for their families, and to perform adequately in their roles as husbands and fathers (15).

Hobbies, sports, and visiting relatives who live in the same community are prevalent activities. Participation in associations is related to the education of the workers: the higher their education, the more likely they are to participate. Some research has shown that the blue collar worker was less likely to participate in voluntary associations than his white collar counterpart. But this essentially correct finding masks some important distinctions. Blue collar workers are more likely than white collar workers to live in the central city. The size of the community depresses their participation. But an even more important factor is the level of education of the workers. Blue collar workers who are also high school graduates are almost as likely as similarly educated white collar workers to participate in associations. In a study involving an upper working class population of Philadelphia, it was found that fully 35 per cent participated in two or more voluntary association (unions and churches were not counted unless the worker had a specific role in either of them) (15).

The Major Source of Segmentation

The history of relations between blue collar workers and the managers of the industrial enterprises in which they work is studded with conflict, violence, and distrust. Betwen 1837 and 1842, a third of the labor force was out of work, and half of the remainder worked only part time (16). During that period wages dropped from 30 to 50 per cent. By the end of that depression it was estimated that half of the factory workers worked eleven or more hours each day. These conditions led to the formation of labor associations that sought to reduce the length of the working day to ten hours. Eventually, the movement was successful, but only at the cost of a decade of struggle with owners and managers.

The fledgling workers'-associations suffered serious setbacks during the Civil War. Strikes were broken by federal troops, and the workers had a difficult time keeping their wages abreast of the cost of living. After the war, management groups used several tactics to repress the workers. Workers were required to sign yellow dog contracts, which made it a condition of employment that the worker was not to join a union. Blacklists of union sympathizers were circulated among managers of different companies; sometimes the companies simply locked the workers out of the plant if the latter were contemplating union action; legislation was passed in several states forbidding the formation of unions.

Events took a violent turn as the nineteenth century moved toward its close. A strike among the anthracite miners in Pennsylvania in 1874 saw battles between strikebreakers and the miners. A series of murders and assaults of mine foremen and officials was perpetrated. Labor unions fell into low public regard as a result of this violence, although it was not clear whether union leaders or people employed by the mine operators committed the crimes (16).

Violence continued in the famous Haymarket Affair, the Carnegie Steel Company strikes, and the Pullman strike. The courts began issuing orders enjoining workers from forming associations and striking. It was not until the 1930's that unions were recognized as the legal bargaining agents of workers, yellow dog contracts were ruled to be illegal, and court injunctions were forbidden.

This pattern of strikes and violence has left a deep impression on the minds of factory workers. They generally have a deep and abiding distrust of management. Violence still occurs during strikes. To limit the harmful effects of worker-management segmentation, several roles have been developed to rationalize the process of negotiation between these groups: labor mediators and arbitrators, public relations personnel, and personnel managers.

THE LOWER MIDDLE CLASS

The similarities between the members of the upper working class and the lower middle class are so great that many social scientists do not make a class distinction between them. Members of the lower middle class work primarily in offices and small business organizations. They tend to work more with their heads than their hands, although that distinction is far from perfect. Included in this category are the clerks, technicians, the owners of small businesses, and the less successful salesmen. They are white collar workers whose jobs are often just as repetitive and monotonous as the jobs of their blue collar counterparts. Since they earn about the same average income as blue collar workers, their style of life is similar to the latter.

Most of the differences between these categories are matters of degree. The average member of the lower middle class is better educated than his blue collar counterpart. Many more of them than blue collar workers have completed high school and gone on to get specialized training. Secretarial, technical, and data processing schools are some of their more common choices. They put an even greater emphasis on stability and responsibility than the blue collar workers (17). They value home ownership and family-centered activities. Since most of them do not have a college education, their opportunities for mobility are extremely limited. They do recognize the importance of getting an education as a means of getting ahead, and they encourage their children to go even further in school than they did. If they are a little more inclined to participate in voluntary associations than blue collar families, much of the difference is attributable to their higher level of education.

Sources of Segmentation

The members of the lower middle class differ radically from the upper working class in one respect: they identify with the interests and values of the upper middle class. Currently, suspicion, distrust, and hostility between white collar workers and their managers is relatively low. These workers perceive themselves as being a part of management in spite of the obvious similarities between their work and the jobs of blue collar workers. They have been extremely difficult to organize into labor unions—much to the consternation of labor leaders.

It remains to be seen what directions this population will take. As automation of office tasks increases, the white collar worker may realize the similarity between his position and that of the blue collar worker. Should he forsake his identity with management and follow the course of the blue collar worker, the upper middle and upper classes will lose some of their influence. For this reason, social scientists watch organizational trends in the lower middle class very carefully.

THE UPPER MIDDLE CLASS

The upper middle class has traditionally been divided into two sections for purposes of analysis: the old middle class and the new middle class. The old middle class is composed of the old professions—law, medicine, university teaching—and the owners of established, successful, but modest-sized business organizations. The new middle class is composed primarily of the highly skilled managerial and technical personnel in the larger bureaucratic organizations: government, industries, unions, and universities. Not included in the upper middle class are the top executives in the largest of these organizations because a far greater amount of influence is lodged in these roles than is found in the typical upper middle class role. The presidents of General Motors and the A.F.L.-C.I.O. have far more influence in the affairs of American society than a physician, professor, or a lesser executive in their own organizations. Because of their great influence, these executives must be placed in the upper class.

Both the old and the new middle class are very career oriented (17). Great value is placed on a life plan that involves getting a college education and either going into the parent's business or into one of the large bureaucratic organizations and climbing the hierarchy of roles. This class contains the largest proportion of people with five or more years of college. In the upper class, getting four years of college is commonplace, but further education is unnecessary in view of the sustaining power of great family wealth. But access to the upper middle class is based primarily on the possession of unusual skills, which are usually obtained through advanced college education. If we think in terms of training rather than formal education, the training periods of the upper middle class are often exceedingly long. After four or more years of college, the executive trainee has only earned the right to begin training for a career in a large organization. Years of on-the-job training *may* eventually lead to a position of great responsibility in the organization.

Work and Leisure

This has been called an age of increasing leisure. We saw earlier that the blue collar worker is increasingly separating his work role from his other roles. When he punches the timeclock at the end of the day, he tries very hard to put his job out of his mind and to turn to the "important" activities in life. This outlook is not found in the upper middle class. The members of this class generally like their work and they do not separate it from the rest of their lives. Work roles and leisure roles blend and blur; the working day never really ends, and leisure time really has no beginning. If he is oriented in one direction rather than the other, he is work centered and uses leisure activities to support his career. When he learns to play bridge and golf in college, he anticipates that many important contacts and contracts can be made in later years at bridge tables and on golf courses. When he selects a wife, her capacity to implement his career is a very important criterion. When he works on a community fund drive or joins the Rotarians, he is at least as concerned about the effects of these activities on his career as he is with the objectives of the organization itself. He is a regular church attender, but he is no more and perhaps less religious than the members of the working class (18). In all of these activities he is concerned with building and maintaining a network of contacts that will enhance his career.

Life Chances

The upper middle class is the polar opposite of the lower working class in terms of life chances. The members of this class live longer, have fewer lengthy disabling illnesses, have better mental health, and get preferred treatment in the school systems and from law enforcing agencies. In spite of their superior physical health, they visit doctors more frequently and spend more money on health care than members of the lower working class (6). They earn an average annual income in excess of $12,000 per year, of which $2,000 comes from investments in income-producing properties (19). This class owns 65 per cent of the income-producing property in the United States.

Value Systems

There are some similarities and some differences between the value systems of the old and new upper middle classes. Both categories place great emphasis on the importance of work and leading "the good life." They enjoy large homes on large lots in suburban or urban residential areas. Many of them prefer the large, expensive apartments in the centers of our cities because they afford them a minimum of housing responsibilities and a maximum opportunity to enjoy the advantages of city life. Every effort is made to provide for the material well-being of the family. Cars, expensive furniture, clothing, and summer cottages are valued acquisitions.

The upper middle class is the locus of conservatism in our society. The members of the old professions and the owners of the established Main Street enterprises share this outlook. The new middle class places less value on the ethic of individualism than does the old middle class. Its members recognize that their careers depend on their performance in group situations.

The upper middle class, particularly the old class, is very much concerned about their waning influence in the society. At an earlier period in our history, they had a virtual monopoly on the centers of influence in the society. The rise of labor unions, the increasing independence of political leaders, and their lessening ability to control the votes of the lower classes are all sources of this increasing sense of helplessness. Even the ministers in the churches that they attend are less compliant. Being primarily Protestants, they have had to listen to their ministers take increasingly stronger stands on social welfare issues: positions that do not reflect the upper middle class point of view. Many social scientists believe that this feeling of waning influence accounts for the heavy upper middle class involvement in the activities of the Radical Right, but evidence to support this interesting idea is not yet available.

The differences in the value orientation of the old and the new upper middle classes are reflected in the way that they socialize their children (20). The old middle class still trains its children to follow the old individualist ethic. Emphasis is placed on self-reliance, internal control of behavior rather than group control, and self-denial. The child is taught to manage his time, behavior, and money carefully and to develop skills at manipulating other people. The new middle class emphasizes social or group skills. The child is trained to work harmoniously and confidently in group settings. He is taught to accept external controls on his behavior and to accept superiors as men of skill and compassion. In other words, he is trained to assume bureaucratic roles.

THE UPPER CLASS

The upper class has been the least studied of the American social classes. The class contains such a small fraction of the total population (less than one per cent, by the definition we will use here) that it seldom appears in samples of the population. The members also exhibit a natural reluctance to reveal or discuss their private lives; a fact that in itself tells us something about them (17).

The upper class also contains two very different categories of people. At the top is the true upper class whose members inherited their wealth. The lower upper class is composed of the top executives in our largest organizations, who wield great influence in the affairs of our society. These executives achieved their positions primarily because they possess unusual managerial skills. Their average *earned* income is in excess of $30,000, which is greater than that of the upper upper class (19). They earn an additional $20,000 from their investments in income-producing property. While this income is adequate to support their children in an upper middle class style of life, it is not adequate to guarantee that they will be in the upper class too.

This impermanence of status is the fundamental difference between the upper upper class and the lower upper class.

The upper upper class family has usually enjoyed its position for two, three, or more generations. Often the family fortune was created by ownership of an industry or through judicious investments in property and other forms of capital. But through the successive generations, the fortune tends to become more diversified in terms of the types of capital investment. Each generation makes every effort to increase the size and security of the family fortune. The average upper upper class family has $1,000,000 invested in income-producing properties. From this investment it receives $50,000 in dividends. This source of income is supplemented by an average of $15,000 in earned income. In spite of the fact that the upper class constitutes less than one per cent of the population, it controls a quarter of the capital in the society.

The size of the upper upper class investment is usually ample to sustain the family in its position over successive generations. This is the second characteristic that distinguishes the upper upper class from the lower upper class. One generation is inadequate to achieve the higher status position. The style of life of the upper upper class is learned through socialization in that class and, therefore, the top executive cannot hope to emulate it easily. The members of the upper upper class have had a whole series of socializing experiences denied to others (17). They have gone to schools that cater fairly exclusively to their needs. They belong to clubs and other associations that are geared to their way of life and have a well-developed sense of corporateness. They have traveled extensively and have become accustomed to deference from others. All of these socializing experiences set the members of the upper upper class apart from the lower upper class.

There are many milieus in which the members of the upper upper class can interact and develop linkages. Regionally, they are linked through social affairs, participation in charitable activities in their communities, and memberships in the same clubs. Nationally, they are linked through attendance at the same schools, memberships on boards of directors for large corporations, or through national associational activity.

Work and Leisure

Life in the upper class is busy but gracious. Their homes are usually large and they usually have more than one. Servants are permanent employees rather than day workers. Lower upper class leisure follows a pattern a little more like that of the upper middle class, because of the heavy career commitments of top executives. The upper upper class enjoys a diversified range of social activities, ranging from world travel to attending social affairs restricted to the members of their class.

But life is not all leisure for the upper upper class either. Maintenance of the family position usually requires that the members devote considerable time to the family financial interests. If none of the members are capable of maintaining the family position, then the task is given to lawyers and other financial advisors. The schedule of the typical upper class family invariably includes involvement in charitable and other civic activities. Their names are customarily found on the boards of trustees of the most prestigious civic and charitable associations in the community and the society. They also attend meetings of the boards of directors of various corporations. For a generation after the signing of the Constitution, the members of the upper classes sought political offices. Service with the government was seen as an ideal culmination of one's life. Jacksonian democracy ended that role. In the century that followed the Jackson administration, members of the upper class were less inclined to run for political offices. We are probably entering an era of active upper class involvement in political affairs once more. The number of Roosevelts, Harrimans, Kennedys, and Rockefellers and others seeking elective offices may be increasing again. There are three major reasons for this drift. The moral tone of politics has improved, which makes political activity attractive to these people once again. The familiarity of their names increases the likelihood that they can win elections. Their wealth gives them a decided advantage because they can use it to buy the television time and the opinion-polling facilities that have become integral parts of the modern political process.

REFERENCES

1   W. Cohen, W. Haber, and E. Mueller, *The Impact of Unemployment in the 1958 Recession* (Ann Arbor: Survey Research Center, 1960). Prepared for consideration for the Senate Subcommittee on Unemployment.

2   M. Harrington, *The Other America: Poverty in the United States* (New York: The Macmillan Company, 1962).

3   B. Bettleheim and M. Janowitz, *Dynamics of Prejudice* (New York: Harper & Row, Publishers, 1950).

4   H. L. Sheppard, L. A. Ferman, and S. Faber, "Too Old to Work—Too Young to Retire: A Case Study of A Permanent Plant Shutdown," Report to the Special Committee on Unemployment Problems, U.S. Senate, 1960.

5   D. Street and J. C. Leggett, "Economic Deprivation and Extremism: A Study of Unemployed Negroes," *The American Journal of Sociology, 67* (1961), 53-57.

6   K. B. Mayer, *Class and Society,* rev. ed. (New York: Random House, 1962).

7   A. B. Hollingshead and F. C. Redlich, *Social Class and Mental Illness: A Community Study* (New York: John Wiley & Sons, Inc., 1958).

8   U.S. Department of Commerce, Bureau of the Census, *Statistical Abstract of The United States: 1963,* 84th ed., p. 120.

9   N. Rogoff, "Local Social Structure and Educational Selection," in *Education, Economy, and Society,* A. H. Halsey, J. Floud, and C. A. Anderson, eds. (New York: Free Press of Glencoe, Inc., 1961).

10   A. B. Hollingshead, *Elmtown's Youth* (New York: John Wiley & Sons, Inc., 1949).

11   St. C. Drake and H. R. Cayton, *Black Metropolis* (New York: Harcourt, Brace, and World, Inc., 1945).

12   M. Axelrod, "Urban Structure and Social Participation," *American Sociological Review, 21* (1956), 13-18.

13   C. R. Walker and R. H. Guest, *The Man on the Assembly Line* (Cambridge: Harvard University Press, 1952).

14   O. Collins, M. Dalton, and D. Roy, "Restriction of Output and Social Cleavage in Industry," *Applied Anthropology, 5* (1946), 1-14.

15   P. Mott, F. Mann, Q. McLoughlin, and D. Warwick, *Shift Work: Social, Psychological, and Physical Consequences* (Ann Arbor: University of Michigan Press, 1965).

16   J. G. Rayback, *A History of American Labor* (New York: The Macmillan Company, 1961).

17   J. A. Kahl, *The American Class Structure* (New York: Holt, Rinehart & Winston, Inc., 1961).

18 G. Lenski, "The Sociology of Religion in the United States: A Review of Theoretically Oriented Research," *Social Compass, 9* (1962), 307-37.

19 J. C. Bowen, "Some Aspects of Transfer Taxation in the United States" (Unpublished doctoral dissertation, The University of Michigan, 1958).

20 D. R. Miller and G. E. Swanson, *The Changing American Parent* (New York: John Wiley & Sons, Inc., 1958).

14 religion in american society

How religious are Americans? Virtually all of them profess to believe in the existence of God; only 5 per cent of the population denies this belief (1). Seventy per cent of the adult population are members of churches, and that figure has been increasing steadily (2). Over half of the adults in our society also claim that they attend church at least once a month, and that percentage is rising each decade (3). Sunday school enrollment is increasing more rapidly than the proportion of children in our society (3). Church and synagogue construction also proceeds at a dramatic rate; 150 to 200 Roman Catholic churches are constructed each year, and comparable statistics are reported by the Protestant and the Jewish church leaders (4). This increase in church construction is spurred by the shift of the population from urban to suburban areas and the growing interest in *organized* religion in our society.

Participation in organized religion has not always been so popular in our society. Only a very small percentage of the population were members of colonial churches (5)—for several reasons. First, many leaders of colonial churches were quick to expel some of their members and to deny the right of membership to others, if they felt that the situation warranted such action. Modern churches take the opposite approach to their members, demanding very little of them, and seldom expelling them from membership. Second, Catholics, Quakers, and even Baptists could not be reported as church members in many of the colonies because the laws forbade the practice of those religions. Third, our colonial cultures contained a heavy element of anticlericism and scientific rationalism. The excesses of established state religions in various countries of Europe had alienated many of the colonists. Others were influenced by the rationalist movement in France, which proclaimed that science and not religion was the route to knowledge of man and the universe. Atheism, or, at best, deism, was probably more prevalent during this period than any other in our history. Finally, the westward expansion of the population was more rapid than the pace of church construction. For these reasons, only one century ago less than 10 per cent of our population were listed as church members; since that time the figure has risen steadily (2).

The figures that show this increased popularity in organized religion may overstate the case somewhat (4). Movement from one part of the country to another is more prevalent today than it was a century ago. Some people are undoubtedly counted twice: once at their old place of residence and again in their new community. There may also be a greater tendency to count children in with the adult members of the church today than there was a few generations ago.

Despite these qualifications, the data undoubtedly do reflect an increasing inclination on the part of Americans to participate in organized religious activities. There are several reasons for this trend. First, contemporary organized religion is easier religion than that of the colonial period; it makes fewer demands for qualitative participation in church affairs. All-day services and other demanding duties are no longer with us. Religious training for church membership has become a relatively brief and undemanding affair. Attendance at services and participation in other church activities is voluntary. Second, the automobile and bus have made churches more accessible now than they were in colonial times. Third, church activities have become very diversified, appealing to the interests of a broader segment of the population. Social, intellectual, recreational, and welfare activities have been formalized into a series of clubs within each church. Fourth, since church membership is least prevalent in the lower working class, the churches have undoubtedly profited from the rising level of education of the population. These and other forces have contributed to making religion a part of the American way of life. In the value system of the society, being a good American involves belonging to a church (3).

The increasing popularity of religion has some elements of a Pyrrhic victory, because it has been accompanied by another trend: the increasing secularization of life. In hunting and gathering and agrarian societies, religion was not restricted to a single role or a single hour one day each week. It pervaded all of a person's roles; it was a part of all his activities. The eminent sociologist Emile Durkheim observed that a major theme in man's history has been the narrowing role that religion plays in his life (6). Behavior has become compartmentalized into religious versus other activities. Business or just plain human relations no longer need be guided by religious precepts. Indeed, religious precepts may be seen as a handicap to successful competition.

Within the church the emphasis may have shifted from theological matters to social activities. The potential of church organizations as social institutions increases their appeal to migrating Americans. Church leaders have capitalized on this fact and developed many programs to accommodate new residents in our communities. Lack of concern for theological matters is evidenced by an increasing willingness on the part of church members to blur denominational lines. In the new suburbs the members may be less concerned about denominational differences than they are about the types of programs that the church offers (7). Will Herberg (3) sums up these trends with the observation that Americans are becoming more secular at the same time that they are becoming more religious.

RELIGION AND THE ECONOMY IN AMERICAN SOCIETY

While Roman Catholics are the largest single religious group in American society, the societal value system is largely a Protestant one. This fact can be traced to the origins of Protestantism during the commercial revival in Europe. Social scientists argue over which came first, Protestantism or capitalism (8). This question has little relevance for us here; it is sufficient to note only that the two movements did gravitate toward each other. The merchants who were also Roman Catholics experienced role conflict. Their economic activities were built on an edifice of profit: a practice that Catholic norms condemned. They were a willing audience for the new Protestant theologians who were migrating to the new commercial centers. The new religious doctrines were not opposed to the worldliness of the merchant class. They had no norms against profit or progress. They preached a doctrine of individualism, which in its most extreme form said that every individual was his own church. They stressed the importance of having a "calling": a requirement that was harmonious with the business orientations of the merchants (9). These doctrines provided a rationalization for cutting away from feudal social ties that impeded commercial activities.

The new religions did not insist that salvation could be obtained only if the person had faith and did good works: faith was enough. This tenet had the effect of divorcing religion from the day-to-day activities of the businessman; if he acted immorally as a businessman, his salvation was not affected. This doctrine found its most extreme form in Calvinism, which said that it really didn't matter what you did on earth—you were either elected for salvation or you were not. This doctrine raised an interesting question in the minds of the merchants: how were they to know whether they were elected for salvation? Still not free of the medieval mentality, they looked for signs that would give portents of their fate. What sign could be more reasonable for indicating election than success in worldly affairs? The idea that the people most likely to be saved were those who were most successful on earth gained wide acceptance among the fledgling capitalists (9). The twin motives of profit and salvation were combined to form a powerful incentive for the new class.

This alliance of capitalism with Protestantism created a cultural tradition that is a major part of the American way of life. In the latter part of the nineteenth century these combined themes were expanded, amplified, and promulgated in all parts of the society. It was virtuous to work hard; it did not matter what your work was so long as you did it well.

If these themes were not adequate, they were combined with scientific darwinism to achieve a new and more powerful synthesis. Successful people were those most fit to survive; less successful people should know their place in life and not interfere with the affairs of the fit. This new synthesis, called *social darwinism*, provided a powerful legitimating myth for societies with private economies.

The alliance of the Protestant churches with capitalism has taken many forms. The pulpit and the religious journal have been used to protect the value system of business. The following passage from an essay by Henry Ward Beecher is illustrative of this relationship.

It is said that a dollar a day is not enough for a wife and five or six children. No, not if the man smokes or drinks beer. It is not enough if they are to live as he would be glad to have them live. It is not enough to enable them to live as perhaps they would have a right to live in prosperous times. But is not a dollar a day enough to buy bread with? Water costs nothing; and a man who cannot live on bread and water is not fit to live. What is the use of civilization that simply makes men incompetent to live under the conditions which exist . . . [10]

In his study of a mill town during a strike, Liston Pope (11) shows that the Protestant church leaders in the community took the side of the mill owners against the strikers. The portrayal of Christ as an astute businessman in the book *The Man Nobody Knows* by Bruce Barton (12) shows how far this alliance has developed. Some of the Protestant *sects* are based on an integral association with capitalism. Advice is given by the sect leaders on investments and business decisions, and prayers are offered for success in business ventures.

Although the above theme has been central in the development of Protestantism and capitalism in America, there have been many dissenting voices. The argument between fundamentalists and modernists has centered on the issue of worldliness. The tenets of national church organizations have often differed from what was actually advocated in the pulpits of the local churches. If the national organization advocated universal brotherhood as a part of the Christian way of life, the issue might be stifled in one local church with an upper middle class or southern white clientele and supported in another church with a less hostile congregation. Beginning in the middle third of the present century, many Protestant churches took a more independent view of social problems, disregarding the beliefs of many of the members. They returned to the older themes of universal brotherhood, advocating equality for Negroes and the right of workers to organize and bargain collectively. Welfare programs also found increasing support from Protestant religious leaders. The reasons for this shift are derived from the larger culture. As we saw earlier, the philosophy of welfarism and collectivism is winning general acceptance in the population. Since this is a wealthy society, many ministers have concluded that the demands of less privileged groups will not impoverish business organizations or their leaders.

RELIGION AND GOVERNMENT IN AMERICAN SOCIETY

In the colonial period, several of the colonies had state religions, and the practice of other religions was restricted if not forbidden. At the time of the Constitutional Convention there were many advocates of a state religion for the new nation that was being created. But since they could not agree on which religion should be the state religion or whether they ought to have one, the writers of the Constitution decided instead to separate church and state.

The separation has been more theoretical than real. The government maintains service chaplains and provides some forms of aid to sectarian schools as well as public ones. Acting as a pressure group, religious leaders have had considerable effects on the laws of our society. Blue laws that forbid business activity on Sunday are a product of the efforts of ministers. Religious identification is a very important factor in voting behavior; a majority of the Catholics and Jews in our society vote for Democratic Party candidates, while Protestants are more likely to prefer those of the Republican Party (13). This fact has been a very powerful factor in the calculations of politicians, both during elections and during debates and votes on legislation.

PROTESTANTS, CATHOLICS, AND JEWS: THE MAJOR AMERICAN RELIGIONS

Two out of every three adults in our society claim to be Protestants, another quarter are members of the Roman Catholic Church, and three out of every hundred are Jews (14). Despite the seeming numerical superiority of the Protestants, their influence in the society is reduced by denominationalism and the spatial location of their membership. There is only one Roman Catholic Church, but the Protestants are divided among the Baptists, Methodists, Lutherans, Presbyterians, and many other groups. And even these major groupings are divided into a myriad of denominations (15). There are 27 Baptist denominations, including the Southern Baptist Church, which is the fastest growing religious group in America. There are 21 Methodist, 17 Lutheran, and 10 Presbyterian denominations. Jews are divided into Orthodox, Conservative, and Reformed patterns of religious observance. Ordinarily a temple or synagogue is organized to serve only one of these populations.

Spatial Distribution

Jews are the most urban of the major American religious groups (4). Virtually all of them live in urban areas. Catholics are also urban dwellers primarily. About two out of every five Protestants live in the rural parts of our society. This clustering has some interesting effects on the relative strengths of the three religions. In most of the major urban centers, the Catholics are the majority. For this reason Catholics have been able to play a very influential role in the political and moral affairs of the cities. Protestants have displayed a similar domination of rural affairs.

Church Attendance

Another reason why Catholic influence is greater than its numbers would seem to merit is the allegiance the Church claims from its members. In a study of the major religious groups in Detroit, Gerhard Lenski found that seven out of every ten Catholics reported that they went to Mass once a week, compared to three out of every ten Protestants who claimed that they went to church once a week (16). He also found that only 12 per cent of the Jews interviewed reported that they went to their synagogue each week. Apparently, even when a Catholic marries someone of another faith, he continues to attend the Catholic Church.

Religion and Social Class

There is a very strong relationship between a person's social class and his religious preference. Jews are a predominantly middle class religious group. Lenski found that eight out of every ten Jews interviewed in Detroit were in the middle class. Herberg says that the figure is nearer to 55 per cent for the entire society (3). Catholicism is primarily a working class religion, with at least six out of every ten members being in that position. The white Protestants are distributed across all of the classes.

Since denominational differences are secondary to class considerations among Protestants, they tend to select churches that have members from their social class. Very few Protestant churches have a cross section of the population within a single congregation (4). With some local exceptions, the upper class and the upper middle class are found in the Episcopal, Unitarian, and Congregational churches. The Presbyterian, Christian Science, and Methodist churches and the various Friends societies have memberships from the intermediate class levels. The Baptists are in a lower position in terms of the social class of the memberships, because many Negroes belong to Baptist denominations. Pentacostal, Holiness, and Jehovah's Witnesses have a predominantly working class membership. The sects—small, less formal, and perhaps less permanent religious organizations—appeal to working class people primarily.

Even within the Roman Catholic Church there are marked social class differences from one church organization to another because of the class composition of neighborhoods and the spatial location of the churches. If the church is located in an upper middle class neighborhood, it will have a predominantly upper middle class membership. This same pattern applies to Jewish synagogues. The picture that emerges from all of the data is that social class is a very important factor in the organization of religion. Congregations do not have mixed memberships. For this reason, religious organizations do not serve to decrease the segmentation that exists among the various social classes.

The norms of each of the major religions contribute to the class differences among them. The Jewish subculture places great emphasis on getting an education and electing one of the more skilled professions such as medicine, law, or teaching. Among the three religious groups, Jews get the best educations, Protestants are next, and Catholics last. Lenski says that Protestants place more moral emphasis than Catholics do on the attainment of advanced education and the more skilled occupations because of the survival of the Protestants-capitalist ethic (16). The Protestants still value high educational attainment, hard work, and success. For these reasons, plus the white Protestant domination of the major business organizations, white Protestant males rise farther in the class system than do Catholics.

RELIGION AS A SEGMENTING INFLUENCE

One of the most extreme examples of segmentation on the basis of religion is provided by Holland. There are three major "religions": Catholicism, Protestantism (two major types), and secularism (including socialists and atheists). The Dutch refer to these religious groupings as the "pillars" (*verzuiling*) that support their society. Religion is the basis for selecting virtually every associational membership. Instead of one cheesemakers' association there are three: Catholic, Protestant, and secular cheesemakers' associations. It is possible, therefore, that the adherent to any one of these religious persuasions will never encounter someone of a different persuasion in an associational setting. Furthermore, Catholics are expected to marry Catholics, and the other groups have the same expectations.

Our own society has not reached this extreme, but it is more polarized on the basis of religion than might be imagined. Religion is a basis for choosing marriage partners, friends, and associational memberships. Let us look at the role of religion in each of these groups in more detail. Marriage to a person of the same religion has declined since 1870, but it is still very high (3). The Jews are the most likely religious group to marry someone of the same faith; data from a 1957 study done by the Bureau of the Census show that in 93 per cent of the marriages where one partner was a Jew, the other was also. Protestants are almost as likely to marry other Protestants; in 91 per cent of the marriages where one partner was a Protestant, the other was also. Roman Catholics are the most likely to marry outside their religion; in only 79 per cent of the marriages where one partner was a Catholic, the other was also. The more frequent out-marriage of Catholics is probably related to the degree of availability of Catholic partners. If Catholics are living in a Catholic milieu, they will marry other Catholics, but if they live in a Protestant milieu, they are more likely to marry Protestants. Even if people marry outside their religion, they report that it is wiser to marry someone of the same religion (16). If the marriage is mixed, one of the partners is likely to convert to the religion of the other: a tendency that increases the religious homogeneity of group memberships.

The chances are better than three out of four that a person's close relatives will be of the same religion (16). Religion is also an important factor in the formation of friendships. In the 1957 study by the Bureau of the Census, each of the 35,000 persons interviewed was asked to name his three best friends. They were then asked to give the religious preference of each of these friends. Seventy-eight per cent of the Jews interviewed said that all three of their best friends were also Jewish; 49 per cent of the Protestants and Catholics reported that all three of their best friends shared their religious preference. The study of religion in Detroit produced essentially the same findings (16). These findings are not too surprising when we take into account the tendency of people to live in neighborhoods with other people of the same religion. Jews have been forced to live in ghettoes, and Catholics have often been excluded from upper middle class Protestant neighborhoods. One simple device for excluding Catholics and Jews from a neighborhood is to refuse their church leaders a permit to build a church or synagogue in that neighborhood.

Segmentation by religion also applies to associational memberships. The early Protestant monopoly of many associations such as country clubs, businessmen's clubs, and other civic associations has been used to exclude Catholics and Jews. Partly as a result of this type of discrimination and partly because of the communal orientation of Catholic and Jewish leaders, parallel Jewish and Catholic organizations have been formed. There are Jewish and Catholic veterans' organizations, boys' clubs and men's clubs, associations for writers, artists, and scientists.

The Knights of Columbus and other fraternal organizations provide Catholic parallels to Protestant fraternal orders. All three religious groups have elaborate welfare agencies that serve the members of their own religious groups. Catholic, Jewish, and Protestant fraternities are found on many college campuses. The Catholics, of course, maintain their own school system.

There is also evidence that occupations exhibit a checkerboard pattern, with some occupations being dominated by one or another of the religious groups. This pattern arose primarily because Protestants have discriminated against Jews and Catholics in the occupations that they dominate. Consequently, the Jews and Catholics have been forced into newer and sometimes less desirable occupations. Police and fire protection agencies of the larger cities have more than their proportional share of Catholics. Jews got into the entertainment industry early and have enjoyed some success in it, but both they and the Catholics are generally underrepresented in the older business corporations.

On the basis of this evidence, we may not have reached the extreme found in Dutch society, but we are not really far removed from it. It is quite likely that all of a person's primary contacts and many of his secondary ones are with persons of the same religion.

THE SOURCES AND CONSEQUENCES
OF SEGMENTATION

We must look back quite far in American history to find the sources of religious segmentation in our society. American religious conflict has its historical roots in medieval Europe (17). Following the Protestant Reformation, Catholics indulged in a wave of persecution seeking to stamp out the heretical faiths. Of the many terrifying events that occurred during that period, perhaps one did more to engender anti-Catholic sentiment than all the others. In 1572, tens of thousands of Protestants were massacred in France in little more than one day. That event is referred to as the St. Bartholomew's Day Massacre, and it was followed by a wave of revulsion in the Protestant countries. In England anti-Catholic laws were passed, and these laws were carried over to colonial America. The practice of Catholicism was proscribed in all but three of the colonies. By 1790, Catholics were permitted to vote in only three of the states.

The Jews were not the objects of discrimination during this period. It is estimated that there were only 10,000 to 15,000 of them in the country at this time, and most of them were living in New York (4).

During the period immediately after the signing of the Constitution, anti-Catholic activity was less common. But when the migrations of the Irish and other predominantly Catholic nationality groups began, the tempo of discrimination and violence rose. Novels were published that purported to expose the depraved activities in convents and seminaries. Badly printed excerpts from some of these novels can still be obtained in some areas in our society. By 1830, destroying convents, burning churches, and religious rioting had become more frequent. In 1854 on "Bloody Monday" in Louisville, Kentucky, 100 Catholics were killed by rioters, and scores of their homes were burned (3).

The influx of immigrants during the mid-eighteenth century gave rise to nativist movements in the United States. In 1852, the most famous of these organizations, the Know-Nothing Party, was formed. The Know-Nothing Party was a secret organization whose members advocated the expulsion of foreigners. Only Anglo-Saxon Protestant immigrants were acceptable to them. The Know-Nothing ward leaders were selected for their unusual physical strength, because they regularly met the arriving immigrants, beat them up, and urged them to return to their "own country." The popularity of this group is attested to by the election results of that period. In 1854 they elected governors in 9 states, 62 United States Senators, and 104 of the 234 members of the House of Representatives (17). They were unable to retain their identity as a separate party, however, and their members joined the two major parties that we have today.

Anti-Semitism was still not so prevalent as it is today, but by the last quarter of the eighteenth century it was beginning to crystallize. In 1877, a wealthy Jew was denied permission to register at a summer resort. The incident was so unusual that it was reported in the newspapers. Americans rallied to the side of the Jew, but the event served to communicate the principle of exclusion to other hotels, clubs, and resorts.

In the early part of the present century a scientific and pseudo-scientific literature developed that "demonstrated" the superiority of Anglo-Saxons over all other racial groups. In the face of mounting migration to the United States of people from eastern and southern Europe, these "findings" provided the needed rationalizations for laws that established immigration quotas for each society of origin. The culture became infused with racialist theories that catalyzed the development of new anti-Semitic, anti-Catholic, and anti-foreigner organizations. After World War I the Ku Klux Klan achieved great influence, and its activities were not restricted to the South. Anti-Semitism became more overt. Gerald L. K. Smith, Father Coughlin, and many others claimed huge followings in the population who supported their anti-Semitic views. By 1939 there were about 800 pro-Nazi and anti-Semitic organizations in the United States.

Contemporary Sources of Conflict

Since World War II, overt violence and anti-Semitic and anti-Catholic activity has subsided. This change is not due to a relaxation of religious tensions; the religious war has simply gone underground. The sources of conflict are almost the same today that they were during the colonial period. Although they are a majority, Protestants are developing a fear of becoming a minority (3). Many Protestants believe that "The Catholics are having large numbers of children simply to hasten the day when they can take over the society and when that happens they will repress Protestantism just as they do it today in Spain." Protestants fear the antidemocratic tendencies in the Catholic Church. They don't like the idea of extending federal aid to parochial schools. They oppose the Catholic views on divorce laws, birth control, and sex education. Rural Protestants particularly dislike the Catholic positions on gambling and drinking.

All of these issues are capable of segmenting the population whenever they become overt political issues. Kenneth Underwood (18) has described the process of religious segmentation in the case of a New England community. An advocate of birth control had been invited to the community to speak on that subject. The Catholic leaders used their influence to prevent her from speaking. Their efforts were successful, but, as a result of the incident, the community was segmented into two hostile religious camps. The event confirmed for the Protestants all of their old beliefs about Catholics, particularly their fears about the antidemocratic tendencies of the Catholic Church.

Other similar incidents could be recounted, but the point is that each issue simply converts latent hostility into overt conflict. There is probably some truth to the fears of Protestants, but only *some* truth. On the basis of our rules of increasing size, it is doubtful that the Catholic Church is a monolithic structure. Diverse viewpoints are being debated within that religious community: some Catholics do espouse a conservative and essentially antidemocratic point of view, but others advocate that the Church must be normatively more in harmony with American society. We must also expect on the basis of our earlier rules that each religion is going to be greatly affected by the norms of the larger society in which it is located. Catholicism has been profoundly influenced by the American way of life (3).

The conflict goes on, and the Catholics have their own axes to grind.

They are profoundly disturbed by the generations of discrimination against them by the Protestants. They are on the opposite side of the issues mentioned earlier. They want aid extended to parochial schools, and they oppose birth control and sex education. They conflict with Protestants over many problems of childbirth and other medical practices. These differences are purely religious in nature—the Catholics do not believe that doctors or any one else should interfere with divine processes. But even these views are being eroded by the conditions of life in postmedieval societies. Today Catholics have a generally favorable view of Protestants. They believe that Protestants are just as fair and honest as other Catholics, but the Protestants do not reciprocate this view (16). The Jews are greater objects of discrimination and segmentation than are the Catholics, for three major reasons (4). First, the role of the Jew in medieval society has left a legacy of stigma. He was an outsider who made a living by violating the norms of medieval societies. Second, the Jews were the people who killed Christ. Third, many American Jews came to this country from the eastern part of Europe. Their swarthiness, the sharpness of their features, and their behavioral mannerisms were foreign to Americans. Americans were and still are socialized to adopt a slim-lipped, controlled, and generally unemotive demeanor in their secondary relationships. The immigrant Jew talked excitedly, waved his arms as he spoke, and insisted on standing within one foot of the face of his auditor. These overt behaviors were sufficient to cool the interest of Anglo-Saxon Christians in assimilating the Jews into their culture.

The Jews have reported that the Catholics, not the Protestants, are their worst oppressors. This attitude is probably derived from greater contact between Jews and Catholics in the cities than between Jews and Protestants. The numerical advantage of the Catholics has undoubtedly been used to prevent the Jews from gaining access to some political positions and influencing other community affairs.

SUMMARY AND CONCLUSIONS

In his book, *Protestant-Catholic-Jew*, Will Herberg says that we are becoming a society composed of three segmented religious communities (3). They are not merely associational memberships; they are each a way of life; they are the basis for choosing a marriage partner, friends, and associations. Herberg thought that these ties would decline in importance among second generation Jews and Catholics as these people sought to become assimilated into American culture. The third generation would return to the church of their grandparents, secure in their status as Americans first, Jews or Catholics second. Thus the potential for conflict would be reduced because the members of these religious organizations would share a primary commitment to the American way of life.

Lenski's evidence for Detroit suggests very strongly that the second generation was no less involved in religious affairs than the first or the third (16). The communal religious life was handed down unbroken through three generations. Given this fact plus all of the evidence on the importance of religion in choosing group memberships, we conclude that religion is probably second only to class and perhaps race as a segmenting influence in our society.

In Chapter 3 we saw that segmentation ordinarily leads to further segmentation: a vicious cycle is created. If subgroups are somewhat segmented from each other and potentially disruptive issues exist among them, then segmentation is likely to increase. Because they are segmented initially, the members of each group have little opportunity to communicate with each other, to understand each other better, and to resolve mutual problems. For this reason, problems may not get solved. Instead, they continue to serve as sources of aggravation, hostility, and lessening contact.

Our religious segmentation is not so complete as it is in Holland, but barring some unusual event, there is no reason to predict a lessening of tension among the various religious groups (3, 16). Divisive issues are continually arising to prevent any immediate resolution of the conflict.

As a segmenting influence, religion is not so powerful as social class differences. We have seen that religious differences are in many ways also social class differences. But even within each religion, social class segments the members. Few churches have a membership that crosscuts social classes. Therefore, within each of the religious segments there are further segments. The combination of social class and religious difference is one of the most fundamental of the influences that segment American society—both vertically and horizontally.

REFERENCES

1   L. Rosten, ed., *A Guide to the Religions of America* (New York: Simon and Schuster, Inc., 1955).

2   B. Y. Landis, ed., *Yearbook of American Churches for 1961* (New York: National Council of Churches of Christ in the U.S.A., 1960), pp. 278-82.

3   W. Herberg, *Protestant-Catholic-Jew* (Garden City: Doubleday & Company, Inc., 1955).

4   D. O. Moberg, *The Church as a Social Institution* (Englewood Cliffs, N.J.: Prentice-Hall, Inc., 1962).

5   W. W. Sweet, *The Story of Religion in American Society* (New York: Harper & Row, Publishers, 1950).

6   E. Durkheim, *The Division of Labor in Society*, George Simpson, trans. (New York: Free Press of Glencoe, Inc., 1947).

7   R. D. Lambert, "Current Trends in Religion—A Summary," *Annals of the American Academy of Political and Social Science, 332* (1960), 154.

8   J. M. Yinger, *Religion, Society and the Individual: An Introduction to the Sociology of Religion* (New York: The Macmillan Company, 1957).

9   M. Weber, *The Protestant Ethic and the Spirit of Capitalism,* T. Parsons, trans. (London: George Allen & Unwin, 1930).

10 H. W. Beecher, *Christian Union*, August, 1877, quoted in Yinger, *Religion, Society, and the Individual,* p. 219.

11 L. Pope, *Millhands and Preachers* (New Haven: Yale University Press, 1942).

12 B. Barton, *The Man Nobody Knows* (Indianapolis: The Bobbs-Merrill Company, 1924).

13 A. Campbell, G. Gurin, and W. E. Miller, *The Voter Dedecides* (New York: Harper & Row, Publishers, 1952).

14 Bureau of the Census, "Religion Reported by the Civilian Population of the United States: March, 1957," *Current Population Reports: Population Characteristics,* Series P-20, No. 79, 1958.

15 Landis, *Yearbook of American Churches for 1961,* pp. 271-72.

16 G. Lenski, *The Religious Factor: A Sociological Study of Religion's Impact on Politics, Economics, and Family Life* (Garden City: Doubleday & Company, Inc., 1961).

17 G. Myers, *A History of Bigotry in the United States* (New York: Random House, 1943).

18 K. Underwood, *Protestant and Catholic* (Boston: Beacon Press, Inc., 1961).

race and nationality

The first large group of immigrants to arrive in the United States from areas other than northwestern Europe were Africans. The influx of Negroes was greatest in the seventeenth and eighteenth centuries, but it continued until the importation of slaves was abolished under the new Constitution. Between 1820 and 1920 millions of migrants entered this country from all parts of the world. Some of them were brought to this country by private companies to supply the manpower needed for our rapidly expanding industrial economy, but most of them left Europe because of droughts, the threat of starvation, or persecution. Both before and after World War I legislation was passed that set severe limits on the number and types of immigrants who would be permitted to enter our country. By these means the tide of immigration was effectively stemmed. But a new form of migration replaced the old one. World War I created intense needs for manpower in the industrial centers of the North. Attracted by the wages and the comparative freedom of the North, many Negroes migrated into the urban centers in search of work and a new life. That migration is still going on.

The discussion in this chapter will focus primarily on Negro-white segmentation. Segmentation between the old Anglo-Saxon immigrants and the newer immigrants from southern and eastern Europe is largely historical and is slowly disappearing (1). Much of the segmentation between the old and the new immigrants was voluntary anyway. Japanese, Chinese, Latvians, and many other nationality groups simply preferred to live with other people of the same nationality regardless of whether they were discriminated against. This fact accounts for much of the remaining clustering still found among certain nationality groups in our society.

With the exception of the Negro, it has been shown that nationality groups are assimilated into the mainstream of American life when their average education, income, and occupational choices approximate those of the older Anglo-Saxon immigrants (1). Residential segregation of the Polish and Italians has declined greatly since their arrival in this country (2). Even the Japanese population of San Francisco is gradually dispersing within the white population of that city (3). The Puerto Ricans are the most recent migrants to the United States, and despite the fact that their average income and education is lower than that of the Negroes, they are already being assimilated into the population to a greater degree than the Negroes. For these reasons, our major focus in this chapter will be Negro-white segmentation.

THE FACTS OF SEGMENTATION

Residential Segmentation

Some communities do not permit Negroes and certain other groups to settle within their boundaries. The satellite communities that surround our major urban centers often have these proscriptions. Many of the residents of these smaller communities moved from the cities to escape contact with minority groups; to maintain the racial homogeneity of their suburban communities they use a variety of formal and informal devices. One of the most elaborate exclusion systems developed was used in Grosse Pointe, Michigan (4). The realtors developed a point system; in order to live in the more exclusive residential areas of that community, it was necessary to score a specified quota of points. A higher point total was required for people of southern and eastern European extraction. Negroes and Puerto Ricans were excluded altogether. Points were given if the applicant was dressed conservatively and was not swarthy. As a result of these highly effective exclusion systems, only 5 per cent of the population of our suburbs is nonwhite. If we remove from this calculation all of the Negro domestics who live in the suburban homes of their employers and the Negroes who live in segregated suburbs, the 5 per cent figure would be greatly reduced.

A less covert struggle to maintain segregation occurs within the central cities themselves. Negroes began moving into the cities of the North in 1917 and thereafter. As with earlier European migrations, the Negroes were encouraged by recruiters from the industrial organizations of the North to migrate to the cities and work in the factories. The war in Europe had created a sudden increase in the demand for workers that could not be met with the available labor supply in the North. When they arrived in the Northern cities, Negroes settled in the tenement districts in the centers of the cities. The owners of the dwellings in these areas prospered by subdividing old houses into smaller units and charging high rents for the smaller rooms. If the subdivision of the housing units was not sufficient to increase the population density of the neighborhoods, the rents were. Families were often forced to live together and pool their money in order to pay the rents demanded (5).

Since 1940, the migration of Negroes from the South into the central areas of our largest cities has continued unabated. This migration creates great pressure to expand the boundaries of the Negro ghettoes into the white neighborhoods. As the Negroes move outward from the centers of the cities, the white exodus begins. Fearing a loss of property values and contact with this disliked minority, the whites sell their homes and move to all-white neighborhoods further from the center of the city. Their property values may decline, but the loss is a function of their actions and the facts of racial discrimination. When so many houses in a neighborhood go on sale at once, the supply exceeds the customary demand and the price must go down. Furthermore, the market for the houses is almost exclusively a Negro market, since very few whites are willing to move into a neighborhood that has Negro residents.

Many organizations operate to maintain residential segregation. Realtors generally refuse to show Negroes homes in all-white neighborhoods. To do so is often contrary to their own biases and would very likely result in punitive action by the board of realtors. Even if a Negro is able to buy a home in an all-white neighborhood, he still may not be able to get a loan from a bank to purchase it. Aside from pure and simple discrimination, the bank often cannot make the loan because of certain banking regulations. Many Negro families can earn enough money to make a down payment on a house only if the wife works. But banks cannot include the wife's earnings in their calculations of a person's ability to meet the payments because of Federal Housing Administration or private bank rules (6). Although such a rule makes economic sense, it affects Negroes more than whites. For these reasons residential segregation of Negroes has been extremely high and essentially unchanged over the last few decades.

With some variations, there is a common pattern of events that results in the conversion of a neighborhood from all-white to Negro. The harbingers of neighborhood change are the working class whites, Jews, Poles, and other ethnic and nationality aggregates of people who are themselves trying to keep ahead of the Negro outward expansion. They can buy a house in an all-white neighborhood, especially if the residents of that neighborhood are anticipating that the composition will change eventually anyway. The Negroes can buy an occasional home in these rapidly changing neighborhoods more readily than they could in the original all-white neighborhood. The initial entry of a Negro family into a white neighborhood is called "blockbusting"; one family buys a home in the neighborhod and then rides out the storm of protest. Some of the other families immediately put their own houses on the market, but many of the more liberal white families decide to stick it out so long as the neighborhood does not have a majority of Negroes in it. But usually a tipping point is reached where the proportion of Negroes in the neighborhood is so great that the remaining whites want to move out. Some of the less scrupulous realtors in the area will use any of a number of strategies to hasten the "tipping" of a neighborhood in anticipation of making considerable money in the resale of the houses. As a result of this process, black belts are created in the centers of our cities. In 1960, the Negro populations of Baltimore, Cleveland, Detroit, Philadelphia, and St. Louis exceeded 25 per cent of the total population of those communities. Negroes are in a majority in Washington, D.C. By 1970 it is estimated that a third of the population of Chicago will be Negro, and 45 per cent of the population of Manhattan will be Negro and Puerto Rican (5). It is estimated that in thirty years, Negroes will comprise 25 to 50 per cent of the population in ten of our fourteen largest central cities (5).

This concentration of the Negroes in our urban areas creates an optical illusion. When whites are asked if the Negro population in the

United States is increasing, they respond that it is. The popular belief is that the Negro birth rate is so high that their proportion in our population is growing rapidly. Actually, the proportion of Negroes in our population has declined since 1790 from 19 to 10 per cent (7). The Negro birth rate is higher, but so are the infant mortality rate and the maternal mortality rate. The resulting growth in Negro population just barely equals the white immigration to this country from other countries. The optical illusion is created because of the migration of Negroes to our largest urban areas.

The creation of these black belts constitutes a major social problem. Cities are required to spend increasing sums of money on a variety of projects. But they face the prospect of diminishing tax receipts, because the central cities are inhabited by low income Negroes and whites, and the higher income groups are moving to the suburbs.

The vanguard of Negroes moving outward from the urban centers is moving into neighborhoods populated largely by working class whites. Contact with upper middle class whites is less common because the latter tend to leave the area well in advance of the Negro movement. Since aggressive behavior is a more common solution to problems among members of the working class than it is in the middle class, the potential for violence in the transition neighborhoods is great (5).

Occupational Segmentation

Although virtually all nationality and all other racial groups are successful in gaining access to the white collar occupations, Negro progress has been very slow. Six per cent of the Negro population, compared to 13 per cent of the white population, are in professional, technical, and kindred occupations (8). But that census category included athletes, dancers, entertainers, and technicians: occupations that do not have even a vague resemblance to the work of the old professions. If these categories of persons were removed from the tabulations, the Negro percentage would be lowered more than the white percentage.

Sixty-four per cent of the Negro population are in semiskilled or unskilled occupations, as compared with 35 per cent of the white population (8). Negroes are the service workers in our society. They are janitors, redcaps, shoe shiners, yard workers, and housecleaners. Their low levels of education account for much of this difference, but even that characteristic is a product of discrimination. Negro schools in the South are poorer than the white schools in the South, although that situation is improving in many areas. Very few of the graduates of Negro colleges could compete successfully in white universities and colleges. But even if schools were available, the Negro traditionally has not been inclined to take advantage of them. Centuries of slavery and discrimination have instilled in him the belief that getting an education is a waste of his time because it will not improve his opportunities to get a job that is commensurate with his training. Census data show that this attitude is reasonable, because when whites and Negroes with similar levels of education are compared, the whites still get better jobs. In the northern and western sections of this country, where occupational discrimination is supposedly less pronounced, 22 per cent of the Negro college graduates are laborers and service workers. A majority of Negro high school graduates are in that same category in the same part of the country (9). Many of the Negroes who do obtain more skilled occupations find them in Negro industries. They are professors in Negro colleges, lawyers in Negro law firms, and insurance salesmen in Negro agencies. So pervasive are the effects of discrimination on the inclinations of Negroes to get an education and on the quality of that education that even when job opportunities do become available in white industries, there often are no Negroes qualified to take the jobs. The Negro is exhibiting greater willingness to get an education today. In 1940, 41 per cent of the nonwhites dropped out of school before they completed the fifth grade. Today only 23 per cent quit that early (10). Since increasing numbers of Negroes are living in the urban areas of the North where the quality of education is higher, they are better prepared to compete for white collar jobs in formerly all-white industries. Governments and private groups are exerting mounting pressure on business organizations to hire Negroes in the white collar jobs. In the meantime, because of their poorer educations and occupations, Negroes have lower incomes than whites. In 1961, the average Negro earned $2,908 while the average white was earning $5,570 (11). Even when educational and occupational differences are controlled, the Negro earns considerably less than the white person.

Associational Segmentation

Negro-white segmentation in associations is still the rule in American society. Negroes are excluded from white country clubs, fraternal organizations, and churches. Eleven o'clock on Sunday morning has often been referred to as the most segregated hour in the week. Actually, churches may be the last association that Negroes wish to desegregate. Negro churches have provided the organization and inspiration for many of the civil rights programs. If churches were desegregated, the civil rights movement might suffer a great setback. Negroes are even underrepresented in the leadership ranks of unions. Because of this associational segmentation, Negroes have developed their own parallel organizations. There are Black Elks, Black Methodists, and the Colored Knights of Pythias. Frazier (12) has provided us with some excellent insights into the associational activities of middle class Negroes. He shows that the Negro has often strived to emulate the dominant white culture, but in doing so, he has created a caricature of white behavior.

Educational Segmentation

We have already seen that residential segregation is very high and has not changed much over the last few decades. Because of residential segregation in the North, school systems also become segregated. As the proportion of Negroes in a neighborhood increases, the proportion of Negroes in the schools that service those neighborhoods also rises. In Los Angeles, 85 per cent of the elementary school students are Negroes or Mexican-Americans in 20 per cent of the schools. In Manhattan, 90 per cent of the students are Negroes or Puerto Ricans in 13 per cent of the schools (13). The presence of growing numbers of Negroes in the same schools with white students heightens the desire of the parents of the white students to move further away from the center of the city. Although it is often not necessary, school segregation can be maintained by gerrymandering the residential boundaries within which the schools will serve the residents. In summary, the segmentation between whites and Negroes is greater than it is between the various social classes and religious groups. With the fact of segmentation established, let us now examine the history of race and nationality relations in American society.

THE HISTORICAL BACKGROUND OF RACIAL AND NATIONALITY SEGMENTATION

Negroes began arriving in the colonies in the seventeenth century. Their position in early colonial society was less extreme in those early years than it was to be in the nineteenth century (14). They arrived in a country that was already full of indentured white people who were working off their indentureship and becoming free citizens. The Negro had the same right; he could become a free man. The myth of Negro inferiority had not yet arisen. During this period in our history, a very popular belief was that a disease had swept across Africa and made the Negro black, but in the healthy climate of the colonies, he would revert to his natural white color.

While their status was not so low as it was to become, the Negroes did not accept it docilely. They revolted on the ships that brought them over from Africa, and they revolted on the plantations where they worked. Failing all else, many of them committed suicide in the belief that they would be reborn in their beloved Africa (14).

The slave system of the classic South and the myth of inferiority that attended it were developed after the economy of the South shifted from naval stores to cotton. Since technological innovations were yet to come, cheap labor was very useful. Negroes could be used to harvest the cotton that had to be handpicked as it ripened. They could also be used for the laborious task of combing the seeds out of the picked cotton. The demand for slaves grew rapidly, and willing slave traders filled the need.

The societies from which the slaves were obtained were not so primitive as is often thought. Most of the slaves came from fairly advanced agrarian societies, not from hunting and gathering societies (14). Often they were the stateless agrarian societies of which we spoke earlier. These societies were generally patriarchal, which leaves us with the problem of accounting for the matriarchal organization of contemporary Negro subcultures. The slaves were obtained through warfare and raids among the villages of the African Negroes. The captives were herded aboard boats, taken to the colonies, and sold at auction to plantation owners and managers.

The experience of slavery eradicated most of the traces of African culture from the Negro's behavior patterns. He still retains some of his African heritage in his interest in shouting religions, but little else (14). Selling Negroes at auctions changed the structure of the Negro family. Marriage among slaves was not deemed necessary; a man and a woman simply began living together. The family was seldom sold as a unit. When the woman was sold, the children went with her. This arrangement accounts for the contemporary matriarchal structure of the Negro family. A lower class Negro woman may still have several "husbands" by whom she has children, and while the males may come and go, the children remain with the mother.

The higher status of the Negro woman also resulted from her role as a sexual object for white men and from her being allowed to work in the house. In general, the lighter skinned Negroes were trained to do housework, and, to this day, the Negro accords greater deference to the lighter skinned members of his race (15).

The Civil War ended the formal system of slavery, but replaced it with the modern system of segregation and discrimination. No amicable theories about blackness being the result of disease existed; Negroes were the primary targets of the racist theories that were fashionable after the Civil War; they were deemed inferior. This outlook has prevailed to the present day in only slightly modified form.

THE NEGRO TODAY

The cultural heritage of the migrating Negroes is often forgotten. They were illiterates imbued with a culture created during two centuries of slave status in a rural setting. The social structure in which they had lived had profound effects on their behaviors. They developed a value system that emphasized short-range thinking and placed no value on self-denial, delayed gratification, or self-discipline and control. They never had been permitted to get educations, so they had never developed any norms that valued it. Theirs was a value system that prevented its holders from improving their occupational positions in an industrial society.

Slavery had converted the Negro family structure from patriarchal to matriarchal. The family was composed of the mother and her children, and fathers were fleeting and vaguely remembered members of this group. Like the members of so many agrarian societies, the migrating Negroes attached great value to having large families; they continued to value them in their new homes in the North. They preferred storefront religions in which the emphasis was on shouting and on personal and often physical religious experiences (16). Their lack of knowledge about some of the most routine aspects of urban living was also a product of this background. For these reasons and others, the Negro was an easily identified alien in urban cultures—a person to whom the dominant value system attached the stigma of failure and one whose behavior seemed to prove it.

The social environment into which the Negroes moved was discussed earlier. They settled in the centers of the cities in the burgeoning tenement districts. The conditions under which they lived then and live now were often unbelievably bad. Landlords subdivided apartments, but seldom provided bath and kitchen facilities for each of the resulting living units. Often several families were forced to share one kitchen and bathroom; a family often had only one bedroom for all of its members. These and other factors created Negro neighborhoods of very high social density. Children are forced to play on the streets because of the lack of home, associational, or municipal facilities.

Even adult Negro life in the tenement areas is centered to some extent on the streets. The heat of the tiny and overcrowded apartments forces them out of doors in the summertime. They congregate on the corners or in front of the taverns visiting with other Negroes. If the neighborhoods look dirty, it must be remembered that when a neighborhood is tipped, city sanitary services usually are provided less frequently. Also, the owners of the tenements are unlikely to paint or repair their apartment houses because such investments would reduce their margins of profit.

The Negro population in the urban slum has many of the characteristics of a mass; it is fairly unintegrated, undifferentiated, and uninfluential. The composition of neighborhoods and apartment buildings changes rapidly as the people seek to exploit new ways of making a living or simply of staying alive (16). Sometimes well-intentioned urban renewal agencies have unwittingly aggravated the mass characteristics of Negro neighborhoods. When old tenement districts are razed in order to construct new housing, even the poorly integrated neighborhood organization found among Negroes is destroyed. Negroes are assigned to the new housing individually rather than by neighborhood groups. At least temporarily, the new housing project is very much a mass organization. In the slums, the crime rate is very high, and heavy police surveillance is required. Welfare agencies must concentrate much of their effort in these congested neighborhoods because of the high rates of various kinds of disease and the abundance of social problems found there.

Changes in the Negro Subculture

We have been talking thus far only about the largest segment of the Negro population—the lower working class. There are indications that some of the behavior patterns described above are changing: others have not altered noticeably. The stability of the Negro labor force is increasing. Union membership and the accompanying privilege of seniority is helping to increase the occupational security of many Negroes. More recently, federal laws and pressures from various associations have forced business organizations to provide more skilled jobs to Negroes.

The lower working class Negro family is still primarily matriarchal, but it will be interesting to see how this arrangement is affected by the increasing job stability of males. The large family is still valued by the Negro who moves to the urban areas from the South, but the second urban generation is having smaller families. The desertion and

divorce rate is still very high. The proscriptions against having illegitimate children are still not strong, and the illegitimacy rate is higher
among Negroes than it is among whites (17). But it is not so high as
official records indicate. In many instances where there *is* a legitimate
father, the mother will report children as being illegitimate to welfare
agencies in order to supplement her income. When these cases are
removed from the statistics on illegitimacy rates, the Negro rate drops
greatly, but is still significantly higher than the white rate (18).

Life chances have been very slow in improving for the Negro.
Negroes are getting better educations today than their parents did,
but they still lag badly behind the whites in this regard. The parents
today want their daughters to complete their educations so they can
get secretarial jobs rather than having to do housework (6). But they
are less optimistic about the opportunities of their male children and
less inclined to encourage them (6). Their reasons are economic; the
sooner a son gets a job, the sooner he can become a financial asset
rather than a liability. Health problems are much more prevalent
among Negroes than they are among whites. Negroes are more likely
to have the serious mental and physical ailments. The infant mortality
rate is twice as high, and the maternal death rate is four times as high
among Negroes as among whites (19).

The Negro today is losing his extended family orientation. Contrary
to popular stereotypes, Negroes are less inclined to live with relatives
in times of economic distress than are whites in similar positions (6).

Negro Social Classes

Not all Negroes are in the working class, although the
overwhelming majority certainly are. In fact, the differentiation in the
Negro subcultures is very great. We have already said enough in this
chapter and earlier ones about the Negro working class, so let us
concentrate on the middle class. The Negro middle class is very much
like the white middle class in terms of values. Its members save their
money, engage in long-range planning, and use a similar pattern of
socialization on their children. They also emphasize respectability,
home ownership, and the importance of family life. Divorce and desertion are far less prevalent in the Negro middle class than in the
working class. Middle-class Negroes try to avoid the slum neighborhoods (if they can) because they believe them dangerous places to go.

The Negro middle class has two very different segments: the old and
the new middle class. The old middle class is composed primarily of
Negroes who have the more skilled white collar jobs in industries that

cater to the Negro markets. These people own or hold positions in Negro insurance firms, colleges, magazines, and other business organizations. They often are in politics. Many of them were educated in Negro colleges in the South. These schools had a strong socializing effect on them (20). They were virtually complete and independent units, with their own stores, cafeterias, and movie houses. Contact with the white populations in the nearby towns was almost unnecessary. Negroes of the old middle class are likely to be committed to the school of Negro thought associated with Booker T. Washington: the Negro should work to prepare himself for status in the white man's world. He should get as much education as his ability permits, and he should accept the white man's culture as his own. The leaders could be militant, but the masses of Negroes were expected to be compromising and acquiescent. For this reason and the fact that their livelihood depends on the continued existence of a separate Negro market, the old middle class has been less willing to fight for Negro civil rights. Their approach has often been compromising, half-hearted, and not very militant.

The new middle class is composed primarily of Negroes who have white collar jobs in previously all-white industries. They have an entirely different outlook (21). They feel more secure in the jobs that they have obtained in the white man's organizations. They believe that it is possible for Negroes to break down the barriers of economic discrimination and to continue to live in American society. They take a much more militant stand vis-à-vis the influential whites in their communities. College students have discovered the enormous influence of the mass media on public opinion and political activity and have utilized this influence to obtain many concessions from white elites (20). These students have also discovered that civil rights activities can increase their deference status among other Negro students. They have discovered, too, that white leaders in most communities are unwilling to sacrifice some fundamental values in order to maintain segregation (22). The whites will often make concessions when faced with the prospect of interracial violence or other actions that are contrary to their basic principles.

The position of the Negro in the new middle class is a marginal one. He may work in a desegregated industry enjoying informal contacts with other whites, live in segregated neighborhoods, and attempt to eat in restaurants whose policy on racial discrimination is not known. His is not the easier life of total segregation, and he must learn to cope with the peculiar problems of these uncertainties in his interpersonal relationships.

The new militancy now crosscuts *all social classes*. It is no longer maintained that working class Negroes should remain silent and inactive behind their leaders. But the lower working class has every reason to be less optimistic about the possibilities of achieving desegregation within the framework of American society. For many of these people, radical solutions are the only possible ones. Appeals to leave American society and form a separate society or to follow a course of violence and attrition against the white man have greater appeal to the pessimistic lower working class than they do to the middle class. The organizational and programmatic consequences of these class differences will be discussed in the next chapter.

THE VALUES OF RACIAL SEGMENTATION

Racial segmentation is costly to maintain. Many types of facilities must be duplicated for each race. Extra police personnel are required. Many skilled occupational roles go unfilled because employers refuse to hire Negroes trained in them. Because of these simple cost factors, there must be some very compelling reasons for the maintenance of segmentation.

Segregation and discrimination are useful to whites because a permanently disadvantaged minority is created. If the occupational status of Negroes is both ascribed and low, they are prevented from competing with whites for valued jobs (23). Negroes also provide a cushion under the white majority whenever economic depressions occur. In depressions it is the Negro who is most likely to find himself out of work.

Segregation and discrimination permit the majority to enjoy a greater share of the resources of the society. By denying the Negro economic equality, there is more wealth available to share among the whites. Perhaps the most obvious advantage of segmentation is that it limits contacts with a minority believed to be inferior. The culture of the white majority is not diluted by Negro norms: a way of life is preserved.

If the Negro is permanently disenfranchised and kept in as near a mass condition as possible, he can never organize to change his status. If he could vote, politicians would have to cater to some of his demands. If he could organize, he might use force or other means to change his status. Finally, discrimination creates a comfortable myth of superiority among the white majority (23).

Segregation and discrimination have advantages for some Negroes too. Negro businessmen often have the Negro markets to themselves. Negro insurance companies, banks, newspapers, and magazines are dependent on the continued existence of discrimination.

SUMMARY AND CONCLUSIONS

In this chapter race and nationality segmentation have been examined with special emphasis on segmentation between whites and Negroes. Historically, many nationality groups from areas other than northwestern Europe have experienced discrimination of many kinds, but they are slowly being integrated into American society as their education and income approximates that of other Americans. Only the Negro and perhaps the Mexican-American have been denied these opportunities regardless of their educational and income statuses. We have seen that Negroes are often prevented from living in suburban communities and all-white neighborhoods, they generally go to segregated secondary schools, they are largely restricted to the less skilled occupational roles in the society, and they are denied membership in many associations.

Most of the contemporary behavior patterns exhibited by Negroes can be traced to their earlier slave status and the contemporary practices of economic deprivation and social discrimination. Their value systems, family structure, and neighborhood organization are products of these experiences.

Two questions must now be raised: What are the consequences of racial segmentation? And what are the prospects for the integration of Negroes into the occupational and social structures of our society? In the next chapter we will take up the first of these questions. In Chapter 17 the factors that lead to greater racial integration will be discussed.

REFERENCES

1   S. Lieberson, *Ethnic Patterns in American Cities* (New York: Free Press of Glencoe, Inc., 1963).

2   K. E. Taeuber and A. F. Taeuber, "The Negro as an Immigrant Group: Recent Trends in Racial and Ethnic Segregation in Chicago," *The American Journal of Sociology, 69* (1964), 374-82.

3   H. H. Kitano, "Housing of Japanese-Americans in the San Francisco Bay Area," in *Studies in Housing and Minority Groups,* N. Glazer and D. McEntere, eds. (Berkeley: University of California Press, 1960).

4   W. Mendelson, *Discrimination* (Englewood Cliffs, N. J.: Prentice-Hall, Inc., 1962; a Spectrum book).

5   M. Grodzins, "The Metropolitan Area as a Racial Problem," in *American Race Relations Today,* E. Raab, ed.

(Garden City: Doubleday & Company, Inc., 1962), pp. 85-123.

6   J. Morgan and M. David, "Race, Economic Attitudes, and Behavior," *1962 Proceedings of the Social Statistics Section of the American Statistical Association*, pp. 2-6.

7   Bureau of the Census, *Historical Statistics of the United States*, 1960.

8   Bureau of the Census, *Statistical Abstract of the United States: 1963*, 84th ed. T 304.

9   Bureau of the Census, *U.S. Census of the Population, 1950*, Special Reports, Part 5, Chapter B, "Education."

10 *Statistical Abstract of the United States: 1963*, T 153.

11 *Statistical Abstract of the United States: 1963*, T 452.

12 E. F. Frazier, *Black Bourgeoisie: The Rise of a New Middle Class in the United States* (New York: Collier Books, 1962).

13 E. Raab, "Foreword: Beginning the Future: Equal Achievement and Integration," in *American Race Relations Today*, E. Raab, ed. (Garden City: Doubleday & Company, Inc., 1962), pp. 79-84.

14 M. J. Herskovits, *The Myth of the Negro Past* (Boston: Beacon Press, Inc., 1958).

15 C. H. Parrish, "Color Names and Color Notions," *Journal of Negro Education, 15* (1946), 124-31.

16 St. C. Drake and H. R. Cayton, *Black Metropolis* (New York: Harcourt, Brace, and World, Inc., 1945).

17 *Statistical Abstract of the United States: 1963*, T 56.

18 W. Pratt, Research Associate, Center for Population Studies, Ann Arbor, Michigan, in a personal communication. This finding emerged indirectly from a study of Detroit welfare agencies.

19 *Statistical Abstract of the United States: 1963*, T 66.

20 C. U. Smith, "The Sit-Ins and the New Negro Student," in *American Race Relations Today*, E. Raab, ed. (Garden City: Doubleday & Company, Inc., 1962), pp. 69-75.

21 L. H. Mayhew, "Law and Equal Opportunity: Anti-Discrimination Law in Boston" (Unpublished doctoral dissertation, Harvard University, 1964).

22   M. Tumin, P. Barton, and B. Burnus, "Education, Preju-
     dice and Discrimination: A Study of Readiness for Desegre-
     gation," *American Sociological Review, 23* (1958), 41-49.

23   H. Blalock, "Segregation" (Unpublished paper, University
     of Michigan, 1959).

the consequences of segmentation 16

In the last four chapters the major factors that segment American society—social class, religion, and race—have been discussed. Social classes and race were described as factors that can segment the society into several "layers" of people. Religious differences divide the society vertically into segments that cut across social class differences. An implicit assumption in those chapters was that segmentation was harmful to the society, but the validity of that assumption was not discussed nor was it demonstrated. In this chapter we will see the consequences of segmentation for a society.

THE BASIS OF PROBLEMS IN SEGMENTED SOCIETIES

The reasons why segmentation can have adverse effects on a large organization, including a society, need be reviewed only briefly here, because they were discussed earlier, in Chapter 3 under

Propositions 10 and 11. Segmentation was defined in terms of the existence of barriers to communication among the parts of an organization. As the number of levels in each hierarchy in an organization increases, problems of communicating up and down each hierarchy may arise, and problems of interaction *among them* also increase. These problems can be solved, but they require the concerted efforts of highly skilled people: people who are not always available. In this instance segmentation develops as a natural consequence of increasing size; it can also be created by other means. Segregation and discrimination against minority groups, conquest, geographical barriers, and historical factors can also produce a segmented condition among the parts of a population.

Unless actions are initiated to arrest the process, a vicious cycle of increasing segmentation is developed (1). In the segmented parts, the populations are facing problems that they would like to solve effectively. Often the solution of these problems requires action by other parts where greater amounts of influence reside. Negroes living in tenement ghettoes would like to have their living conditions improved, but such a change would require the assistance of governmental officials. But if segmentation exists among the parts, the members of the more influential parts may not even be aware of the problems of the members of some of the other parts. Or if segmentation has proceeded far enough, they may not be able to appreciate the significance of the problems that the members of the other parts face. The quotation from an essay by Henry Ward Beecher, on page 234, clearly shows that he had little understanding of the real impact of poverty on the lower working class. This lack of understanding permitted him to take the callous position that he did without any qualms of conscience. One need not look so far back into our history to find examples of callousness induced by lack of first-hand knowledge of the meaning of problems faced by people in other parts of the society. How many people have you heard say they had no sympathy for the poor because anytime they want to improve themselves they can? Such a statement is naïve, but it provides a comfortable rationalization for inaction. If segmentation has proceeded even further, and conflict or hostility exists among the affected parts, then the possession of information, even if it is accurate, will seldom result in problem-solving action.

But if the problems persist, the members of the affected parts will have to cope with them as best they can. In other words, they will have to form new norms. This process increases the subcultural variation between parts of the society and further decreases the possibility of interaction among them. Language and behavioral differences appear that further impede interaction among the parts. A sixty-five-year-old upper class woman and a thirteen-year-old lower working class boy will experience great difficulty communicating with each other; their problems, their outlook on life, and even their vocabularies are so divergent that communication is almost impossible. Thus, segmentation can often lead to even greater segmentation. It is on the foundation of these conditions in organizations that the problems segmentation creates for a society are built.

SEGMENTATION AND SOCIAL CHANGE

In Chapter 5 we saw that the greater the segmentation among the parts of an organization, the less likely are changes initiated in one part to be adopted by the members of other parts. If communication barriers exist, the members of the other parts may not even know that the innovation has been made. If hostility or conflict exists among the parts, the members of the one parts are unlikely to want to adopt the innovations of another, hostile part unless the innovation is essential to its survival. The teachers in segmented secondary school systems are less likely to adopt their colleagues' innovations in teaching techniques than are the teachers in integrated school systems (2). In segmented hospitals, the staff members are less likely to change their routines or to adopt new equipment at the request of the administrator or director of nursing than are the employees of integrated hospitals (3, 4). Similar conditions exist in societies. There are many reasons why France industrialized more slowly than England during the early part of the nineteenth century, but one of them was the existence of barriers to communication and hostility between the agencies of the national government and the owners of private industries (5). Some of the governmental agencies had achieved remarkable innovations that would have improved the productivity of certain French industries. The owners of these industries seldom adopted these innovations into their technological processes, preferring to continue using older methods.

It must be remembered that it is the *parts* that are segmented and that these parts contain varying amounts of influence. Since they do possess influence, they often cannot be forced to accept changes, and their relationships with other parts are more of a bargaining nature than they are of a hierarchical or command nature. Any proposed change in the pattern of relationships among the parts of a segmented system will cause the members in each segmented part to examine the proposal for the implications it has for *that part* rather than for the system as a whole. A change that might be beneficial for the entire system but not for the part will generally meet the resistance of the part (4). This problem is especially severe for modern societies where the parts are highly interdependent and where the society must often react promptly and in a unitary fashion to the actions of other societies. The realities of modern warfare and diplomacy, for example, require such prompt and unitary reactions to the activities of other nations. The existence of segmentation impedes the ability of the society to make these prompt responses.

Often the attempts of influential parts to solve the problems of *other parts* (rather than those of the total organization) are resisted by other equally influential parts. Programs to alleviate poverty, sickness, or racial discrimination have in the past been vetoed by influential parts of American society. The problems are permitted to remain, and the potential for conflict or violence is not reduced.

SEGMENTATION AND DEVIANCE

Deviance and the protection of deviants is increased in segmented systems (4). We have already seen that the members of segmented parts may develop norms designed to help them to cope with their problems. Often these norms violate the norms of the total society. If the problem is poverty, then stealing and prostitution may become increasingly prevalent among the poverty-stricken members of the population. If the problem is maintaining job security, the solution may be underproduction, failure to report errors in performance, unwillingness to make independent decisions, or any of a large number of behaviors that deviate from the norms of the organization involved. Other similarly situated members of the organization are not inclined to report the deviance of those around them even though they may not participate in deviant activities themselves. To whom should they report deviance? To the authorities who have allowed the problem to persist in the first place? In social-psychological terms, we would expect a greater proportion of the members of such organizations to be *alienated* from the elites. Alienated people are unlikely to support the norms of the elites seen as responsible for the conditions of the other members of the organization.

Segmentation and Juvenile Delinquency

A contemporary illustration of the relationship between segmentation and deviance is provided by the case of juvenile delinquency. The number of juvenile delinquency court cases has doubled in the period between 1948 and 1957. About 2.3 per cent of all the children in the vulnerable age group—10 through 17—have been referred to juvenile courts in the United States (6). And the increase is expected to continue (7).

There are a great many, often conflicting, theories about the causes of delinquency in our society (8). Rather than discuss each major theory here, we will select the elements from a number of them that are relevant for the theme of segmentation being developed here. In modern industrial societies, the roles of young people and the problems they face differ greatly from those of young people in agrarian villages. The children in peasant villages are very closely tied to their families and have little opportunity, after they are five or six years old and able to be involved in productive activity, to interact with other children in the village. The boys follow the father to the fields and learn to help him with farming; the girls learn to do housework from their mother. These children, having minimal contact with other children in the village, develop no special problems of their own that cannot be handled within the family.

The emergence of industrial society changes this relationship between parents and children. Children in industrial societies are not productive assets to the family (except in the unusual family that is still a productive unit). The father cannot take his children to work with him and teach them his trade. Housework in industrial societies is not the arduous activity it is in agrarian societies, and it does not require the dawn to dusk commitment from the female members of the family. The training that children formerly received at home is now given to them by members of large bureaucratic organizations—the school system. In the schools a large cohort of young people is created; these children can interact easily, and they are freed from the kinds of task responsibilities that agrarian children have. The members of this cohort face common problems. They must learn how to relate to one another, to cope with the requirements of the school system, to use the leisure time that their role enforces upon them, and to develop new roles in the absence of a task role. Interaction among these youngsters has led to the development of the youth culture, which for all of its dynamic qualities is nonetheless distinct from the other parts of American society (1). The members of the youth culture have devel‹
their own variations on the English language, styles of dress, heroes, leisure time activities, and a seemingly endless variety of other patterns of behavior. Their perspectives are often so different from those of their parents that interaction between parents and children become less qualitative and more easily misunderstood or not understood at all.

Deprived of their task responsibilities, the members of this youth culture seek solutions to the problem of boredom. Some devote great energies to their school work or athletic activities; others engage in clique-based social activities. For many teenagers, however, the problem of boredom is never effectively or permanently solved. Young people often spend their time searching for something to do, and their behavior very much resembles the milling behavior of a crowd. They drive up and down the main streets of town or from one drive-in restaurant to another looking for something to do. They congregate on corners or in stores, sharing their mutual boredom, hoping for a suggestion that will provide some fun. Sometimes "fun" can take the form of deviant activities. Drag racing, breaking the windows at a school, sexual activities, or stealing are some of the many forms of deviance practiced. Juvenile delinquency is practiced in all social classes; it just varies in content from one class to another. The lower working class child often cannot afford the kinds of delinquent activities engaged in by upper class children; e.g., drag racing.

The lower working class child faces a special set of problems and a different environment that help to create the particular type of delinquency found in that class. He must go to school, but as we have seen, he is not socialized appropriately for the requirements of a school system; he receives little support from his family or peers in his school activities, and he himself does not value an education (1). He would like to have fun, but he cannot buy it as easily as the children in higher social classes because he does not have enough money. The acceptance of deviant solutions to his problems is made easier by the presence of deviant elements in his social environment. He sees prostitution, gambling, graft, and other illicit activities around him (9). He sees that the agents of organized crime have the clothes, cars, and women that he would like to have. He and the other children in his neighborhood often have a well-developed hostility to authorities of the larger social system. The schoolteacher, police, and social workers represent a system that makes demands on him he cannot or does not want to meet (1, 10). The police chase him from the corners, and teachers sanction him negatively for many of the behaviors he exhibits in school.

In such an environment stealing can be a promising source of money and gambling a means of increasing it. Breaking into private property, destroying it, and many other activities can be a source of fun. Never trained to control his physical aggressions and always zealous of his masculinity, the lower class youth finds that these deviant outlets are appropriate for his particular set of skills.

Working class delinquency is seldom gang delinquency. While it is true that gangs do exist, most of the juvenile crimes are committed by single individuals or ephemeral cliques of young people (11). These young people are very effective in segmenting themselves from the established channels of communication in their communities. Therefore, one of the problems faced by authorities in coping with delinquency is finding the delinquents. Some communities have developed programs designed to reintegrate the delinquents into the established channels of communication. In one such program college students with working class backgrounds are hired to work with the young people in certain sections of the community. Each of these group workers is expected to act as an intermediary between the youthful offender and legal agencies. These workers will often intercede with judges, police, and school authorities, explaining the circumstances of the young people. They also try to legitimate the actions of these agencies to the young people. By these means the communities involved hope to reverse the process of segmentation that exists. While it is too early to evaluate the effectiveness of these and other programs, it is apparent from our earlier discussions that *the problem will continue to exist so long as the conditions that gave rise to it are allowed to persist.*

SEGMENTATION AND SOCIAL CONFLICT

All of our earlier discussions suggest that the potential for conflict in segmented systems is very high. Persistent and unsolved problems can create a reservoir of hostility within a segment. Occasionally, this hostility will be manifested in overt violence or conflict. In highly segmented hospitals, the staff members report greater tension, conflict, and friction among the departments that must work together than is reported in integrated hospitals (3, 4). The propensity to strike is greater in industries where the characteristics of the technology and geographic location help to create segments (12). In our discussion of segmentation on the basis of religion, we saw that violence and conflict often occur among religious groups. Swastikas are painted on synagogues, Catholic churches and homes are burned, and sometimes rioting based on religious differences results in killings. These events are not confined to American society; they occur in many societies and with greater severity whenever religious segmentation exists. Even in Holland, where relationships among the various religious groups are highly institutionalized, issues come up that lead to the outbreak of conflict and hostility.

Conflict and hostility also occur between the social class and racial segments of the population. Sometimes a seemingly insignificant event can trigger a riot. A fight between a white man and a Negro at a public beach can arouse latent hostility and spread the conflict until it is necessary to call out police units or even the National Guard. Negroes are beaten or lynched by whites, and retaliation is inevitable. The homes of integration leaders are bombed, and Negro churches are destroyed. When a Negro moves into a white neighborhood, he is sometimes greeted by violence. Many Negroes feel no compunction about committing crimes against whites because of the ever present hostility between them.

Violence is contrary to the values of American society, but some forms of conflict can be useful for the society generally and for the parts containing persistent problems in particular. Interpart conflict may be the only means available to the populations of segmented parts to call their problems to the attention of the other parts of the society. During the early sit-in demonstrations, the participating Negroes found that their problems were being publicized through the mass media that reported the events. Americans were made aware, often for the first time, of the problems of the Negroes.

Conflict *sometimes* results in the development of new channels of interaction among the parts of the organization and thereby provides a means for the peaceful solution of problems. The history of American labor relations is instructive in this regard. Early labor-management relations were frequently marked by violence, but out of the conflict has emerged a plethora of institutionalized means of resolving labor disputes before they erupt into violence.

Conflict can also have the effect of integrating the parts internally. If some members of a part are the objects of violence, the others may rally around them. The added strength that this integration provides is useful for ensuing interactions. If the conflict is on the international level, then the nation as a whole may become more integrated and capable of unitary response to the actions of other nations.

These advantages of interpart conflict are mentioned because they are not readily apparent; it is generally assumed that all conflict is "bad." From the perspective of the American value system conflict should be resolved by peaceful, legitimate means, but as we have seen, the existence of segmentation can preclude the use of these means. Segmentation, therefore, can create conditions that run counter to the overt values of American society.

SEGMENTATION AND WITHDRAWAL BEHAVIOR

The existence of persistent unsolved problems in the population of a segment can result in apathy or withdrawal behavior in the population. Unable to affect their fate or to achieve their objectives through the existing channels of decision making, the members of a segment often resort to withdrawal from involvement in the larger social system. Sometimes the form of withdrawal involves non-participation in any type of associational activity or in citizenship roles. The lower working class population generally and the Negro portion in particular exhibit high rates of this form of withdrawal behavior. This segment of the population is less likely than any other to read books and magazines, to belong to churches or other voluntary associations, or to vote in national elections (13, 14).

Organizations designed to support this tendency to withdrawal and apathy often develop in the segments. Illicit organizations that distribute opium derivatives are taking advantage of the withdrawal tendencies of segmented populations. Other organizations such as cults and religious sects develop rituals compatible with the withdrawn population. The organization of Father Divine, a Negro movement that commanded a sizable following in the East, goes one step further and provides both economic security and insulation for its members. This organization is a collectivist response to discrimination and deprivation (15). The members pool their money and other resources to create economic organizations designed to service their members. They own stores, farms, barbershops, and other types of businesses that the members are expected to patronize exclusively. These establishments also provide a place of employment for the members. By these means segmentation is increased, but so too is economic security.

A more dramatic Negro movement that aimed at the complete withdrawal of the Negro population from the affairs of American society was the Garvey movement that flourished after World War I (16). Marcus Garvey was a Jamaican who advocated that the Negroes should leave the United States and return to Africa. He formed an organization called the Universal Negro Improvement Association which he claimed had two million members recruited primarily among lower working class Negroes. His efforts to move the American Negro population to Liberia were opposed by the governments of England and France. The emissaries of these two countries exerted great pressure on the government of Liberia to reject the Garveyites, which they did. Garvey also encountered the resistance of the Negro middle class in the United States, whose members were far less pessimistic than the lower working class about the opportunities for eventual assimilation into American society. Garvey himself was finally convicted by the federal government for using the mails to defraud, and he was sentenced to a five-year term in a federal prison. With this event the Garvey movement collapsed, but the cause he espoused is not dead. Today the Black Muslim movement constitutes a carefully organized and highly influential counterpart to the Garvey movement.

The Black Muslims advocate the complete rejection of the white man's culture and seek to separate themselves physically from the white man. Their organization also has many of the features of the Father Divine organization. Muslimism is built on a religious cornerstone: a black man's religion that is a variation of the Moslem religion of the Arabic cultures. The members are required to dress neatly, comport themselves well, and to work hard. They must have jobs, and these jobs are often provided by Muslim businesses. These aspects of their programs provide the members with a sense of economic well-being and personal worth. A paramilitary wing of the organization—the Fruit of Islam—trains the male members in the techniques of self-defense. Muslims are taught to restrain themselves in the presence of white people, but if attacked, they can assert themselves effectively. Many whites are very much concerned about the implications of the Fruit of Islam for racial violence in American society, because it is not clear that the objectives of this subgroup are totally defensive.

The leaders of the Muslim movement would like to have four or five states allocated for the exclusive use of the Negro population of this country. But they also expect that it will be several years before they can marshal sufficient strength to force the white population to accept this plan. Until then, they insist that their members avoid social interaction with whites.

Despite the extremeness of their appeal, the Black Muslims have in excess of 100,000 members today and have set a goal of 5 million members by 1970. Like the Garvey movement before it, the Black Muslim movement recruits members primarily from the Negro working class. The main resistance to the movement comes from the Negro middle class and from Negro organizations that advocate working within the legal framework of the United States to obtain their rights.

Perhaps the real impact of the Muslim movement lies not in its own strength, but in the indirect effects it has in strengthening other radical Negro movements. As in most segmented situations, there are many radical organizations competing for the allegiance of the working class Negro. Many of them are only a shade less radical than the Muslims, but these subtle differences make them attractive to many Negroes. In other words, the existence of the extremely radical Muslim movement legitimates other radical movements (17).

SEGMENTATION AND PROTEST BEHAVIOR

Persistent segmentation can also give rise to protest organizations that attempt to establish communication linkages with the major centers of influence in the community or society. Through the use of these communication channels, the leaders of the protest organizations hope to create greater awareness of the problems faced by the populations they represent and to obtain aid in solving those problems. Since it is not always possible to build channels of interaction between segmented parts, some organizations will advocate the use of *any* means to achieve their objectives—legal or illegal.

The National Association for the Advancement of Colored People (NAACP) has based its programs on legitimate means: lawsuits that seek to remove the barriers of discrimination in the society, and negotiation with the elites of the communities for increasing Negro rights. The outstanding achievement of this organization was the 1954 Supreme Court decision that struck down segregation in public educational institutions. Since that time, several organizations have come into existence that have used a broader strategy than the NAACP has been willing to use. The economic boycott of the bus system in Montgomery, Alabama, in 1955 by the followers of Martin Luther King introduced a new weapon in the arsenal of protest movements. The success of the bus boycott led to the formation of the Southern Christian Leadership Conference (SCLC) and the subsequent widening of protest activity in the South. The techniques of the SCLC and of other similar organizations (the Congress on Racial Equality and the Student Non-Violent Coordinating Committee) have included sit-ins, freedom rides, demonstrations, and economic boycotts, to mention a few. Behind each technique is the basic strategy of publicizing the conditions of the Negroes in the United States through the mass media. By these means, the leaders of these movements hope to bring collective public prssure to bear on local elites in order to obtain concessions for Negroes.

Historically, the role of labor unions is similar to that of contemporary Negro movements. Associations of workers used a variety of strategies to win concessions from the owners and managers of American industries. Often these techniques violated state and local laws. But with the passage of time, unions came to be recognized as legal bargaining agents for their members. In other words, these organizations were able to establish communication links between the owners and managers and the workers.

In each of the major religious groups there are organizations designed to establish communication linkages with the other parts of the society. Often these organizations seek the passage of legislation designed to increase the civil liberties of their members. Such organizations as the Anti-Defamation League are designed to combat prejudice against Jews. The strategy of this organization is centered on educating the population, either through the mass media or through other channels. The major religious organizations in our society have formed joint agencies designed to combat religious prejudice and conflict in American society.

SEGMENTATION AND COUNTERPROTEST

An axiom of political science is that organization generally leads to counterorganization. The various movements that have sought to increase the influence possessed by Negroes, blue collar workers, and various religious groups have been somewhat successful in wresting influence away from the traditional centers of influence in our society. This loss of influence is often the basis for counterorganization among the more influential segments of the population. These organizations also vary in willingness to use illegal as well as legal means to achieve their objectives.

At various times in American history organizations have developed that sought to maintain segmentation between white Anglo-Saxon Protestants and other racial and ethnic groups. These groups were discussed in earlier chapters. The Know-Nothing Party, the Ku Klux Klan, and the Silver Fascists are examples of this type of organization.

Today, numerous organizations seek to maintain the hegemony of whites, Protestants, or the middle class. The Ku Klux Klan still exists and functions in many areas of the country besides the South. If this organization is less visible and active today, it is owing in part to the extensive surveillance of its members by government agencies. White Citizens Councils have formed in many communities, particularly in the South, to prevent the Negroes from increasing their influence in community affairs. Numerous small organizations with programs similar to that of the Ku Klux Klan have sprung up in the South, recruiting working class whites in local communities.

Some organizations have developed in the middle and upper classes as a consequence of particular problems that impinge upon the members of these classes (18). The threat to the continued existence of the United States posed by the Soviet Union and mainland China is one problem that has led to organizational responses. Isolationism is still a very strong ideology in the midwestern and southern portions of the

United States, and it is particularly strong among the members of the middle class in those sections of the country. Many of these people resent the internationalist orientation of the middle and upper classes in the East. This resentment is aggravated by the fact that the internationalists dominate the foreign policy–making agencies of the government. Many members of the middle class are also disturbed by the increasing tendency of Protestant clergymen to become advocates of aspects of welfarism and universal brotherhood. They are alarmed by the growing influence of labor unions, the expansion of the Negro ghettoes into white neighborhoods, and the expanding role of government in the activities of the society.

Fearful of losing their traditionally high influence status, these people are often attracted to many social organizations and movements that advocate various means of dealing with these problems. When Senator Joseph McCarthy announced that he would expose and remove the Communists in the State Department, Harvard, and in our delegation to the United Nations, he was invoking themes that appealed to these elements in the society. The John Birch Society recruits its membership primarily from the middle class because of its overt concern with Communist infiltration into the government, the eastern elites, and among Protestant ministers. It must be remembered that this overt concern with "the Communist threat" probably masks the real concern of the members with their loss of influence status in the society (18).

SEGMENTATION AND TOTALITARIAN SOCIAL MOVEMENTS

From the point of view of the democratic value system of American society, the worst threat of segmentation is the possibility that it will spawn totalitarian social movements. A totalitarian movement has great appeal to persons in segments that have the characteristics of a mass. These movements appeal to the unintegrated members of the population by offering them an organizational membership. They solve the problem of being undifferentiated by giving their members roles and statuses in an organization. They make a previously incomprehensible world more understandable by providing an ideology and scapegoats. Scapegoats are categories of people—Jews, Negroes, capitalists—who are accused of being responsible for the conditions of the mass. They provide an object for the accumulated hostility of the people in the mass. The ideology offers the members a common perspective for making judgments about events in the social world, and it provides a program for the creation of a new social order that will remove the old vexations. These organizations also remove the sense of powerlessness that pervades a mass population by demonstrating that, through the totalitarian organization, they can influence the affairs of the society.

The events in Germany that culminated in the victory of the Nazi Party illustrate this relationship between segmentation and the development of totalitarian movements. After World War I several masses developed in German society (19). One mass was composed of the soldiers who returned home from the war to experience unemployment rather than national gratitude. For them the postwar years were marked with bitter frustration and poverty. A second mass developed in the lower middle class. In the early 1920's Germany experienced a crippling inflation. It cost millions of marks to buy a pair of shoes; people took wheelbarrows of money to go shopping. The lower middle class Germans who had been raised to believe in the virtues of thrift and industry were disillusioned when the savings that they had accumulated from a lifetime of work and frugality were wiped out by the inflation. A third mass was composed of young Germans who were disillusioned in the society of their fathers. They shared the idealistic and romantic notions of Germany that predominated in their culture, but how was the dream to be compared to the reality of a defeated Germany?

Hitler was able to appeal to all of these segments of the population. To all of these segments he offered a scapegoat: the Jew. He said that it was the international Jewish conspiracy (which was allied with the Communists) that had brought Germany to its low state. It was they who were responsible for the surrender of Germany and the manipulation of the financial markets to produce the inflation. To the unemployed ex-soldier he offered the prospect of employment and membership in a paramilitary organization. To the lower middle class he held out the prospect of a stable economy. To the youth he promised the resurgence of Germany as a world power. His appeals to the youth also combined the music of Wagner with an abundance of pageantry with conspicuous success.

The effect of these appeals is apparent in the voting behavior of Germans between 1928 and 1932 (20). In 1928, 810,127 people voted for the candidates of the Nazi Party. By 1930 the vote for that party had increased to 6,379,672, and the Nazis won 107 seats in the Reichstag. During the same period, another radical paramilitary party—the Communist Party—received over a million more votes than it had in 1928. In other words, almost 7 million new votes were cast for these two radical parties. Many of these votes came from the 2,440,990 people who voted for the first time in their lives in the 1930 election although they had been eligible to vote in previous elections. These essentially apathetic and withdrawn people saw radical movements as the only solution to their problems and therefore supported them. The more than 1,700,000 young people who were eligible to vote for the first time also contributed heavily to the radical vote in this election. By 1932 the Nazi Party had doubled its vote over the total for 1930 and became the ruling party in Germany.

We have already seen earlier that segmentation in American society has led to apathy and withdrawal on the part of large segments of the population. We have also seen that paramilitary organizations often arise in these segments. Crises such as the depression of the Thirties or the threat of communism could aid the causes of these organizations until they could play an even more influential role in American society than they do today. The persistent problems of unemployment, racial discrimination, and the Cold War have created and vitalized many such movements; a serious crisis could empower them.

SUMMARY

Some systems can function adequately even if they are segmented provided that there is no great need for the parts to operate in a highly interdependent fashion. But if the problem-solving ability of the members of one part is greatly dependent on other parts, then segmentation can produce some serious effects. Many persons in segmented parts of the population will withdraw from active participation in the total society and its institutions. They generally become apathetic, but they may join an organization that provides them with a means of escaping from the problems posed by the society. If the problems of these people are not solved and crises occur that aggravate their condition, protest organizations may develop and win supporters in these segments of the population.

The potential for conflict and violence is very great among segmented parts. The violence that occurs may be spontaneous, or it may be a part of the programmed activities of a radical organization. The development of protest organizations and of counterorganizations can heighten these possibilities of violence. The most serious threat of segmentation is that it can provide the basis for creating masses in the population to which totalitarian movements will often have considerable appeal.

REFERENCES

1   A. Cohen, *Delinquent Gangs: The Culture of the Gang* (New York: Free Press of Glencoe, Inc., 1955).

2   R. Lippitt and R. Fox, "The Innovation of Classroom Mental Health Practices," in *Innovation in Education,* M. Miles, ed. (New York: Bureau of Publications, Teachers College, Columbia University, 1964).

3   J. Cummings and E. Cummings, "Social Equilibrium and Social Change in the Large Mental Hospital," in *The Patient and the Mental Hospital,* M. Greenblatt, D. Levinson, and R. Williams, eds. (New York: Free Press of Glencoe, Inc., 1957), pp. 51-76.

4   P. E. Mott, "Sources of Adaptation and Flexibility in Large Organizations" (Unpublished doctoral dissertation, The University of Michigan, 1960).

5   T. A. B. Corley, *Democratic Despot: A Life of Napoleon III* (London: Barrie and Rockliff, 1961).

6   U.S. Children's Bureau, *Juvenile Delinquency: Facts and Facets* (Washington: Department of Health, Education, and Welfare, 1960), Publication No. 4.

7   U.S. Children's Bureau, *A Look at Juvenile Delinquency* (Washington: Department of Health, Education, and Welfare, 1960), Publication No. 380.

8   For an excellent discussion of the characteristics, strengths, and weaknesses of these theories, see D. J. Bordua, "Delinquent Subcultures: Sociological Interpretations of Gang Delinquency," *The Annals of the American Academy of Political and Social Science, 338* (1961), 119-36.

9   D. J. Bordua, *Sociological Theories and Their Implications for Juvenile Delinquency: A Report of a Children's Bureau Conference* (Washington: Department of Health, Education, and Welfare, 1960), Publication No. 2.

10   R. A. Cloward and L. E. Ohlin, *Delinquency and Opportunity* (New York: Free Press of Glencoe, Inc., 1960).

11   J. F. Short, Jr., R. A. Tennyson, and K. I. Howard, "Behavior Dimensions of Gang Delinquency," *American Sociological Review, 28* (1963), 411-28.

12   C. Kerr and A. Siegel, "The Interindustry Propensity to Strike—An International Comparison," in *Industrial Con-*

flict, A. Kornhauser, et al., eds. (New York: McGraw-Hill Book Company, 1954).

13 M. Janowitz and D. Marvick, *Competitive Pressure and Democratic Consent,* Michigan Governmental Studies, No. 32 (Ann Arbor: The University of Michigan, Bureau of Government, Institute of Public Administration, 1956).

14 G. Knupfer, "Portrait of the Underdog," *Public Opinion Quarterly, 11* (1947), 103-14.

15 S. Harris, *Father Divine: Holy Husband* (Garden City: Doubleday & Company, Inc., 1952).

16 C. E. Lincoln, *The Black Muslims in America* (Boston: Beacon Press, Inc., 1961).

17 L. E. Lomax, *The Negro Revolt* (New York: The New American Library, 1963).

18 D. Bell, *The New American Right* (New York: Criterion Books, 1955).

19 H. Arendt, *The Origins of Totalitarianism* (New York: Harcourt, Brace, and World, Inc., 1951).

20 R. Bendix, "Social Stratification and Political Power," in *Class, Status, and Power: A Reader in Social Stratification,* R. Bendix and S. M. Lipset, eds. (New York: Free Press of Glencoe, Inc., 1953).

some sources of integration

In view of the powerful segmenting forces that affect American society, how has it remained intact? There must be integrating forces of almost equal strength to the segmenting ones. In this chapter several integrative influences will be discussed.

DIFFERENTIATION AMONG THE PARTS

As the differentiation of the parts increases, the span of activities performed by each part narrows, and the parts become more interdependent. The interdependence found in highly differentiated organizations is an important factor for maintaining their solidarity.

American society is a highly differentiated organization. Communities are often highly specialized in terms of the functions they perform. New York is primarily a commercial and financial center; Chicago is a manufacturing and transportation center; Detroit is an automobile manufacturing center; Los Angeles is an electronics and aircraft manufacturing center. Each of these subgroups in the society is dependent on a rural hinterland to provide the food the urban residents do not make. Each is also dependent on other communities to provide products that are not manufactured there. The necessity of maintaining the flow of goods among our highly specialized communities is so great that federal legislation has been passed to minimize the possibility of a transportation strike.

Other types of subgroups—business organizations, work teams, associations—are highly specialized. The role structure is also exceedingly refined. The differentiation of the parts is so pervasive at all levels of our society that it is our single most powerful integrative factor.

The division of labor enhances social integration in another way. Associations are often formed among those people who occupy the same role. The associations of physicians, lawyers, engineers, and blue collar workers are well-known examples. These organizations provide an important communication link between their members and the other parts of the society. Through them the members can inform others about their problems and avoid some of the consequences of segmentation.

This communication link is a two-way street; it also can be used to communicate the needs and problems of others to the members of the association via their leaders. The union leader can provide information to the members of his union on the state of the economy in general and the company in which they work in particular. These reports provide the members with interpretations of events that they might not otherwise get.

The existence of associations is a key characteristic that separates a mass from an integrated organization. Without associations, mass behavior, alienation, and anomie would be more prevalent in the organization. Since vital economic and political institutions cannot function properly if mass behavior is prevalent, the value of the integrative and stabilizing association becomes more apparent.

Integration among the parts of the society is also maintained by interaction among the elites of associations, industries, and governmental agencies. The members of these types of organizations—blue collar workers and company executives, for example—may be highly segmented from each other, but their leaders are not. The head of a labor union and the director of labor relations for the company interact frequently. Each is aware of the needs and problems of the other's constituents, and each is aware that the success of his career is largely dependent upon the other. These factors make it difficult for either person to take an extreme position in a bargaining situation.

The members themselves are unlikely to support radical solutions to their problems. The members of an association often belong to other organizations in the society as well. Union members are often members of churches, political parties, and social clubs. Each of these other subgroups has norms that usually support those of the total society, and each socializes its members to obey them. For this reason, if the leader of the union should propose the violent overthrow of the government or of management as a solution to the workers' problems, he would probably lose the support of many of his members.

This heterogeneity of group membership found among the members of the larger associations creates a dilemma for a revolutionist. He needs a large membership if he is to exert great influence, but the larger the membership, the greater will be the number of people who will resist his radical appeals. If the membership of an organization has a variety of overlapping group identifications, the leaders will be forced to mitigate their appeals if they wish to continue to be leaders.

NORMATIVE INTEGRATION

Although increasing size and the elaborate division of labor do not permit the degree of normative integration that is found in many smaller societies, normative integration is not absent in our society. Americans share many cultural values. The values of free enterprise, democracy, liberty, and the maximization of individual potentialities are supported by most of the population. They are built into our Constitution and our other bodies of law. Structural features have been created to resolve conflicts over the primacy of each of these values and the manner in which they should be implemented. The electoral process is intended to resolve conflicts over values peacefully. The legislative process is a means for resolving conflicts among subgroups over which values will be implemented without resorting to unlegitimated conflict and violence.

CONFLICT

It was noted earlier that conflict can be an integrative as well as a segmenting influence (1). Conflict among the parts may be the only means available to some parts to communicate to others the fact that they have problems that are in dire need of problem-solving action. Often conflict can result in the formation of institutionalized means of problem solving where none had existed before.

International conflict was also mentioned as a source of integration. It can sometimes unite the members of a society in the face of a threat from another society. In the face of the current international conflict with Communist nations, the problems of the Negro are cast in a new perspective. It is difficult to maintain the luxury of racial discrimination in view of the gravity of the present international situation. Every major racial incident in the United States is reported in the mass media of the race-conscious uncommitted countries of Asia and Africa. The problem is aggravated when the representative of one of the countries personally experiences the problems of racial discrimination in his travels in this country. Since these nations hold the balance of world power and since they do not like our practice of racial discrimination, continued racial conflict in America increases the difficulty of maintaining the status quo in international affairs.

International conflict also requires the efficient mobilization of the manpower of the society. Many more engineers, mathematicians, and other highly skilled personnel must be trained than currently are being trained. But because of racial discrimination, Negroes remain a virtually untapped source of skilled personnel.

THE USES OF AUTHORITY

The persons who occupy extremely influential roles in the major centers of influence—church, business, and political leaders—can exercise their authority to prevent segmentation or to integrate segmented parts. Church organizations have developed a number of subgroups designed to eliminate religious prejudice. Community councils of churches are often the most prominent and active backers of activities intended to eliminate racial as well as religious prejudice and segmentation. During the period of the heavy immigration of Catholics from the southern and eastern parts of Europe, the Catholic Church played a central role in helping the immigrants to adjust to the culture of American society (2). One expert on American religious history has speculated that Catholic control over the immigrants probably held down the crime rate (2).

The efforts of church leaders are not uniformly successful. Once segmentation has occurred, church leaders experience great difficulty in reaching their members in the affected parts. Their efforts to contact juvenile delinquents and reintegrate them into the society encounter as many barriers as do other agencies' efforts in the same cause. Testimony to the difficulties experienced by church leaders in dealing with the problem of the segmented youth culture is provided by the fact that juvenile delinquency is at least as high among church members as it is in the general population and perhaps higher (3).

The leaders of business organizations can and sometimes do use their authority to maintain the integration of the society. By advocating nondiscriminatory hiring policies, they assist Negroes, Jews, and Catholics in getting jobs commensurate with their abilities. But their efforts in this direction have not been universal and persistent. Their authority can also be used to integrate an existing work force. Some instances where managerial authority has been used this way have been studied by social scientists (4). They have found that when Negroes and whites are required by management to work together, they generally have maintained harmonious relationships on the job. In one study of a company where southern whites and Negroes were integrated into work teams, it was found that the whites did not change their attitudes toward the Negroes, but they did cooperate with them when they were in their work roles (5).

Business leaders are only beginning to use their vast influence to assist in the process of integrating the parts of the society. Agencies of the government have had to force many of them to change their discriminatory hiring policies. They also have been reluctant to use their influence to assist in the elimination of racial segregation in the South.

Unions have been able to use their authority to break down some segmenting barriers. We have already seen how their leaders can operate to minimize segmentation between the managers and the workers. They also help to remove some of the barriers to interaction between Negroes and whites. By including Negroes in their membership and by insisting that the privileges of seniority be extended to this race, they have helped the blue collar Negro to achieve a position of some security. They sometimes use their authority to see that racial differences are not used by the companies as criteria for distributing better jobs. At the national level, unions have exerted their influence to obtain the passage of a variety of legislation intended to solve the problems of people in the segmented parts, particularly in the working classes.

As in the case of business and church leaders, the leaders of unions have not exerted the full measure of their influence to eliminate segmentation. Although the evidence is not decisive, it is likely that Negroes are underrepresented in the leadership roles of unions (4). Often in factories in the South unions will agree to maintain racial discrimination in hiring practices in order to organize the white workers.

Although the records of the organizations discussed above have not been too impressive thus far, they are likely to improve in the future. It has only been in the last decade that governmental agencies have recognized the value of working through these organizations to reduce racial and religious segmentation. Civil rights groups have discovered this potential even more recently. The public relations minded leaders of these organizations are beginning to find the costs of segmentation greater than the rewards.

Public Authority and Integration

There are three major ways in which the authority of national, state, and local governments *can* be used to integrate the parts of the society. They often can eliminate barriers by issuing directives or executive orders to eliminate segmenting conditions. They can solve the problems that segment the society. And they can provide mediators to rationalize interactions between the representatives of segmented parts and help them to solve their problems.

One of the classic uses of executive orders to eliminate segmenting barriers occurred during and after World War II, when executive orders were issued to integrate racially segmented military units. During the war, experiments had shown that the white members of integrated platoons exhibited less racial prejudice than whites who were in segmented platoons (6). These same experiments also showed that the Negroes in integrated platoons had higher morale and were more effective soldiers than the Negroes in segregated platoons. Subsequent to this successful venture in racial integration, the executive branch of the government has used directives to integrate factories holding contracts for government work, military hospitals, and communities that service military bases.

Various legislative programs are intended to solve the problems of people in different segments in order to prevent further segmentation or to help eliminate it. Housing, social security, and medical aid programs are designed to alleviate some of the most severe problems of the lower working class. Social scientists and the leaders of the national government now recognize that these programs have not really helped the people who need the most help—the lower working class—and greater effort is now being expended to assist these people. Governments at all levels have concerned themselves with the problems of the youth culture: delinquency and dropping out of school. Funds for research into these problems and to support action programs have been made available.

In addition to solving potentially segmenting problems, political leaders also use their authority to create institutionalized linkages between the segmented parts. In the 1930's the federal government and some state governments passed legislation that recognized the right of workers to organize and bargain collectively with management groups. The federal government also fostered the organization of the Farm Bureau: an organization designed to establish communication linkages between the farmers and the national government.

Governments also maintain elaborate facilities to mediate disputes between the representatives of different segments of the society. The Federal Mediation Service maintains a large staff of experts trained to mediate labor-management disputes; most of the states have parallel agencies. Court systems are an obvious application of governmental influence to settle disputes between parts of the society. By these means disputes can be settled without resort to violence.

The courts also function to break down the segmenting barriers in the society. The United States Supreme Court demonstrated this use of federal authority in the 1954 decision that proclaimed educational segmentation of Negroes to be unconstitutional. Since that decision, the court has continued to exercise its authority continuously to remove the barriers of discrimination in the school system. It has also declared other forms of racial segmentation unconstitutional.

THE MEDIA

The technology of industrialism has been used to create a variety of types of media; newspapers, magazines, books, radio, television, and motion pictures are the major ones. Each caters to vast audiences and to a variety of different tastes. The primary role of the media is to provide entertainment, but they are also a significant integrating influence in American society.

The media can help to make us aware of the problems existing in the segmented parts of the society; they can provide us with the communication linkages needed to expose these problems to the population. Consider the problem of young people dropping out of school. Most American families have not had direct experience with this problem because it is most common in the lower working class. Data that described the magnitude and consequences of dropping out of school existed in publications of the U.S. Bureau of the Census. The data showed that the dropout problem was becoming increasingly serious. The number of children dropping out of school by the time they had reached the tenth grade was increasing. These children were inadequately trained to obtain jobs in a society that placed increasing emphasis on the possession of a special skill. The census data showed that these youngsters waited a longer average time before they obtained their first job than did young people who completed their high school training. Census data are not read by very many Americans, so this esoteric form of the media did not inform the general American public of the seriousness of this problem. But census data are read carefully by social scientists, writers for magazines, reporters, and other communications specialists. Not long after the publication of the census data, articles discussing the problem of the dropout appeared in many magazines and newspapers. These articles were written to communicate to various audiences in terms that were meaningful to them. But still nothing approaching direct knowledge of the impact of dropping out of school was available to the general population. The graphic media, particularly television, picked up the problem from these other sources and presented highly personal studies of the effects of dropping out of school on *individuals*. We were permitted to "live with" a dropout for a half hour. The problem now had greater direct impact on the population; a public opinion favorable to government action to deal with the problem was formed. Agencies of governments at all levels have been pressured into creating programs to reduce the dropout rate.

The media also help to coordinate activities in the society. The publishers of newspapers that service subcommunities in our largest cities regularly scan the media in search of information of importance to their readers (7). They inform their readers of the relevance of certain events for their subcommunities. They also support community charity drives and other integrative activities through the medium of their newspapers. The integrative influence of the community newspaper publisher is also exerted directly on the political and economic decision makers who guide the affairs of the subcommunity and the larger city in which it is located. The publisher interacts with these other leaders directly in social and organizational settings, and most of the other leaders are regular readers of his newspaper.

The publication of the results of scientific research is another way in which the media are used to coordinate the activities of the members of our society. Medical findings are converted into medical practice after they are published. Social scientists, engineers, lawyers, and other professionals are greatly dependent on the media to provide them with information that has a crucial bearing on their routine actions.

The media are also used to reinforce the norms of the society. The most popular media provide an almost unbroken succession of morality plays in which moral dilemmas are discussed and solved. Family situation stories provide solutions for the problems of relating to our wives, husbands, or children. Other plots provide us with orientations to our other interpersonal relationships. Virtually all of the media reinforce the norms of the society by rejecting radical solutions to human problems. During the economic depression of the 1930's, numerous motion pictures were released that treated the problems of the unemployed workers sympathetically. These themes were often designed to soften the blow of the depression; they suggested that poor people were happier, wiser, and mentally healthier than rich people and that poor people eventually received their just rewards. An optimism about the future was maintained; a young man could open a garage and become the successful owner of a chain of garages or the salesgirl in the department store could marry the owner's son.

SOCIAL MOBILITY

People who have experienced upward mobility have had the unique experience of participating in some of the subcultures found in each social class. Some of these people may have lived in working class neighborhoods when they were children, lower middle class neighborhoods in the early stages of their careers, and upper middle class neighborhoods at the culmination of those careers. A more common pattern is to move from the lower middle to the upper middle class. Many of these upwardly mobile people have learned the nuances of language in each social class, the life styles of the members, and a variety of other information about the subcultures. They have the capacity to communicate meaningfully to the members of more subcultures than do the preponderant majority of people, who have not experienced mobility in their lifetimes. They are also capable of providing others with insights into the problems and behaviors of people in different subcultures.

Before the significance of this relationship between upward mobility and social integration can be understood, we must first discuss the emerging role of the middleman in our society. On two earlier occasions it was noted that segmentation can lead to the development of marked subcultural differences among the segments and a consequent further decline in the ability for the members of the segmented parts to communicate with each other. If the organization is to remain intact, roles must develop that have as their chief function the maintenance of two-way communication and problem solving among the affected parts: the role of the middleman. These people can mediate disputes, communicate meaningfully to the members of each of the disputing parts, and provide each with insight into the needs and problems of the other. The bona fide middleman must have considerable knowledge of the life styles, habits of thought, and manners of communicating of more than one subculture or segment in the society. We would expect a high proportion of the occupants of middleman roles, therefore, to have experienced upward mobility in the society.

There are many specific middleman roles in American society: politicians, mediators and negotiators, public relations experts, advertising executives, and writers are among the most important and well known. Since the days of Andrew Jackson, and up to the 1950's, the major recruitment base for politicians was the working class. Many persons in the working class saw politics as an excellent way to obtain a maximum of influence with a minimum of education. The successful politicians headed a party organization that linked the neighborhoods in his community with the key centers of influence. Like the other associations we have discussed, this party structure provided a two-way communication path that could be used to minimize the effects of segmentation.

The successful politician was very often a man who could trace his origins to the working class but who was now a member of the upper middle class. This mobility experience helped him to understand the needs and problems of people at various class levels. He could allocate the resources at his command to them to help solve those problems, and he could communicate the needs and problems of people in one segment of the society to people in another.

Since World War II, the upwardly mobile politician has steadily been replaced by women, lawyers, public relations firms, and people with ascribed wealth in the elite roles of party organizations. Lacking any genuine understanding of various subcultures, these people prefer to manipulate the electorate through the mass media rather than through a ward organization. Theirs is the politics of personalities rather than party organizations. If they allow the precinct organizations to atrophy, they destroy one of the communication links between various segments and the centers of influence. It is not clear yet whether this trend to mass media rather than associational politics will continue, but the consequences for social integration are both clear and negative.

Since World War II there has been an enormous increase in the number of practitioners of another of the middleman roles: the public relations specialist. This expert performs integrative activities that are sometimes superficial in their effects and other times profoundly useful. If he represents an industrial concern, he may devise a series of superficially integrative programs to increase the popularity of the company in the communities where it has plants and among the workers in those plants. Motors are given to high schools for use in auto shops, land is given to the city for use as a sanitary land fill, or a beach is purchased on a nearby lake for the use of the employees of the company. A more useful integrative function is performed by the public relations specialist when he prevents his client from performing a potentially segmenting act by advising him of the consequences of that act.

The key skill of the public relations specialist (just as it is that of the advertising executive) is his ability to predict the reactions of various parts of the population to different activities and to communicate meaningfully to those populations. Leila Sussman submitted questionnaires to a sample of public relations specialists (8). The questionnaires delved into the backgrounds, career patterns, and value orientations of these people. She found that most public relations specialists had experienced upward mobility. They come from lower middle class families in the urban areas of the northeastern part of the United States. The great majority of them went to college, where they took many courses in literature and composition. After completing their college training, they experienced occupational and social mobility that sensitized them to other subcultures in the society. Sussman reports that they believe business management is the core of society and that their task is to maintain open channels of communication between the groups they represent and the other segments of the society in order to prevent misunderstandings. Unfortunately, their programs sometimes obscure misunderstandings rather than prevent them: a tendency that impairs the exercise of their full integrative potential.

Among the most interesting of the middlemen are the writers. Some ply their trade by writing books, others by writing movie scripts, and still others are reporters. Good writers possess the ability to communicate to others the thoughts, feelings, problems, and needs of people in different subcultures. A Richard Wright or a James Baldwin can tell us what it is like to grow up in a Negro subculture and give us insights into the problems of being a Negro. An Ernest Hemingway can capture the verve as well as the pathetic aimlessness that characterized the lives of many of the people who grew to adulthood in the 1920's. An F. Scott Fitzgerald can portray life in the upper class with a lucidity that has escaped subsequent generations of writers. Television writers and newspaper reporters can perform a similar function. The human interest story is an attempt to personalize the impact of seemingly impersonal events. One article in the newspaper reports a two-car collision in which several people were killed, but the human interest story tells us the effects of this incident on the families of the deceased in highly personal and universally understood terms.

Like the public relations man, the writer very often comes from a working class or lower middle class family background (9, 10). He experiences a pattern of upward mobility similar to that of the public relations man. He possesses the unique ability to communicate to us the thoughts and problems of people in segments other than our own; he provides us with social insight.

VIOLENCE AND COERCION

George Orwell, in his *1984,* gives us an extreme and fanciful example of how violence can be used to keep the members of the society from developing deviant subcultures that would be segmented from the rest of the society. The hero, Winston, is alternately tortured by some sophisticated machinery and subjected to verbal coercion until he readjusts his cognitive processes to admit that "two plus two equals five." At the end of the novel the tormented Winston comes to love the people who have tortured him. Fanciful as the specific events are, they are based on the sound principle that violence and coercion can be used to maintain the integration of a social organization. Bruno Bettelheim's studies of prisoners in concentration camps showed that under these conditions of extreme deprivation and violence, the prisoners often developed strong positive emotional attachments to their guards—the very people who were bent on their destruction (11).

Totalitarian elites make use of this integrative effect of terror on the populations they control. The threat of terror is often sufficient to prevent the vast majority of the population from deviating from the norms. The occasional visible exercise of terror can be used to remind the people that it exists and can be used against them too.

SUMMARY

Of the many integrative influences examined in this chapter, the differentiation of the parts is undoubtedly the most important one. Specialization makes populations interdependent, often in spite of the fact that they might prefer greater segmentation. Conflict, violence, and coercion can also be used to unite a population or to prevent it from forming subgroups that deviate from the norms of the total society. The mass media help to coordinate the routines of distant parts of the society and to provide us with social insight. In order to maintain open channels of communication between segmented parts of the system, the role of the middleman is developing in importance, and the occupants of that role are increasingly numerous. Because the role requires skill at communicating with people in different segments of the society, it is very often filled by people who have experienced upward mobility.

REFERENCES

1 L. A. Coser, *The Functions of Social Conflict* (New York: Free Press of Glencoe, Inc., 1956).

2 W. Sweet, *The American Churches* (New York: Abingdon-Cokesbury Press, 1947).

3 M. L. Barron, *The Juvenile in Delinquent Society* (New York: Alfred A. Knopf, Inc., 1954).

4 Many of these findings are summarized in H. Blumer, "Recent Research on Race Relations: United States of America," *International Social Science Bulletin, 10* (1958), 403-47.

5 L. M. Killian, "The Effects of Southern White Workers on Race Relations in Northern Plants," *American Sociological Review, 17* (1952), 327-31.

6 S. A. Stouffer, "A Study of Attitudes," *The Scientific American, 180* (May, 1949), 11-15.

7 M. Janowitz, *The Community Press in an Urban Setting* (New York: Free Press of Glencoe, Inc., 1952).

8 L. A. Sussman, "Personnel and Ideology of Public Relations," *The Public Opinion Quarterly, 12* (1949), 697-708.

9 L. C. Rosten, *The Washington Correspondents* (New York: Harcourt, Brace, and World, Inc., 1931).

10 L. C. Rosten, *Hollywood: The Movie Colony, The Movie Makers* (New York: Harcourt, Brace, and World, Inc., 1941).

11 B. Bettelheim, "Individual and Mass Behavior in Extreme Situations," *Journal of Abnormal and Social Psychology, 38* (1943), 417-52.

the family as an integrative influence

Rivaling the differentiation of the parts as an integrative influence is the family. The continued existence of an organization is dependent on the recruitment of new members to replace those who have died or retired from active participation. Before they can fill vacated roles, the new members must possess fundamental linguistic and physical skills. They must learn the norms and values that govern social behavior. The family is the basic unit that performs these functions.

Not all families perform this integrative function adequately; sometimes they train their children in patterns of behavior and thought that are detrimental to the integration of the society. As was shown earlier, lower working class socialization often fails to inculcate the appropriate skills and values in children for successful performance in the society. But most families perform their integrative functions well.

The mechanism of integration used by the family is *socialization:*

the process of converting a human organism into a skilled person. One cannot perform this process for oneself; nor does it occur automatically as a child grows up. The case of Isabelle illustrates the necessity of human interaction if the child is to become a skilled person (1). Isabelle was the illegitimate daughter of a mentally defective farm girl. In order to hide their shame from others, the grandparents locked Isabelle and her mother in a darkened room. For the next six and a half years the child experienced little human contact. The grandparents satisfied her basic biological needs, but otherwise avoided contact with the child and her mother. The mother was an inadequate source of human interaction because she was a deaf mute as well as mentally defective. When the authorities found Isabelle, she was more like an animal than a human being; she crawled on her hands and knees, emitted gutteral sounds, and was obviously frightened by the presence of other human beings. The child was placed under the supervision of a team of specialists, and during the next two years she progressed rapidly to being a normal eight-and-a-half-year-old. Later tests revealed that she was mentally normal. Isabelle's earlier condition was attributable to her lack of human contact, interaction, and socialization.

The next part of this chapter discusses the mechanics of familial socialization. In order to gain maximum insight into this process, we will think in terms of individuals rather than populations. In other words, our approach will be social-psychological rather than strictly sociological. Following that discussion, we will examine the changing role of the family in modern society on a more general basis.

THE FAMILY AND SOCIALIZATION *

The newborn child is an autistic organism; he is unable to distinguish objects in his environment—much less interact with them; he cries when he is hungry and sleeps when he is not; he is completely self-absorbed. With very few exceptions his physical and verbal behavior is random. He kicks his feet, moves his arms, and emits purely random sounds.

The child's awareness of his social environment gradually increases; he learns to recognize his mother's face and her voice. He begins to respond to her. The child becomes aware of the fact that he is utterly dependent on this other person to remove his discomforts, but also learns that she does not always remove them immediately. He learns that when his mother is busy with certain tasks, his crying will not

* This discussion is based primarily on T. M. Newcomb's *Social Psychology* (New York: The Dryden Press, 1954).

elicit the response from her that he desires. When she is busy, she may even sanction him negatively with harsh, loud words. Gradually, he learns that his parents are pursuing objectives of their own and that he must modify his behavior in order to get what he wants. His physical behaviors become less random as he discovers that some of them are useful for obtaining things. He learns to grasp objects and draw them to him, to throw them, to turn them in his hands, to sit up, and to crawl. He practices each of these behaviors endlessly, energetically, and with great fascination. Every mother ruefully recalls instances when her child threw toys out of the crib repeatedly in spite of frequent admonishments to stop. The mother assumes that the child is being mischievous, but at this stage he is merely experimenting with his new-found physical skills. Later he will learn the nuisance value of his behavior. His development is usually assisted and even led by his admiring parents. Each successful mastery of a physical skill is an occasion for effusive rewarding behavior: being picked up, hugged, and generally given attention.

Verbal skills develop simultaneously and in a similar manner to his development of physical skills. The child learns that some of the sounds he uses are more influential than others; they cause others to respond to him. This discovery causes the child to learn other sounds that have the same effects. His parents are eager helpers in the development of his vocabulary. Gradually, through the use of certain facial muscles, the child masters the common sounds and words of his parents' language. He loses his natural ability to make sounds that are not relevant for his parents' language. This lost ability is evident to us whenever we try with indifferent success to learn to make the different sounds of a foreign language: sounds made with ease during the first year of life.

After the child masters individual behaviors, he begins to integrate them with each other. He learns to skip a rope, bounce a ball while walking, and to talk while he is eating. This difficult process of learning to integrate behaviors will continue until very late in his life. It is accomplished by the use of a few important interpersonal mechanisms. The first of these is the use of sanctions by the parents. Parents reward their children for the mastery of certain behaviors and punish them for others. By these means they guide his selection of behaviors. The child also discovers that his parents are never wrong; their predictions of the consequences of his actions are unfailingly accurate. If he is about to put his hand on a hot stove, his mother tells him that it will hurt him. If he does it anyway, he learns that she was correct. Because of his parents' uncanny accuracy, the child learns to accept their views. As he confronts some of the more nebulous problems of life—ethical and value issues—he accepts the viewpoints of his parents, who are obviously experts. He learns that it is good to be honest, to work hard, and to respect his elders. Whether he will be a conservative or liberal, religious or an atheist, out-going or withdrawn is usually determined in these early years. The child also uses his parents as a model for his own behavior; he loves them and he wants to be like them. He wants to learn to walk because they do; he wants to use a spoon rather than his fingers because they do; he wants to dress and talk like his daddy because he is "his boy."

CHANGES IN THE FAMILY FROM AGRARIAN TO INDUSTRIAL SOCIETY

Obviously, the family plays a vital role in the preparation of children to assume skilled roles in the society. Yet for all its importance, the family has undergone some fundamental changes that have impaired its effectiveness as an integrative organization. These changes occurred at the same time that societies were shifting from an agrarian to an industrial form of organization. In this section the structure and functioning of the agrarian family is compared with that of the industrial family.

But before we begin that comparison, a few observations must be made about the relationship between industrialization and the structure of the family. For many years, the vogue in sociology was to examine the technological factors that *caused* changes in the structure of the family (2). The introduction of machine technology, for example, took productive activities out of the home and relocated them in factories. As a result, family size declined, because children were no longer needed in productive activities; in fact, they detracted from the economic position of the family, since they were in nonproductive roles. This relationship between the technology and the family is important, but it is not the whole story. It fails to take into account the dynamic relationship of the parts of a social organization. We might ask, for example, how rapidly industrialization would have occurred in western Europe or the United States if the agrarian families in these areas had been organized similarly to the agrarian families in the Middle and Near East. The fact is that the particular structure of the preindustrial family in Europe and the United States may have contributed to the rapid industrialization of these societies. Even after industrialization had begun in Europe, the effects of changes in the family—changes that were in many respects independent of industrialization—accumulated in such a way as to cause changes in the development of the factory system (3). We conclude, then, that the relationship between the economy and the family has been one of parallel and interactive development in which the economy is a dominant influence, but not an overwhelming one (4).

The Agrarian Family

The agrarian family is relatively multifunctional. It is primarily a producing unit whose members produce the food they eat, the clothes they wear, and many of the tools they use. It is also the center of religious observances: a responsibility it might share with a priest or a small religious association. It is *the* educational institution in the community. In addition, the family is the center of recreational activity and companionship.

The emphasis on production affects the structure and functioning of the family in many ways. Marriages are viewed more as business alliances than as love matches. Spouses are selected for their ability to assist in productive activities, their physical health, and their reliability. Attributes such as friendliness and sexual attractiveness are secondary. The Mexican peasant husband actually prefers to marry a woman who is disinterested in sex, because he feels more confident that she will not be promiscuous with the other men in the village when he is away working in the fields (5). Social interaction in the agrarian family is characterized by far less warmth than it is in the successful American marriage.

If the size of the landholdings and the level of technology require it, the agrarian family is large. Sometimes large size is obtained by extended family living; other times the family is nuclear, but there are many children. The agrarian family is usually, though not always, patrilocal. The husband has inherited his land from his father, and the wife has moved into his house. The father is expected to assert the masculine aspects of his role. He is an autocrat, although his wife can mitigate his decisions occasionally. He hopes to demonstrate his masculinity by producing many sons, working hard on his land, and demonstrating his capacity for drinking with the other male members of the village. The norms of agrarian society support this performance by clearly differentiating his work from women's work and by inculcating in young women the virtues of the patriarchal arrangement. Divorce is uncommon and often proscribed. Where it is permitted, the grounds are usually the wife's inability to produce children or either partner's unwillingness to perform the expected productive functions.

The roles of agrarian children are quite different from those of children in industrial societies. Children are valued as additional workers. In unmechanized agrarian societies they are essential if the family is to survive. Without them, the couple would face the prospect of having no one to care for them in their old age. So crucial are children to survival that they are often believed to be gifts from God: an attitude that explains some of the resistance to birth control programs in the underdeveloped countries. In medieval Europe, small children were thought of as animals similar to the other ones that were raised on the farm (6). As soon as they were old enough to help with the work, they were then thought of as young adults. The medieval farmer had no concept equivalent to our notion of "child"; there were babies and adults. When the children are old enough, the parents begin training them. The boys spend their days with their father in the fields and the daughters in the house with their mothers. At this very early age, then, the children develop definite sex identifications.

If the economy features settled agriculture, the family is not spatially mobile. The children grow up in the village of their parents: a pattern that will be repeated each generation. The position of the family and of its members in the village social structure seldom changes. The family roles are relatively clear and consistent. Life in agrarian society is relatively unambiguous and unchanging.

The Industrial Family

The family in an industrial society presents a sharply contrasting picture. It has lost to large, bureaucratic organizations (or must share with them) many of its older functions. Productive functions are controlled by large industrial organizations. Few husbands own the organization that they leave home to work in every day. Many family educational activities have been taken over by school systems; religious training is provided primarily by church systems. Even recreational activities are increasingly being provided by outside agencies: Little League sports teams, athletic associations, and the myriad other organizations that cater to the tastes of young people. Since the husband's place of work is often changed, the modern family is more mobile. It is increasingly common for the family to live in two or three different communities and many neighborhoods in the course of its existence. This mobility increases the ambiguity of the family position in the social structure.

The stripping away of many of the central activities of the agrarian family has changed the marriage relationship and the bases for selecting marital partners. Partners are now selected for their potential as companions. Physical appearance and personality dimensions increase in importance. The career-oriented young man also looks for a girl who will be an asset to his career: a girl who has developed smooth social relationships. But the opportunities to choose a suitable marriage partner are very restricted. The mobility of the family and the great size of communities decrease the likelihood that couples knew each other when they were growing up. The courting system is usually inadequate to give young people any deep insights into the prospects for a successful marriage. But in spite of the functional weakening of the family and the difficulties in making a good choice for a spouse, *more* young people are getting married today than formerly and at an increasingly young age.

Marriage creates at least as many problems as it solves for the partners. The norms that govern the division of labor in the modern family are less clear and consistent than they are in agrarian societies. As a result, the modern family is less integrated functionally than the agrarian family. The importance of masculine performance is still inculcated in male children, but norms of the society and the family no longer support this position unequivocally. The virtue of equalitarian decision making is stressed, so the husband must resolve the conflict between his masculine role and sharing decision-making activities with his wife. His role as a husband is no longer clearly delineated. His wife expects him to perform many activities around the house that he considers to be women's work. In the earliest years of the marriage, most of the arguments will be over role expectations: who will take out the garbage, who will wash the windows on the outside and who on the inside?

If the functional integration of the family is reduced, the happiness of the relationship is very likely to suffer (7). Studies of marital happiness among American couples show that between 15 and 20 per cent of the married couples interviewed are unhappy in their present marriages and another 20 per cent are neither happy nor unhappy (8, 9). The increased instability of the modern marriage is reflected in the data on divorces and annulments. At the turn of the present century, there was one divorce for every 12 marriages. By 1950, 3 out of every 12 marriages ended in divorce or annulment (10). That rate has been fairly stable for the last decade. Not included in these statistics are the separation or desertion rates, which are not insignificant. For every four marriages that are formally terminated, there is another one ended by desertion of one of the partners (11). Accurate data on the prevalence of separations are not available.

The family roles of children have also been affected by the shift from agrarian to industrial society. Young people no longer have productive roles in the family; they have had to develop new ones for themselves. Their roles also lack clarity and certainty. The son is seldom trained by his father in the latter's trade. Since the father works away from the home, the sons have no real comprehension of his job. Since the male children cannot go to work with their fathers, they are usually trained by their mothers, with the result that they often learn a female version of the male role. Young girls are now being taught to develop their own vocational skills rather than to wait to become homemakers. Many women attempt to maintain both marriage and work roles. But their careers are interrupted by pregnancies and the necessity of caring for their children. Forced to withdraw from the world of work, the wives must choose between new avenues of individual effort and becoming a housewife who satisfies her personal ambition by identifying with her husband's career. Many wives who worked before they had children return to the labor force as soon as they can arrange for the care of their children or when the children have grown up. Others pursue their ambitions in the status hierarchies of voluntary associations, golf and bridge tournaments, or other organizations in the world of feminine leisure.

Since children are not necessary as workers, the size of the modern family has decreased dramatically. Compare the size of families of women born between 1900 and 1904 (who would have completed their families by now) with women born between 1835 and 1839 (12). Table 18-1 shows that comparison. A third of the families in agrarian America contained seven or more children, compared to only 7 per cent of the families today. Six out of every ten modern families have two or less children, compared with one out of every four in the earlier period.

TABLE 18-1

PERCENTAGE DISTRIBUTION OF EVER-MARRIED WOMEN
BY NUMBER OF CHILDREN BORN TO THEM

Number of	Year of birth of women	
children	1835-1839	1900-1904
0	8 %	20 %
1–2	17	42
3–4	20	23
5–6	19	8
7–9	21	5
10 or more	15	2
	100 %	100 %

Source: Department of Commerce, Bureau of the Census, *Historical Statistics of the United States, Colonial Period to 1957*, Series B 19, p. 24.

THE ROLE OF THE MODERN FAMILY

Because of the erosion of family functions, some social scientists have speculated that the family may eventually disappear as a social unit. To support their argument they call attention to certain socialist societies where more of the functions of the family have been assumed by the state. On the collective farms in Israel—the kibbutzim —the care of children was assigned to trained specialists rather than to the parents (13). The parents visited their children at the nurseries maintained by the collectives. The parents themselves ate in communal dining rooms and shared general recreational facilities. Their private quarters were a single room adequate only for sleeping and sexual intercourse. Immediately after they had established themselves in power, the leaders of the Soviet Union instituted many similar programs, some of which still exist despite a growing emphasis on the importance of the family.

The fact remains that the family does play a vital role in the affairs of the society and in the lives of its members. The structural weaknesses of the contemporary family may be merely transitional: symptoms of changes in the organization of the larger society. The family provides a means for transferring wealth through the mechanism of inheritance. One reason that some socialist leaders have de-emphasized the role of the family is to avoid the development of a self-perpetuating class system by removing the possibility of inheritance. The family is still *the* primary group in virtually all societies. It is still the most important source of emotional support and companionship: a trait that makes it extremely attractive. It is still the most important institution for socializing children, which makes it particularly useful to the other parts of the society. It also simplifies interpersonal relations. Social activities are likely to be more regularized and predictable in a marital relationship than outside one. Marriage provides sexual protection for the wife. It also offers the only legitimate means of satisfying the desire to have children. Finally, the family organization can be used to cope with some of the complexities of modern living by developing an appropriate division of labor. Many wives have become specialists in making consumer decisions. They have developed considerable knowledge of the price structure of commodities: they are informal comparison shoppers. They are assisted in this task by a variety of women's magazines and consumer bulletins. Wives also have become specialists in the management of their homes. Freed from detailed involvement in these activities, husbands can devote their energies more fully to the pursuit of their occupations.

Relationships Between the Family and the Economy

The family is locked in a series of interdependent relationships with other parts of the society. We have already seen the important role that the family plays in preparing children for the school system and in sustaining their performance in it. The family and religious organizations also work together to support each other's values and those of the total society. But perhaps the most important of the interdependencies is between the family and the economy. The family supplies workers for industries and markets for the goods, and the industries provide income for the family. And not only the husband works: the working wife is becoming increasingly prevalent. In 1890 only 1 out of every 20 married women worked: today 7 out of 20 work (14). Another increasing trend is for the husband to take a second job: a practice known as "moonlighting." Between 5 and 7 per cent of workers have second jobs. Although the family is no longer a producing unit, it is a working unit. The complex work relationships that can develop in the family are illustrated if we look at the family's life cycle. When a young couple gets married, the common practice is for the wife to withdraw from the labor force and to devote her full time to the homemaking role. This pattern is being modified currently by an increasing tendency for the wife to remain in the labor force after her marriage. In a recent study of 1,000 blue collar workers and their wives, it was found that among wives who were less than 35 years old and who had no children, over 50 per cent were working (15). Of these working wives, half had working hours different from their husbands', which meant that they did not see each other very often on working days. These young people are accumulating money as rapidly as possible to realize a family life plan. The husband is not likely to have a second job during this period. When the first child is born, the wife usually drops out of the labor force and the husband becomes the sole provider for the family. It is during this period after the birth of the first child that the husband is most likely to get a second job. As the number of children increases, the probability of getting a second job also increases. In young families where there are three or more children, over 20 per cent of the husbands had a second job (15). As the children grow old enough to take care of themselves or leave home, the wife who worked before she had her first child is likely to return to work, and the moonlighter is likely to quit his second job.

Changes in the economy can have profound effects on the structure and functioning of the family. When the economy is depressed and unemployment rates increase, the family of the unemployed worker is seriously affected (16). Loss of income is the most immediate problem, but other consequences are equally important. The husband has failed to maintain the role that the norms of the society ascribe to him. His wife may take in work or get a job and become the most influential member of the family. The husband loses much of his ability to control the behavior of his children. Quarreling and declining involvement in social activities further threaten the integration of the family.

A second illustration of the effects of economic decisions on the family is provided by the phenomenon of shift work. Workers are often required to work during hours other than the usual 8 A.M. to 4 P.M. Twenty per cent of the workers in our major cities work either from 4 to 12 P.M. or from 12 P.M. to 8 A.M. (17). Many more workers must be on their jobs during a different span of hours *each week*. Companies could not maintain these shift schedules if the workers' families did not make the necessary adjustment to them. The wife must make many more meals each day, and she must do her housework at unusual times when her husband and children are not sleeping. Shift work changes the structure and functioning of the family in other ways (18). It increases the difficulty of performing the husband and father roles. The shift worker cannot provide companionship for his wife during the normal evening hours and, if he is an afternoon shift worker, he seldom sees his children, except on his days off. Since he cannot fulfill the normal male role in family activities, serious problems of coordinating family activities develop. Among the families of afternoon and night shift workers, functional integration is lower and conflict among the members is more prevalent than it is among day shift workers.

Relationships Between the Family and the State

The family is a key institution for training members of the society in the value of loyalty to the state. The children are also taught the responsibilities of their roles as citizens. Their future voting behavior is largely determined in the family setting. The role of the family in shaping these citizenship values and activities is so fundamental that the leaders of totalitarian societies see the family as a threat to their objectives (19). Totalitarian leaders desire absolute normative homogeneity among the members of the society; the relatively diverse teachings of families are totally unsatisfactory to them. Therefore, the leaders have sought means to destroy the family as a viable institution. In the Soviet Union, church marriages were not legal (19). A legal state marriage could be obtained by signing a registry in a government office. Either partner could obtain a divorce simply by filling out a form in another bureau. Marriages lasting a single day were not uncommon. Children were enrolled in state-sponsored associations where they were taught to inform on their parents if they made seditious remarks. Parents were told that it was illegal for them punish their own children. With the parents living in fear of their own children and only very loosely attached to each other, the Soviet family devolved into something less than *the* primary group.

The importance of the family in the lives of its members is demonstrated by the fact that in those societies where the state has sought to eliminate it as an effective unit of socialization, it has persevered and after an initial period of weakness regained its strength. On the collective farms in Israel the family is becoming a stronger unit (20). The apartments of the parents are more spacious, meals can be eaten in the apartment rather than in the communal dining rooms, and children are permitted to live with their parents. Soviet leaders became alarmed at the decline in the birth rate and the increasing prevalence of abortions during the period of the eclipse of the family. The policy of de-emphasizing the family was reversed. Today in the Soviet Union, the family is a very strong unit.

The state provides the family with many services. It provides protection for the family and welfare services that are designed to help it in periods of economic or psychological distress.

SUMMARY

The family is the major socializing institution in most societies. It prepares young people to assume roles in other subgroups in the social system. It is also the major source of companionship and a contributory source of recreational and religious activities.

In spite of its attractiveness and importance, the family has undergone some changes that have weakened it as an institution. It has lost many of its older functions to large bureaucratic organizations. In the present transitional period, the norms governing the roles of its members are not clear. The development of the youth culture due to the withdrawal of young people from productive roles and placing them in schools has segmented parent-child interaction. Because of the operation of these and other factors, family integration and happiness are far less than perfect. Divorce rates have increased. Nonetheless it is concluded that the family is not a dying institution; it serves too many important functions for its members. As this unit adjusts to the demands of life in an industrial society, it will probably reassume some of its earlier stability.

REFERENCES

1 K. Davis, "Final Note on a Case of Extreme Isolation," *The American Journal of Sociology, 52* (1947), 432-37.

2 W. F. Ogburn, "The Family and Its Functions," in *Recent Social Trends* by the President's Research Committee on Social Trends (New York: McGraw-Hill Book Company, 1943), 661-71.

3 N. J. Smelser, *Social Change in the Industrial Revolution* (Chicago: The University of Chicago Press, 1959).

4 W. J. Goode, *The Family* (Englewood Cliffs, N.J.: Prentice-Hall, Inc., 1964). Foundation of Modern Sociology Series.

5 O. Lewis, *Tepoztlan: Village in Mexico* (New York: Holt, Rinehart & Winston, Inc., 1960).

6 P. Aries, *Centuries of Childhood; A Social History of Family Life,* R. Baldick, trans. (London: Jonathan Cape, Ltd., 1962).

7 P. Mott and D. R. Warwick, "Shift Work and Social Relationships." Paper read at the *Meetings of the American Sociological Association,* August, 1963.

8 L. M. Terman, *et al., Psychological Factors in Marital Happiness* (New York: McGraw-Hill Book Company, 1939).

9 E. W. Burgess and L. S. Cottrell, Jr., *Predicting Success or Failure in Marriage* (Englewood Cliffs, N.J.: Prentice-Hall, Inc., 1939).

10 J. L. Hirning and A. L. Hirning, *Marriage Adjustment* (New York: American Book Company, 1956).

11 R. E. Baber, *Marriage and the Family* (New York: McGraw-Hill Book Company, 1953).

12 U.S. Census Bureau, *Historical Statistics of the United States, Colonial Period to 1957,* Series B 19, p. 24.

13 M. E. Spiro, *Kibbutz, Venture in Utopia* (Cambridge: Harvard University Press, 1956).

14 U.S. Census Bureau, *Historical Statistics . of the United States, Colonial Period to 1957,* Series B 19, p. 57.

15 These data were taken from two studies done at The Institute for Social Research, The University of Michigan, Ann Arbor, Michigan. The first study obtained questionnaire

data from 8,500 workers in a utility company (1948). The second study obtained questionnaire data from 1,000 continuous process workers and from their wives in two continuous process companies.

16   E. W. Bakke, "The Cycle of Adjustment to Unemployment," in *A Modern Introduction to the Family,* N. W. Bell and E. F. Vogel, eds. (New York: Free Press of Glencoe, Inc., 1960), pp. 112-25.

17   U.S. Department of Labor, Bureau of Labor Statistics, *Wages and Related Benefits: 82 Labor Markets, 1960-1961,* Bulletin No. 1285083 (1961), 78-80.

18   P. E. Mott, F. C. Mann, Q. McLoughlin, and D. R. Warwick, *Shift Work: The Social, Psychological, and Physical Consequences* (Ann Arbor, The University of Michigan Press, 1965).

19   N. S. Timasheff, "The Attempt to Abolish the Family in Russia," in *A Modern Introduction to the Family,* N. W. Bell and E. F. Bell, eds. (New York: Free Press of Glencoe, Inc., 1960), pp. 55-63.

20   M. E. Spiro, *Children of the Kibbutz* (Cambridge: Harvard University Press, 1958).

part four THE
CENTRALIZATION
OF INFLUENCE AND THE
EMERGENCE OF
THE TOTAL SOCIETY

the centralization of influence in contemporary societies

The major trends that have shaped western societies have been urbanization, the development of an industrial technology, the increasing size of organizations, and the shift from a value system centered on individualism to one of welfare-collectivism. But to understand the directions that industrial societies are taking and will take in the future, another trend, which is becoming increasingly significant, must be examined: the centralization of influence.

THE NEED FOR UNITARY ACTION

Because of the unique problems faced by modern societies, their parts must act in such tight concert that their members must give considerable authority to a central part to act on their behalf. The increasing need for *unitary action* by societies is primarily

responsible for the growing centralization of influence. Central governments have always been vested with some authority to act with a minimum of consultation, but these areas are expanding, and the amount
of consultation is declining. The allocation of authority is not an act
without substance; it is not a mere exchange of communications. It can
be translated in terms of objects: more numerous personnel and agencies, larger budgets, and other resources. As the size and resource base
of a part grows, the other parts increasingly are required to adjust their
activities to its rhythms: its influence grows (1).

These trends seem to contradict Proposition 13, which says that decentralization of authority will accompany increasing organizational
size. Actually, they do not. The authority that has been accumulated
from the smaller units of the society has ordinarily been decentralized
within the social organization of the government itself. The political
elites cannot hope to retain all of the governmental authority in their
hands. Furthermore, there are many areas in which the national governments have created highly decentralized methods of wielding their
newly found influence. In the United States, for example, federal funds
are granted to the states for local administration provided that the
state agencies meet certain nationally established standards of behavior.

The need for unitary action comes as a result both of dramatic
changes in intersocietal relations and of problems occurring within
societies.

External Sources

The technologies of modern communication and war-
fare have heightened the pace, intensity, and seriousness of international interactions. Prior to the twentieth century, diplomatic exchanges and troop movements were slow enough that the elites of each
nation had some time to discuss alternate courses of action. That situation no longer exists; today diplomats can carry on conversations with
each other even though half of the world separates them. These rapid
interactions often require prompt decisions: there is little time for
prolonged discussions among elites representing the various parts of
the society. As a result, the agencies of the central government have
either taken the initiative or been given increasing authority to act for
the populations they represent.

The need for unitary action is greatest in wartime. Modern wars are
total wars involving the total mobilization of populations and resources. Vast authority is given to national governments or expropri-
ated by their agents. The past century has been marked by a series of

such conflicts. In each instance national governments were granted broad authority to regulate the activities of the population. But after each conflict, many governments did not relinquish completely their wartime authority. As a result, many of them have emerged from each war larger and more influential than they were before the war.

The continuing threat of total war and the conditions under which such a war would be fought have also increased the need for unitary action. A permanent state of semimobilization is one consequence of the ever present possibility of war. The military budget of the American federal government hovers around 50 billion dollars annually. It has become a key industry: one that requires considerable centralization of influence. Since nations can be destroyed in a matter of minutes, the authority to respond to nuclear threats must be given to a small number of people who must make a decision for the entire population.

Internal Sources

The causes of the centralization of influence that come from within the societies themselves are often less obvious. Yet unitary action and its consequence, the centralization of influence, are necessary today because of the increased needs for centralized social planning. Human populations have always sought to control the processes of social change within their societies in order to achieve their collective objectives, but their planning was necessarily more limited in scope than it is in modern industrial societies. The ancient Egyptians cleared the swamps that bordered the Nile and developed irrigation systems to water the reclaimed land. But those impressive projects do not compare with modern efforts to reshape the environment and the social structure. Industrial populations have at their command a more facilitative technology, vaster resources, and greater expert knowledge. Modern man can contemplate projects about which the ancients could not even dream. Using his tools and his knowledge, he can control rivers thousands of miles long, convert vast tracts of desert into crop-producing land, or alter the social organization radically.

This same technology also permits centralized agencies to plan for the entire society. In the larger preindustrial societies the means of communication and transportation were so rudimentary that active control over a wide range of projects by a central agency was not possible. Today the remotest parts of societies can be linked to the central planning agencies so that actions can be monitored, decisions requested, and answers transmitted.

Centralized social planning has become increasingly necessary because the parts of industrial societies are highly specialized and extremely interdependent. Changes in the functioning of one part can have important consequences for the other parts, even the most remote ones. Planning becomes essential to control the pace and types of change that take place in or among these parts. The planning must be centralized because the parts themselves are ill-equipped to cope with modern problems. The parts are often highly segmented from each other, their resources are too limited to support unilateral solutions to the problems that they face, or their influence or authority is insufficient to command the necessary responses from the other parts. The effective solution of the problems faced by industrial societies generally requires the coordinated efforts of all of the parts of each society. Some pooling of resources and allocation of authority from the parts to the central planning agencies is required. These planning activities have generally been performed by the national governments in each society. The influence exercised by national governments has grown as their authority and resources have increased.

SOCIAL PLANNING IN THE UNITED STATES. There are many internal reasons for increased social planning and centralization of influence in the United States: three of them are of major importance. First, national political institutions are being used to overcome some of the problems of social segmentation that were discussed earlier. The government as an interested third party can mediate disputes between segmented parts of the society or it can pass legislation that regulates their actions or institutionalizes ways for them to solve their joint problems. The leaders of labor unions, for example, sought and received the assistance of the national government in the passage of legislation that protected certain of the interests of blue collar workers. Other segments of the population—the aged, poor, and racial and religious minority groups—have also looked to the federal government for solutions to their problems. Federal responses increase the number of agencies and the size of the federal budget: influence is centralized.

Second, the problems faced by the parts of American society have often been too vast in scope or cost to be solved by them separately. The problems of controlling floods in the Tennessee Valley or the Missouri-Mississippi river basin are too great for the individual states involved. Federal action and federal authority often have been required to cope with these problems. A parallel form of centralization is occurring among cities. Metropolitan problems are no respecters of city or even state boundaries. The cities and the suburbs that ring them face problems that they can solve only through joint action. Metropolitan authorities are being formed to handle these problems. The range of authority of these metropolitan organizations is growing as additional problems are assigned to them for solutions. This growth in metropolitan authority occurs at the expense of that of the individual communities that comprise them.

A third type of problem has resulted from the early American emphasis on an economy essentially free of social regulation. This principle was built into the Constitution of the United States. The powers of the federal government were explicit and limited; all other powers were reserved for the states and the people. The Constitution erected fences around the economic sector of the society designed to protect it from the encroachments of the federal government. The states were generally unable to regulate the economy. If a state passed stringent child-labor, health, safety, or tax laws, it faced the threat of losing some of its industries to other states and the prospect of not gaining any new ones. Therefore, state legislators were reluctant to pass adequate legislation to protect the disadvantaged members of the population. The pressing nature of these problems has led to the creation of federal authority to cope with them. The relation between the political and the economic sectors of American society can be summarized as follows: under the laissez-faire system, economic activity is naturally diffused among the millions of interactions that take place each day in an industrial society, but political control is limited to certain types of interactions among people. Today, political authority is gradually being extended to include the regulation of more areas of economic interaction.

THE CENTRALIZATION OF INFLUENCE AND THE UNDERDEVELOPED NATIONS

The centralization of influence is not restricted to industrialized societies; it is also strikingly apparent in those underdeveloped societies whose leaders have decided to industrialize *as rapidly as possible.* The centralization of economic, social, and political influence is often required in order to solve the severe problems that accompany rapid industrialization. These nations often have large populations that seldom produce more capital than they use for their personal needs. Yet industrialization requires that each year a 10 per cent surplus of wealth be created for investment in new economic growth (2). The population must be mobilized carefully in order to create the necessary surplus wealth. Often the natural resources of the underdeveloped societies are very limited. A central authority is needed to plan the use of these resources in a manner that will optimize the rate of industrialization. Capital goods must be produced before consumption goods. In a society where steel mills are few in number and low in productivity, resources cannot be used for the construction of a chain of ice cream stands. Because of its small size, the skilled labor force in these societies must be mobilized effectively. If there are only three economists in the society, permitting one of them to be in private practice, another to work for the government, and the third to work for an opposition political party is a luxury that cannot be afforded. All of these skilled personnel must be mobilized to achieve the objectives of the whole society *so long as the leaders insist on rapid and efficient industrialization.* For this reason, among others, opposition political parties are not tolerated in many underdeveloped societies; they divide needed manpower that must be concentrated on the central tasks of the society. Consequently, there is often only a single mass political party in which virtually all of the skilled members of the society are enrolled. Finally, centralization is essential to creation of a national plan of development and to the coordination of the activities of the parts to see that they perform the tasks assigned them in the plan.

THE CENTRALIZATION OF INFLUENCE AND THE TOTAL SOCIETY

The preceding discussion would seem to imply that the centralization of influence is coming about by a gradual, evolutionary process. Sometimes it does, but often this process has been catalyzed by the advocates of a variety of social philosophies who share the belief that increased centralization of authority is essential to solve human problems. The extent to which these political activists would centralize influence varies. The most extreme position is taken by the proponents of the total society in which *all* influence would be concentrated in the hands of a political elite. Such a concentration of influence would involve necessarily the destruction or withering away of all the other subgroups in the society, since these groups contain influence, and since they would also provide a breeding ground for norms that might deviate from those desired by the political elite. Ideally, in the total society the only primary tie would be between *each* member of the society and the elite; the nonelite members would have no such group ties with each other. The state might create groups, but they would be mere front organizations through which the elite could propagandize the members. They would not provide a basis for primary relationships among the members. Possessing all influence and all authority, the elite would regulate all human behavior either directly or indirectly. The total society is a mass society in its most extreme form, but it is one that is purposely created by a political elite.

Although the extreme form of the total society is probably unattainable, close approximations to it could develop *in a variety of ways.* The gradual centralization of influence that is occurring in western industrial societies could lead to the development of a kind of total society. If the range of both influence and authority exercised by the central governments increases and this trend is accompanied by diminished associational and family life, a mild, paternalistic form of the total society could develop. As we have seen, there are social forces that have weakened associational as well as family ties in American society. In the concluding chapter of this volume the possibility of developing a total society in the United States will be discussed.

Another route by which the total society can be and has been developed is that used by the totalitarians. Totalitarian elites differ from other advocates of forms of the total society by their willingness to use terror. They are not concerned as much with the solution of human problems through the centralization of influence as they are with obtaining complete control of the society for themselves. This form of society will be discussed in detail in Chapter 21.

Other political thinkers and activists are less extreme in their proposals. The American liberal desires increased centralization of authority in the hands of the federal government, but there are important limits to the types and uses to which he would put federal authority. To regulate economic activity, for example, general preference is given to passive regulation rather than outright nationalization of enterprises. Socialists prefer a greater concentration of authority and influence in the national government. They hope to solve many human problems by nationalizing some industries and assuming direct control of other human activities. But socialists disagree considerably over the degree of centralization required. Some of them would nationalize only a few key industries while retaining a democratic election system. Others want to nationalize all of the means of production and to control the economy through a system of centralized planning. This type of socialist more nearly approximates the advocate of the total society.

Implicit in the design of all of these ideologies, whether socialism, totalitarianism, or even modern liberalism, is an acceptance of the basic hypothesis of sociology: the structure of organizations will influence various rates of human behavior. The followers of each persuasion believe that man can manipulate his society in order to achieve the behaviors that he desires for his fellow man. Socialists are concerned about man's alienation from his work, the loss of his sense of creativity, and his lack of economic freedom. To remake him into an active, participating, creative member of society they have proposed a number of changes in the social structure. The social structures they have proposed and the effectiveness with which they have achieved their objectives will be discussed in the next chapter. The totalitarians have devised a series of social structural means of maintaining their control over the populations they rule. These structures will also be examined in some detail. In the concluding chapter of this volume, the implications of these isms for American society will be discussed, particularly with reference to the possibility that our society will become a total society.

SUMMARY

In the last century there has been an increasing centralization of influence in many societies. In industrial societies centralization has developed because of the greater need for unitary action today than at any previous period in history. Unitary action is required to cope with the unique circumstances of modern diplomacy and warfare. It is also required to handle some of the internal problems encountered by societies: segmentation, the increasing interdependence among the parts of each society, and the need to solve problems of such scope that they are beyond the capabilities of the individual parts. Underdeveloped countries are also resorting to the centralization of influence in order to hasten the pace of industrialization.

The existence of these problems has given rise to a series of ideologies designed either to solve them or to take advantage of them. Many of them share an advocacy of greater centralization of influence in the central government. Among the more prominent of these isms are the various forms of socialism, totalitarianism, and modern liberalism.

REFERENCES

1   R. Bierstedt, "An Analysis of Social Power," *American Sociological Review, 15* (1950), 730-38.

2   W. Rostow, *The Stages of Economic Growth: A Non-Communist Manifesto* (Cambridge: Cambridge University Press, 1960).

socialisms **20**

Social structures that can be included under the rubric of socialism have existed since antiquity. But most of the early forms of socialism differed considerably from the modern versions because they were developed to solve different problems or they were limited by the rudimentary communication and transportation facilities of preindustrial societies. For this reason, we will limit our discussion to the modern forms of socialism. But to obtain a useful perspective of these socialisms, we must examine the cultural backgrounds in which they developed. We will find a common theme: laissez-faire capitalism and the problems it created. Contemporary socialisms developed primarily as responses to the problems created by laissez-faire capitalism in industrial societies.

THE CAPITALIST BACKGROUND

Like contemporary socialisms, laissez-faire capitalism is a relative newcomer to the history of social relationships. In hunting and gathering societies the economy was seldom separated from regulation by the other parts of the society (1). To make economic exchanges serve societal objectives, they were regulated by traditional, societal norms rather than by the laws of the marketplace.

The integration of the economy into the society was equally apparent in most of the agrarian societies that have existed, including the societies of medieval Europe. The economy was not divorced from political influence: the political elite and the economic elite were generally composed of the same people. But even when these elites were separate, the political leaders were free to regulate economic activity to any desired detail. The key motive of capitalism—production for a profit —was proscribed in these societies.

This tradition of political control of economic activity prevailed at the time of the industrial revolution. State bureaucracies regulated the developing industries in almost unbelievable detail. In the wool industry in France and England, the weight, breadth, and color of the cloth produced were regulated, and the products were subjected to inspections by state agents. This detailed political control of economic activity had some harmful effects. It was difficult to innovate or to take advantage of innovations in manufacturing techniques when detailed regulations burdened the productive process. If the breadth of the cloth was legally restricted, then it was futile to use a new machine that permitted the weaving of broader pieces of cloth. The new class of industrialists had every reason to resent the interference of the state in economic activity.

But the desire of the industrialists to be free from governmental interference had other sources. It must be remembered that the new industrial-commercial class was a deviant subgroup in feudal society. Its members were viewed with suspicion and treated with hostility by the landowning nobility. Conflict between the two groups was commonplace. To protect themselves and to guard their growing strength, the capitalists advocated the protection of the economy from influence of the other parts of the society, particularly governmental institutions. This laissez-faire value is central to the structure of capitalism.

The type of society advocated by the early capitalists was a new and unique social arrangement. The most important subgroups in the ideal capitalist society were the markets in which commodities, labor, and land were bought and sold according to the laws of supply and demand, unfettered by manmade laws. Political institutions were viewed as passive subgroups that facilitated economic activity by coining money and raising armies and navies to protect international trade and foreign investments. Governments could also provide certain types of social control, such as police forces, courts, and prisons, but the main source of control was the market mechanism. Since government regulation of market activities were proscribed, the question was asked: Why wouldn't the capitalist system degenerate into a war of all against all? Wouldn't the greatest success go to those competitors who violated social norms? How would their behavior be regulated? The economist Adam Smith provided a somewhat mystical answer to these crucial questions. He said that every individual would be "led by an invisible hand to promote an end which was no part of his intention" (2). The competitors would be guided by their self-interest, but that self-interest would be enlightened; it would be enlightened by an awareness of the social consequences of economic acts.

What the early theorists of capitalism failed to realize was that it is virtually impossible to maintain free competition in the markets of an industrial society unless there is an impartial and influential subgroup that regulates economic activity. Without this independent subgroup, competition is stifled. Certain of the competing companies will be more successful in their market activities than others. The less successful companies will go out of business, and the more successful ones will increase their business volume and their organizational size. The theorists of capitalism certainly envisaged that the less efficient producers would go out of business, but they did not contemplate the consequences of the growth in size of the remaining organizations. As was shown earlier, the more units that mass production organizations can manufacture, the lower the cost of each unit. This fact creates a cycle of success: having competed more successfully than other companies in existing markets, the remaining companies could produce a greater volume of goods at an even lower unit cost, which in turn permits them to compete even more successfully in the markets. Any new company seeking to enter the market in this second stage of economic development finds that the ante is higher; it must make a larger initial capital investment in order to start a company with any prospect of success. As a consequence of the cycle of economic success, many markets gradually became dominated by a few giant corporations whose leaders were quick to choke off any competition from the remaining smaller firms or from new firms. Competition among the remaining corporations was replaced by cooperation: prices were fixed and markets were allocated among them.

Enlightened self-interest did not materialize either. A competitive advantage was enjoyed by capitalists who were guided by self-interest rather than social interest. In their drive to minimize costs, the owners of many factories paid very low wages, used child labor in order to pay even lower wages, and maintained long working hours and poor working conditions. The conditions of the workers, while not so bad as many of the social writers of that period would have us believe, were bad enough. A few industrialists, such as Robert Owen, insisted that by paying adequate wages, reducing working hours, and using safety equipment the productivity of the workers was greatly increased: so much so that unit costs were actually lower than if prevailing labor policies were followed. Their argument was generally neglected, however, and the conditions of the workers remained largely unimproved.

THE DEVELOPMENT OF SOCIALISMS

It was at this historic juncture that socialist ideologies began to develop. The common theme in all of them is the desire to reinstitute societal regulation of the economy: to use it to serve public rather than private ends. Beyond this single characteristic the programs of socialists vary greatly. Some socialists advocate state ownership of industries; others favor the formation of cooperatives that are relatively free of state regulation. Among those who favor state ownership, some want to nationalize all industries, others would nationalize only certain key industries. Some socialists propose central planning for the nationalized industries; others prefer to decentralize planning.

Integral to the thinking of all modern socialists is an acceptance of the assumption that social structure influences rates of human behavior. By reorganizing the structure of societies along socialist lines they hope to increase some rates of behavior while decreasing others. The behavioral objectives of socialists and the structural devices advocated to implement them will be discussed in this section of the chapter.

Freedom in Work

One characteristic of socialists that is especially difficult for Americans to understand is the great importance they attach to factory life. In the United States few blue collar workers are interested in their work roles; a major objective of a large majority of these workers is to minimize the number of hours that they work and maximize their free time. Socialists, by contrast, want to convert the factory into an organization in which the workers can realize many of their abilities. They maintain that under capitalism man has become alienated from his work. This alienation results in part from the fact that the worker does not own the place in which he works. It also results from the use of mass production techniques that suppress the sense of creativity the worker derives from making the entire product himself.

To increase the worker's creativity, morale, and involvement in his work, most socialists advocate public ownership of at least the key industries in the society. There are many ways that this objective can be accomplished. The workers can form producers' cooperatives by pooling their wealth, buying a factory, and operating it themselves. Another solution is to nationalize the industries and form workers' councils in each factory. The members of a workers' council are chosen from among the workers in the factory by their fellow workers. These representatives are authorized to make the policy decisions necessary to operate the factory. They are expected to consult with their constituents whenever very important decisions are being made. Whether by using producers' cooperatives or nationalizing industries, socialists expect that the worker will become more involved in his work because it is *his* factory. He will use his creative ability in order to contribute his share to the success of *his* enterprise.

Economic Freedom

Socialists also want to maximize economic freedom and equality. Many decisions that people make involve the expenditure of money. The less money they have, the narrower the range of alternatives they can consider; they are being denied one kind of freedom. A family's decision about whether to send their child to college presupposes that they have enough money to consider sending him. But if the family is supporting their retired parents or a disabled relative, or if the husband is unemployed, the resulting shortage of funds may preclude the possibility of sending a child to college.

Socialists are acutely aware of the abundance of goods and services that industrial capitalism has produced, but they have always been disturbed about the existence of poverty amidst this abundance. To maximize economic freedom, socialists propose to maintain full employment and to institute a number of welfare programs. These welfare programs include old age assistance, medical insurance, and disability assistance. Sickness, old age, and unemployment will not be allowed to impair economic freedom to any great extent. Some socialists also hope to equalize economic freedom through the use of heavily graduated income taxes and confiscatory inheritance taxes.

Freedom of Opportunity

The limited occupational mobility found in many industrial and agrarian societies is also a source of concern to socialists. They want the social structure to be arranged so that every individual has the opportunity to actualize his potential skills. If a child has the potential to become a factory manager or a pianist, then the society should be structured to facilitate the development and use of those skills. His social class position must not serve as a barrier to his self-actualization. To achieve freedom of opportunity, socialists propose some fundamental changes in the structure of society. First, they would provide equal educational opportunity for all the members of the society. Second, they would limit or eliminate the effects of social classes. Heavily graduated income taxes and inheritance taxes are one means of accomplishing this objective. Third, through a process of education, they hope to develop a value system in which all occupations are equally valued because they are contributing to the welfare of the society. Fourth, some socialists would develop a more comprehensive state nursery school system that would involve the socialization of very young children by trained personnel rather than by the parents of the children. By this means they hope to inculcate a set of values in the children that will permit them to function effectively in the society: a task they think not all parents are capable of performing. Nurseries of this kind have been adopted on the collective farms in Israel and in the Soviet Union. Fifth, a few socialists advocate the destruction of the family as a viable unit in the society. They recognize that the family is the single most important basis for the ascription of wealth and occupational roles. Therefore, they believe that by destroying the family they can eliminate highly integrated social classes.

Political Freedom

Some socialists, but by no means all of them, believe that political as well as economic freedom should be maximized. The population should have the right to choose which among the political elites in the society will rule them. This objective has some important social structural implications. First, it implies that the population has a genuine *choice* among elites. The political elites must represent some differences in value orientations; political competition will not be destroyed. Information about the effectiveness of the ruling elite and the platform of opposition elites must be available or genuine political freedom is not possible. This requirement poses a serious problem in socialist societies because the mass media may be nationalized and, therefore, subject to pressures from the ruling elite to distort or suppress information.

As was noted, not all socialists are in sympathy with this objective. Some of them believe that real political freedom occurs only when the population is freed from being concerned about political decisions. They envisage a rather paternalistic system in which the needs of the population are cared for, but in which they need not concern themselves with policy decisions. Table 20-1 summarizes the objectives and social structural proposals of the majority of socialists.

TABLE 20-1

OBJECTIVES AND STRUCTURAL PROPOSALS OF MOST SOCIALISTS

Rates of behavior that socialists wish to maximize	Social structures needed to implement desired behavior
Freedom in work *The reduction of alienation Increasing involvement Expressing creativity*	Public ownership of the means of production Full employment
Economic freedom	Full employment Welfare programs
Equality of opportunity or maximizing *self-actualization*	Removal of social class differences *High inheritance and income taxes Equalizing prestige of all occupations Limiting the role of the family in the society Equalizing educational opportunities Socialization of small children by trained specialists*
Political freedom *	Protecting political competition among opposing political parties Maintaining free media Protecting the rights of others to investigate the actions of the ruling elite and to publish the findings

* There is less agreement among socialists about the value of this objective than there is about the others.

THE SOCIAL STRUCTURE OF MODERN SOCIALISM

The various modern socialisms did not spring into existence fully developed; they are the product of over a century of thought and experimentation. Among the earliest forms of socialism proposed, and perhaps the most atypical, was *syndicalism*. The proponents of syndicalism sought to return the economy to the fabric of society by means of trade unions. Their strategy called for the use of general strikes by the workers in order to wrest control of the factories from the owners. In each factory the workers would elect representatives from their own ranks to form a council (syndicat) charged with the responsibility of operating the factory. Representatives from each syndicat in a community would be selected to participate on the community council, which would coordinate economic and political affairs for the community. Regional and national councils were also envisaged by some of the syndicalists. But syndicalism was unique in proposing that the locus of influence should be the factory or the community. Such a system has obvious drawbacks (3). First, like all organizations constructed from the bottom up, syndicalism increases rather than lessens the problem of coordinating the activities of the parts in each community and in the nation as a whole. In post-industrial revolution societies the parts have become so interdependent that greater coordination among them is required, not less. Coordination among the various independent syndicats would be extremely difficult if not impossible to achieve. Second, even though the workers controlled the factories, there is no reason to assume that they would run them in the interest of other workers in the society rather than for their personal interests. The syndicalist argument that workers would never do anything contrary to the interests of other workers sounds like an ill-disguised version of the "enlightened self-interest" theme of capitalism, and equally unlikely to be realized. Third, the workers seldom have the technical, administrative, and commercial competence to run the enterprises in which they work. Fourth, there is little reason to believe that syndicalism would produce workers' democracy. Trade unions are not notoriously democratic organizations; they are usually run by rather well-entrenched oligarchies, who seldom permit a counterelite to exist. Yet the existence of a choice among elites is essential to a democratic system. There is no particular reason to assume that the elite would suddenly become democratic after it had assumed authority for operating the factories. The advantages for the worker of trade union authoritarianism as opposed to entrepreneurial authoritarianism are not clear.

Syndicalism captured the imagination of many social reformers because it had a feasible strategy for the assumption of worker control of the means of production. But it was clearly out of step with social trends. It was a system based on the decentralization of influence at a time when social forces required increased centralization of influence.

For this reason, syndicalism never became a major force for the re-shaping of society. In some communities, particularly in Spain, the general strike and other means were used to set up syndicats and communes, but they were invariably quashed by the forces of the national government if they did not fall from the weight of their own defects. Some of the elements and part of the aura of syndicalism are still retained by labor unions. But they have been translated into strategies for gaining worker rights and privileges rather than control of the factories themselves.

Cooperativism

A second type of socialism, also somewhat anomalous when compared with modern state socialism, is cooperativism (4, 5). There are two basic types of cooperatives: producers' and consumers' cooperatives. To form a producers' cooperative, several persons pool their money by buying equally valued shares in the cooperative. The money is then used to purchase facilities, equipment, and materials. This form of organization differs from a joint stock corporation in two ways: all of the shareholders are workers, and their dividends are determined by the amount of work that they do rather than the amount of stock they hold. The shareholding workers are expected, but not required, to participate in the management of the organization or to serve on committees of various kinds. Some of the profits of the organization are withheld from distribution as dividends; they are retained in a fund to provide welfare services for the members and their families when they are ill, disabled, or retired. The producers' cooperatives in Sweden have built resort hotels, apartment houses, and retirement villages for their members. This form of organization does implement freedom in work and economic freedom, but it is a very decentralized form of socialism. It often is found in societies that also have capitalist and state-owned enterprises, as in Sweden, England, Denmark, and France. During the nineteenth century, producers' cooperatives were sometimes formed by disgruntled American workers, but they were seldom successful enterprises. They usually failed because the workers did not have the knowledge and skills to operate a business or because the leaders of competing private organizations were able to prevent them from getting the supplies they needed.

The process of forming a consumers' cooperative is similar to that of the producers' cooperative. Interested persons buy equally valued shares in the venture and use the money to buy a store and stock it with merchandise. These stores range in size from the small corner variety store to the large department store that one finds in the metropolitan centers of industrial societies. The member receives a share of the profits in proportion to the amount of money he spent in the cooperative during the year. Nonmembers are encouraged to shop at cooperative stores; they can become members by purchasing a specified number of dollars of goods from the store. Consumers' cooperatives have essentially the same form of organization as the producers' cooperatives. The members are responsible for the operation of the cooperative; they may serve on committees or participate directly on the management board. As in the producers' cooperatives, a certain proportion of the dividends is set aside for welfare activities.

Many consumers' cooperatives have been formed in the United States; student book stores and employee credit unions are common examples. But cooperativism has never been so popular in the United States as it is in Europe. One reason for the extensive European development of both producers' and consumers' cooperatives was the prevalence of cartels of privately owned companies in several key industries. These organizations set production quotas and prices for the individual companies that joined the cartels. The prices for certain products, such as light bulbs or footwear, were often multiples of their actual value. Producers' cooperatives were formed to manufacture these overpriced commodities. Sweden offers an excellent illustration of the development of cooperatives (4, 5). Consumers' cooperatives had existed there before the turn of the present century. In 1899 the consumers' cooperatives formed the Cooperative Union, which bought goods at wholesale prices for the participating stores. The Union found that prices for some commodities were being maintained at unreasonably high levels by the cartels. The leaders of the Cooperative Union decided to form producers' cooperatives to supply their participating stores with goods that were being overpriced by the cartels: margarine, electric lights, footwear, and a host of other goods. Their actions forced the private companies to reduce their prices in order to compete for the Swedish markets. The Cooperative Union also formed insurance and banking firms. Today this Union is an extremely large organization. Its producers' cooperatives are really joint stock organizations, but they are run efficiently and with primary concern for the interests of their members. The Cooperative Union has its own school system for training store and plant management personnel and for training people to work in the Union bureaucracy. Worker democracy is maintained by a system in which the members of the Cooperative Union elect eighteen board members from thirteen districts to supervise Union activities. The board is responsible for hiring directors who fill the actual administrative roles in the organization. Most of the directors are selected from within the organization. They are socialized in and committed to the principle of cooperation, which is the binding force of the organization. Sweden has often been referred to incorrectly as a socialist society; it is not. It has a mixed economy in which the cooperatives compete side by side with privately owned organizations and with state monopolies.

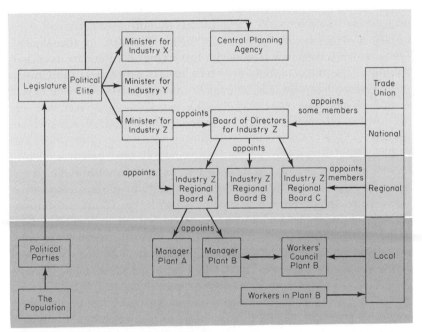

FIG. 20-1 Democratic state socialism.

Democratic State Socialism

When Americans use the term *socialism* they are generally referring to the more centralized version of this highly variable phenomenon. In democratic state socialism, the institutions of government are retained in their existing form, and some or all of the industries in the society are nationalized: the government assumes ownership of these industries for the people. The industries become state monopolies. To describe democratic state socialism, we will use a very general scheme because the details vary from one country to another as well as from one socialist to another. Figure 20-1 provides a simplified outline of the structure of democratic state socialism. In this scheme democratic institutions for the resolution of conflict are retained so that political elites representing different policy orientations can compete for the support of the electorate. The leaders of the majority party organize the national legislature; they are the elite of that organization. The members of the elite allocate among themselves the various ministries of the government. Some of these ministries are concerned with the operation of the nationalized industries. In England there is a minister for transportation industries, one for fuel and power, and one for civil aviation (3). The ministers usually appoint most of the members of the boards of directors for each industry. In England, a few board members are selected by the leaders of the national organization of the trade unions (3). The national board sets industrywide production quotas, decides how much money is to be spent on capital improvements, and other major policy issues. It also selects, with the approval of the minister, the members of the regional boards for the industry.

The regional boards translate the production, labor force, and equipment objectives of the national boards into regional and factory or mine quotas. In addition, they perform certain administrative functions, such as appointing and evaluating the performance of plant managers. Although the plant manager is charged with the technical and administrative responsibilities for his plant, his actions are often subject to the approval of a workers' council.

The authority of the workers' council varies greatly from one socialist society to another. Ordinarily, the members of the council are expected to take part in discussions about the operation of the plant. They are often charged with major responsibility for the maintenance of adequate safety equipment, the hiring of new workers, and making rules governing the activities of the workers in the plant. In some socialist societies, the workers' council is the key policy and administrative unit in the factory; it may even have the authority to hire its own manager. In other societies, the council is a mere facade: a front group used by a political elite to placate and propagandize the workers. To the democratic socialist, the workers' council is an institutional device of major importance; it is at the very heart of the attempt to reinstate popular control of economic institutions. The extent to which this device has been an effective experiment in social integration will be discussed later in this chapter.

Democratic socialism contains several avenues of public access to control of economic activity. The public elects the members of the national legislature, which is charged with ultimate authority for economic policy making. Control is also obtained through the trade unions, whose members can appoint representatives to the various boards that operate the nationalized industries. Another device used in Great Britain is the consumer advisory board: a group of private citizens who receive the complaints from consumers about the products, service, and other activities of the nationalized industries (3). These complaints are forwarded to the national or regional boards of the industries for study and action.

To assist the national boards in their decision making, there is often a central planning agency that provides each industry with relevant information. The planning agency may make available data on foreign buying and manufacturing trends, the condition of other interdependent industries, and the general state of the economy. But in the more centralized versions of democratic socialism, the central planning agency is vested with greater authority. It is responsible for the creation of a national plan for the entire economy. It sets production quotas for each industry in the society. The annual plan created by this group is transmitted to the national legislature for approval, and, once it is approved, it generally has the force of law. The national boards for each industry are expected to draw up their own plans to implement the national plan. This planning activity is transmitted down the hierarchy of each industry, and at each level the plan is worked out in increasing detail. Monthly as well as annual production quotas are set for the plant manager. The size of his bonus and his promotional opportunities often hinge on his success at meeting these quotas.

Authoritarian State Socialism

Not all state socialisms are democratic. In the so-called communist countries of eastern Europe and in China are found authoritarian state socialisms. Authoritarian state socialism differs from democratic state socialism in fundamental ways. There is no multiple party system to serve as a means of resolving conflict among competing elites in the society. All conflicts are resolved within the single elite party that rules the society. The party maintains some of its members in the key positions in the government and in the economic sector of the society. A council of economic ministers, which is charged with the operation of the economy, is appointed by the political elite. This council and the central planning agency are responsible for implementing the national economic objectives of the political leaders. The central planning committee collects data on the performance of each enterprise in the society. These data are used by the national council of economic ministers to develop the annual plan for economic development. Once the national plan is outlined, the planning agency establishes production quotas for each industry or each enterprise in the society. These national agencies are also responsible for the development of new industries.

There are no effective labor unions to monitor the activities of the national boards of each industry on behalf of the workers. The party, however, does maintain staffs whose members monitor the actions of the governmental and economic bureaucracies to see that they are in accord with the objectives of the political elite. This form of

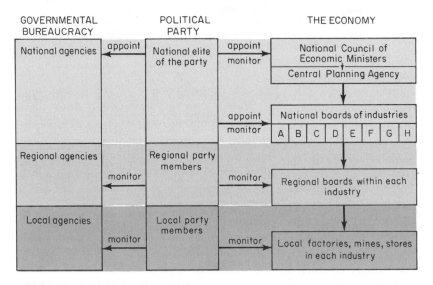

FIG. 20-2 Authoritarian state socialism.

socialism maximizes the centralization of influence and the integration of the economy with the rest of the society; it approaches the extreme form of the total society. Figure 20-2 outlines the structure of authoritarian state socialism.

The Accomplishment of the Objectives of Socialism: A Balance Sheet

We have seen the objectives of socialisms and the social structures proposed to realize them. How effective have these structures been for achieving the purposes for which they were intended? Since state socialisms are the most prevalent forms of socialism today and are likely to be more widespread in the future, we will restrict our discussion to them.

The Achievement of Freedom in Work

Probably no single objective is more central to the interests of the majority of socialists than obtaining freedom in work. Socialists have sought to reshape the place of work into a setting in which the worker could become personally involved and express his creative ability. To accomplish these objectives, they have nationalized industries and established workers' councils. How useful have these social arrangements been for achieving freedom in work?

NATIONALIZATION AND THE SIZE OF BUREAUCRACIES. In our discussions of the effects of increasing population size on the structure of organizations, we saw that increasing size can be accompanied by an even faster rate of growth in the bureaucratic component of the organization. Bureaucratic growth can be forestalled if authority is decentralized or work is contracted out to independent organizations. We also saw that the increase in size can give rise to serious problems of communication, coordination, and legitimacy. All of the more centralized versions of state socialism—for example, those of the Soviet Union, Poland, Czechoslovakia, and, to a lesser extent, Great Britain—have experienced this growth in the size of their economic bureaucracies and the problems that attend it. The additional levels of hierarchy required to bind the individual enterprise with governmental agencies add to the problems of communication up and down hierarchies. Messages take longer to reach their destinations, and decisions are correspondingly delayed. This problem is particularly severe if decision making is a highly centralized activity; long periods of inaction can exist between the discovery of a problem and the receipt of a solution for it.

NATIONALIZATION AND MANAGERIAL INITIATIVE. How does this problem of increasing bureaucratic size affect freedom in work? It can have the effect of dampening managerial initiative as well as preventing its recognition when it is used. Virtually every plant manager is a careerist who is interested in being promoted to higher positions in the industrial bureaucracy. He is unlikely to engage in behaviors that will seriously hurt his chances of promotion. Since there are more levels of hierarchy, there are more people who must approve his promotions. An innovative act on his part is a decided gamble. One superior may see the action as a demonstration of talent while another sees it as an unauthorized exercise of influence. Many managers decide to play it safe; they feel that their chances for being promoted are greater if they stay inside the known boundaries of their roles (3). Rather than use their own initiative, many managers refer their problems to their superiors in the bureaucracy, requesting decisions from them. Decisions by these remote authorities are not always the most appropriate ones because they often fail to take into account the unique features of the local situation.

In the very highly centralized state socialisms, managerial initiative has been minimized purposely. This de-emphasis of local initiative decreases the flexibility of the economy. The problem can be illustrated by the Polish economy. It is difficult, if not impossible, for the central planners to anticipate all of the consequences of their decisions. Since prices in Poland are determined by the planners rather than by market mechanisms, the planners can create some serious problems by setting arbitrary prices for commodities. In Poland, the planners underpriced coal to such an extent that it was highly profitable for a plant manager, whose performance was being evaluated in terms of his costs of production, to continue to use coal as a fuel rather than some other source. As a consequence, hydroelectric facilities were not developed, although in the long run they are essential to the Polish economy. The factory managers refused to take advantage of many fuel-saving innovations because the price of coal was so low that the innovations were not worth the investment (6). An advantage of the free market system for determining prices is that it forces the manager, as well as other personnel, to use their ingenuity to devise means of cutting costs.

NATIONALIZATION AND DEVIANCE.   If state socialisms, particularly the more centralized varieties, are to function effectively, then a valid set of standards must be created that can be used to judge the performances of the industries and their personnel. But socialists and capitalists alike have learned that these standards are difficult to create and often easy for the plant manager to subvert.

In the late Thirties Soviet planners became aware of some of the perils of developing single measures of managerial and factory performance. The Soviets had used factory productivity as a measure of the effectiveness of factories and management teams. Managers were meeting their production quotas, but often incurring unreasonably high production costs. Some of them overlooked machinery repair and safety in the rush to meet the production quotas (7). Some failed to produce adequate numbers of spare parts for the equipment that they produced in order to concentrate on meeting their machinery production quotes (7). If it was impossible for the manager to meet the quotas for all product lines, they often concentrated their efforts on those lines that were easiest to produce, although other lines might be more essential to the entire economy (7). To overcome these problems, the central planning agencies in the more centralized versions of socialism now use several criteria to judge the effectiveness of factory management teams. These criteria take into account production costs as well as productivity and a variety of other factors.

Even though the criteria for judging performance have improved, the central planning agencies still have difficulty getting feedback communications from the factories. In order to take some of the strain out of meeting quotas, some managers have underrepresented their productive capacity and overstated their needs for supplies (7, 8, 9). While this distorted information may solve problems for the factory management team, it does not maximize the effectiveness of the general economy. Plant management teams have reported that they have almost met their quota and that the remainder of the quota "is currently in production" (7). If their costs have been unusually high, they may "lease" their machinery to another factory with a cooperative manager whose costs have been unusually low. The machinery never really leaves the first factory, but credit is received from the second one that is entered on the books of the first factory as an asset. The image that the central planners have of the state of the economy can be quite distorted.

Where centralized planning has failed to provide the factory manager with the necessary equipment, supplies, and other essentials of production, informal networks of communication and influence have developed among managers. In order to obtain supplies, Soviet factory managers hire specialists who are skilled at obtaining them (7). These specialists (*tolkach* or supply expeditors) work for a commission, often for several companies. Generally, they maintain their headquarters in Moscow, where they maintain social and business contacts with their clients' suppliers. This role is illegal in the Soviet Union, but it is essential to the operation of the economy; while official protests of the practice are frequent and loud, it is not stopped.

In order to pay the fee of the *tolkach*, the manager has to falsify his books. And he usually has little trouble obtaining the cooperation of his chief accountant because of another informal norm. The members of a management team will usually cooperate with one another to hide deviant activities from the central agencies. Managers of different plants have been known to cooperate with one another also.

Even in England, where planning and authority are relatively decentralized in the nationalized industries, some of these problems have developed (3). Inaccurate information was being sent up the economic hierarchies to the parliamentary elite. As a result, the key decision makers often did not have the proper information on which to make policy. The managers often demonstrated an unwillingness to use their own initiative in decision making, preferring instead to refer their problems up the hierarchy for decisions. As a consequence, the parliamentary elite has ordered the boards of the various nationalized industries to assume greater responsibility for economic policy making and if necessary to oppose the stated objectives of the political leaders. Similarly, plant managers are expected to assume more responsibility for the operation of their factories. In other words, they are seeking to solve the problem with greater decentralization of authority.

THE EVOLUTION OF WORKERS' COUNCILS.   Another structural device upon which many socialists place great reliance for the achievement of freedom in work is the workers' council. The seeming promise that this device held for worker control of the means of production has seldom materialized. In the Soviet Union, immediately after the revolution, the workers were allowed to select their own supervisors and foremen, and soldiers elected their officers. But these luxuries of worker democracy had to be revoked as one emergency succeeded another. Greater emphasis had to be placed on technical and administrative competence of army officers and management personnel than the workers had given it. As a result, a hierarchical arrangement was reinstituted in which plant managers were appointed by the relevant central ministry and officers were selected by other, higher ranked officers. Gradually the workers' councils atrophied as the system became increasingly centralized; today they are merely front groups that have no authority for making factory policy.

In Poland, the workers' councils, which were instituted in 1956, suffered a similar fate for different reasons (7). The authority granted the councils included the sale of surplus machinery in the factory, distribution of workers' shares of the profits, creation of internal regulations, and the development of norms for giving bonuses. They also could *review* the policies and operations of the management personnel. But their role in policy formation was vague. The managers quickly discovered that the interests of the members of their workers' councils were very narrow; they were interested only in wages, bonuses, and working conditions. For this reason the professional managers became opposed to the workers' council idea, and their opposition led to the demise of the institution. Another reason for its demise can be traced to the existence in each factory of a member of the Communist Party who is responsible for reporting on activities in the factory to party leaders. Since the party controls all of the important resources in Poland, the local party representative has become the key person in policy determination at the local level. Plant managers are unwilling to initiate new programs until they have discussed them with the party representative.

In England, the narrow range of interests of the members of the workers' councils has been one of the problems leading to the disuse of this form of worker representation (3). In council meetings with the manager, the workers wanted to discuss wages and working conditions rather than plant policy, future objectives, and financial performance. Many of the elected representatives of the workers simply did not have the technical competence to discuss these problems. The members of the council also found themselves in a position of serious role conflict. Instead of being wage bargainers, they were expected to dictate wage policies to their constituents. If a worker violated a plant rule, the workers' council was expected to judge him rather than support him. Being good trade unionists, the members of the councils gradually decided that their role was to represent the interests of the workers if those interests were contrary to those of management. In such a situation, they had an obligation to oppose management. The workers' councils fell into disuse.

THE YUGOSLAVIAN EXPERIMENT.   In Yugoslavia a new approach is being taken to the problem of achieving freedom in work (9). When the Yugoslav socialists came to power after World War II, they installed a highly centralized form of socialism modeled after that of the Soviet Union. By the early 1950's they had encountered all of the drawbacks of centralization that we have just described and some that we have not. To solve these problems, they revamped the structure of their economy completely, replacing it with a highly decentralized version of public ownership.

Today each factory is owned by the workers in it. They elect a workers' council with broad authority to operate the plant. The members of the workers' council elect from among their ranks a management board of three to eleven people, depending on the size of the organization, which together with the manager actually runs the enterprise. The manager is not appointed by the state bureaucracy; he is selected jointly by the workers' council and the council of the commune (city) in which the factory is located. Each enterprise is free to determine what it will make, to whom it will sell, where it will buy, what to import and export, and how much its workers will earn (9).

Thus far, this structure resembles syndicalism, but it is not. There are many ways in which the state controls the activities of each enterprise. A central planning agency creates a national plan for the economy each year. This plan is discussed at all levels of the society, but no production quotas are set for the individual enterprises. The plan serves as a guideline to each workers' council for what it *ought* to produce; it creates a set of economic and social *priorities*. The workers' council cannot disregard the plan completely, however. Bank loans are a necessity in any modern business for expansion of facilities and for short-term purchases. The banks are more likely to lend money to an enterprise that intends to further the objectives of the national plan than to one that has no such intention. The virtue of this system is that it allows each workers' council and each commune to adjust its productive activities to local problems and needs without deviating too far from the national objectives: it decentralizes authority and decision making and introduces an element of flexibility not found under centralized planning. The relative autonomy of each enterprise in the Yugoslav system is reflected in the appearance of brand names and a greater emphasis on quality of production rather than on meeting a quota.

CONCLUSIONS.   In evaluating the effectiveness of socialist institutions for achieving freedom in work, it is easy to give free rein to our cultural prejudices. Every failure can be interpreted as another proof of the superiority of capitalism as a method of organizing an economy. It would be a mistake to draw such a conclusion. It is important to remember that socialist experiments have a very brief history. Although they have encountered many problems, most socialists have been willing to learn from their experiences and to adjust their social structures accordingly. Yugoslavia provides a dramatic illustration of this willingness to be flexible. Another problem that has affected the development of socialism is the fact that socialists have seldom been given a healthy, stable economy to operate. Socialist economies have often been emergency economies; they have had to face the problems of international wars, industrializing agrarian societies, or operating failing enterprises. In these situations, greater centralization of authority was required more often than the socialists themselves would have desired under more normal circumstances. To meet these emergencies, it has often been necessary to forego the development of freedom in work at least temporarily.

Nonetheless, the evidence is clear that mere public ownership of the means of production and the establishment of workers' councils does not create freedom in work. In Stalinist Russia this objective was simply discarded as socialism was overlaid with the most thorough version of totalitarianism ever experienced by a large society. In many other socialist societies new approaches are being considered to create greater freedom in work. Two solutions currently being tried are greater decentralization of *authority* and the reintroduction of a few selected mechanisms of capitalism. Bonuses, rather than ideological appeals, are being used as production incentives. Piece work systems have been instituted in which the worker is paid according to the number of pieces that he produces. In Yugoslavia, the utilization of the techniques of private enterprise has been very great. The workers' councils divide the profits of the productive organizations among the workers, they sell their products in an open market system, and they can create new product lines. It is interesting that since the introduction of this amalgam of capitalist and socialist practices, the economy of Yugoslavia has developed at an exceedingly rapid rate.

The Achievement of Economic Freedom

Compared to their achievements in the area of freedom in work, socialists have been very successful at reaching their objective of economic freedom. They are developing economic freedom by maintaining full employment and by introducing a series of ambitious welfare programs. Most socialist societies have been able to maintain virtual full employment. Since socialism often has been introduced in agrarian societies and in others that had suffered greatly from the destruction of World War II, full employment has been needed. In agrarian societies where a large proportion of the population is necessarily involved in agriculture, the problem has been to find enough people to fill the growing number of roles in industries. To meet this demand, a large proportion of the female population has been kept in the labor force. In a few socialist societies full employment has been maintained only by overhiring. But concern for efficiency often has a lower position on the value scale of socialists than the maintenance of economic freedom.

Welfare programs are abundant in these societies. Medical care and old age assistance are usually provided by the state. These programs are often so extensive as to include free summer camps for children and inexpensive summer resorts for the worker and his family.

The Achievement of Equality of Opportunity

The two major means by which many socialists have sought to achieve equality of opportunity have been the reduction of social class differences and the equalization of educational opportunities. They have not been as uniformly successful at achieving this objective as they have at achieving economic freedom. Social class differences have been retained or extended rather than modified. In the Soviet Union after World War I, influence was highly centralized in the hands of the party elite. But the distribution of rewards was fairly equal: the wages of skilled workers were almost identical with those of unskilled workers (10). But as social differentiation increased, a stable class system appeared. Ten distinct strata have been identified: the ruling elite, superior intelligentsia, general intelligentsia, working class aristocracy, white collar workers, well-to-do peasants, average workers, average peasants, disadvantaged workers, and forced laborers (10). This class system persisted through the vicissitudes of World War II, and the government has instituted many laws to perpetuate it. Since the government is the recipient of the profits from every state-owned productive enterprise in the society, it does not have to rely on taxes as a source of income. Therefore, income taxes are low and not steeply graduated, but there is considerable variation in earnings from one part of the population to another. It is possible for a family to accumulate considerable wealth for its private purposes. Furthermore, this wealth can be passed on to the offspring almost intact, because the inheritance taxes are extremely low.

The development of a class system has also been accompanied by practices that have the effect of reducing mobility within or between generations. In order to complete the last three years of secondary school and to continue on into college, Soviet youths are required to pay tuition. Any youth in the society can obtain an adequate scholarship to cover his tuition and other costs of getting an education if he competes successfully in the national scholarship examinations. But the children of wealthier families do not *need* to compete for state scholarships in order to obtain an advanced education. Admission to certain schools is also restricted to certain classes of people—sons of highly ranked military officers are given preference for admission to certain elite military training schools. It is also becoming increasingly difficult for semiskilled blue collar workers to move up the factory hierarchy to assume foreman or other managerial roles.

We saw earlier that the Soviets have changed their policies with regard to the family, seeking now to strengthen it rather than to weaken it. The family has become an important unit in that society for the maintenance of class differences: through inheritance, and the use of elite positions to structure the laws to the advantage of the elite.

In England, attempts to equalize opportunity were not eminently successful. Although some industries were nationalized, the same people who were charged with operating them before nationalization generally continued to operate them. Heavy income and inheritance taxes have been imposed and have had some leveling effect, but not the spectacular results that the socialists had hoped for. The maintenance of class differences has continued largely because of the character of the English secondary school system and its relation to selection into universities. The highest quality secondary schools are the private schools whose students are best prepared for and most likely to be accepted into the best universities. The quality of education obtained in the public school system is not so high as it is in private schools. Since the wealthy families are the ones who can afford to send their children to the private secondary schools, these children are more likely to be admitted to the best universities. The socialists attempted to solve this problem by creating a national scholarship program. Any student who could compete successfully in the national examinations would receive a state scholarship. The unanticipated consequence of this program has been that the higher the applicant's class position, the more likely he was to pass the examination. A disproportionately large share of the scholarship money has been used to educate members of the middle and upper classes.

The Achievement of Political Freedom

Not all socialists have been concerned with the maintenance of democratic institutions in which the right of the electorate to select their rulers is maintained. In fact, there are very few cases of societies where there is almost complete public ownership of the means of production *and* an emphasis on the institutions of democracy. In Sweden, India, and Great Britain, only a fraction of the economy is nationalized. In all of these societies, however, the institutions of democracy have largely been maintained. The problem that has arisen, particularly in Sweden, has been that competing parties try to outbid each other in promising larger welfare programs. Grand promises can help a party to get elected, but they also can interfere with rational economic planning after the election is over.

SUMMARY AND CONCLUSIONS

The basic purpose behind the development of social-isms was to return the economy to the fabric of society where it could be used to promote the interests of all of the people. Some of the different structures proposed by socialists to achieve their objectives of economic, vocational, and political freedom and social equality have been syndicalism, cooperativism, and democratic and authoritarian state socialisms.

It is difficult to evaluate accurately the effectiveness of these various forms of socialism for achieving these objectives. Socialist economies often have been emergency economies that have been subjected to the stresses of war and rapid industrialization. Whatever weaknesses these systems have displayed must be interpreted within a framework of success. In the Soviet Union, Israel, and other agrarian societies, social planning has increased the rationality of the industrializing process. In England the nationalization of weak industries has often resulted in the revitalization of those industries. The best testimony to the successes of socialism is provided by the fact that virtually the entire populations of most socialist societies are probably firmly and voluntarily committed to these forms of economic organization. One evidence for this assertion is the fact that even among defectors from the Soviet Union there is almost unanimous agreement that state ownership and centralized planning are superior to capitalism as a means of organizing an economy.

Nonetheless, it is apparent that the various socialist institutions have undergone some very unsocialist changes. In some societies, authority has been decentralized in an attempt to solve the problems of communication feedback, flexibility, managerial initiative, and economic efficiency created by centralization. By far the most ambitious attempt to decentralize authority has occurred in Yugoslavia—an experiment that must be watched with great interest by social scientists.

It has been a fairly general experience that the majority of workers cannot be motivated to produce by appealing to their sense of social responsibility. As a result, economic motivations have been reinstated; managerial teams are paid large bonuses for exceeding their production quotas, and workers are often paid piece rates. In Yugoslavia the factory profits are distributed by the workers' council among the workers in it. The Yugoslavs have also recognized the value of a market system to encourage production in certain areas and to establish prices for some commodities.

The creation of socialist forms of organization has not yet produced the desired results in terms of other rates of behavior. Crime, delinquency, apathy, and other types of deviance are becoming increasingly serious problems in the Soviet Union, Great Britain, Sweden, and elsewhere. The existence of these problems must provide cause for serious reflection among socialist leaders. Socialists argue effectively that these problems exist because socialists have never had an opportunity to run a healthy economy nor to run a society long enough to change the value patterns of the people. They have had to operate in situations of great stress rather than situations of cooperation and harmony. The tendencies to deviance are a product of this stress and the residue of "capitalist mentality" in the population.

But perhaps the most fundamental observation that can be made about socialism has to do with its widespread adoption by the elites in underdeveloped countries. Socialism provides an organizational format that helps underdeveloped nations to industrialize rapidly. It provides for central planning, the ability to coordinate the activities of all parts of the society, the mobilization of the labor force in accordance with the plan, and an ideology to sustain the population (8). But as these societies are successful in raising their level of technology, the number of subgroups or centers of influence in the society increases (Proposition 2). The middle class, composed of the technical and professional workers, increases in size and professional ability. Under these conditions the centralization of authority becomes increasingly difficult to maintain, because the political leaders simply cannot absorb all of the knowledge essential to effective economic decision making (Proposition 13). Decisions about the allocation of resources in a socialist society require a knowledge of such economic concepts as paretomarginality; the political leaders simply do not have training in these esoteric areas of human knowledge. Increasingly, the political leaders must look to professional economists, engineers, and other highly trained personnel to devise the appropriate means for achieving their objectives. Some decentralization of authority is required.

There are, in fact, fewer compelling reasons for maintaining the centralization of authority as the economy improves. It is sometimes maintained simply because of the desire of the political elite to retain its share of both influence and authority. In Chapter 3 we saw that the decentralization of authority is a rational method for coping with the problems of increasing population size and technological complexity. If the political elite fails to decentralize authority after the economy has improved, it must expect to have the types of problems we have discussed.

REFERENCES

1   K. Polanyi, *The Great Transformation* (Boston: Beacon Press, Inc., 1957).

2   A. Smith, *The Wealth of Nations.*

3   H. A. Clegg, *Industrial Democracy and Nationalization: A Study Prepared for the Fabian Society* (Oxford: Basil Blackwell, 1955).

4   M. W. Childs, *Sweden: The Middle Way* (New Haven: Yale University Press, 1936).

5   C. B. Mamoria and R. D. Saksena, *Co-operation in Foreign Lands* (Allahabad, India: Kitab Mahal Private Ltd., 1963).

6   J. M. Montias, "Producer Prices in a Centrally Planned Economy—The Polish Discussion," in *Value and Plan: Economic Calculation and Organization in Eastern Europe,* G. Grossman, ed. (Berkeley: University of California Press, 1960), pp. 47-75.

7   J. S. Berliner, "The Informal Organization of the Soviet Firm," *The Quarterly Journal of Economics, 66* (1952), 342-65.

8   J. M. Montias, *Central Planning in Poland* (New Haven: Yale University Press, 1962).

9   A. Waterson, *Planning in Yugoslavia: Organization and Implementation* (Baltimore: The Johns Hopkins Press, 1962).

10   A. Inkeles, "Social Stratification and Mobility in the Soviet Union: 1940-1950," *American Sociological Review, 15* (1950), 465-79.

totalitarianism **21**

Throughout most of human history, many people have lived under dictators or despots. These forms of rule are not to be confused with totalitarianism. In totalitarian societies, virtually all influence is concentrated in a single elite; it approaches being a kind of total society. In a dictatorship, a ruling elite allows no effective opposition to its right to rule, but the amount of influence that it actually controls can be very limited. In the most limited form of dictatorships an elite assumes control of the government, the police, and the military forces. Through the control of these agencies of coercion and violence, the elite hopes to maintain itself in its position of great political influence. But in this limited form of dictatorship, very little influence is exercised over nonpolitical interactions. Family, religious, and economic life go largely undisturbed. A more ambitious dictator might extend his influence to include control over some key aspects of the economy such as the banking system. But he still leaves most sectors of life essentially undisturbed. The oriental despot, despite the vastness of his influence, could not monitor or control effectively the behaviors of all his subjects. The technology of agrarian societies was so rudimentary that he was forced to leave most sectors of life unregulated.

A totalitarian elite suffers from no such limitations. The same technology that created the material blessings of modern societies has also ushered in the possibility of the total society. In 1948 George Orwell wrote his famous novel, *1984*, in which he speculated on life in a total society. When he reversed the last two digits of the year 1948 to create the title of his novel, he implied that the characteristics of the total society that he was describing already existed in their embryonic form in 1948. In his mythical society, Oceania, the level of technology had reached a degree of sophistication that enabled the elite to monitor every behavior of its members. 1984 is still almost two decades away, but already the techniques of monitoring human behavior are reaching a level of refinement anticipated by Orwell. It is now possible for a specially equipped truck driving up a street to record which television stations the people in the houses on that street are listening to. The value of such a device in a totalitarian society is obvious. Private conversations between people in their houses can be monitored from hundreds of yards away. Business organizations are using these devices to monitor the activities of their competitors as well as their own employees. A few business organizations require polygraph tests as a condition of employment. Governments are using these devices increasingly. It is becoming more difficult to live a truly private life. The techniques and tools of modern communication can be used by the totalitarian elite to propagandize the entire population. The same technology can be used to receive messages almost instantaneously from its agents in the remotest parts of the country. The rifle mounted over the fireplace is no longer an effective means of counterrevolution. The instruments of warfare have become so complex and devastating in their effects that only the state can afford to manufacture them, and the population cannot defend itself against them. Other technological innovations, such as electronic data processing equipment, enable state bureaucracies to handle volumes of information about the population that were formerly impossible. All of these innovations created the possibility of constructing the total society, a variation of which is totalitarianism, in this century. It is possible for a small elite to control not merely the instruments of violence or the economy, but all the behaviors of man. The social structural devices for accomplishing this objective are the subject of this chapter.

THE DEVELOPMENT OF TOTALITARIANISM

There are three stages in the development of a totalitarian society (1). First, there has to be a mass to which the totalitarian elite can appeal. Second, the totalitarians must enlist enough members of the mass into their organization to make it an effective political force. Third, the elite of the totalitarian movement must establish itself in the positions of authority either by revolution, coup, or legal election. Let us examine each of the elements in this process.

The Existence of a Mass

Earlier, the mass was defined as an unintegrated, undifferentiated, and powerless element in a population. In Germany the economic catastrophes that followed World War I led to the development of a mass. Unemployed soldiers, disenchanted youths, and the bankrupted lower middle class were the major elements in this mass. In the Soviet Union no comparable masses existed at the time that Stalin came to power; he had to create one (1). Under Lenin every effort was being made to *differentiate* the population. Greater formal recognition was extended to the different nationality groupings in the society, and some nationality differences were created where none actually existed. Under Lenin's New Economic Policy, social and economic differentiations of the population were purposely developed. In order to achieve his totalitarian objectives, Stalin had to destroy these differences and reduce the population to a mass. He eradicated social class differences by eliminating many of its elements from the population. Six million wealthy peasants (kulaks) were killed, elements of the middle class were liquidated and many of the remainder lost their wealth and positions, and the nobility was liquidated or fled voluntarily. Under Lenin regional administrative units called Soviets had been created and given considerable authority; Stalin removed their authority. The channels of influence were made to run directly from Moscow to every sector of the society. To forestall the development of worker solidarity, Stalin created the Stakhanovite system. Workers were rewarded with special recognition and status as labor heroes for exceeding production quotas. Cooperation among the workers was replaced by competition for these valued status positions, which workers hoped would shield them from arrest by the secret police. Stalin also prevented the governmental bureaucracy from becoming a source of independent influence by removing many of the members of this organization. Half of the members of the bureaucracy were removed from their offices. Many elements of the military elite were liquidated following a series of show trials. Even the Communist Party was subjected to this program of massification; the ranks underwent repeated purging. Reduced to a mass, the population of the Soviet Union was now prepared for the introduction of totalitarianism.

The Totalitarian Movement

The leaders of the embryonic totalitarian movement concentrate their energies on winning members for their organization from the masses. They take advantage of the sense of aloneness and disillusionment that characterizes a mass. A variety of emotional appeals are utilized. Audiences are offered scapegoats for their problems. They are told that the "international Jewish conspiracy" was responsible for the surrender of Germany during World War I and that the Jews had also manipulated the money markets to cause the inflation that followed the war. Stalin offered the capitalists, the revisionists, and the deviationists as scapegoats for the Russian people. In making this type of appeal, both Hitler and Stalin took advantage of the inability of the mass man to test the validity of their explanations. Being unintegrated, the mass has no readily available means of testing the accuracy of these assertions. The scapegoating strategies of Hitler and Stalin called for constant repetition of "the big lie" until the masses believed it.

Other forms of emotional appeals are also used in the process of winning the allegiance of the masses. Torchlight parades, martial music, advocating violence as a means of resolving problems, and making utopian promises are all part of the strategy. Emotional slogans and symbols are geared to the emotional state of the masses. The advocacy of violence is appealing because it is an excellent outlet for the pent-up feelings of the mass man. Yet on the horizon is the promise of a better society in which the mass man becomes the central focus of attention.

The organization of the totalitarian movement is often paramilitary in character. The ordered military life with its rank system and formal norms appeals to the disorganized mass. It offers the prospects of definition of position and security. The paramilitary organization also has the advantage of institutionalizing or legitimating the use of violence. A feeling of strength replaces powerlessness as mass men learn to act in concert with each other to achieve their objectives.

The Coup, Election, or Revolution

A totalitarian movement that competes successfully for the allegiance of the masses can be a very large and threatening organization. If it becomes large enough, it can assume control of the state by legal election. If its opportunities for legitimate access to authority are blocked, it can capture the agencies of government by the use of force. The paramilitary totalitarian movement is ideally designed for subverting weak governments. First, it has little regard for the means used to achieve its ends of complete victory. Second, with its emphasis on discipline and complete commitment to the objectives of the movement, it can utilize the energies and loyalties of its members to a degree that other organizations cannot emulate. Secret members of the organizations can infiltrate the agencies of the state and then obtain jobs for other members. The committed member working twenty-four hours a day and placing his party obligations above those of family and job is an awesome competitor in the struggle for power. Third, if violence is necessary to achieve control of the state, the military emphasis of the organization ideally prepares it for this type of activity.

THE OBJECTIVES OF TOTALITARIAN ELITES

There is a single overriding objective pursued by every totalitarian elite: to organize the society in such a way as to maintain itself in power. To pursue this ultimate objective, certain programmatic objectives are followed. The elite must be able to control virtually every aspect of human behavior. If there are other agencies that can influence human behavior, potential sources of deviance and counterrevolution exist. Effective subgroups cannot be allowed to develop or persist since each one constitutes a center of influence: a fragmentation of state influence. If family interaction remains a private sphere separated from state control, it could threaten the stability of state authority. Children could be socialized in patterns of behavior that deviate from those desired by the state. Therefore, the family must be destroyed as a socializing agency and as a source of qualitative human relationships. Similarly, all associations are potential sources of deviance, so they must be rendered impotent. Ironically, it is this condition of being unintegrated and powerless that drove the masses into the totalitarian movement to begin with. But totalitarian elites are masters of the art of creating illusions; the individual is powerless, but he feels that he is very powerful because he is taught to identify with the leader, who is all-powerful. The individual is alone and separated from other people, but he does not feel alone because he identifies directly with the leader. He also feels that he is a part of an effective organization and that his highest obligation is to perform his role properly. He is a member of the mass, but he does not realize it.

The potential source of opposition to the totalitarian movement comes from people who are outraged by the actions of the leader. To be outraged, they must have a sense of personal worth, dignity, and an awareness of their individualism. The programmatic objectives of the totalitarian elite include necessarily the destruction of the sense of individualism, dignity, and personal worth. No one must see himself as being separate from the state or the party; only one primary relationship will be fostered: the one with the leader.

External threats to the monopoly of influence enjoyed by the totalitarian elite also exist, whether real or imagined. Therefore, the program of the elite usually includes world domination among its objectives. The position of the elite is truly secure only when it dominates the entire world. The exceptions to this objective occur only when the totalitarian society is too small for the elite to dream of world conquest.

THE SOCIAL STRUCTURAL MEANS OF IMPLEMENTING THESE OBJECTIVES

To achieve its objective of a complete and perpetual monopoly of influence, totalitarians reshape the structure of their societies thoroughly. These are the social structures they use.

The Official Ideology

The cause of the elite is aided considerably by an official ideology (2), designed to cover all the important aspects of human existence. It explains the conditions that existed prior to the elite's assumption of power. It offers an explanation for the social forces that are at work in the world. But its primary focus is on the millennium—a perfect final society—and the programmatic means for achieving it. Thus the official ideology has the effect of marshaling all human activity to realize the millennium by spelling out the roles and obligations of every member of the society. Hitler's ideology focused on the world society that pure Teutonic Germans would rule. All impure or less perfect racial strains would be eradicated or reduced to slavery. This ordered empire would last for a thousand years at least. Stalin had the advantage of the ready-made ideology of communism as expounded by Marx, expanded by Lenin, and subsequently modified by Stalin himself. Each member of the Communist Party was thoroughly indoctrinated with this ideology. He devoted his energies to his assigned tasks because he believed that he was assisting in the coming of the millennium. If he suffered from personal privation, he understood that he must do so in order to make life better for future generations of the population.

Control of All Centers of Influence

The elite cannot destroy all the centers of influence in the society. They would not destroy the economy simply to remove it as a center of influence. In the ideal total society these indispensible centers of influence are controlled by the ruling elite. In Hitler's Germany the accumulation of total influence by the elite was never achieved because some of these centers of influence did remain somewhat autonomous (3). The state never assumed ownership of the major means of production in German society, although they did regulate it in many ways by controlling supplies and credit. Some productive organizations were created by the Nazis—the Hermann Göring Works, a munitions producing complex, is an example. The offices in this organization and others similar to it were filled with members of the Nazi Party, but it was a venture that represented only a small proportion of the total German economy (3). Hitler never destroyed the influence of the state bureaucracy or the military, since both organizations were basically sympathetic to his objectives anyway (3). It is difficult to predict whether this state of relative independence would have continued had the Third Reich lasted longer than it did. The Göring Works may have served as a model for future totalization. In any case, Germany under Hitler was far from the perfect example of the total society.

Stalin was much more successful in achieving a total society. The Communist Party controlled all of the centers of significant influence. Party members occupied all the key roles in the state bureaucracy. Since the economy was public property, the party controlled it directly and through the state bureaucracy. The military hierarchy was controlled by the use of purges, secret police reports, and the assignment of party members to command roles or as political attachés. Some of the means Stalin used to destroy other forms of qualitative association are described below.

The Paternalistic State

Viewed in one way, every social structure represents a dynamic solution to the problem of freedom versus order. If a population is perfectly free, there are no encumbrances on the members' abilities to decide their own courses of action. But social organizations *are* encumbrances on the complete freedom of the population because they *order* some of its actions through the exercise of influence or norms. Therefore, the more order that is built into the social structure, the less freedom the members of the population have. The advocates of laissez-faireism sought a social structure that would maximize the freedom of the individual members of the population and that correspondingly minimized the amount of order in it. The architects of the total society resolved this problem of freedom versus order in the opposite way; they forsook freedom as it has been defined customarily in order to achieve the ordered society. Freedom was redefined as the release of the population from the restrictions on action caused by such organizations as the family, the churches, and other associations. But the definition of this term was extended even further; the population was truly free when its members did not have the onerous responsibility of making decisions. The function of making decisions would be assumed by the state.

Because these definitions help the totalitarian elites to accumulate influence, the elites incorporate them into their official ideologies. The totalitarian society is a paternalistic society. In order to increase the freedom of the individual, totalitarians destroy all subgroups intervening between the individual and the state. They reserve to themselves the difficult task of making decisions for the members of the society. They provide for all the needs of the population. Welfare programs, which increase the security of the population, are developed in abundance. Recreational facilities and many varieties of entertainment are provided by the state.

This paternal character of the totalitarian society is far more apparent to the members than the terroristic and violent elements that have been so well publicized elsewhere. For most Germans living under the Nazi regime, Hitler was the man who created full employment and prosperity, built good highways and summer camps, and who restored the desired image of the Fatherland. The provident paternalism of the elite helps to account for the fact that the populations under them were unwilling to overthrow them.

A Single Mass Party

In totalitarian societies there is only one political party; a legitimated opposition would drain away some of the influence of the elite. A political party is an almost indispensible device, however. It has the advantages of a status system, and status systems can be used as mechanisms to control a population. Ambitious party members will conform rigidly to the norms of the party in the hope that their conformity will be rewarded by promotions. They are also willing to use their superior positions to control those people who are under them. This status advantage of the party is heightened by accepting only one or two per cent of the population as members. The attractiveness of party membership is further enhanced by the simple device of restricting the key roles in the economic and political institutions to party members. The ambitious person wants to become a party member in order to be eligible for the better occupational roles and the rewards attached to them.

The single party is also an excellent device for winning the allegiance of the talented young people in the society. It is these people who pose the greatest potential threat to the elite. By taking them into the party, indoctrinating them thoroughly in the official ideology, and rewarding them for proper performance, the elite can control this element in the population.

Elite Control of Weapons and the Mass Media

If the elite controls the instruments of violence, a counterrevolutionary group has less chance of success. When a totalitarian movement captures control of a society, its leaders usually seal the borders of the country to prevent the influx of arms to aid counterrevolutionaries. Often a house-to-house search is made to locate private arms. The thoroughness of this effort to stifle armed opposition is illustrated in a study of a Chinese village during the Communist transition (4). The Communist soldiers made a systematic search of the village for arms. One farmer truthfully told a search party that he had no weapons. He was immediately arrested, interrogated, and tortured. His enterprising wife obtained his release by purchasing an old rifle from another villager, burying it in her yard, and informing the police where it was buried.

Control of the mass media is equally essential. Free media could be used by antiregime organizations to undermine the totalitarian elite. But control of the media also serves a positive function for the totalitarians. The total society is a new way of life, and the population must be indoctrinated to accept it and to behave according to the new norms. By controlling the mass media, the elite can indoctrinate the masses in this new way of life. Studies of persuasion have shown that *repetition* of the same point of view can be an effective method of persuasion *if the audience is not exposed to any other point of view* (5). By controlling the media consumption of the population, the elite can mold public opinion most effectively. The effectiveness of this method of ideological control is apparent from interviews with defectors from the Soviet Union (6). Although the defectors are often critical of some aspects of the regime, their analyses involve an uncritical use of Marxian concepts. Nazi propaganda was so effective that the German population continued to believe that Germany was winning the war long after it had begun to lose.

The Institutionalization of Terror

Integral to the objective of maintaining complete control of the population is the systematic use of terror (1). The central institution for the application of terror is the secret police, whose operatives are found at all of the key positions in the society and in many of lesser importance. The range of surveillance of this organization is increased by an elaborate system of informing. Children are taught in school and in their state-sponsored clubs to inform on the political deviances of their parents. Adults inform on one another in order to increase the security of their own positions. Finally, the individual informs on himself. The elite often requires each person, particularly party members, periodically to write a self-criticism, which is forwarded to the appropriate superior. Public confessions are also a part of the system of informing.

The exercise of terror takes on new and subtle forms in order to achieve equally new and subtle means of controlling the population. One such device is the random or capricious use of terror. In the concentration camps, the inmates were sometimes told to line up and count off "by fives." All persons who shouted the number "three" were shot. On another day it might be the people who had shouted "one" or "four." This random use of terror had the effect of removing any sense of individual dignity, meaning, or worth. The person is deprived of dying for something; he dies because he shouted "three." The awesome power of the state and the insignificance of the individual is apparent.

The random application of terror can take much subtler forms. One of the projects Hitler envisaged for Germany after the successful conclusion of the war was embodied in his Health Bill (1). According to this piece of legislation, extermination and sterilization would be extended beyond the Jews and various nationality groups to all Germans who did not meet required health standards. Every member of the society would be given a comprehensive physical examination. A person with a suspicious shadow on his chest X-ray might find himself in a concentration camp preparatory to extermination. Although this exercise of terror might not appear to be random to the untrained observer, doctors would be horrified. Doctors often do not agree on a diagnosis when presented with the same medical evidence, even when that evidence includes X-rays.

Associated with the random use of terror is the mechanism of keeping the standards for arrest unclear. People are arrested for no apparent or predictable reason and never seen again. For those who remain behind, the event is almost as impressive as it is for the person arrested. There are no guidelines to predict the arrest; why was such an inoffensive person arrested? Neighbors become doubly guarded in their behavior and less willing to associate with one another; terror increases the mass character of the population.

The lack of guidelines benefits the elite in other ways. If a party member is asked to prepare a report on another member, he can interpret the request many ways. The party elite is planning to arrest him, it is going to arrest another party member who is also preparing a report on the same person, it simply wants the information on the other member, or it is providing busywork. Fearing the exercise of terror, this person will conform as closely as he can to the desires of his superiors, he will question his own personal worth or importance, and the state will get a useful report.

The capricious and unpredictable exercise of terror is self-reinforcing. The individual is frightened, but he is also ashamed of himself for being frightened. He commits acts that violate older principles of human dignity. He reports others in order to save himself; he chooses among murders. Hannah Arendt tells of the Greek woman who pleaded with the Nazi police to spare her three sons. They offered to spare one child chosen by her. She made the choice, but she was thoroughly humiliated by the experience. The guilt, shame, and humiliation that results from these violations of principles of human dignity cause the person to question his own personal worth. Is he really any better than the secret police? At least they are strong! Once this attitude is developed, the ability of the elite to control the population is greatly increased.

The Shapelessness of the Social Structure

The notion of the rigid hierarchy of offices in totalitarian bureaucracies is more a figment of the imaginations of movie producers than it is an accurate portrayal of the social structure. The social organization of totalitarian societies is shapeless and even bewildering. *This shapelessness is another means of achieving elite control of the entire population.* Shapelessness is created by two devices: duplicating offices and organizations, and shifting authority from one office or organization to another.

In Nazi Germany the individual lived in several overlapping administrative districts. The leaders of each district could issue orders, but the limits of their authority were not clear. Since the threat of arrest was always present, the members of the population had to decide which orders to obey or which ones had the highest priority. They read and listened to elite propaganda for clues to approved behavior. Editorials critizing an organization or announcements of the arrest of its leaders were useful in helping people to decide whom to obey. But more important, this device oriented the population directly to the elite.

State-sponsored associations often existed in duplicate. The members were never sure which one was more favored by the elite. Arrests of members in one association signaled that it had fallen into disfavor. Later, arrests might be made among members of the second organization. To protect themselves, the members of these organizations would not form primary group ties in either association: the population remained individuated and confronted directly by the totalitarian elite.

The duplication of offices had special relevance for the exercise of terror. In the Soviet Union under Stalin, the secret police maintained a special department for every enterprise in the society. But the Communist Party also had a similar organization that spied on each subgroup, including the secret police. Within the secret police organization there was a special department that reported on the activities of the other secret police. The Central Committee of the Communist Party received several different reports on the activities of people in any given organization. Since discrepancies among these reports were investigated with special care, each agent protected himself by filing more thorough reports than the other agents.

In spite of the duplication of offices and the difficulty in determining which is the most influential, there is one useful rule of thumb: the more visible the agency, the less influence or authority it probably has. The populations in totalitarian societies learn to conform to the perceived wishes of the least visible agencies.

Shapelessness is also maintained by shifting the location of authority. While the confusion and duplication created is very great, this mechanism increases the control of the leader. He can use different channels to exercise his will. He can order the arrest of an individual through any of a variety of channels and cause the other arresting agencies to wonder if they are falling from favor. This device ensures the conformity of the bureaucrats. Every bureaucrat competes for favor; he informs on other people in his office, including his superiors. He chooses among murders and is humiliated by the experience. The mass character of the society even extends up the hierarchies of the party, governmental, and police organizations. Even the members of the elite are not safe from the exercise of terror and the other techniques of totalitarianism. Practically every member of the ruling elite of Nazi Germany and Stalinist Russia was liquidated and replaced by some equally insecure person (1).

SUMMARY AND CONCLUSIONS

Reading about totalitarian societies has a certain never-never-land quality for the American student because this form of organization is so alien to our culture. Yet those structures have been created and used to control enormous populations over long periods of time. The evidence shows that the mechanisms of totalitarianism are effective for maintaining absolute control over populations.

Many questions about totalitarianism remain unanswered. One reason for the limitations of our knowledge is the limited number of societies in which totalitarianism has occurred. The Soviet Union under Stalin and Nazi Germany are the best-known examples of this type of social structure. Yet in Nazi Germany a complete totalization of society was not achieved, since the economy, the military, and the ministerial bureaucracy remained fairly independent centers of influence and authority.

The most fundamental question we can ask about totalitarianism is whether it can maintain its stability. Is it possible to keep a population organized permanently in the manner described in this chapter? This question has relevance for predicting the course of social change in the Soviet Union and some semiindustrialized societies where this type of social structure is used. The question is not experimentally answerable. On theoretical grounds there are reasons to expect that it is extremely difficult to maintain a totalitarian society as that society increases its level of technology and population size (Propositions 2, 4, and 13).

In an industrial society, the political elite cannot hope to maintain absolute control over the population. The problems of these societies are often extremely complex, demanding the esoteric knowledge and skills of professional workers. The political elite is dependent on these professionals to provide guides to its decision making. Because of their special skills, professionals acquire the authority to make some classes of decisions. In the language we have used earlier, the number of centers of influence increases: a fact that limits the authority of the totalitarian elite. For the student of social organizations, the direction of social change in the Soviet Union and other quasi-totalitarian societies must be watched with great interest. These societies are industrializing, and the number of centers of influence in them is increasing. The effects of these changes, born of economic success, on the actions of the political leaders will be crucial for the social development of these societies.

REFERENCES

1   H. Arendt, *The Origins of Totalitarianism* (New York: The World Publishing Company, 1958; a Meridian book).

2   C. J. Friedrich, "The Unique Character of Totalitarian Society," in *Totalitarianism*, C. J. Friedrich, ed. (Cambridge: Harvard University Press, 1954).

3   F. L. Neumann, *Behemoth: The Structure and Practice of National Socialism, 1933-1944* (New York: Oxford University Press, 1944).

4   C. K. Yang, *A Chinese Village in Early Communist Transition* (Cambridge: The Technology Press of the Massachusetts Institute of Technology, 1959).

5   C. I. Hovland, I. L. Janis, and H. H. Kelley, *Communication and Persuasion: Psychological Studies of Opinion Change* (New Haven: Yale University Press, 1953).

6   A. Inkeles and R. A. Bauer, *The Soviet Citizen: Daily Life in a Totalitarian Society* (Cambridge: Harvard University Press, 1959).

the changing shape
of american society 22

The problems that have led to the centralization of influence in other societies also impinge on American society. The scope and complexity of domestic problems and the nature of contemporary international relations require unitary action. In spite of the need to centralize influence, neither totalitarianism or any of the forms of socialism have been adopted as methods of centralization.

There are three major reasons for this reluctance to use these social structures to solve problems. First, Americans experimented fairly successfully with relatively passive means of controlling the economy and of solving other large-scale problems. The excesses of business organizations have been blunted by a host of legislation—antitrust laws, securities exchange regulations, and bank credit control, for example. None of these laws provides for direct government ownership of the means of production. The central government can regulate the activities of business enterprises without assuming direct ownership of the companies involved. Many, but not all, government projects are administered through state agencies rather than directly from Washington. Even the publicly owned utility—the Tennessee Valley Authority —is highly subject to the wishes of local political leaders in Tennessee. The general effect of this form of regulation and control has been the stabilization of economic interaction and social change.

Second, Americans value minimal governmental intervention in the activities of the parts of the society. This value is incorporated in the Constitution of the United States and is continually reinforced in the educational system and elsewhere. Socialism and totalitarianism are anathema to the vast majority of the population. But it must be remembered that the luxury of our opposition to these isms is dependent upon the success of the present approach to the centralization of influence by social regulation. If this more passive approach had not been successful, radical social movements might have been more successful than they were.

Third, perhaps the most fundamental reason for the failure of the socialist or totalitarian social movements in the United States derives from the peculiar structure of the American political system. A series of checks and balances built into the Constitution of the United States makes it very difficult for any collection of parts in the society to form a permanent majority. In order for any political organization to win an election, it must have a broad base of support in many parts of the society (1). Its backing must crosscut social classes, states, and regions. But there have been very few times in American history when conditions existed that were disturbing to broad sections of the population. Unless these conditions exist, the totalitarians and socialists have very little chance of obtaining the needed support. They will remain a class, religious, or regional interest group. Today there are some categories of people who are susceptible to the appeals of socialism or totalitarianism, but they cannot muster the broad base of support essential to winning because the other parts of the society do not share their problems and can use the system of checks and balances to veto their efforts (2). Another tendency that undercuts these social movements is for the national political parties to capture the issues of minority parties if they do come to control a sizable portion of the electorate. The fledgling social movement finds its issues stolen, its leadership still excluded from the positions of authority, and its membership dwindling.

AN AMERICAN TOTAL SOCIETY

Although socialisms and totalitarianisms are not likely methods for the centralization of influence in American society, another form of the total society may develop. Alexis de Tocqueville, a French observer of American life, wrote about this possibility over a hundred years ago (3). He believed that a total society would develop because of our emphasis on social equality. He reasoned that if men achieved equality, the society would assume greater importance to them than the individuals in it. The individual would be lost in that greater entity—"the people at large." If the society assumes greater importance than its individual members, then the prerogatives of the society are more important than the rights of the members. The rights of the latter become secondary to the privileges of the able, knowledgeable, and foresighted elite of the total society.

Whether or not our belief in social equality is actually a factor in the emergence of a total society in America, many of the characteristics of our present society are similar to those predicted by de Tocqueville and which he ascribed to a total society. He expected American society to develop some of the characteristics of a mass society. The members would be self-centered or at best family-oriented. Other associations would exist, but they would provide instrumental rather than primary relationships. Subtle social pressures to conform to detailed group standards of behavior and thought at the expense of exhibiting individuality and creativity would be exerted on the individual. The task of standardizing his behavior would be simplified by the availability of vast quantities of material wealth. The individual would be inundated with commodities that would have the effect of dulling his critical senses, reducing his frustrations, and leaving him with seemingly little to ponder. Overarching the society would be a provident, paternalistic central government, vested with all authority and influence, and allowed to rule absolutely because it gives the population what it wants.

Many members of the population are disturbed by the pressures for behavioral conformity or standardization, the fragmentation of social life, our spiritual decline amidst material abundance, and the increasing centralization of influence and authority in the political sector of our life. These similarities between de Tocqueville's predictions and certain aspects of American culture are both amazing and alarming. Yet it would be superficial to conclude that the total society is here. Individual autonomy still exists, social life is not completely individuated, and influence and authority are still fairly decentralized. These characteristics of the total society are present, perhaps in increasing prevalence, but we recognize them and are often disturbed by them because we do have something with which to compare them. Let us now examine some of the social forces that have led to the increased prevalence of these characteristics of a total society.

THE DEVELOPMENT OF A TOTAL SOCIETY

The major forces that are compelling us to centralize influence were discussed in Chapter 19: the quickening tempo and increasing seriousness of international affairs, the problems of an economy separated from social regulation, and the existence of problems beyond the capabilities of smaller units to solve. Although these problems account for much of the trend toward centralization, they do not help us to account for some of the other features of the potential total society. In American society, behavior is being standardized and voluntary associations are being rendered impotent without the use of a secret police force. Behavior is being totalized almost without governmental coercion; something far more pervasive and informal is at work. Certainly increasing population size is an important contributing factor, but greatly aggravating the effects of size is the rationalist-individualist value system that is a part of our tradition (4). A cornerstone of the American value system is that the society should be structured so as to facilitate the development of the individual. This idea has no precedent in medieval Europe. There, as in most classic agrarian societies, the individual had no real meaning outside the organizations with which he associated. Even his name reflected his organizational affiliations: his village and his occupation. The fabric of medieval life was woven of groups, not individuals, and the groups were autonomous, self-sufficient units: the guilds, manors, and monasteries. When the philosophers of the seventeenth and eighteenth centuries talked of creating a society in which the autonomous, self-sufficient individual would be exalted, *they were actually ascribing to persons the characteristics of these medieval organizations* (4).

The ideology of laissez-faireism supported the rationalist-individualist conception of society. The early capitalist philosophers conceived of society as a collection of individuals who in their economic activities were subjected only to the workings of the markets and not to social or political restraints. In both ideologies, associations were seen as influences that unduly restrained the actions of the individual. The position taken by the rationalist-individualists and the laissez-faireists is ironic, since the associations they disdained are actually essential to the development of individualism and to the maintenance of the capitalist system. Just at the time when the individual was told to free himself from the restraints of associations, he found himself face to face with a new society that made it impossible for him to exist without such groupings. The industrial society with its giant bureaucratic organizations was and is too much a match for the individual (4, 5). In the guild or monastery he could interact easily and readily with his superiors, but in a modern industrial society how was he to obtain redress for his grievances? The organizations were both large and impersonal; alone he had little hope of influencing his superiors. He became less than an individual; he was a member of the "labor force." To achieve *his* objectives he had to form associations with others in similar positions. Yet this collectivization occurred in a society where joint action was far less esteemed than individual accomplishment. There was no value system that showed him how to maximize his individuality in organizations. Lacking this value system, one has no behavioral guides to achieving autonomy in organizational settings. Therefore, his strategy in organizations is often to cooperate minimally in order to fulfill his personal needs rather than to structure the organization to provide a milieu for maximizing the autonomy of the members (6).

The irony continues: The continued existence of the capitalist system is dependent upon the organizations that the ideology of early capitalism abhorred (4). Associations provide a means by which people can develop attachments to the larger units of society. Through them the individual learns about the problems of the larger organizations and can participate in their solution. He can also use them to communicate his own problems to the elites of these organizations who have the ability and the influence necessary to solve them. These opportunities to interact with the leaders of larger organizations through association aid in the development of allegiances between the individual and the larger organizations. Viewed in this light, such organizations as labor unions are essential to the maintenance of private industry. Without labor unions the individual worker would have fewer ways available to him for forming and maintaining allegiances with the company in which he works. Without this type of association the company would become even more impersonal and remote than it is already. In such a situation threats to nationalize the industry would be met with unconcealed apathy on the part of the workers. What difference would it make to them if one impersonal and remote elite is replaced by another? The continued existence of capitalism is dependent upon the existence of viable and effective labor unions—organizations that many industrialists would like very much to do without. Samuel Gompers, the founder of the American Federation of Labor, showed that he understood this role of unions by referring to his union as a "handmaiden of capitalism." Lenin belatedly discovered this function of unions. When he tried to increase popular support for communism in Germany, he found that the major sources of resistance to his appeals were the labor unions.

The Erosion of Associational Life

One trend that led to the development of the welfare-bureaucratic society was the shift from a mass to a bureaucratic form of organization. Associations appeared, and many people joined them. These associational ties have helped to solve human problems and heighten the stability of the society. Whether this trend toward associational integration will continue is now open to question. Lacking an ideology of organizational life as a means of fostering individual development, this life has undergone some erosion. Religious institutions have experienced a loss of some of their older functions. The separation of religious activities from secular activities was noted earlier. For many people, religion is a Sunday ritual and little more. But the decline in viability goes much further. Members of congregations often are critical when their ministers, priests, or rabbis step over the boundaries of the spiritual and involve themselves in secular affairs. The participation of religious leaders in civil rights demonstrations and in the passage of fair-housing legislation often engenders this reaction. The compartmentalized behaviors of the members of congregations is expected of the clergy and rabbinate also. But the limitations placed on religious institutions do not end there; an increasingly vocal segment of the membership in religious organizations want their ministers to limit their sermons to "spiritual" matters and not to dwell on the ethical issues involved in secular affairs.

The social class system has undergone drastic changes that have removed just about all of its organizational functions. Interclass relations in medieval Europe were governed by the principle of *noblesse oblige,* which stated that the nobility were bound in a web of reciprocal relations with the peasants who worked their lands. This value is illustrated by the lord's normative act of taking a basket of food to the cottage of a sick peasant. He was recognizing his obligation to provide for the security of those who worked for him. Social class relationships are no longer characterized by *noblesse oblige* or anything similar to it. The task of providing for the welfare of the population has become primarily a governmental or an individual one. But there is an important difference between medieval and modern bureaucratic relationships: medieval relationships were individualized and personal, whereas bureaucratic relationships are relatively standardized and impersonal.

This standardization and impersonality heightens the mass quality of the society.

Another form of association that was of great importance at an earlier period in American history, but that is declining in importance today, is the political party. For all of their excesses, the political parties did perform some valuable functions at the turn of the present century. They did link the individual with the affairs of the larger society; they provided an avenue of upward mobility for many working class people; and they were a modest welfare agency. It was virtually impossible to get elected to political office without the backing of one of the party organizations. But the role of political parties in public affairs has changed since the decline of the spoils system and the advent of modern mass media and political polling techniques. It is possible for a candidate to win an election without the direct support of a political party. If the candidate is wealthy enough or his supporters are, he can buy the necessary television and radio time, buy political polls, and build his own organization. He can engage in mass rather than organizational political strategy. His chances of success hinge largely on the funds available to him and his ability to "sell himself" in the media. We live in the age of the mass media candidate, where the attractiveness of the candidate can transcend all other requirements. It is doubtful that many of the candidates who are being elected to public office today would have been nominated by the parties at an earlier period in history. The shift in styles of campaigning is emasculating the parties. They have become more nearly fund-raising organizations, providing money for the all-important media exposure. The older group functions of parties have not disappeared completely, but they have become much less important. Today political parties are more nearly ephemeral groups that mobilize their members just before an election and then lapse into passivity until the next one: they are October organizations.

Many more illustrations of the erosion of group life in American society could be presented, but perhaps one more will suffice to make the point. Social life in an earlier period took place primarily in the family or in fairly stable friendship groups and associations. This social life took many diverse forms, such as the family musicale or a group of peasant farmers getting together on a Friday night to talk and drink wine. Much of the stability of this group life has been lost because of the mobility of the American population and the development of newer forms of entertainment. We move to new neighborhoods or new cities as our jobs require. Under these conditions, the composition of neighborhoods is in flux, and it is difficult for the new arrival to form friendships and for the older residents to maintain the ones they have. The content of social life is in some ways less variable from one group to another. On any given evening many millions of Americans are watching the same programs on television, going to the same movies, or reading the same books and magazines. Small group entertainment is succumbing to mass entertainment. In eight out of every ten homes either the television or the radio or both are on for an average of four hours each day (7). The mass media are a potent force for the fragmentation of social life.

The associations that do exist have undergone some changes that have contributed to the development of the total society. The associations that exist are often large and few in number. They often have experienced increases in their size and developed oligarchical patterns of control. Labor unions are generally oligarchical organizations; there is usually a small, self-perpetuating elite in which the greatest share of influence is concentrated. Business organizations are oligarchical by design, and we have already discussed the trend toward the centralization of influence in governmental institutions. These are the major subgroups in American life, and yet they are little models of the total society itself. How is the human potential that surely exists in the mass of the members of these subgroups to be developed if they are total organizations themselves?

MAINTAINING FREEDOM AND AUTONOMY

A complete description of American society would not be as negative as that given above. It must be remembered that the objective of this chapter is to select for discussion those social forces that are impelling us toward a form of the total society. In an earlier chapter, the broader character of contemporary American society was discussed. Our society is still essentially pluralistic, relatively integrated, and facilitative of autonomy and individualism. In a sense, one of our problems is very similar to that of the socialists. The socialists have found that their system does not automatically give rise to the autonomous individual, and they are casting about for ways to improve their performance. We have found that the early capitalist system did not foster the autonomy that is cherished and that the form of government we used in order to remove the excesses of capitalism aggravated the problem in some ways while it relieved it in others.

How, then, is the maximization of individual potentialities we prize so highly to be obtained in a society where considerable centralization of influence is required? There are many proposals offered in answer

to this question. But virtually all of them are offered by the adherents
to one or another of the older ideologies, which may have been appropriate for past social and technological situations but are impractical
for the conditions of the present. Very few new ideas are emerging;
primarily, there is a simple recognition of the need to develop an
ideology for our postconsumption society.

Surely one ingredient in such an ideology must be a set of values
supporting the notion that individual potential can be realized in
organizations. In contemporary organizations such as business enterprises, unions, and governments, a premium is placed on harmony
rather than conflict, conformity rather than originality. This emphasis
reflects a lack of confidence in exactly what a large organization ought
to be doing (8). A new value system must support the older notion
that diversity in ideas and competition for their implementation are
valuable both for the organization and the individuals in it. It must
provide guidelines so that the organization does not stifle the creative
efforts of its members, and so that the individual himself knows how
to act to maximize his objectives in a social perspective. The alternative
of impersonal bureaucratic organizations run by conforming specialists
who have no sense of the broader social implications of their actions
or no interest in them is not attractive.

Another structural device that can help us to eschew the total society
is the decentralization of authority (9). It is quite possible to centralize
influence and yet decentralize authority (Proposition 13). We can delegate to some other person the right to perform a certain set of tasks,
but we can always remove him or reassume the delegated authority if
necessary. Many industries have shifted to a decentralized authority
structure after finding that their most successful executives came from
those factories where authority was decentralized. In a decentralized
industry the manager of a factory is provided with a few guidelines for
his behavior. He is evaluated in terms of his ability to hold or increase
his share of the market in the commodity his plant manufactures, to
stay below certain cost levels, to develop the personnel under him,
maintain good labor relations, or some combination of these and other
standards. Within this framework the manager is expected to make his
own decisions and to demonstrate his own initiative. He has better
opportunity to develop his individual skills in this situation than he
does in one where his decisions are always made for him or monitored
closely by his supervisor. Interestingly, the Soviets have had a similar
experience whenever they have decentralized decision making within
their economic system (10).

The elements of decentralized authority are still evident in our governmental institutions. Many federal programs are administered through local units of government within a framework of broad federal regulations. But alongside this approach is the continuing abrogation of the authority as well as the influence of the smaller units of government.

We have operated often on the assumption that authority has to be centralized along with influence; that assumption is not true. Greater decentralization of authority in other areas of our associational life could produce benefits for their members similar to those found in industrial situations. The oligarchical structure of most labor unions, for example, leaves little opportunity for local leaders or members to develop their individual skills. The decentralization of authority should be protected where it exists and developed where it does not.

These are only two of the many ways in which the total society in its implied American form can be avoided: many others will be proposed from time to time. We are not at the end of ideologies, we are simply between them. Perhaps as the sophistication of the knowledge being developed by social scientists increases, they can play a useful role in the development of a society that maximizes our values of freedom and autonomy. But in the ideal American society this task cannot be delegated to social scientists or any other experts; it is a task in which all of the members of the population must participate.

REFERENCES

1 E. E. Schattschneider, *Party Government* (New York: Holt, Rinehart & Winston, Inc., 1942).

2 D. Street and J. C. Leggett, "Economic Deprivation and Extremism: A Study of Unemployed Negroes," *The American Journal of Sociology, 67* (1961), 53-57.

3 A. de Tocqueville, *Democracy in America.*

4 R. A. Nisbet, *The Quest for Community* (New York: Oxford University Press, 1953).

5 E. Fromm, *Escape From Freedom* (New York: Holt, Rinehart & Winston, Inc., 1941).

6 D. Riesman, *The Lonely Crowd: A Study of the Changing American Character* (New Haven: Yale University Press, 1950).

7 G. A. Steiner, *The People Look at Television* (New York: Alfred A. Knopf, Inc., 1963). Cited in H. L. Wilensky, "Mass

Society and Mass Culture: Interdependence or Independence?" *American Sociological Review, 29* (1964), 173-97.

8   V. A. Thompson, *Modern Organization* (New York: Alfred A. Knopf, Inc., 1961).

9   P. F. Drucker, *The Practice of Management* (New York: Harper & Row, Publishers, 1954).

10 D. Granick, *The Red Executive: A Study of the Organization Man in Russian Industry* (Garden City: Doubleday & Co., Inc., 1960).

index

a

Aggregates, 34, 153, 158
Agrarian societies: analysis, 123-137; comparative wealth, 180; development, 42-44; economic regulation, 316; England, 143-145; family, 81, 294-296; influence, 194-195, 196; Marxian theory, 169; mass-industrial transition, 161, 163; Negroes, 252, 253; religion, 232; socialism, 335, 338; submarginal economy, 109-112; values, 118; welfare-bureaucratic society, 174
Agricultural potential approach, 41-42, 67
American society: changing shape, 355-364; family, 291-302; integration sources, 278-290; introduction, 187-190; planning, 310-311, 313; race and nationality, 245-258; religion, 230-243; segmentation, 261-275; social classes, 191-227
Anomie, 154, 156, 158
Associations: agrarian society, 130; American society, 188, 189, 357, 358-362, 363-364; integration source, 279-280; mass organization, 153, 156, 157, 161; middle class, 222, 223-224; protest movements, 271-273; racial basis, 250-251; religious basis, 237, 238-239; social class development, 197, 198; status mobility, 205; subgroup type, 77-80, 84; totalitarianism, 345, 348, 350, 352; upper class, 226, 227; welfare-bureaucratic societies, 178-179, 181; withdrawal behavior, 269-270; working class, 216, 220
Attitudes, 17, 211, 216-218, 225, 282
Authoritarian state socialism, 327-329
Authority hierarchies: American society, 357, 363-364; associations, 78; central-

ization of influence, 307-314; coordination, 65-66; definition, 32; integration source, 281-284; interaction problems, 61-64; planning, 332; population size, 58-61; pre-urban society, 116; productive organizations, 81; ranking systems, 57-61; segmentation, 262, 264; socialism, 320-321, 329-330, 336, 338, 339; totalitarianism, 343-354; welfare-bureaucratic society, 177, 182, 183; workers' councils, 332-334
Authors, role of, 288-289
Automation (see also Technology): lower middle class effects, 222; welfare-bureaucratic society, 175, 176; work pattern changes, 95, 98

b

Brands, 115-121, 124-125, 127
Barriers, interaction, 33 (see also Interaction)
Behavior (see Human behavior)
Belief systems, 27, 70, 89, 90 (see also Value systems)
Birth rates: agrarian society, 129; family size, 298; industrialization, 142, 161; Negroes, 249, 255; pre-urban society, 112-113; welfare-bureaucratic societies, 181
Black Muslims, 270
Block busting, 248-249
Bureaucratic organization: American society, 358-359, 360-361, 363; family relations, 296, 302; juvenile delinquency, 265; mass-industrial society, 163; socialism, 329, 330; totalitarianism, 353; trends, 87; upper middle class socialization, 225; welfare society, 165-183; definition, 176-177

c

Capitalism, 315-318, 335, 338
Caste system, 126, 134, 198-199, 206
Centers of influence, 20 (*see also* Influence)
Centralization of American society, 355-364
Chain organizations, 21
Chain-reaction effect, 90-91, 102
Channels, accommodating, 49-50
Classes of society (*see* Social classes)
Cliques: lower working class, 216; mass-industrial society, 161; social class development, 198; subgroup type, 75-77; youth, 265, 266-267
Cohort phenomenon, 94, 102, 130, 265
Collectivism, 179-183, 234, 269 (*see also* Socialism)
Committees, 78, 79, 84
Communication: acceptance of change, 99-100; American society, 188, 189, 361; associations, 79-80; authority hierarchies, 61-64; centralization of warfare, 308-309; channeling, 49-50; diffusing information, 89-90; influence patterns, 19-20; integrative source, 284-286, 287-289; interaction basis, 18-19; mass organization, 156, 158-159; normative behavior, 55; protest behavior, 271-272; segmentation, 262, 263; socialism, 329, 338; totalitarianism, 342, 349-350; welfare-bureaucratic society, 175-176; definition, 18-19
Community relations: American society, 188, 199-200; centralized influence, 310-311; differentiation, 278-279; immigrant roles, 152-156; influence status, 31; juvenile delinquency, 267; key industry influence, 46; mass-industrial society, 162, 163; rank systems, 60-61; residential segmentation, 246-249; subgroup type, 82-83, 84-85; welfare-bureaucratic societies, 174
Composite bands, 115
Conflict: American society, 189-190, 363; class differences, 218, 220-221; coordination, role of, 65-66; costs of interaction, 92-93; integration, 280-281; marriage, 297, 301; Marxian theory, 170; mass organization, 157; norms and roles, 26-27; organizational change, 102; rate of change, 95, 100; religious basis, 232-233, 239-243; segmentation, 64, 262, 263, 264, 267-268, 271-275; socialism, 326, 327; violence, use of, 289; workers' councils, 333
Conservatism, 224, 225
Cooperativism, 323-325
Coordination: acceptance of change, 99-102; population size, 64-66; small organizations, 75; welfare-bureaucratic society, 175-176
Corporateness, 191-192, 198, 226
Corporate organization, 148-149

Costs of business, 172-173
Counterprotest movements, 272-273
Culture: agrarian societies, 124, 126; bureaucracy, 177; cohort phenomenon, 94; Negro, 252-258; norms, 27-29; organizational relationships, 70; segmentation, 63-64; socialism, development of, 315-318; subculture (*see* Subcultures); welfarism, 234; youth, 265-266; definition, 27

d

Death rates: agrarian society, 129; industrialization, 142, 161; Negroes, 249, 255; pre-urban society, 113; welfare-bureaucratic societies, 181
Decentralization: American society, 357, 363-364; social planning, 332, 333-334, 338, 339
Democratic state socialism, 325-327
Demographic transition, 142
Deviance: agrarian society, 135-136; American society, 189; segmentation problems, 264-273; socialism, 330-332, 339; totalitarianism, 345, 350
Dialectic materialism, 167
Differentiation (*see* Specialization)
Diffusion, 89, 124
Discrimination: integration sources, 278-290; racial, 246-258; religious, 239-243; segmentation, 262
Divine, Father, 269
Division of labor (*see* Labor, division of)
Dropout problem, 214-215, 284-285

e

Ecologists, 29, 170
Economic organization: agrarian society, 123-124, 128, 136-137; American society, 200-207, 355-356, 358-359, 362, 363; capitalism, 316-318; centralization of influence, 311-312, 313; chain-reaction effect, 90-91; changing, 87; environmental determinism, 40-44; family relations, 294-295, 296, 300-301; industrialization, 139-149; integrative sources, 282, 286; lower middle class, 222; Marxian theory, 167-172; political elite relationship, 60-61; religion in America, 232-234; social environment, 40, 67-68; socialism, 318-320, 321, 322, 323, 325-328, 329-335, 338-339; social organization, 44-48, 69-70; studying, 11-12; subgroup types, 74, 75, 80-81, 82, 83, 84; submarginal economy, 110-112, 117-118; totalitarianism, 341-342, 347, 349; upper working class, 218-219, 220-221; welfare-bureaucratic society, 172-177, 182
Education: dropout problem, 284-285; family relations, 295, 296, 300; middle